History of Korean Modern Retailing

History of Korean Modern Retailing

Repressed Consumption and Retail Industry, Perceived Equality and Economic Growth

By

Jong-Hyun Yi

BRILL

LEIDEN | BOSTON

Cover illustration: Seoul's premier shopping district, spring 2014. Courtesy Sean Pavone/Shutterstock.com.

Library of Congress Cataloging-in-Publication Data

Yi, Jong-Hyun.
History of Korean modern retailing : repressed consumption and retail industry, perceived equality and economic growth / by Jong-Hyun Yi.
pages cm
Includes bibliographical references and index.
ISBN 978-90-04-27421-1 (hardback : alk. paper) -- ISBN 978-90-04-27422-8 (e-book) 1. Retail trade--Korea (South)--History. 2. Department stores--Korea (South)--History. 3. Economic development--Korea (South)--History. 4. Social stratification--Korea (South)--History. I. Title.

HF5429.6.K6Y5 2016
381'.1095195--dc23

2015028925

This publication has been typeset in the multilingual "Brill" typeface. With over 5,100 characters covering Latin, IPA, Greek, and Cyrillic, this typeface is especially suitable for use in the humanities.
For more information, please see www.brill.com/brill-typeface.

ISSN 0169-9563
ISBN 978-90-04-27421-1 (hardback)
ISBN 978-90-04-27422-8 (e-book)

Contents

Acknowledgements

The birth of this book would not have been achievable without the contribution of many others. First and foremost this book would not have been possible without the distinct Korean history in which the contemporary individuals had lived and died. The significant achievements and distinctiveness of modern Korean history are testaments to their fierce struggle for survival both on a national and international level. This book attempted to trace a small part of their history.

Along with them, I have to profusely thank Dr Jim Hoare. He spared no efforts to publish this book from the outset. Whenever the work for publication was delayed, usually from my indolence, he endlessly encouraged me and reminded me of the value of this work. Needless to say, without his guidance and help, this publication would not have been possible.

There are numerous traces of the influence of Professor Janet Hunter in this book. Janet was my supervisor during the writing of my Ph. D. thesis, on which this publication is primarily based. She taught me scrupulously the significant principles of research.

I should also express my thanks to Mr Paul Norbury who arranged and guided the process of publication as the editor of Asian Studies in Brill.

My father who would have felt the utmost joy in seeing the publication of his youngest son's book passed away last year. He was one of those contemporary individuals who contributed in moulding modern Korean history. Moreover to us, he was the enduring guardian of our family, silently and ceaselessly pulling us through the most testing of times and warmly encouraging us with his earnest delight through the best. I cannot find worthy words to express my gratitude to my father. I dedicate this book to him.

List of Figures and Tables

Figures

Tables

List of Abbreviations

APC	Average Propensity to Consume
BOK	Bank of Korea
CAEO	Citizen's Action for the Expulsion of Over-consumption
CFA	Credit Finance Association
CKER	Center for Korean Economic Research
CPI	Consumer Price Index
DEI	Daewoo Economic Institute
DTI	Department of Trade and Industry
EPB	Economic Planning Board
FKI	Federation of Korean Industries
FSA	Financial Statement Analysis
FSS	Financial Supervisory Service
GMS	General Merchandise Store
GNDI	Gross National Disposable Income
GNI	Gross National Income
HCI	Heavy Chemical Industry
IKDI	Institute of Korean Distribution Industry
KAMA	Korea Automobile Manufacturers Association
KCA	Korea Consumer Agency
KCCI	Korea Chamber of Commerce and Industry
KDS	Korean style Discount Store
KDSA	Korea Department Store Association
KDI	Korea Development Institute
KFTC	Korea Fair Trade Commission
KIEP	Korea Institute for International Economic Policy
KIET	Korea Institute for Industrial Economics and Trade
KIF	Korea Institute of Finance
KIPF	Korea Institute of Public Finance
KISS	Korea Institute of Social Science
KOFOTI	Korea Federation of Textile Industries
KOCA	Korea Chainstores Association
KOSA	Korea Iron and Steel Association
KOSPI	Korea Composite Stock Price Index
KNSO	Korea National Statistical Office
KOSCA	Korea Super-Chain Association
KRX	Korea Exchange
MOCT	Ministry of Construction and Transportation

MOF	Ministry of Finance
MOGAHA	Ministry of Government Administration and Home Affairs
MOL	Ministry of Labour
MOLEG	Ministry of Government Legislation
MRFTA	Monopoly Regulation and Fair Trade Act
NB	National Brand
OECD	Organisation for Economic Cooperation and Development
PB	Private Brand
PFCE	Private Final Consumption Expenditure
POS	Point-of-Sale
SITC	Standard International Trade Classification
SK	Statistics Korea
SMSTR	Small and Medium Sized Traditional Retailer
SSM	Super Supermarket
SWEHS	Salary and Wage Earners Households
TFP	Total Factor Productivity
VAT	Value Added Tax

Laws and Regulations of the Retail Industry

1949 Sangpyo-beob [Trademark Law]

1951 Jung-angdo-mae-si-jangbeob [Law of the Central Wholesale Market]

1959 Jeongchal-je [Price Tag System]

1961 Si-jangbeob [Law of the Market]
Sangpumgwon-beob [Law of the Gift-Voucher]
Bu-jeong-oe-lae-pum dan-sog [Measure to sweep away fraudulent foreign goods]
Jeongchal-je [Price Tag System]

1962–1966 Je 1cha gyeongje-gae-bal 5gae-nyeon gye-hoeg [First Five-Year Plan for Economic Development]

1965 Jo-se-gammyeon-gyu-je-beob [Regulation Law on Tax Reduction and Exemption]
Jeongchal-je [Price Tag System]

1966 Yu-tonggu-jo gae-seon-e gwan-han jangdan-gi jonghab-dae-chaeg [Comprehensive Measures in the Long and Short Term for the Improvement of the Distribution System]

1967 Bu-dongsan-tu-gi eog-je-e gwan-han teug-byeol-jo-chi-beob [Special Measure concerning the Repression of Real Estate Speculation]

1968 So-bi-ja bo-ho yo-gang [Outline for Consumer Protection]

1967–1971 The Second 'Five-Year Plan for Economic Development'

1969 Yu-tong geun-dae-hwa 5gae-nyeon gye-hoeg [Five Year Plan for the Modernisation of the Distribution System]
Dae-lyang pan-mae-jo-jig wan-bi gye-hoeg [Plan for the Completeness of the Organisations for Large Sales] (DTI)

1972 Yu-sin-heon-beob [Ushin Constitution]

1972–1976 Je 3cha gyeongje-gae-bal 5gae-nyeon gye-hoeg [Third Five-Year Plan for Economic Development]

1974 Jonghab-mul-ga-an-jeongdae-chaeg [Comprehensive Measures for the Stability of Prices]
Gug-min-saenghwal-ui an-jeong-eul wi-han dae-tonglyeong gin-geub-jo-chi [President's Emergency Measures for Stability of People's Living]
Pyo-jun-yu-tongma-jin-je [System for the Standardisation of Retail Margins]
Teug-byeol-yeon-swae-hwa-sa-eob-gi-jun [Special Criteria for Chain Businesses]

1975 Yu-tonggeun-dae-hwa chog-jin-beob [Law for the Stimulation of the Modernisation of the Distribution Industry]

Jungso-sang-in jo-jig-ui teug-byeol yeon-swae-hwa sa-eob-e gwan-han gi-jun [Special Criteria for Chain Businesses Created through the Organisation of Small and Medium Sized Retailers]'

1977–1981 Je 4cha gyeongje-gae-bal 5gae-nyeon gye-hoeg [Fourth Five-Year Plan for Economic Development]

1977 Bu-ga-ga-chi-se-geum [Value Added Tax]

Han-gug-jungso-sang-in-yeon-swae-hwa-hyeob-ui-hoe [Korean Council for the Chain Businesses of Small and Medium Sized Retailers]

1978 Han-gug-su-peo-ma-keshyeob-dongjo-hab [Korean Cooperative Association of Supermarkets]

1980 Dog-jeomgyu-je mich gongjeonggeo-lae-e gwan-han beob-lyul [Monopoly Regulation and Fair Trade Act]

Yu-tongsan-eob geun-dae-hwa chog-jin-beob [Law for the Stimulation of the Modernisation of the Distribution Industry]

1981 Junghwa-hag-gong-eob-tu-ja-jo-jeongjo-chi [Measure of Rearrangement of Investment in HCI]

Establishment of the Korea Fair Trade Commission

Hal-in-pan-mae-un-yongjun-chig [Working Standard of Discount Sales]

Si-jangbeob jeon-myeon gae-jeong-an [Whole Amendment of Law of the Market]

1982 Si-jangbeob si-haenglyeong (Dae-tonglyeonglyeong 10887) [Enforcement Decree of Market Law (the Presidential Decree No. 10887)] which made, for the first time, a legal definition of the department store

1982–1986 Je 5cha gyeongje-sa-hoe-bal-jeon 5gae-nyeon gye-hoeg [Fifth Five-Year Plan for Economic and Social Development]

1983 Yu-tong-eob-gye hal-in-teug-byeol-pan-mae-haeng-wi-e dae-han bul-gongjeong geo-lae-haeng-wi ji-jeong go-si [Specification on Behaviour of Unfair Trade concerning Discount Special Sales by Retail Companies]

1986 Do-so-mae-eob jin-heungbeob [Law for the Promotion of the Wholesale and Retail Industry]

1987 Je 6cha gyeongje-sa-hoe-bal-jeon 5gae-nyeon gye-hoeg [Sixth Five Year Plan for Economic and Social Development]

1987 Si-jangbeob si-haenglyeong (Dae-tonglyeonglyeong 12211) [Enforcement Decree of Market Law (Presidential Decree No. 12211)]

1991 Do-so-mae-eob-jin-heungbeob si-haenglyeong (Dae-tonglyeonglyeong 13411) [Enforcement of Decree of Law for Promotion of Wholesale and Retail Industry (Presidential Decree No. 13411)]

1995	Do-so-mae-eob jin-heungbeob jeon-myeon gae-jeong-an [whole Amendment of Law for the Promotion of the Wholesale and Retail Industry]
1997	Yu-tongsan-eob bal-jeon-beob [Law for the Development of the Distribution Industry]
	Sogieob mich sosanggongin jiwoneul wihan teugbyeoljochibeob [Act on special measures for the development of small and micro enterprises]
2004	Jaeraesijang yugseongeul wihan teugbyeolbeob [Special act on the promotion of traditional market]
2009	Jeontongsijang mich sangjeomga yugseongeul wihan teugbyeolbeob [Special act on the promotion of traditional marketplaces and shopping districts]

Note on Romanization

The romanization system used in this book is the 'Revised Romanization of Korean' (RRK) introduced by the Republic of Korea's Ministry of Culture and Tourism in July 2000. This system is different from that previously in use, which was very similar to the McCune-Reischauer romanization system, and it reflects more accurately the characteristics of Korean sounds. It is also considered to be more convenient in computer typing as it excludes the breve which has been used to show short vowels in the McCune-Reischauer romanization. Predictably, therefore, there was considerable confusion in the early period of the first publication of the RRK system. It was natural that people who were used to McCune-Reischauer romanization stuck to that format in spite of the promulgation of the new system. However, a long time has passed since its first appearance and the Korean government has constantly tried to spread its use as much as possible. As a result of these efforts, the new romanization rule is now broadly used in South Korea both in official documents and in academic writing, where it is now becoming the required method of Korean romanization. Furthermore, it is expected that its use will spread more widely over time. Accordingly, this book uses the new romanization system.

CHAPTER 1

Theories and Framework

1 Introduction

The process of the distribution of goods is essential in order to ensure the circulation of goods following production, because continuous production cannot exist without the distribution of goods. This applies to the operations of a company. A company can only survive in the market when the goods that it produces are put into circulation – two factors which operate consecutively, whether they are integrated within its organization or not. However, in the field of economics, there is generally a tendency for the study of the distribution sector to be considered as less important than that of the production sector. The distribution process is seen as a factor that automatically follows the production process, or as dependent on the production process. This tendency is also found in studies of the South Korean economy. Most such studies have focussed on the structures of production, export, and investment and have endevoured to analyze the relationship between these factors and rapid economic growth (Luedde-Neurath 1988; Amsden 1989; Wade 1990; Park 1992; Koo and Kim 1992; Chang 1996). This may reflect circumstances in the real world, because the Korean economy has certainly achieved rapid economic growth through investments and exports. Since the 1970s, the heavy and chemical industries have also been a driving-force. In particular, it is believed that the Korean government has also played an important role in economic growth. It is unsurprising, therefore, that this perception of Korean economic growth has been accepted by a number of scholars.

However, the distribution sector in the Korean economy has received increasing attention as the domestic market has been expanding in line both with the increase of income, and with consumption liberalization dating back to the 1980s. Some *chaebols*,[1] which had concentrated on the manufacturing sector for a long time, became involved in the distribution industry, in particular, the retailing sector, because they discovered a chance for more profit in this sector. As the influence of domestic consumption on the Korean economy increased, its importance grew. This change in economic circumstances also

1 This term refers to Korean conglomerates like Samsung and Hyundai which have various subsidiary companies in addition to their main interests. They are somewhat similar to the Japanese *zaibatsu*.

 | DOI 10.1163/9789004274228_002

influenced the relationship between manufacturer and consumer. Until then, it was a fact that manufacturing companies had not considered domestic consumers' preferences to be as important as those of the export market. However, the growth of the domestic market, and the profits it has generated, has boosted the significance of internal consumers' behaviour. Manufacturing companies have had to address the preferences of domestic consumers given the extent of their strategic importance to their businesses. Thus Korean economic growth cannot be fully explained without due consideration of the distribution sector. In particular, this work is premised on the belief that an economic history approach to studying the evolution and development of the distribution industry in Korea since the 1970s will yield key benefits. This approach will significantly assist in an examination of the Korean economy's various characteristics, and provide some predictions regarding its future. The study of the distribution industry has been lacking in the field of economic research, although it has received some attention in the discipline of marketing in management studies. However, even here, the process and rationale behind the development in retail institutions has received little attention. Instead, such studies have mainly concentrated on the marketing strategy of manufacturing or retailing companies. As a result, the management studies approach has not been wholly successful in analyzing the characteristics of Korean retail institutions and the domestic market.

This book will examine the evolution of Korean retail institutions, and their interaction with aspects of the macroeconomic environment, such as economic growth, and changes in government policy and consumer behaviour. It may be useful to review the distinctive characteristics of Korean retail institutions. It is believed that this approach will help us to understand the Korean economy more fully and, in particular, the major changes that have taken place since the middle of the 1980s. Research concerning the evolution of retailing is also understood to be an important field in the study of retailing, whether it be theoretical or empirical, because it is fundamental to other types of research into retailing, such as the modelling of its role in economic growth. In particular, since the 1990s, as globalisation has led to the internationalisation of retail institutions, research concerning the evolution of retail institutions in developing countries has received scholarly attention. In line with this trend, this work will contribute to the development of the study of the retail system in developing countries. It also analyses the evolution of retail institutions in Korea from the viewpoint of the environmental theory of retailing and in part the conflict theory of retailing. This approach illustrates the strengths and weaknesses of theories in the study of the evolution of retail institutions in developing countries. In addition to this, it broadly tries to look at the relationship between the stratification of the consumption market and economic growth.

The work focuses on the department store (*baeg-hwa-jeom*), a retail establishment that sells a wide variety of goods under the same roof. This is one of the representative institutions, even though other types of retail institutions are also examined in relation to the department store. I define the department store in Korea as a luxurious retail format that primarily sells luxuries. It also means a format which develops into a type of the chain store from a single outlet. Accordingly, 'department store' indicates a department store format or a department store as a single selling unit, while 'department store company' denotes its company as the owner of one or more units. In addition, I often use the term 'traditional market' (*jae-lae-si-jang*) to define another retail outlet, namely a type of permanent market where a great number of independent retailers are clustered. Most retailers in the market sell their goods by traditional methods such as haggling without fixed pricing.[2]

I concentrate on the department store for the following reasons:

Firstly, the department store in Korea is the retail institution which, except for traditional markets, has the longest history among various types of institution. The first department store in Korea appeared as a branch of a Japanese department store in 1935 after Japanese imperialism colonised Korea. After the establishment of the Japanese store, Korean department stores were created and began to compete in the domestic market. Even though they did not take a dominant position in the domestic market, they were the only modern retail institutions[3] even in the 1970s – the period that this work focuses on. Therefore, they are the most appropriate institution to study in order to examine the evolution of retailing in Korea. Secondly, department stores have become one of the most important objects of government policy among retail institutions since the 1970s. This is related to their status as the first retail institution which

2 More concrete definition and shape will be described in various examples later on.

3 In general, modernization of retailing is understood to begin from around 1850 in Western countries such as the UK, the US and France, etc. and the department store is one of its representative formats. Alexander and Akehurst point out that the department store format as a modern one is different from existing traditional retailers in terms of its operation and management even if there are individual differences between various countries (Alexander and Akehurst 1999: 11, etc.). Particularly, they note fixed pricing and clear labelling as differences between both modern and traditional ones. In this respect, some Korean department stores in the 1970s can be said to be a modern retailer which was different from traditional retailers at that time. Of course, the meaning 'modernized' has more implications in reality than in an academic definition like that. It would be understood as a something advanced, good and clean, compared with the traditional retailer.

adapted the framework of modernization among Korean retailers. On the one hand, the government, applied measures to impose its policies, but on the other hand, it made department stores the focus of regulation. In this respect, they have become the most significant retail institutions for better or for worse. Thirdly, the department store is the institution which has experienced the most dramatic change in terms of the status of retail institutions since the mid-1980s. While it had experienced explosive growth since the mid-1980s, the period of boom had been relatively short, lasting for about fifteen years. The path of the rise and fall of the department stores may reflect changes in the socio-economic circumstances of the Korean economy, such as a transition from government to private leadership, from government to market liberalization, and from production to consumption. The drastic change in department stores meant a fundamental change for all of Korea's retail institutions, and the beginning of a new era in retailing. Finally, in terms of practicability for research, as we have seen, the data concerning the department stores are easier to collect than the data concerning other retail institutions, because most of them are big businesses and are listed on the stock market. Therefore, they have to periodically make most of their financial data public, and submit data concerning their trade and financial operations to government institutes such as the Korea Fair Trade Commission (KFTC) whenever any problems occur. Of course, even though all data is not made public at such a time, some will later become available in the public domain.

This book covers the period from the 1970s to the present, in which there are three distinct eras according to the developmental stage of the consumer market: the period from the 1970s to the middle of the 1980s; from the mid-1980s to the middle of the 1990s, and the period following that.

2 Literature Review

2.1 *Existing Studies of the Korean Economy*

Most of the existing studies focus on the manufacturing sector. They primarily consider the manufacturing sector and its development of technology to be at the center of Korean economic growth, even though there was a change in approach to research after the 1997 crisis. Most of the scholars mentioned earlier, whether neo-classical or developmental, who have led the controversy surrounding reasons for the rapid growth of the Korean economy, hold similar views in terms of their concentration on the manufacturing sector as the main factor of Korean economic development. This phenomenon may be related to conventional studies which purport to show that rapid economic growth in

Korea could be achieved by the mass export of manufacturing goods. In fact, a number of scholars who have studied the Korean economy have connected the rapid economic growth with exports. The World Bank[4] has pointed out that the rapid growth of exports, as a result of the export-push policies of the high-performing Asian economies, combined with the superior performance of these economies in creating and allocating human capital, provided the means by which they attained high rates of productivity-based catching up and total factor productivity growth (The World Bank 1993: 316). A number of publications from institutes sponsored by the government, have also concentrated on the manufacturing sector. Some books (Jo Dongseong 1990; Choe Jeongpyo 1993) written about *chaebol* or its subsidiary, discuss the contents of the distribution sector because they usually show the developmental and structural changes of *chaebol*. However, they also focus on the development and changeover of the manufacturing, rather than the distribution, sector in each *chaebol* group.

These trends in academic research reflect change in the real world. After the financial crisis in 1997, the focus of research concerning the Korean economy changed from an analysis of the previous success to finding the reasons for the failure. In this process, research concerning the firm, instead of government or policy, became prominent. This was because the problem of firm structure was identified as one of the causes of the crisis (Song Mingyeong 1998; Gim Seongsu 1998, etc.). However, most studies also focus mainly on the structure of the *chaebol* and the relationship among the subsidiaries in terms of corporate governance. There was little research that paid special attention to the retail company in relation to the crisis, even though the distribution sector was also, directly or indirectly, connected with the crisis. In particular, after the crisis, research concerning the Korean economy concentrated on the financial sector, including corporate finance. A number of Korean scholars (Gim Sangjo 1998; Jeong Unchan 1998, 1999) focused on the problem of the financial sector, including banks, non-bank financial companies, and the relationship between the corporate and financial sectors. In addition, some scholars (Chang et al. 1998; Jeon Changhwan 1998; Park 1998) paid attention to the relationship between the crisis and liberalization and globalisation in the financial sector. Even if it is clear that the topic of study varied with the crisis, the distribution sector still remains outside the attention of scholars.

4 The World Bank book was unique among publications from international economic institutes in that it emphasized the role of the state. However, it was said that it was too late in that it was published when the retreat of the state was already under way in the Korean economy.

2.2 *Existing Studies of the Retail Sector*

The trends of research concerning retail institutions cannot avoid reflecting the real world in which the study of the manufacturing sector is dominant. As has been mentioned, there are not many studies of the retail sector compared with studies of the manufacturing sector in Korea. In particular, there is little study of the retail sector from the standpoint of economics and economic history. For example, there are a number of studies of the car or electronic industries from the standpoint of economics. However, researchers have not paid attention to the retail sector even in the field of labour economics despite the retail industry labour force accounting for about 20 percent of the whole labour force in Korea (SK Economically Active Population Survey, annual). This phenomenon has been almost the same in the field of management. Even though the retail industry is an important field of marketing, most researchers concentrate on other fields such as strategy or consumer satisfaction. In these circumstances, books or dissertations regarding retail institutions are very rare. Therefore, most publication concerning the retail sector in Korea have pointed out the shortage of experts as one of the most serious problems preventing the development of the retail industry (Okubo 1992: 127–130; Min Gyeonghwi et al. 2000: 101, 251–252).[5]

Existing studies concerning the retail sector can be classified as follows. First of all, most of research on the distribution sector in Korea adopts the viewpoint of manufacturing companies. From this perspective, the distribution sector is not a crucial factor for the survival of the companies but is one of the tools enabling them to grow efficiently. Therefore, if the manufacturing company thinks that outsourcing the distribution sector is better for its profits than ownership then, unlike the production sector, the distribution sector could be hived off. This means that the studies of the distribution sector from the viewpoint of the manufacturing companies mainly pay attention to the role of the distribution sector as an object of marketing strategy in terms of the company's efficiency. If a manufacturing company considers outsourcing the distribution sector as the next step, this is directly connected with its hegemony over the process of distribution. Most studies projecting this view concentrate on how manufacturing companies, as the leaders in the process of distribution, can play a leading role in the relationship between manufacturing and retail companies. Jeong Byeonggwon (1996) and I Seoktae (1998) emphasized cooperation between manufacturers and their retailing agents in

5 In particular, most of the policy-reports by the government have indicated the need for education of experts as a desperate task. As a result, there is lively discussion around the establishment of an educational institute for a special retailing course.

order to improve their competitiveness. Gim Beomsu (1997) found that the relationship between manufacturer and distributor depended more on mutual understanding and respect than just trust through the empirical study.

Secondly, there are a few studies from the standpoint of distribution companies. Most of these studies try to analyze the issues surrounding the performance of management in retail companies in accordance with the change of economic environment (Jo Changuk 1991; I Sanghyeon 1996; Gang Aeri 1996; Bak Jinyong 1998). Jo (1991) emphasized that the spread of the POS (Point-of-Sale) system was needed to improve productivity of the distribution sector as he indicated that the POS system was not popular in the Korean economy. Gang (1996) pointed out that the strategy of discount stores (*Hal-in-jeom*) was the systemisation of cost reduction and the establishment of new relationships between producer and distributor. Bak (1998) paid attention to the role of trust and commitment as factors to achieve and maintain long-term relationships in distribution channels. In particular, some of them take notice of the influence of the openness of the Korean retail market. Jeong Ho (1996) indicated that it was necessary that distributors of small and medium size home appliance businesses should establish cooperative systems at the level of the region or even nationwide, to survive given the openness of the Korean retail market. I Inpyo (1999) emphasized the importance of Korean retailers strategically penetrating small and medium sized cities rather than big, already well-commercialized cities. He pointed out that big foreign retailers implemented strategic close relationships with local consumers. Even though most researchers in this field possess distinctive ideas and arguments, with the exception of Bak (1998) and I Inpyo (1999), their work would be classified as low-level academic research rather than advanced academic work because these studies were dissertations written for Masters' degrees. Bak's writing is a kind of a modelling work which argues that trust is a major determinant of relationship commitment between retailer and supplier. Although this work implies managerial lessons for good performance of the retailer, it does not have implications for retail evolution and perspectives of socio-economic environments. In comparison, I Inpyo's work examines the strategy of retailers under conditions of the open market as an economic circumstance. Even if this work suggests some managerial ideas such as a global sourcing to the retailers, it seems to limit itself to describing differences between domestic and foreign retailers.

There are very few books which study the retail sector from an historical viewpoint. Those that exist are works written to influence government policies rather than providing an academic treatment. Therefore, even though these studies contain historical data concerning the Korean retail industry, they concentrate mainly on broad explanations and suggestions of policy rather than concrete analysis. For example, the Korea Chamber of Commerce and Industry (KCCI), which has been the most important body concerning the retail industry, pointed out in the book *Han-gug-ui yu-tongsan-eob* (*The Korean Distribution Industry*) (1985), that the distribution sector in the Korean economy was far too weak in relation to the manufacturing sector. The book argued that problems would result from the strong regulation of the distribution sector, due to the manufacturing-driven economic policy of the Korean government. It insisted that the Korean economy could continue its successful growth when the distribution sector also became more efficient proportionate to the manufacturing sector. The book used different historical data for analytical purposes. However, the goal of this kind of writing is likely to reflect the interest of the retail industry in obtaining more support from government. Accordingly, it is hard to say that its view is academically rigorous. *The Korean Distribution Industry – in terms of the response to the liberalisation of retail sector* (1992) by the Japanese author Takashi Okubo, who had worked for a Korean retail company for a long time, also tried to analyze the industry's characteristics and its response to the liberalization of Korean retail companies. The author, who also had experience of the Japanese retail industry, suggested the support of middle sized manufacturers and the investment of human capital to improve retail expertise in order to develop the Korean retail industry. He also argued that retail companies could develop when they were made to fit the unique culture and tradition of Korea. This kind of suggestion is quite different from most Korean writing in that it stressed a Korean idea of retail strategy instead of the Western standard. This work also has various data concerning the Korean retail industry. However, even if it gives some interesting insights into the Korean retail industry, these are mainly based on subjective views rather than on academic analysis. In this regard, it is unlikely to be considered a substantive piece of academic research.

Han-gug-ui yu-tongsan-eob (*The Korean Distribution Industry*) (Nam Ilchong 1992) suggested ways in which the Korean retail industry could be improved, to face the opening of the domestic market. In pointing out that the productivity of the Korean retail industry was much lower than the manufacturing sector, it suggested that the Korean government should remove or weaken many of the strong regulations within the retail sector in order to develop the industry. In particular, the study focused on the growth in competitiveness of the retail industry in response to increased market openness. However, this is restricted to research on regulation in the retail industry. Nam's work did not pay attention to the structural characteristics of the Korean retail industry, but instead stressed the positive effects of deregulation on increases in competitiveness. Recent research concerning openness of the domestic market, in works by

Gim Jundong et al. (2003) and Baek Insu et al. (2006), should also be taken into account. These books used some historical data. However, even though this research drew on historical data, it mostly concentrated on policy lessons. This is probably an inevitable limitation of works written as policy reports, which are not concerned with the basic reason for changes in retail institutions.

There is also a tendency in such studies, particularly in the writings of Korean authors[6] (KCCI 1999: 23–26; Seo Yonggu 2006: 9–12; Baek Insu 2006: 204, 211, etc.), to introduce the dichotomy that large Western modelled retailers are better for economic growth, whereas traditional institutions are not so good, even though the traditional market has played an important role in the Korean economy. However, the role of traditional institutions should not be disregarded given that it is one of the two forces responsible for rapid economic development in Korea. In fact, it is believed that the underdevelopment (backwardness) of large retailers was the result of the Korean government's industrial policy. That is to say it was another side of developmental policy. The government had constrained consumption to concentrate money within the industrial sector for the early period of development. It also intended to control the social atmosphere in order to increase production by strongly repressing consumption.[7] It is natural that the underdevelopment of the retail industry, and in particular, large retailers, resulted under such circumstances. Therefore, it is clear that there has been a close relationship between rapid economic growth and the underdevelopment of the retail industry for the 1970s at least. Furthermore, it is believed that the traditional market played an important role in two or three aspects. First of all, it provided an interim market place for the labour force which moved to the industrial sector from agricultural regions. Because there were hardly any barriers to entry with respect to capital and technology in the traditional market, it could play a role in maintaining a reserve industrial labour force for various industries. In this respect, it is also understood that the traditional market performed the role of buffer to mitigate the problem regarding the imbalance of supply and demand in labour force proportionate to business fluctuations (Jeong Geonhwa 1987: 53–58). Additionally, as we shall see, the traditional market was able to provide a

---

6 On the other hand, the Japanese scholar, T. Okubo, emphasized in his book that the Korean retail industry had to develop with the life-style of the Korean people not with the example of developed countries.

7 At that time, there were a number of metaphorical expressions which compared production and export to war such as an industrial soldier (labourer), a soldier for export, and the battle front of export etc. and slogans urging frugality were often seen even in private companies as well as administrative institutions.

convenient shopping place for the public because most traditional markets were located in residential areas. Therefore, it was one of the key aspects of the economic and social life of the public. However, some existing studies have a propensity to disregard this role of the traditional market, and related policy reports at times fail to suggest appropriate ideas for the development of the Korean retail institution. As a result of this attitude, such studies have demonstrated an inability to grasp the characteristics of the Korean retail sector.

In addition, some Korean writings tend to attribute the underdevelopment of the retail industry to the immaturity of the socio-economic environment even while stressing that the role of the government was crucial in the 1970s (Im Jongwon 1989; Hwang Myeongsu et al. 1992; KCCI 1999, etc.). In contrast, my argument will emphasize the government's repression of the retail industry as the primary reason for its backwardness and that the socio-economic conditions necessary for the emergence of mass retailers with their associated rapid economic growth, were already in place, at least from the middle of the 1970s.

2.3 *Existing Studies of Department Stores*

There has been hardly any research exclusively concerned with the department store in Korea. Hence, there is little published research focused on the department store except for a book on one company's history and some books about the retail industry which deal with the department store as one of many retail institutions. In spite of these limitations, one of the most significant pieces of research concerning department stores is the 1987 publication, *Sin-se-gye 25nyeon-ui bal-ja-chwi* (*The25 years' History of Shinsegae*),[8] which focuses on a single retail company. Some papers concerning department stores are mainly theses for a master's or doctor's degree, and even so the history of this research is very short (Gu Hyeongsuk 1995; U Eunyeong 1996; Choe Ilhyeong 1997; Gim Jeongeun 1998). In the case of the Shinsegae history, the research minutely describes the process of development of a department store. It has historical value in terms of the development of department stores, in that it was an in-depth work based on a good empirical foundation. However, there is no doubt that it has limitations. Although it was based on the evidence, one cannot expect that the company history would include unfavourable evidence about the process of its development.

Most academic papers concerning department stores have been submitted since the middle of the 1990s. This is related to the period of openness of the

8 This is a book commissioned from an independent work and so it is inevitable that data quoted from the book needs to be cross-checked. This is possible from newspapers and interviews.

domestic market in the 1990s because it became an important social issue at that time. Most of this research concentrates on the response of internal department stores to the openness of the market. Some contain various suggestions to the Korean government on improving the competitiveness of domestic department stores. In sum then, these studies were designed to analyze the survival strategy of department stores. Gu Hyeongsuk (1995) carried out research into the matter of the store's image through a case study of a department store. She argued that intangible benefits such as various types of service and the attitude of staff were more important factors in creating a store's image than the quality and variety of goods in a Korean department store. U Eunyeong (1996) suggested four kinds of marketing strategy concerning the price and promotion of domestic department stores, introducing the management of department stores in developed countries as good examples.

Apart from these studies, there are a few articles regarding the internationalisation of domestic department stores (Choe Ilhyeong 1997) and the prospects of private brands (PBS)[9] in the stores (Gim Jeongeun 1998). Choe (1997) dealt with the example of the entry into the Chinese domestic market of Shinsegae Department Store, and emphasized the long-term necessity of targeting the domestic market. Choe also suggested differing strategies across regions. Gim (1998) discovered that the goal of PB development in department stores lacked clarity and thus consistency of management. Gim pointed out that it was very important to both educate PB specialists and to develop CEOS' (Chief-Executive-Officer) receptiveness to PBS.

Most existing studies have not concentrated on the nature of the evolution of department stores. In particular, they have something in common with policy orientation. Therefore, even if it is a fact that some of them have dealt with factors affecting the evolution of department stores, it may not be enough for them to explain the process of their evolution comprehensively. Furthermore, it would be impossible for them to analyze the main reasons for the evolution and the relationship between several aspects of the environments and the change in department stores.

3 Theoretical Framework

Generally speaking, as it is said that one of the most significant characteristics of retailing is just to change, theories abound explaining the institutional

9 Private Brand (PB) means goods planned by retailers' own intention unlike National Brand (NB) provided by manufacturers.

change and evolution of retail companies. However, most theories are unable to explain fully all aspects of change in retail institutions, because they analyze processes of change in limited terms. To overcome this problem, Brown (1987) tried to classify the existing theories into three categories: environment, cycles and conflict theory. He constructed these categories in the belief that they provided robust axes of analysis for studying the change and evolution of retail institutions. Brown explained that researchers needed to combine each category with the other two categories in order to provide a comprehensive analyze of the evolution of retail institutions. He suggested that there would be an environment-cycle, environment-conflict, and environment-cycle-conflict theory. This study examines the evolution of Korean retail institutions using this concept, but focussing on the environment as the main element.

3.1 *Environmental Theory: Convergence or Divergence in the Evolution of the Retail Institution*

The environmental theory is broadly described by two categories: convergence and divergence. In general, the environmental theory that decides the stages of development in the retail institution according to the level of industrialization was broadly accepted among researchers by the early 1970s (Brown 1987: 7). Bucklin (1972)[10] identified five stages of institutional evolution from the periodic markets of pre-industrial societies to the conglomerate retailing of a developed economy. Wadinambiaratchi (1972)[11] also suggested a theory of six stages from a similar point of view. These theories could be classified into a kind of theory of convergence because it was understood that a similar type of retail institution appeared in other societies according to the level of economic development. Therefore, it was believed that marketers would be able to predict retail trends in one nation on the basis of developments in other, more developed, economies with such a model[12] (Cundiff 1965: 59–60).

10 Bucklin identified five stages of institutional change in retailing in accordance with the level of economic development as follows: Periodic Markets-Prebusiness Era, Permanent Markets-Prebusiness Era, Fragmented Markets-Petty Capitalism, Vertically integrated Markets-Industrial Capitalism, Conglomerate Retailing-Financial Capitalism.

11 Wadinambiaratchi's six stages are as follows: Itinerant Traders-Tribal Stage, Exchange Markets-Peasant Stage, Storekeepers-Early Commercial Stage, General Stores-Highly Commercial Stage, Specialised Stores-Early Industrial Stage, Mass Merchandising Stores-Highly Industrial Stage.

12 Even though Cundiff says that the shape of retailing is affected by a number of factors, such as the political and legal framework as well as the culture, he emphasized that the basic trend of evolution of retailing by way of economic development is very similar.

However, another group of scholars in environmental theory insisted on the divergence of the evolution of retail institutions through the study of comparative retailing. They emphasized that the shape of a retail institution in an individual country was different from that of another country because it was influenced by different environments, such as cultural, political, historical and legal forces. One of the representative theories to consider such things is political economy theory. Political economy theory, as a representative theory of divergence, understands the social system as comprising interacting sets of major economic and socio-political forces which affect collective behaviour and performance (Stern and Reve 1980: 53). From this point of view, political economy theory may be used in the study of distribution channels because the political economy worldview has proved reasonably flexible in conceptualising organizational behaviour. Its usefulness has been documented in the analysis of individual organizations as well as of inter-organizational networks (Zald 1970; Benson 1975). Stern and Reve (1980) have extended the political economy framework by adapting it to the super-organizations of distribution channels. Thus, political economy theory provides a basic framework for analyzing the evolution of retailing institutions as determined by factors such as internal polity and external economy.

3.2 *Cyclical Theory*

Cyclical theory holds that retail institutions change in line with regular patterns. Pattern analysis of this kind has taken pride of place in the investigation of institutional change (Brown 1987: 9). In this category, there are two classical theories concerning the evolution of the retail institution: the wheel of retailing and the retail accordion.

3.2.1 The Wheel of Retailing

The wheel of retailing is undoubtedly the most famous and frequently cited theory of institutional change (Brown 1987: 10). The theory, which was conceptualised by McNair (1931, 1958, 1976, 1978) explains the evolution of retailing through the change of price and service. New types of retailers cut their prices by reducing or eliminating customer services, but once they are established they increase prices and customer services, and so themselves become vulnerable to new, low-price retailers. According to the wheel of retailing, retail institutions would experience three stages, i.e. entry, trading-up and vulnerability phases, from the birth to the death of the institutions. The retailer at the stage of entry provides goods for customers at a low price as an innovative retailer with a minimal service. It is poor in facilities and offers only a limited product range. Because of its low status, these conditions are not a problem and its administrative costs are also low. However, as it becomes an established retailer, in the trading-up phase, the retailer faces different environments from those of the entry stage. It has to provide a higher level of service for customers and to equip elaborate facilities in order to compete with new entrants. It cannot help raising the price in order to make these changes and extend product offerings. In general, retailers at this stage would move to higher-rent locations and show a propensity towards fashion orientation. Most of these changes are related to higher prices and services in accordance with the change in their status. Finally, the innovator in retailing becomes a mature retailer. The return on investment gets lower and lower and conservatism becomes stronger and stronger in this phase. In the end, it disappears and another innovator replaces it as the dominant retailer. This theory tends to be well applied to the US and European cases and is empirically supported by work on department stores, supermarkets and discount stores (Rosenbloom and Dupuis 1994: 149–151). However, it has also induced a great deal of scholarly debate particularly surrounding the causes of trading up. Stressing the importance of demand factors instead of competition among retail formats, some scholars point out growing consumer affluence as a decisive demand factor for the cycle (Pioch and Schmidt 2000: 184). In addition, this can not be applied to the Korean department store format because its starting position was not low price and less service.

3.2.2 The Retail Accordion Theory

This theory which was conceptualised by Hollander (1966), explains the changes of retail institutions in terms of the pattern of merchandise assortments. He argued that individual retail institutions widen and narrow their inventories over time. Furthermore, he pictured retailing as an orchestra or band of accordion players, in which, as he says, at any one moment some of the players are compressing their music boxes while others are extending them. This is useful to analyze the process of change in American department stores which developed from specialist establishments to the diversification of merchandise, and then returned from the latter to the former again. This is also appropriate in explaining the development of shopping centers and supermarkets which developed in the process of oscillation from diversification to specialization.

3.2.3 Other Theories

With these theories, the retail life cycle theory (Davidson 1970; Davison et al. 1976) which argues that retail institutions evolve through stages of birth, growth, maturity and decline has also attracted attention. It analyzes the process of institutional evolution in terms of the change of retailer's volume in profitability and market share while the wheel of retailing pays attention to the change of price and service as crucial factors of evolution of retailing. Based on product life cycle conceptualisation, however, the retail life cycle is similar to the wheel of retailing in the process of evolution although its analytical points of evolution are different.

The polarization principle explained by Dreesman (1968) is also an important theory which is useful for the analysis of the change in retail institutions. It argues that two different types of retail institutions, in terms of size, exist together. In fact, as large institutions become dominant in most developed countries, small institutions also exhibit a tendency to increase conversely. When the supermarkets developed into bigger units, the small supermarket obtained a new lease of life because supermarkets cannot be built in areas where the market is small. Therefore, the more the supermarkets grew in size, the greater the increase in potential for small and more versatile units (Dreesman 1968: 80). The polarization principle can explain the phenomenon that small convenience stores may also prosper even if large retailers become dominant in the market.

3.3 *Conflict Theory*

It is said that vigorous competition between the old and the new is capitalism's driving force, and retail institutions are also permanently exposed to keen competition if they are in a lively capitalist system. Once new retail institutions appear on the market, it is natural that severe conflicts occur between new and old institutions, as they contend for consumers. In this process, the new entrant as an innovator would make use of new technology, while the older entrant acting as a defender would reform existing management or sales skills. As a consequence, innovation in retailing continues through the process of conflict. For example, institutions such as department stores, discount stores, supermarkets and hypermarkets obtained dominance in the market and either retained it continuously or else lost it in such processes of conflict.

The dialectical theory of Gist (1968) is an example of a theory which explains the change of institutions according to the conflict view. Derived from Marxist philosophy, dialectical theory argues that the existing retail institution is a type of synthesis resulting from the conflict between two types of retailers, i.e. the thesis and antithesis, in the past. According to Gist, the dialectical process continues because the synthesis becomes another thesis for a new round of negation by a new antithesis. Apart from the dialectical theory, Coughlan, Anderson, Stern and El-Ansary (2001) suggested four stages[13] in the action-reaction sequence of the conflict which 'actually strengthened and improved a channel' according to conflict theory (Coughlan et al. 2001: 237). Izraeli (1970) also examined the change of retailers in terms of crisis-response by institutions. This theory may be open to various kinds of possible ways of retail evolution because it concentrates just on the action-reaction sequence as a process of its evolution. Unlike the cyclical theory which suggested the direction of retail evolution, it suggests the pattern of conflict as a driving force for retail evolution. Thus, its direction can be changeable in accordance with the character of conflict. However, it may be that this kind of theory lacks consideration of the socio-economic factors as environmental conditions (Pioch and Schmidt 2000: 185).

3.4 *Combined Theories*

Even though a number of the theories mentioned have analytical power concerning specific aspects, none of the three basic perspectives provides an entirely satisfactory explanation of institutional evolution. This is because the theories have a tendency to be overly conceptual while the nature of the retail industry would be dynamic. In addition to this, the fact that these theories concentrate mainly on experiences of the US can be pointed out as a limitation of application to other cases (Brown 1990: 51). In general, the environmental theory may make light of the role of the institution as an innovator even if it is not passive. On the other hand, it is possible that the cyclical theory falls into a danger of determinism, due to its preoccupation with pattern because it emphasizes only the role of the innovator. Conflict theory is also incomplete in explaining the evolution of the institution. Concentrating only on the interaction between institutions, it may be unable to explain the origins of institutions, the form that they take and the reasons for their initial and continued success. Because of these problems, it is not surprising that combined theories, such as environment-cycle, environment-conflict and environment-cycle-conflict theories, have been developed (Brown 1987: 20–21).

---

13 These four authors classified a number of types of conflict between institutes into four kinds, i.e. latent, perceived, felt and manifest conflicts, in accordance with the level of perception and reaction against the competitor.

3.5 *Theoretical Framework for this Study*

In this work, I will analyze the structure and the evolution of the retail institution in the Korean economy basically within the framework of the combined theory suggested by Brown. In the case of analysis of retailing in developing countries, there is a propensity to base the analysis on the environmental theory (Goldman 1974, 1991, 1992, 2001; Shimaguchi and Rosenberg 1979; Campbell 1985; Trappey and Lai 1996). First of all, this could be related to the fact that developing countries are not innovators in retailing in the world market and they import a number of types of retailing from the developed countries. For example, the department store, which began in France, faces a different environment from those in France, particularly in the countries that import it as a new type of retailing. The import of a new retailing institution is similar to the graft of a plant to a different land. Therefore, the future of a department store is crucially dependent on the specific environment of the new country. The same case can be applied to the supermarket, which started in the US, but became one of the most popular types of retailing around the world. However, as a consequence, it became one of the most varied retail institutions in terms of the forms that supermarkets took because they adapted themselves to different environments in individual countries. A similar phenomenon could appear even in developed countries if a retailer in those countries is not an innovator. However, because there are a lot of similarities between developed countries, transplantation between them could cause much less trouble, compared with that between developing and developed countries. Thus evolution of the retail format in a developing country as an importer would be enormously influenced by the environment around the retail industry. Secondly, it would be related to the fact that most developing countries try to reform the structure of retailing artificially rather than allowing them to change naturally according to the trend of the market. In general, they may think that traditional markets in their countries are so inefficient that they can inhibit more economic growth.[14] Therefore, the countries make efforts to change the structure of retailing in order to avoid the problems which stem from the backwardness of the retailing system. In this process, it is inevitable that the policy of the government, rather than any existing retailer, plays a more important role in changing the retail institutions and so the policy environment becomes a very important factor affecting the evolution of retailing in developing countries.

14 Many developing countries, including Korea, are likely to import retail institutions from western countries as an instrument for reform of the retailing system. In the case of Korea, a number of policy reports emphasized that the government had to take the lead in reform of a western type in the retailing sector (KCCI 1999: 23–26).

Taking account of such factors, I will take environmental theory as one of the most significant theories among the combined theories. In particular, political economy theory is useful for the analysis of the evolution of the Korean retailing system because its process of evolution has been influenced by internal responses as well as by external environmental factors. This theoretical framework would help to analyze the characteristics of the Korean retailing system, whether it is similar to the Western model or not, because there are a lot of cases where even their similarities stem from other reasons.

First of all, Korea's situation appears very unusual, in that there was hardly any modern retailer operating in the second half of the 1970s. This was at a time when Gross National Income (GNI) per capita was up to over 1,600 US dollars with rapid industrialization, and there were six cities with populations over 0.5 million, and twenty-eight cities with populations over one hundred thousand (SK Population and Housing Census, annual). Korea's situation cannot be explained by Bucklin's argument which is the convergence view among environment theories. This extreme delay in the emergence of modern retailing should be examined within its particular socio-economic and legal context. Here in particular, the political economy theory view seems useful in explaining the Korean evolution of the retail format. Cyclical theory does not explain the unusual evolution of the department store format from its position as a luxury retailer to its position toards the cheaper end of the market. This transition, which appeared in the mid-1980s in Korea, demonstrates a reverse trend to that proposed by cyclical theory. Therefore, this phenomenon should be examined through analysis of environmental characteristics present at that time.

In addition to these matters, the relationship between the department store and the discount store also has unusual characteristics. In the 1990s, with the appearance of the discount store, following the department store, the conditions of retailing in the Korean economy became similar to the evolutionary process of retailing in Western countries. Thus, it is possible for the evolution of the Korean retailing system to be interpreted in terms of conflict theory. In fact, it is said that the Korean retailing sector became an area of conflict theory with the appearance of the discount store (O Sejo and Sekine Takasi 2002: 141). However, even though it was clear that conflict between institutions took place in the retail sector and that they were influenced by each other, it is doubtful whether the conflict was a driving-force of change in retail institutions. In the case of Korea, the large retailing companies, which owned department stores, entered the discount stores' marketplace as part of their survival strategy. For instance, the domestic companies of discount stores, which are dominant in the market of discount stores, such as E-mart and Lotte Mart are owned by department store companies, which are dominant in their own market as well. This kind of ownership of the companies produces a different result from conflict between individual companies which only own department or discount stores, because a retailing company as a conglomerate could choose one or both in accordance with its circumstances. An individual company owning the old type of retail institution would reform its management to compete with a new retail format as a contender. In this case, therefore, the driving-force of the change and evolution of the old retail institution can be said to be a competition and conflict with the new retail formats. This is a result from the situation that one company has one retail format. In contrast to this, the company which owned both types of retail institutions would manage them in terms of a portfolio for profit maximization. Needless to say, here, the most significant reason for being of both types is to increase the company's profitability. The old retail format is more likely to be cooperatively reformed for their common goal. Therefore, the driving-force of the change and evolution of the old one would be not conflict but cooperation with the new one. This aspect will be explored in terms of the market segmentation strategy by big businesses with respect to the conflict between retailing formats. That is to say, I will try to establish what environmental factors are at work. In fact, there has been a tendency for some large retailing businesses in Korea to concentrate more on the discount store, rather than the department store format. Future trends will depend on the expansion of the market, and the availability of funds within the company. On this point, even though it is true that the era of conflict between retail institutions began with the appearance of the discount store in Korea, the analysis of the Korean retail institution would be clearer if it were supplemented by the viewpoint of political economy as a part of environmental theory.

In spite of these particular contexts, other theories cannot be said to be totally inappropriate for the exploration of the evolution of Korean retail formats. The emergence and rapid growth of modern retailing in Korea, despite its relative lateness, seems to correspond to some extent to convergence theory in the environment theories. With the appearance of the discount store, the repositioning of the department store as an upmarket entity, in which higher prices are offered with quality customer service, is also consistent with the evolutionary logic of the wheel of retailing by McNair as a cyclical theory. Additionally, it cannot be said that aspects of competition and conflict do not exist even in the cooperative relationship between the Korean department store and the discount store. Therefore, I will pay particular attention to the usefulness of political economy theory to examine the Korean case as being based on combined theories such as the environment-cycle-conflict theory.

4 Hypotheses

This work focuses on a number of questions which will be addressed on the basis of this political economy approach.

4.1 *Why didn't the department stores take over the position of traditional retailers in the Korean domestic market by the mid-1980s in spite of their long history? – The period of dominance by policy*

It is said that the prerequisite for the department store is the concentration in the city of a middle-class with purchasing power, because a large retail institution cannot be run without a huge amount of demand (Pasdermadjian 1954: 2; Shaw 1992a: 17–18). In terms of this pre-condition, the groundwork may well have been laid within the Korean economy for the new retailing system to apply to mass-consumption from the middle of the 1970s, or at least by the end of the 1970s. For instance, in particular there were already seventeen cities[15] which had populations greater than 100,000, including six cities with populations over 0.5 million in 1975 (SK Population and Housing Census; BOK National Accounts). The income of these urban residents was presumed to be higher than the average income level of the country as a whole, because most of them resided in highly industrialized cities such as Seoul and Busan. These indicators are at higher levels than those of the developed countries when this type of mass–consumption developed rapidly. For example, in the UK, there were twenty-eight cities with populations over 100,000 in 1879–80, and mass retailers, including the department store, emerged and developed around the middle of the nineteenth century (Fraser 1981: 128–131; Shaw 1992a: 18). However, the prosperity of large retail institutions did not become a reality in Korea. Even though there were a few department stores in Seoul as retailers modernized, they covered just a small part of consumption in the market, while traditional small retailers were dominant. Even though the department store was the first type of modernized retailer, and given that it had also encountered the proper conditions for development since the middle of the 1970s, why did it not function as a springboard for the development of modern retailing? First, I argue that this could be explained by the policy of the Korean government. The government had been carrying out its third 'five-year plan for economic devel-

15 A city is defined as administrative districts which are authorised by the government among administrative districts where their populations are over 50,000 (SK Population and Housing Census). So, the ratio of urbanization, which will be used later on, denotes a proportion of the population living in such cities to the whole population.

opment' since 1972.[16] It urged the following goals: the improvement of the international balance of payments, the advance of industrial structure through the development of heavy chemical industry, the development of human capital and technology, and an average of 8.6 per cent economic growth rate in the period, etc. The goal given greatest priority by government was the economic growth rate, and its main tool was the speeding-up of the development of industry, in particular heavy chemical industry (HCI). To achieve this goal, the government selected the steel, nonferrous metal, mechanical, shipbuilding, electronics and petrochemical industries as six strategic industries to be developed in the period (Gang Gwangha 2000: 58–72; Im Hwicheol 1998: 26). In this process, the distribution sector was disregarded, because the government tried to concentrate internal capital on HCI investment. Furthermore, it produced an atmosphere which considered domestic consumption a sin because a huge part of the money for the investment had to be provided from external consumption (exports).[17]

Si-jangbeob (The Law of the Market), which was enacted in 1961, was the basic law for the distribution industry in Korea at that time. This law was required as there were a lot of problems such as the unclear definition of retail institutions and thus inappropriateness of regulations due to their unclearness of definition (KCCI 1999: 45). However, it continued until 1986 when *Do-so-mae-eob jin-heungbeob* (the Law for the Promotion of the Wholesale and Retail Industry) was enacted, even though a number of the policies concerning the distribution industry had already been published. This means that government perception of the distribution industry changed for the first time after the mid-1980s. Most policies in that period concentrated on the protection of consumers and stability of prices rather than on the development of the distribution industry (Shinsegae Department Store 1987: A Chronological Table of Retail Policies, 1971; EPB 1974; DTI 1974a). The government also paid attention to the reform of traditional retailers even providing a little support for the distribution industry, rather than the development of new institutions such as department stores (Ibid, DTI 1970, 1972, 1974b). A senior government official in charge of the distribution industry policy said that the government disregard-

16 The Korean government had started a 'five-year plan for economic development' in 1962 and had upgraded it every five years. By the way, the government had changed the title of the project to 'the five-year plan for economic and social development' since the fifth project of 1982. It is believed that the change has comprehensive meanings, including the change of both the government's viewpoint on economic development and the relationship between the public and private sector, etc. (Gang Gwangha 2000: 87).

17 At that time, the Korean government displayed a slogan in President Park Chung Hee's calligraphy extolling 'National Foundation through the Exports'.

ed the industry and that most of the policies concerning it concentrated on consumer protection and the stability of prices (Jeon Sangu 1995: 22–23).[18]

Secondly, faced with strong government intervention, retailers, whether modernized or traditional, were barely able to promote their interests. For example, the Korean government imposed the prohibition of gift-vouchers as part of the goal of imposing constraints on consumption, and thus triggered social tension in 1975 when the Korean economy experienced recession after the oil-shock. It was understood as an extraordinary measure in that the gift-voucher not only had a long history but also had accounted for around 35 per cent of department stores' total sales (Shinsegae Department Store 1987: 140). This meant that the government's policy could sometimes deal a serious blow to a company's survival. The department stores accepted the policy as a first-step because they could not directly protest against government policy. The department stores, which suffered a severe blow as a result of the prohibition, made a proposal to the government to lift it in 1976, which was about one year after the implementation of the policy. However, the government firmly refused to budge (Ibid: 140). In particular, retailers were unable to try a strategy of expansion because the government imposed a number of regulations related to the establishment of stores.

Thirdly, it will be shown that, related to the second point, it was difficult for the *chaebol* to enter the retail industry given that the government encouraged them to invest in the manufacturing sector. The *chaebol* could not fail to be obedient to the government in the early period of development because they possessed insufficient capital. At that time, the fact that the *chaebol* could not enter the retail industry meant that there was no capital available to target the mass-consumption market in Korea. Thus we can see that the political environment in which Korean department stores operated during the 1970s, was not conducive to their development and expansion.

On the other hand, the government maintained support for traditional retailers though this was partly because it recognised an important role for the traditional market as a stopover for populations moving from rural to urban areas. The traditional market was also a familiar shopping place for most people in Korea. Therefore, in spite of its modern characteristics, the department store as a retail institution did not experience a boom period in the 1970s.

To sum up, the policy environment was the most crucial factor contributing to the backwardness of large retailers such as the department store even if economic and social circumstances were appropriate for their development. As a

---

18 Jeon Sangu was a director of industrial distribution in the Department of Trade and Industry when he wrote the article.

result, the underdevelopment of the retail sector continued in contrast with rapid economic growth through the manufacturing sector.

4.2 *After the mid-1980s, why did the department store grow rapidly? – The period of explosive expansion of consumption and the ratification of the policy*

The Korean economy experienced dramatic economic growth of about 10 per cent per annum from 1976. After a three year economic boom, from 1979, it faced a comparative recession with th economic growth rate averaging 6.8 per cent per annum. However, as GNI per capita increased to US$ 1,431 in 1978 (BOK National Accounts, annual), some of the large companies, concentrated mainly in the manufacturing sector, began to pay attention to retailing. Lotte, which is the largest *chaebol* group, concentrated on retailing in Korea, and established its first department store in 1979. Subsequently, other *chaebol* began to consider taking part in the retail sector.

One of the most important changes in macroeconomic data related to retailing was the trend of annual income and expenditure per urban household. While the annual average growth rate of real income per urban labour household, which had been 7.2 per cent in the 1970s, had exceeded that of its expenditure of 5.1 per cent, it had been reversed for the 1980s as that of income was 5.7 per cent, and that of expenditure was 7.2 per cent (SK Monthly Income and Expenditure per Urban Household, annual). The reversal of the relationship between income and expenditure meant that government measures to constrain consumption could no longer be effective. It will be shown that the change in consumption patterns, such as the rise in the consumption of durable goods, and the preference for quality goods became highly evident in the process (Jeong Geonhwa 1998: 193–194). There was a close relationship between such new phenomena and the development of department stores. Urban populations formed an increasing part of the total Korean population, rising from 41.1 per cent in 1970, to 57.4 per cent in 1980 (SK Population and Housing Census, annual). This expansion of urban and commercial areas considerably influenced the structure of the retail industry. In this process, the number of members per family was also decreasing continuously, falling from 5.0 in 1975, to 4.5 in 1980, 4.18 in 1985, and 3.97 in 1990 (Ibid.).

Faced with these developments, the Korean government had to reform the laws relating to the retail sector. At the end of 1981, it undertook a major revision of *Si-jangbeob* (The Law of the Market), which had played a basic role in the retail sector since 1961. The reformed law established the legal basis for a retailing chain. It also re-defined the market in terms of the function and size of the market. For example, while the large retail institutions such as the department store and shopping centers came under the label of general market in the old law, the new law classified them in terms of function and size. This change meant that the government tried to take a more concrete view on a policy concerning the retailing sector, whether it was a matter of regulation or support (MOLEG 1981). The government had already enacted *Yu-tongsan-eob geun-dae-hwa chog-jin-beob* (the Law for the Stimulation of the Modernisation of the Distribution Industry) in 1980 for the protection of producers as well as consumers (MOLEG 1980). The fact that the perception of the Korean government concerning retailing was developing was shown in the new law which replaced *Si-jangbeob* as the basic law concerning retailing. The new law named *Do-so-mae-eob jin-heungbeob* (the Law for the Promotion of the Wholesale and Retail Industry), enacted at the end of 1986, embodied a supportive attitude to the distribution industry in general. However, the law also highlighted the fact that the government wished to regulate large retail institutions for the protection of small- and medium-sized operators. Even though the government perception of retailing had changed, and its stance was more supportive, a greater emphasis was placed on helping small- and medium-sized retailers rather than large retail companies.[19]

The big change in retailing was brought about primarily by the economic environment and not through government policy. Even though the perception of the government had changed rapidly during the 1980s, the economic environment was the prime catalyst for change. The economic environment had dramatically changed from 1986 to 1988, and this pushed the government to adapt policy to changing economic realities. The annual average economic growth of Korea in the period was recorded as over 10 per cent, and GNI per capita rose to the level of over 5,000 dollars in 1989 from 2,643 in 1986. Following the rise in incomes, total retail and wholesale sales had shown a sharp annual increase of about 17.4 per cent for five years, from 1986 to 1990 (SK Wholesale and Retail Trade Census with the Overall Establishment Statistics, 1986; Wholesale and Retail Trade Survey, 1990). Despite government regulations, a change of environment like this stimulated the department store

19 The law was different from the old law in that it aimed at the modernization of the Korean distribution industry comparable to the market modernization of the old one. For this purpose, it is said that the definition of retailers was made clear and general regulation in the old one was changed to selective regulation and support in the newlaw.

companies, which had tried to expand their operations since the early 1980s. Existing department store companies tried to increase the number of branches and a number of new department store companies were established in the 1980s. As a result, the number of department store companies rose to sixty-six in 1991, and ninety-one in 1995 (KCCI *So-mae-eob gyeong-yeongdongtae jo-sa-bo-go* (Analysis of Current Retail Management) annual). The drastic growth of department stores was well demonstrated by the change in the ratio of department stores sales to total retail sales. In the case of 1986, the proportion of department stores was merely 4.3 per cent, but the figure increased to 4.7 per cent in 1988 and 11.7 per cent in 1996 (SK Wholesale and Retail Trade Census with the Overall Establishment Statistics, 1986; The Wholesale and Retail Trade Survey, 1988; The Wholesale, Retail Trade and Service Industry Census, 1996). Thus the change in status of department stores in the retail industry resulted partly from their response to environmental changes. For example, department stores, which had had an image as a luxury retailer since their establishment, tried to target the middle-classes using the chain store strategy. In particular, this phenomenon was shown clearly as they entered sub-centers of cities. Before the 1980s, department stores were placed mainly in the suburban area and their primary goods were luxury clothes. However, as will be discussed in chapter five, most department stores in Seoul, which had been built since the mid-1980s, sold merchandise which was a mix of clothes and popular food; their location was also diversified to the sub-center of the city. This phenomenon has spread to other cities since the 1990s. As we have seen, having experienced rapid economic growth since the mid-1980s, the Korean economy has faced an explosive expansion of consumption. Under the influence of changes in the economic environment, the Korean government began to reform regulation impacting on retailing. Over the fifteen years in which this change took place, department stores increased their market share drastically with this amendment of strategy, thereby heralding what could be called the golden age of department stores in Korea.

To sum up, I will examine the way in which the Korean economic environment became the crucial factor triggering the development of the retail industry, and in turn impacting on government policy. Thus, I explore how Korean department stores responded to changes in the environment, changes in government policy and consumer behaviour.

4.3 *Why has the growth of department stores been moderate since the mid-1990s? (Why was the golden age of department stores so short in Korea?) – The drastic change of environments around the retail industry and the strategic choice of retailing big business*

It was the opening of the distribution industry, which occurred by the end of the 1980s that was the lynchpin for dramatic changes in the industry in the middle of the 1990s. The international pressure to open up economically had been growing since the middle of the 1980s because of Korea's rapid economic growth. In 1989 the Korean government initiated the process of liberalizing the domestic market. This process, comprising five steps, reached its peak in 1996 when the domestic market was completely opened, allowing foreign retailing companies to enter the market (KCCI 1999: 30). In 1997, the Korean government enacted Yu-tongsan-eob bal-jeon-beob (The Law for the Development of the Distribution Industry). Unlike previous laws, this was a law which concentrated on the support and, particularly, the deregulation of the large retail institutions rather than those of a small size (MOLEG 1997). In the course of deregulation, foreign companies within the distribution industry entered the Korean domestic market by means of alliances with domestic companies as a first step, but from 1996 they invested directly in discount stores. Discount stores achieved greater recognition after foreign companies entered the market, even though they had been in operation from 1993. They made an impact on the consumer as well as on existing retailers such as department stores and traditional markets. As modernized retailing institutions they bridged the gap between department stores as luxury shops, and traditional retailers as popular shops.[20] In particular, the economic crisis in 1997 was a crucial factor enabling discount stores to thrive dramatically in the Korean domestic market, because consumers became much more sensitive to prices.[21] The crisis, one of the most serious since the economic development of the 1970s, was a severe shock to Korean people as they faced changes in their traditional institutions such as the industrial relationship and the industrial policies. In particular, the breakdown of employment stability after the crisis strengthened the tension in everyday life. Under the influence of the economic environmental change, the

---

20 E-Mart, which is the largest discount store company, has implemented a policy of double compensation for the lowest price, the first in the Korean market to do so, in order to guarantee its lowest price (Im Yeonggyun et al. 2002: 53).

21 *The Economist* reported that the Korean people were more cautious about price and more interested in practical value as the consumers' tastes were changing in the economic crisis (1997: 65).

growth of discount stores has been fast, surpassing department stores in total sales in 2003, after operating in Korea for ten years (SK Wholesale and Retail Trade Survey, 2003).

As discount stores increased their market share, a conflict between retail formats emerged in the Korean domestic market from the mid-1990s. The department stores, first of all, adapted the strategy of retreating upmarket with high quality services such as expansion of space for leisure. In the case of the main store of Shinsegae Department Store, facilities for the convenience of consumers were changed to luxurious services and they made the atmosphere like that of a luxury hotel. They also strengthened the services for the consumer through the intensive training of employees, and they improved decorations in large halls for special events (Shinsegae Department Store 1996a: 18–22). There was also an example of change in a department store which specialized in clothes through the restructuring of the store. Shinsegae's Youngdeungpo Store expanded the space for women's clothes and created a large hall focused on clothes for the young. A store manager said that he tried to change the image of Youngdeungpo Store to a department store specializing in clothes (Shinsegae Department Store 1996b: 54–55). In other words, the department store was to return to being an upmarket retailer. In general, this situation was the result of severe conflict between both retail formats. However, the outcome in the Korean context was very natural, even if it was not without any quarrel between both formats. This distinctive phenomenon was closely related to the structure of ownership of Korean big business, which owns both retail formats. It can be a kind of diversification of the big business under the same roof. Presumably this is linked to the short heyday of the department store industry.

4.4 *Is the conflict theory useful to explain the Korean evolution of the retail format?*

As we have seen, the structure of the Korean retail industry in which two different types of modern retailers exist and compete might, seemingly, be consistent with the claims of the conflict theory. Once a new retail format appears on the market, it is natural that severe conflicts occur between new and old ones, in order to maintain market share. However, in the Korean situation, caution needs to be exerted over the character of ownership and thus the governance of the main retail companies. The oligopolistic character of the Korean economy due to the existence of the *chaebol* should be considered in the case of the retail industry as well. Most of the main retailers, such as the department stores and the discount stores form part of *chaebol* ownership. For example, the Shinsegae Department Store Company owns E-mart as a division of the discount store and the Lotte Department Store Company also owns Lotte Mart as a division of the discount store. They are all the main competitors in each type of mass retailer. Due to the comprehensive structure of ownership, two different types of retailers in the same company might largely be in a co-operative relationship rather than in a survival game, although there is to some extent internal competition. In particular, given a differentiated consumer market resulting from increases in income differentials since the middle of the 1990s, the different types of retailers can be instruments which carry out the strategy of price differentiation in order to maximize the profits of big retail companies. In other words, they can be components of an asset portfolio for a comprehensive retail company. The main driving force for their evolution may not be conflict but their cooperation with each other in accordance with the situation of the consumer market.[22]

5 Data and Methodology

This work broadly draws on four kinds of data in each different category such as the policy of the government, the economic index, the individual company or industry of retail institutions and the consumer. Additionally, for comparison, it will use some foreign data concerning the policy of the government and the economic index.

5.1 *Government Policy*

The data concerning government policy consists of the law and the minutes of proceedings in government or parliament. There are also some interviews and testimonies recorded by ex-senior officers as supplementary data. The center of this category of data would be the government's official action implemented through a number of regulations. First of all, as we have seen, there are three basic regulations applicable to the distribution industry: the Law of the Market, the Law for the Promotion of the Wholesale and Retail Industry, and the Law for the Development of the Distribution Industry. The Law of the Market

22 Despite being a single company, there would be strong conflict between the different stores in the same format as well as between department stores and discount stores. In fact, as mentioned earlier, most of the companies have separated department stores from discount stores in terms of business divisions, and may encourage competition between stores in the same group for profit maximization. However, it is inevitable that group matters such as the choice of leading business, and the fund raising priorities are decided by headquarters.

was enacted in 1961 and was the first basic law for the distribution industry in Korea. Despite problems of definition and applicability, this law continued until 1986, when the Law for the Promotion of the Wholesale and the Retail Industry was enacted. Of course, the government imposed a number of reforms concerning the distribution industry before the establishment of the new law. These laws play a basic role in showing the change of viewpoint towards the distribution industry in the government policies.

Apart from these laws, the government imposed a great number of enforcement ordinances. These included regulations concerning the new establishment of institutions, the use of gift-vouchers, and department stores' sale periods. Most of these came from the Department of Trade and Industry (DTI). Additionally, regulations concerning prices, fair trade, tax and the protection of the consumer are also often related to the policies of the retail industry. For example, whereas a price tag system (*Jeongchal-je*), which was first enacted in 1965, was a regulation for the protection of consumers, it had an influence on the reform of the price system in retailing. The Fair Trade Act, which was launched under the name of *Dog-jeomgyu-je mich gongjeonggeo-lae-e gwanhan beob-lyul* (Monopoly Regulation and Fair Trade Act) in 1980, also had a huge effect on retail institutions as well as on manufacturing companies. In particular, a 1977 Value-added Tax boosted department stores' turnover, and negatively impacted on traditional markets. Such regulations concerning the general economy were enacted mainly by the Economic Planning Board (EPB), which had played a leading role in Korean economic development during the period of rapid economic growth.

The characteristics of these regulations can be examined through their original publication and then through handbooks, newspapers and journals at that time. Apart from these sources, the minutes of the proceedings of government or parliament are also very useful for the understanding of the atmosphere at that time. In particular, parliamentary stenographic records concerning the laws may help to provide a balanced perspective, because they contain the pros and cons of issue among rival parties. Additional material includes testimonies and interviews recorded by former senior officials and others concerned.

5.2 *Industry and Individual Company*

This work draws on a huge amount of retail industry data. Most comes from the Statistics Korea (SK) and the Bank of Korea (BOK), Korea's Central Bank. Additional data concerning retail institutions can be obtained from institutes such as KCCI.

SK data concerning the retail industry includes:

Wholesale, Retail Trade and Service Industry Census: Name and Physical Location of Establishments, Type of Legal Organization, Head or Branch Office, Opening Year and Business Period, Industrial Classification, Floor Space, Annual Sales, etc. (The first reference year: 1968, Period: Quinquennial). The first title of this census in 1968 was 'Commerce Census'; this changed to 'Wholesale and Retail Trade Census' in 1971. The present title has been used since 1996, reflecting the change of industrial structure. The first census in 1968 was followed by others in 1971, 1976, 1979 and 1982. Two censuses since 1982 were covered by by the 'Wholesale and Retail Trade Census with the Overall Establishment Statistics' in 1986, and the 'Wholesale and Retail Trade Census with the Establishment Census' in 1991, which surveyed all companies in all industries. After this, 'Wholesale, Retail Trade and Service Industry Censuses' were carried out in 1996, 2001 and 2005. This census provides the most basic and significant data for the wholesale and retail industry even if it is impossible to detect short term change because the survey takes place roughly every five years. In particular, it is the only available data on the retail industry in the 1970s, one of the most important periods focused on in this thesis.

Wholesale and Retail Trade Survey:

Name and Physical Location of Establishments, Type of Legal Organization, Kind of Business Activities, Business Period, Regular Holidays, Employment and Compensation, Floor Space, Expenses, Annual Sales, etc. (From 1988, annual). This is a type of sample survey in the wholesale and retail trade industry and was not carried out when the census concerning the same industry was held in 1991, 1996, 2001 and 2005. This statistical data shows us the structural and environmental changes of the retail industry in the short term. However, this data only begins in 1988. It is relatively less reliable than the census, because it is a sample survey. Nevertheless it plays a basic and important role in analyzing trends in the industry. This data is used with the census in order to make up for weaknesses in both the census and the annual survey.

Current Wholesale and Retail Trade Survey (Wholesale and Retail Sales Index): Name of Establishment, Type of Legal Organization, Business Period, Number of Workers, Floor Space, Monthly Sales, Inventories, Major Commodities Dealt, etc. (From 1970, monthly). This survey began as the 'Wholesale and Retail Sales Index of Seoul' in 1970 and expanded to become the 'Wholesale and Retail Sales Index' covering the whole nation since 1980. It is carried out in order to investigate the consumption sector as a part of the Composite Index rather than in order to analyze the trends of the retail industry. Thus it can not be considered as data to examine the concrete state of the retail industry. However, it is useful just to know rough trends of sales in the industry because it maintains consistency of samples in continuous surveys. The information provides is a useful supplement to other returns.

BOK produces data concerning the retail industry as follows:

Financial Statement Analysis (FSA): the main items of the balance sheet, including assets and liability, and income statement (profit and loss statement), including revenues and expenses (Begins in 1962, annual). The purpose of this sample survey is to know financial conditions and business performances of main industries. It can be considered as one of the most reliable forms of data on the financial statement of main industries because the Bank of Korea carries out this survey in accordance with legal regulation. This data is published at the level of the industry rather than the individual company and so is used here to examine the performances of the department store industry.

Most analysis of the retail industry can be achieved using the above data. However, it needs more micro data to examine the changes of structure and of strategy of the industry. The annual survey concerning the retail industry which is carried out by KCCI can make up for these kinds of problems. The 'Analysis of Current Retail Management' from KCCI plays an important role in understanding specific aspects, for example, of the proportion of the sale of individual items in each institution, the number of employees engaged in each task, and even some management strategies of the institution, because they contain more details than those of SK. Aside from this data, figures produced by Korea Super-Chain Association (KOSCA) are also used.

The most important data source for individual department store companies are reports to the Korea Exchange (KRX) because most of the major department store companies are listed on the stock exchange. They have to submit financial data such as a balance sheet, and a profit and loss statement to KRX periodically and declare changes of business, which may influence the property-rights of shareholders, to the public through the internet or by the printing of KRX. Therefore, the information concerned, including new investments, and changes of strategy, etc. can be obtained from KRX. The data, however, is limited to the period of listing. In this respect, the time series data concerning individual companies is not sufficient because most department store companies are listed after the mid-1980s. This information could be complemented in two ways: in the case of financial data, through newspapers, journals, and data from SK and institutions concerned, such as KCCI; in the case of management strategy, through published firm history, internal documents, newspapers, and journals. Magazines, which have been published by individual companies, may also provide important data even though they may distort facts. To avoid using biased data, internal data, such as magazines and internal documents, needs to be cross-checked.

5.3 *Consumers*

It is rare to encounter time series data concerning consumers' behaviour. Therefore, it is difficult to establish the process of change in consumers' behaviour accurately. The further back in time we go, the more difficult it is to track consumer behaviour patterns. The circumstances of the 1970s are worse than the 1980s and those of the 1980s are worse than the 1990s. Furthermore, it is impossible to get historical data through surveys at the present. Despite these restrictions, there is data concerning income and expenditure as a result of the collective behaviour of consumers that can be analyzed. Time series data can show trends of consumers' behaviour even though it would be difficult to analyze their specific characteristics. For this, I will use the concept of Average Propensity to Consume (APC) and examine the changes on the basis of general characteristics of APC in accordance with Keynesian absolute income hypothesis. Three different levels of data will be used to explore characteristics of the consumption attitude; Penn World Tables Version 6.2 (PWT 6.2) for comparison in the international level, National Accounts for the national level, and Monthly Income and Expenditure per Urban Household for the urban sector.

PWT 6.2: This provides purchasing power parity and national income accounts transferred to international prices for 188 countries, including South Korea, for the years 1950–2004. Thus this is very useful for comparison of Korea's level and characteristics of consumption with other countries on the basis of the same income level. These comparisons indicate that Korea's APC is even lower than that of developed countries and Latin American developing countries, and changes dramatically before and after the middle of the 1980s.

The National Account and the data of Monthly and Expenditure per Urban Household will be used for analysis in the national level.

National Accounts (BOK from 1953, quarterly): This contains the production, income and expenditure of the economic actors in a national economy.

Monthly Income and Expenditure per Urban Household: Household Type, Household Size, Number of Earners, Generation Type, Major Source of Income of Household with No Occupation, Yearly Current Income, Type of Living Quarters, Number of Automobiles, Incomes, Expenditures, etc. (SK from 1963, monthly).

These two kinds of data at the national level can show a difference between the trends of the whole country and more commercialized urban areas. For this, I will trace chronologically the APC trend in both sets of data. In addition to this, the difference between both sets of data can be a significant factor to suggest differences of consumption behaviour between the rich and the poor, because average income in the urban area is higher than that of the country as a whole including the rural area. For this, I also use income quintile data in urban areas even if there is limited data within the period.

Secondly, some surveys taken by the government or researchers are also vital to establish consumers' behaviour at that time, even though this is just one set of time data for a policy or for articles. The data concerning consumers' behaviour has been much better since the late 1980s. The Korea Consumer Agency (KCA), which was established in 1987 as a certified government organization under the Ministry of Finance and Economy, has been taking surveys concerning consumers' behaviour and consciousness annually. Institutes such as KCCI have also developed their survey structure by adding items reflecting consumers' consciousness. As we have seen, even though it is a fact that the historical data relating to consumers is insufficient, it would not be a serious problem because it traces the change in consumers' behaviour as only one factor in analyzing the evolution of retail institutions. I will analyze the relationship between the evolution of retail institutions and consumers' behaviour mainly through the change in their income and expenditure by drawing on a number of surveys undertaken by government, institutes or researchers.

5.4 *Socio-economic Data*

Socio-economic data is required since it indicates and provide results of the change in retail institutions.

Population and Housing Census: Place of Residence One Year and Five Years Ago, Employment Status, Industry, Occupation, etc. (SK from 1925, quinquennial). This is also significant data in that the population is a consumer base. This provides the size of the population and households in big cities through which we can presume the degree of development of the big retailer. The change of family composition provided from this census is also quite important data to examine the environment surrounding the retail industry.

The Survey of Land Prices: the change of land prices in each region such as Big City, Small and Medium City and Rural Area in the whole country (MOCT from 1975, Monthly). Land is one of the most important assets and so the change in land prices would influence consumption attitudes. Its price had very rapidly increased over the country during the period of the 1970s and 1980s but the increase in land prices left disproportionately large gaps between regions. Thus the change in land prices helps to explore changes in consumption.

In addition, material such as the Annual Number of Strikes surveyed by the Ministry of Labour (MOL), and SK's Economically Active Population Survey is used.

5.5 *Quantitative or Qualitative*

As indicated, this work uses qualitative as well as quantitative data. Most data provided by SK and BOK is quantitative, while the bulk of the internal data of companies would be qualitative. The data from government will be both quantitative and qualitative.

In general, the quantitative data has to be consistent in terms of statistical criteria and methodology in order to be compared. In this respect, there would be no problem in using the data from governmental organizations such as SK, BOK because their data is credible. What should be noted is the means used to modify the raw data in order to fit research goals. Indexes are sometimes calculated based on a specific criterion for comparison, and a rate of change to look at the trend. Such modifications of the data will be clearly stated wherever it is done. It might be thought that the data from institutes relating to companies differs from government organizations' data in terms of credibility. However, such data has for a long time been accepted by government, researchers and analysts in the stock market. In the case of listed companies, most of the data can be cross-checked automatically because it has to be submitted to the Korea Exchange (KRX) through audit reports. Therefore, this data is as credible as the data from government organizations. However, the qualitative data must be approached with caution. There is no problem in using data obtained from the government and its various organizations as a source for research in the same way as quantitative data. Qualitative data from companies and institutes, however, may sometimes be biased in accordance with their interests. To avoid this problem, data from companies will be cross-checked with other data from sources such as newspapers, journals and official literature.

CHAPTER 2

Backward, Unstratified Retail Industry and Rapid Economic Growth in the 1970s

1 Introduction

The goal of this and the following chapters is to examine the structure of the retail industry and socio-economic parameters such as economic growth and policies on consumption in the 1970s. For efficiency of analysis, this chapter concentrates mainly on the description of socio-economic environments influencing the structure of the retail industry, together with an analysis of the existing structure of the retail industry. It focuses on the action of the three actors – government, retailers and consumers – which make up the existing retail structure. In this process, this chapter shows an unusual incongruity between backwardness of the retail industry and economic development in the 1970s. This approach is different from most existing research which attributes such backwardness to immaturity of economic conditions.

This chapter briefly looks at the state of the retail industry, and eco-political environments before 1970 as a preliminary basis for the industry's conditions in the 1970s. This preliminary work is essential for understanding initial conditions within the retail industry in the 1970s. Then I will explore important topics of the 1970s. Most of these topics will provide evidence to justify the goal of this chapter, which is to show inconsistencies in rapid economic growth, and the backwardness of the retail industry. In general, industrialization is accompanied by various kinds of socio-economic changes. As one of the main factors relating to consumption, the retail industry is a key indicator of such socio-economic change. There are many factors which induce changes in the retail industry during industrialization. Increases in income proportionate to economic growth, may be one of the most important factors. Urbanization which provides the retailer with various kinds of new markets can be a decisive factor. An increase in society's income gap can also be an influential factor to change the structure of the retail industry. Broadly speaking, the Korean economy in the 1970s differed little from other general cases of the period, which were accompanied by economic growth. In particular, Korea in the 1970s experienced a very successful period of economic growth when average growth per annum was over 8 per cent. Under these conditions, rapid economic growth was linked to rapid increases in income as the most important factor

 | DOI 10.1163/9789004274228_003

concerning consumption and the retail industry. The Korean economy changed in industrial structure, and Korean society changed in urbanization and family composition in the 1970s. This kind of development can be said to share strong similarities with developed countries when modern retailers emerged in those regions. In fact, its change was as dramatic as developed countries in terms of scope and speed.

However, as will be seen, the structure of Korea's retail industry hardly changed in the 1970s. While the expansion of quantity was fast in terms of the amount of sales and the number of retailers, structural change was rare, and only found in the traditional market system. I believe that this is an unusual case which could not have occurred without strong intervention in accordance with clear motivation. I will also trace how differences in initial conditions influenced the evolutionary path of the retail industry. Thus this chapter illustrates the relative backwardness of the retail industry, compared with other sectors developed in the 1970s. In this respect, the word 'backwardness' is key in characterizing the Korean retail industry in the 1970s. Another significant term which explains the Korean retail industry in the 1970s is 'unstratified'. In general, development of the retail industry is accompanied by stratification. Retailers try to engage in market segmentation according to different services and thus different prices and this results in the emergence of different types of retailers (Coughlan et al. 2001: 63). However, this phenomenon did not happen to the Korean economy in the 1970s although the income gap increased rapidly with the general increase in income. This could be an important point relating to the relationship between the evolution of the retailer and consumer behaviour, which will be examined. Accordingly, this chapter also pays attention to the unstratified shape of the Korean retail market in the 1970s.

2 Brief History of the State of Distribution and the Retail Industry before the 1970s

2.1 *The Eco-Political Environments in the Korean Economy before the 1970s*

After gaining independence in 1945 from Japanese imperialism, South Korea's modern history was confronted by continual crises, such as the Korean War and political disturbance, which was the result of both internal and external factors. Korea, which experienced US Army military administration for three years after independence, was founded as a completely independent country in 1948. However, the Cold War divided the Korean peninsula into South and North, and such an unstable foundation involved the Korean people in a severe war: the Korean War. The war, which continued for the three years from 1950 to 1953, expanded into a proxy conflict as part of the Cold War, not merely one between the two Korean states. Some twenty-three countries, including the US, the UK, China and the Soviet Union, took part in the war on one or other of the two sides. Even after the end of the Korean War, the political situation did not stabilize with the establishment of a new system of democracy. As a result, in 1960 a new government took office following demonstrations by the revolutionary student movement after the breakdown of the previous administration. The new government, however, soon lost authority to a military regime led by General Park Chung Hee after a military coup in 1961 (Jeong Yunjae 1995; Gim Myeongseop 2003; Bak Taegyun 2007a).

Despite the chaos, the Korean economy gradually returned to normal. The average growth in GDP recorded between 1954 and 1959 was over 4 per cent, mainly as a result of the government's economic resurgence. The BOK classified the Korean economy of the 1950s into three stages: the period of the war economy (June 1950-July 1953); the period of the reconstructive economy (August 1953-December 1956); and the period of stable economy (January 1957-December 1959) (BOK 1960: 23–38).

TABLE 2.1 *Economic growth in the 1950s*

	1954	1955	1956	1957	1958	1959
Rate of increase of GDP (%, Constant price of 1975)	5.6	4.5	-1.3	7.6	5.5	3.9

Source: BOK, National Accounts, annual.

The government's policy for economic growth took just three years to return the country to normal conditions after the war, in which the amount of damage was calculated at US$3 billion. In particular, as the manufacturing sector grew steadily in the 1950s, the secondary industry's ratio in all industries increased to 15.9 per cent in 1960 from 10.1 per cent of GNP in 1953, while that of the primary industry shrank to 36.8 per cent from 47.3 per cent of GNP in the same period (BOK, National Account, annual). While political instability continued throughout the 1950s, the 1961 military coup provided the momentum for political stability in spite of its negative effect on the development of democracy in the long term. It was also clear that economic development plans led by the government started to show results, for the first time, in the 1960s, although the way had been paved for it in the 1950s.[1]

TABLE 2.2 *Economic growth in the 1960s*

	1960	1961	1962	1963	1964	1965	1966	1967	1968	1969
Rate of increase of GDP (%, constant price of 1975)	1.2	5.9	2.1	9.1	9.7	5.7	12.2	5.9	11.3	13.8

Source: BOK, National Accounts, annual.

Park's regime began a 'Five Year Plan for Economic Development' in 1962, one year after the coup, and with it established a strategy of export-driven development. The first 'Five Year Plan' was successful in recording an annual average economic growth rate of 7.8 per cent. The second economic plan, from 1967 to 1971, was also successful in that the annual average growth rate was 9.7 per cent.

2.2 *Equality or Inequality: The Distribution of Income and Wealth*

The most important policy concerning the distribution of income and wealth was the land reform that began in the late 1940s. After the land reform, which finished in the late 1950s, the distribution of landownership improved dramatically. The destruction that resulted from the Korean War was also regarded as a crucial factor that rearranged the situation of distribution (Haggard 1994: 225). An initial condition like this is often argued to be an example of the positive causal effect of equality on subsequent economic growth (Rodrik 1995: 76). While research on equality matters in the 1960s is quite scarce due to lack of data, most research concludes that there was an improvement in income distribution. Ju Hakjung (1979: 34) calculated that the Gini Coefficient of income changed from 0.3439 in 1965 to 0.3322 in 1970. Also, Gim Daemo and An Guksin noted that it changed from 0.37 in 1965 to 0.35 in 1970 (I Jeongu and Hwang Seonghyeon 1998: 159). On the basis of this research, it is generally accepted

1 *Bu-heung 5gae-nyeon gye-hoeg* (Five Year Plan for Reconstruction) in the late 1950s was the original version of 'Five Year Plan for Economic Development'. This plan, implemented by the military power and the Economic Planning Board (EPB), the main department for the economic plan in the 1970s and 1980s, originated in the Department of Reconstruction in the 1950s. (Bak Taegyun 2007b: 298–300)

that it improved slightly in the 1960s (I Jeongu and Hwang Seonghyeon 1998: 160; Choe Gwang and Hyeon Jingwon 1996: 22–23).

However, if landownership as wealth is considered, the distribution of wealth might be different from that of income. In general, the rise of land prices is regarded as having a redistributive effect due to differentiation of wealth. In particular, this phenomenon becomes more serious if landownership is uneven (I Jinsun 1993: 110–111). Accordingly, the rise of land prices during the process of industrialization is likely to engender the same problem because it is concentrated in the urban and industrial areas. In this respect, it is doubtful whether distribution in Korea was relatively equal in the 1960s because land prices increased rapidly with industrialization. The rate of increase of land prices in twelve big cities was over 35 per cent yearly between 1962 and 1968, and it rose to 80.7 per cent at its peak in 1969 (I Jinsun 1993: 116–118). A strong regulation, 'Special Measure concerning the Repression of Real Estate Speculation' which was published in 1967, showed the degree of seriousness of the situation (Yu Haeung and Gim Wonhui 1997: 86). Even though the precise level of the Gini cannot be calculated due to the limitations of the data, in this regard, it is difficult to claim that the distribution in the 1960s was good if it contained landownership as wealth. Furthermore, it is even more doubtful whether or not the effect of land reform on equality was maintained during the 1960s.

2.3 *The State of the Retail Industry*

2.3.1 Policy Environments around the Retail Industry

Extreme political changes in a society in which the market is not well organized may, first of all, give a destructive shock to the retail network because people wish to secure the necessities of life and do not trust the exchange and trade system. In this respect, the Korean economy from 1945, the date of national independence, to 1953, the end of the Korean War, operated in an atmosphere of extreme unfriendliness towards the retail industry. The end of Japanese imperialism, which had dominated Korean territory for thirty-six years, had been accompanied by a breakdown of the retail network. In particular, the US military administration, which served as an interim government following the Japanese retreat, had tried to change the socio-economic system, introducing capitalism. Therefore, it followed that the existing economic network scarcely operated during the period of military administration. During the interim government the Korean economy could be described as going through a period of extreme shortfall in the supply of foodstuff, and high inflation. Total production of the manufacturing sector by value in 1948 was merely 26.0 per cent of that in 1940, and the price of staple crops such as barley and beans was extremely unstable. By 1946, the monthly average rate of inflation was above 10 per cent (I Daegeun 2002: 135–141). Responding to these problems, the US military administration imposed a rationing system on the main necessities of life, together with strict price regulations.

With the foundation of an independent nation in 1948, the new government tried a plan of economic reconstruction. The main points of the policies relating to the distribution sector were stability of prices and the stable provision of foodstuffs, especially grain. With the implementation of these policies, the government tried to build up the norm of the commercial sector through various methods, including a trademark law in 1949 and the price tag system[2] in 1959. In 1951, it introduced the first market law, the 'Law of the Central Wholesale Market' (MOLEG 1949, 1951; Jo Byeongchan 1993: 201). However, the unstable situation which permeated the whole of society continued because of various eco-political problems, including the disposal of enemy properties, land reform and a reduction in the legitimacy of the government due to the division of the Korean Peninsula. In addition, a shortage of goods had not yet been resolved. Accordingly, it was still difficult to say that conditions were ready for the development of the retail industry. Moreover, the wartime economy during the Korean War had further reduced any possibility of developing the retail industry. What was worse, the image of retailers deteriorated because many of them received exorbitant rates of interest in making use of the shortage of goods.[3] Even after the war, circumstances scarcely changed. Even though the Korean government pushed their economic development plan and the economy slowly returned to normal, the shortage of goods still continued. This prevented the development of the retail industry as an important industry in the 1950s.

Park's military coup provided the momentum for drastic change in the Korean economy in the sense that the political power, led by the government, appeared able to promote economic development. However, this did not apply to the retail industry because, as in the past, the industry was not given priority for economic development. Of course, it was a fact that the environment around the retail sector improved continuously through the 1960s with rapid economic growth, and so the size of the sector gradually grew. Nevertheless, the fact that the retail industry was not placed in a priority position in the

2 The Price Tag System entails a situation in which the retailer is obliged to sell a commodity at the indicated price, rather than the sale being subject to bargaining and haggling, thus reducing the possibility of profiteering.

3 This time became known as the period of distribution without production (I Daegeun 2002: 148).

1960s meant that it was impossible for it to develop normally because, in the circumstances of limited resources, most of these economic resources were concentrated on the priority sector. In particular, the fact that in its early period the military government suppressed the retail industry on the grounds of consumer protection showed its attitude towards the retail sector and, simultaneously, intimated the trend of its policies concerning the retail industry in the future. The protection of consumers was one of the important goals, together with price stability, of the policies towards the retail sector from the early 1960s; the fact that protection of consumers was considered seriously as a policy goal was very unpredictable even at that time (Hwang Myeongsu et al. 1992: 305). This might illustrate that the government did not regard the retail industry as a sector deserving of support and, moreover, the government had a negative image of retailers. The military group's first policy concerning the retail sector was the 'Law of the Market', enacted at the end of August 1961. This classified the market into just two categories: the periodic market, which was operated by independent merchants every five to seven or more days, and the permanent market, operating daily in the same place. A characteristic of this law was that the market was defined by the criterion of place. For example, it defined a permanent market as a place where over twenty merchants traded in the same building, or a place which was equipped with the proper facilities such as sanitary and fire prevention requirement in accordance with the regulation concerned (Article 2). Although this law was a reflection of the circumstances of the retail sector at that time, it eventually became out of date because it did not cover new types of retailers, such as supermarkets and department stores. It was also impossible to regulate the behaviour of the trade in line with the law because there were no provisions relating to behaviour, only provisions concerning the place and facilities (Hwang Myeongsu et al. 1992: 282–283). As a result, it could not cover the whole area of the retail industry and thus needed complementary regulations.

Therefore, apart from the basic law, the military government imposed two kinds of additional regulations at almost the same time. The first was the measure to sweep away fraudulent foreign goods, which was effective from 1 September 1961, and the second was the price tag system on 1 October, the same year, in which it announced a fixed price for goods. These regulations, which were intended to reform the existing retail system, however, greatly shocked retailers who did not break off traditional practices. Following the introduction of those policies, the government still tried various methods relating to the retail industry in the 1960s. For example, DTI established a plan for 'Comprehensive Measures in the Long and Short Term for the Improvement of the Distribution System' in 1966 and the authority of the City of Seoul, the Korean capital, devised a plan for the modernization of the Dongdaemun and Namdaemun Markets, which were two of the largest traditional markets at that time. In particular, it seemed that the modernization of the two markets was desperately needed because they also acted as national wholesale markets as well as retail markets for the region of Seoul. As an extension of such policies, there were several further ones, such as the 'Plan for the Completeness of the Organizations of the Large Sale' by the DTI in 1969, and the 'Five Year Plan for the Modernization of the Distribution System' in 1969 (Shinsegae Department Store 1987: A Chronological Table of Retail Policies; DTI 1966, 1969). One of the characteristics of the retail policy in the 1960s was, as mentioned, an approach from the view of consumer protection. The EPB formulated 'An Outline for Consumer Protection' in 1968, which covered subjects such as price regulation of the main necessities of life, the expansion of the price tag system and the establishment of consultation offices in individual markets. Emphasizing commercial norms, it also expressed support for the consumer movement in the private sector and recommended the establishment of consumers' organizations (Hwang Myeongsu et al. 1992: 306).

In brief, it is clear that the government established the basic structure of a policy for the retail sector in the 1960s. However, it seemed that its view of the retail sector was not positive, especially concerning its prospects for economic development as an industry. There was a tendency to regard the retail sector as merely a supplementary tool to stabilize economic circulation, rather than an industry to be developed. Because of this attitude, the main trends of the policies were regulation for price stability and consumer protection rather than the encouragement of the retail industry (KCCI 1999: 44; Hwang Myeongsu et al. 1992: 303).

2.3.2 The Backwardness of the Retail Industry

Paradoxically, the 1950s was a period when the distribution industry rather than the manufacturing industry predominated, even if this was due, not to the prosperity of the distribution sector, but the backwardness of the manufacturing sector. The ratio of the wholesale and retail industries in the gross national product (GNP) was greater than that of the manufacturing sector by the end of the 1950s. While the ratio of the wholesale and retail industries continued at their level of about 16 per cent in the 1950s, that of the manufacturing industry reached 9 per cent in 1953 and had increased to 14.1 per cent by 1959. The ratio of the tertiary industry, including the wholesale and retail industries, was around 45 per cent and the remainder was accounted for by primary industry (BOK, National Accounts, annual; I Daegeun 2002: 423, 445–446). In terms of the employed population, the ratio of the wholesale and retail industries in the whole industry sector was also greater than that of the manufacturing industry in the 1950s. While the former was approximately 5 per cent, the latter was about 2 per cent in the 1950s. However, it was estimated that many more of the population than the official figures showed were employed in the distribution area of the informal urban sector, which did not require either much capital or particular skills, because a large number of people had moved from the agricultural sector to urban areas.[4] Therefore, most of them were shown as unemployed or latently unemployed in the informal urban sector (I Daegeun 2002: 449).

It was inevitable that in such circumstances the distribution sector, particularly the retail industry, would be both poor and small. The situation was further aggravated after the Korean War because a large number of refugees migrated to urban areas. In the case of Namdaemun Market, the number of shops increased from 252 before the war to 500 in 1953 and Dongdaemun Market expanded to 320, twice as many as before the war (KCCI 1954: 13). As the individual markets expanded in size, the number of markets in Seoul also increased to forty-four in 1961 from thirty-two in 1946 (Hwang Myeongsu et al. 1992: 283–285).

One of the most important indexes which show the degree of the development of the retail industry is the type of market that was dominant. According to Bucklin (1972), the developmental stages of the market were as follows: periodic markets – pre-business era; permanent markets – pre-business era; fragmented markets – petty capitalism; vertically integrated markets – industrial capitalism; and conglomerate retailing – financial capitalism. According to a survey in 1966, the number of permanent markets in Korea was only 248, compared with 1,090 periodic markets, making a total of 1,338 markets in Korea.[5] The degree of concentration of markets in Seoul was very high, with eighty-five (34.3 per cent) permanent markets in the capital (FKI 1967: 422). Even though Bucklin's developmental stages could not be applied directly to the Korean case because of environmental differences, it is clear that the backwardness of the retail industry in Korea was severe in that the main part of the market sector comprised periodic markets rather than permanent ones, even in the 1960s after industrialization had begun and was progressing rapidly.

4 In terms of the employed population, the population engaged in agriculture and fishing in relation to all industries fell to about 70 per cent in 1960 from about 80 per cent in 1950 (I Daegeun 2002: 449).

5 These numbers are a little different from the number of traditional markets shown in Chapter 3 due to the difference in survey methodologies, but the trend shown by the data was the same in terms of the relationship between permanent and periodic markets.

The first census of the wholesale and retail industry was carried out in 1968. Even though accurate statistical data were the basic materials for formulating policy as well as carrying out research, there had been no comprehensive collection of data concerning the distribution industry in Korea until then. Therefore, the first census was accepted by the distribution sector as very good news. According to the census, the total number of companies in the wholesale and retail industry was 278,039, made up of 95 per cent retail companies (264,100) and 5 per cent wholesale companies (13,939). As one of the indexes to show the poverty and informality of the distribution industry, we find that in the retail industry merely 0.1 per cent (349) of the companies were incorporated, while the equivalent figure for the wholesale industry was comparatively higher at 6.6 per cent (920) (SK, Commerce Census, 1968). This meant, however, that 99.9 per cent of the retail industry was private business which was much less regulated by the legal system, compared with incorporated enterprises. Nevertheless, the government carried forward a scheme to reform the distribution industry based on the census. This included improving facilities in existing markets, recommending the formation of chains to poorer shops, and the construction of new buildings for the center of the distribution industry (Hwang Myeongsu et al. 1992: 307).

2.3.3 The Department Store as a Fictitious Department Store

In 1955 there were merely six department store companies in Seoul, formed through the process of restructuring the department store industry after national independence in 1945. The Shinshin Department Store was founded in late 1955 and as a result the three major stores, Midopa, Donghwa and Whashin, became competitors. Apart from these stores, according to the 1954 survey by KCCI, there were five department store companies in Suncheon, five in Chuncheon and ten in Gunsan.[6] However, most of them were regarded as just big shops rather than department stores (Hwang Myeongsu et al. 1992: 293–294). Most Korean department stores in the 1960s were merely collections of small shops under one roof where the owners of the building rented spaces to the individual proprietors, rather than one business coming under direct management. This was little different from the other markets except that there was an overall manager for the facility. Therefore, it was no exaggeration to say that most of the owners of department stores were actually letting businessmen, rather than retailing specialists. Furthermore, it could hardly be said that these

6 These cities were much smaller than Seoul in terms of population and the size of their economies, etc., even though they played important roles as the economic centers of their regions.

were department stores as per the true meaning of the term, because their operating systems were different from those of a typical department store. In general, the characteristics of a department store as a modern retailer are fixed pricing and clear labelling within the store (Alexander and Akehurst 1999: 11). However, the department stores in Korea at that time did not enforce such institutions and in some cases, the same goods were traded at different prices even in the same department store (Shinsegae Department Store 1987: 72). Nevertheless, most consumers usually regarded the department stores as shops which usually sold luxury goods. Their luxurious image in the period of Japanese Occupation remained in people's memory and they sold mainly upmarket goods,[7] even after national independence.

After national independence in 1945, the retrogression of the department store industry was due first to the strictly controlled economy and rationing system resulting from the socio-political chaos and political instability following the Korean War in the early 1950s. Department stores were suffering from a lack of goods and, to make matters worse, they could not help becoming smaller because of the expansion of the black market in the unstable economy. In these circumstances, it seemed that the owners of the department stores chose to let their shops to individual owners because they would have to take an enormous risk in the direct management of a big shop (Hwang Myeongsu et al. 1992: 294). Even the 1960s was not a good period for department stores. They received a formidable shock from the retail industry policies enforced by the military government. As we have seen above, measures to sweep away fraudulent foreign goods and the introduction of a price tag system in 1961 were a crucial blow to them. A newspaper published in Seoul around the time of the introduction of the policies sketched the horrible situation of the effect of the policies on department stores under the title of 'Department Store Becoming Vacant Due to Closing up Stores':

> Over half of the shops in the first and second floors, which had been evaluated as the better places for sales in the Whashin and Jongro Department Stores became vacant and, in addition, the Shinshin Department Store encountered a fatal situation where two-thirds of its first and second floors became vacant (Seoul-gyeongje-sin-mun 11 September 1961).

---

7 Most of the shops in a department store sold contraband goods or fraudulent foreign goods as a luxurious retailing institution strategy. Thus, they got a great shock when the military government prohibited the sale of fraudulent foreign goods in 1961 (*Seo-ul-gyeongje-sin-mun* 11 September 1961).

The department stores narrowly maintained their positions in the retail sector during the 1960s. One event during that period was that the Shinsegae Department Store, which was previously the Dongwha Department Store, introduced the system of direct management in 1969, whereby the department store company directly owned and managed departments for sales in the outlet. The Dongwha Department Store, which used to be a part of the Japanese Mitsukoshi group and was the first department store in Korea established in 1930, was merged into Samsung Group in 1963. Samsung changed the name to Shinsegae Department Store and made efforts to change it to a modern retailer of the Western type. This kind of change influenced other stores which followed the same management strategy. In the case of Shinsegae, the ratio of direct management started at 12 per cent in 1963, increased to 50.3 per cent in 1966 and reached 85 per cent in 1969. It also implemented institutions such as a price tag system, a free return and refund system, and free window shopping, which all had an effect on its competitors (Shinsegae Department Store 1987: 78–82). As a result, it can be said that department stores in Korea, in a strict sense, began in the late 1960s even if they still did not get a particular position as a retail format in accordance with legal definition.

3 Overview of Rapid Economic Growth in the 1970s

3.1 *General Government Policy and Rapid Economic Growth*

The Korean economy began the early 1970s in a dismal situation following the depression in the world economy at the end of the 1960s. Moreover, political circumstances, which were one of the most important factors in economic growth, were very unstable because President Park Chung Hee sought to remain president for a third continuous period by revising the constitution. Even though Park, who had already amended the constitution in 1969, won the presidency in 1971, he faced severe resistance from the Korean people. However, by managing the social atmosphere through tools such as the creation of fear concerning North Korea, he brought strong pressure to bear on the resistance and, furthermore, enacted a new constitution, the Yushin Constitution, in 1972, to ensure he retained power. The new constitution, which it was suggested should be called a constitution for Korean unification, removed the limitation on presidential reappointments with the establishment of an indirect election, and greatly strengthened the authority of the president. It also contained a number of the limitations relating to human rights and democracy (MOLEG 1972; Gim Yeongmyeong 1992: 288–309). Later in the decade, Park's assassination in October 1979 threw Korean society into political turmoil, as well as leading to a severe economic depression.

President Park had linked his presidential fate with economic growth and national security against North Korea (Koo 1994: 174; I Byeongcheon 1998: 48). In fact, the possibility of the withdrawal of the US forces stationed in Korea, which was discussed in the early 1970s, might have partly contributed to the establishment of the new constitution by aggravating the uneasiness felt by the Korean people regarding security.[8] It was also understood that the importance of the heavy and chemical industry (HCI), which was a pillar of the defence industry, was also related to such a situation in that the President stressed the independent national defence capability at that time.[9] His intentions for the defence industry appeared in his emphasis on the HCI as a strategic industry in the Third Five-Year Plan for Economic Development, which began in 1972. The Korean plan had the following goals: improvement of the international balance of payments; advancement of the industrial structure through the development of the HCI; development of human capital and technology; and 8.6 per cent average economic growth rate in the period. The most prominent goal was the economic growth rate, and the main tool in achieving its improvement was the speeding-up of the development of industry, in particular the HCI. To achieve this goal the government selected the steel, nonferrous metal, mechanical, shipbuilding, electronics and petrochemical industries as six strategic industries to be developed during this period. There were several events in which the basic infrastructure of the Korean HCI was developed during the third plan as follows: the completion of POSCO, which developed into the second largest integrated steel mill in the world, the Changwon machine industrial complex, the Kumi electronics industrial complex, and the Yuichun petrochemical industrial complex, etc. (KISS 1998: 15).

However, the Korean economy was not immune to various problems from which the world economy suffered, such as a worldwide depression and a suspension of specie payment in the early 1970s. Economic growth in 1970 fell to 8.8 per cent from 13.8 per cent in 1969, and was recorded as 4.5 per cent in 1972. The Korean economy showed a short recovery to 12 per cent in 1973 but fell again to 7.2 per cent, with a 42.1 per cent increase in the consumer price index in 1974, falling yet further to 5.9 per cent in 1975, having suffered badly from the

8 The Yushin Consitution was passed with an approval rate of 91.5 per cent in a referendum on 17 December 1972.

9 The independent national defence capability promoted by President Park Chung Hee was a policy linked with the *Nixon Doctrine* (1970) which stated that the matter of Asia had to be solved by the Asian people (*I Samseong* 1993: 84).

effects of the first oil shock (BOK, National Accounts, annual). In this time of difficulty, the impetus given by the government to the HCI did not weaken. This was reflected in the fourth 'Five-Year Plan for Economic Development' which began in 1977. At that time, the world economy was showing signs of recovery from the severe depression of the first oil shock and the Korean economy was taking advantage of these global trends. The government planned for an annual average growth rate of 17.3 per cent in the HCI, while the goal for the general annual economic growth was 9.2 per cent during the fourth development plan and as a result, the ratio of the HCI to the manufacturing sector would become 52.1 per cent by 1981, the final year of the fourth plan (Im Hwicheol 1998: 27). The growth strategy led by HCI was successful. GNI per capita in 1977 reached the level of US$1,000 and exports were recorded as being over US$10 billion at that time. Such a boom continued into 1978 when the economic growth rate was recorded as being 9.3 per cent. However, there was no exception to the rule that a boom is reason for a depression. The Korean economy settled into a depression from 1979, when its growth rate was 6.8 per cent, and following this the annual economic growth rate recorded, for the first time, minus 1.5 per cent in 1980 after the establishment of the developmental plan. This miserable result was closely related to an excessive boom[10] and the second oil shock in 1979 dealt it a fatal blow (KISS 1998: 17).

In general, an economic crisis is accompanied by political uncertainty and the situation gets worse and worse if the political leadership, particularly authoritarianism, becomes unstable (Przeworski et al. 2006: 193). The Korean economic-political situation at the end of the 1970s followed a worst case scenario. There had been keen political tension between the government and social movement groups advocating the development of democracy and the enlargement of the right to labour in Korea since the early 1970s. Park's regime suppressed the activists, and, what was worse, some of them were killed. As the political situation deteriorated, the social movement also became more active. The economic crisis at the end of the 1970s occurred in such a situation. The combination of economic depression and severe political tension exploded in a social crash and induced a split in political powers. The conflict between the hawks and the doves in power eventually involved people in quite unexpected quarters, and the shock of the assassination of President Park in October 1979 made the Korean economy worse (Gim Ilyeong 1995: 208).

10 In particular, it was understood that excessive investment in the HCI resulted in its overcapacity beyond the amount of exports and, consequently, made the Korean economy fall into a severe recession (Bak Jingeun 2000: 102–105).

In sum, even though the Korean economy faced difficult circumstances, the economy developed continuously in the 1970s. Its momentum for rapid economic growth was an economic plan concentrated on the HCI in the early 1970s which was driven by the government. The HCI had been the center of a driving force for economic growth during the period of the 1970s. Its successful development, however, was remarkably shaken by the second oil shock in 1979 with excessive investment and economic instability aggravating political uncertainty. In contrast to this, the retail industry found it difficult to grasp the momentum to develop because of the government's concentration on the HCI. In particular, although the environment for the development of the retail industry was improving rapidly with the increase of income, the government's negative attitude towards it which we will see in the future constrained its development. Because of this, a distinct phenomenon where the backwardness of retailing coexisted with the prosperity of the manufacturing sector appeared in the Korean economy in the 1970s.

3.2 *The Change of Socio-economic Environments*

3.2.1 The Increase in Income and Expenditure

Rapid economic growth is usually accompanied by the other changes in the socio-economic sector. First, it results in an increase in income, to which we have to pay attention when considering the development of the retail industry.

According to Figure 2.1, the GNI per capita was only 90,000 Korean *won* (US$ 254) in 1970 but had increased to 220,000 *won* by 1974, having taken only four years to more than double. Furthermore, as the income level increased ever more rapidly, GNI per capita reached 500,000 *won* in 1977 and 840,000 *won* by 1979, that is to say it took just five years to achieve around four times the level of GNI per capita in 1974[11] (BOK, National Accounts, annual).

The Private Final Consumption Expenditure (PFCE) shows a similar trend to GNI. The PFCE which was just 2,058.5 billion Korean *won* (US$ 6.03 billion) in

---

11 The reason why the Korean *won* is used as the unit of money is to avoid distortion caused by the exchange rate. In particular, this is needed to keep consistency of statistics used in this work because of the dramatic change in the exchange rate at the time of the financial crisis around 1997. The value of the US dollar calculated in Korean won changed from 804.78 Korean won per US dollar in 1996 to 1,398.88 *won* per US dollar in 1998 (BOK, Foreign Exchange Rate, annual). Accordingly, the valuation of Korean GNI based on the US dollar may well be distorted. Further, the situation of the income in a national economy which may be related to consumption, not by comparison with another country, should be valuated in terms of its own currency. However, this work uses US dollars which are valuated by annual standard exchange rate as a supplementary currency to estimate the amount roughly.

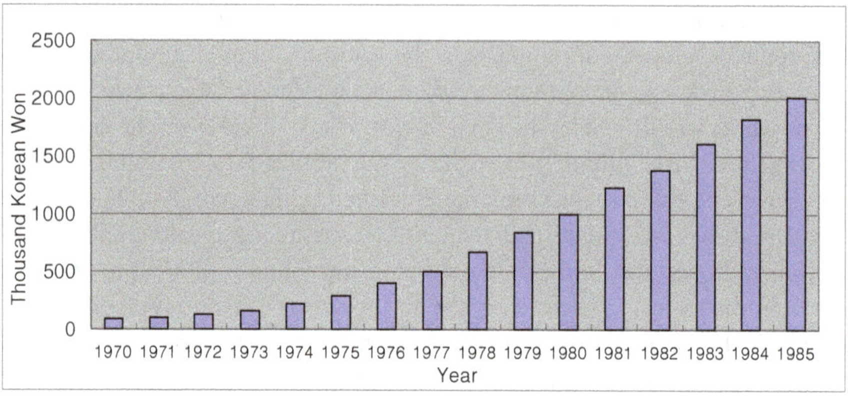

FIGURE 2.1 *Trend of* GNI *per capita (nominal term of* GNI *per capita: thousand Korean* won). SOURCE: BOK, NATIONAL ACCOUNTS, ANNUAL.

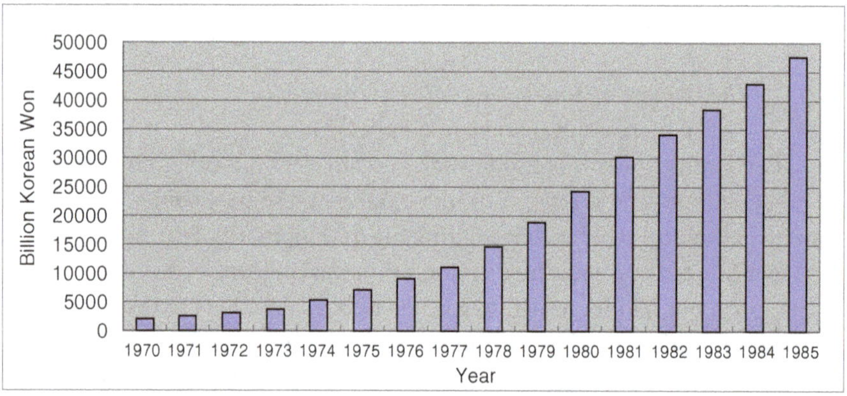

FIGURE 2.2 *Trend of the Private Final Consumption Expenditure (nominal term of the Private Final Consumption Expenditure (*PFCE*): billion Korean* won). SOURCE: BOK, NATIONAL ACCOUNTS, ANNUAL.

1970, increased to 7,164.2 billion *won* in 1975. Increasing continuously, it rose to 24,250.6 billion *won* in 1980.

According to Figure 2.3, the monthly income of salary and wage earners' households in urban areas (SWEHS) continuously increased since 1970. It was 28,200 *won* (US$ 82.5) in 1970, 65,500 *won* in 1975, 144,500 *won* in 1978, and rose to 281,000 *won* in 1981.

According to Figure 2.4, monthly consumption expenditure of urban labour household was not hugely different from the monthly income, rising from 24,700 *won* (US$ 72.3) in 1970 to 56,900 *won* in 1975. The monthly consumption expenditure rose from 108,900 *won* in 1978 to 211,800 *won* in 1981.

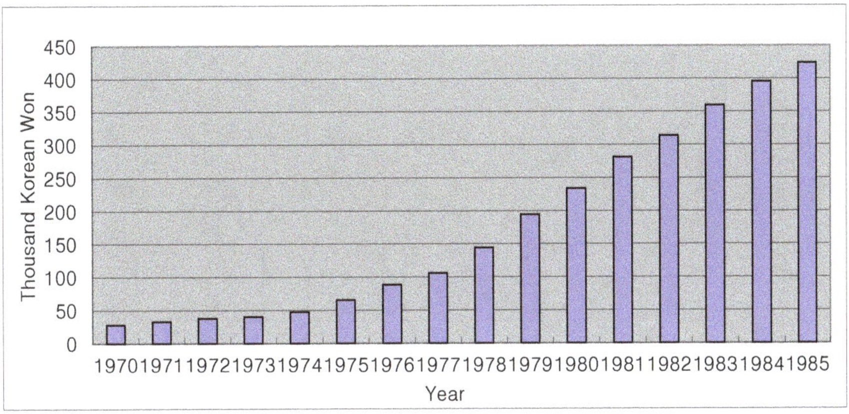

FIGURE 2.3 *Trend of income of urban labour household (nominal term: thousand Korean* won). SOURCE: SK, MONTHLY INCOME AND EXPENDITURE PER URBAN HOUSEHOLD, ANNUAL.

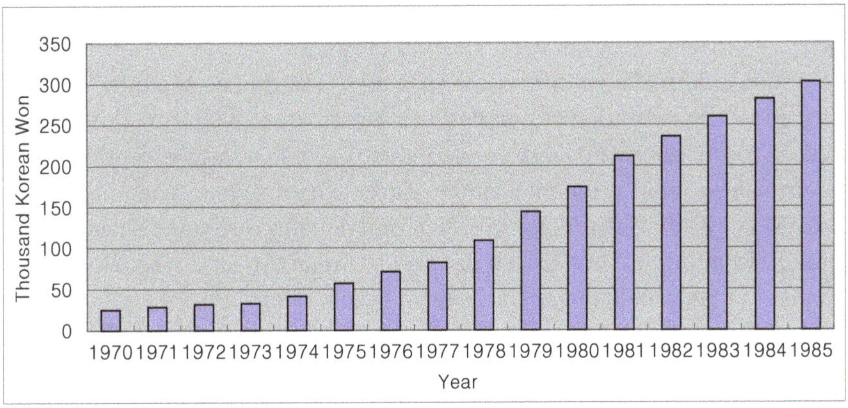

FIGURE 2.4 *Trend of Consumption Expenditure of Urban Labour Household (Nominal Term: thousand Korean* won). SOURCE: SK, MONTHLY INCOME AND EXPENDITURE PER URBAN HOUSEHOLD, ANNUAL.

Figure 2.5 shows that the expansion of consumption expenditure on the basis of increase in income was necessarily linked to the rise of sales of retail industry.

The Wholesale and Retail Trade Census shows that total retail sales were 608 billion *won* (US$ 1,681.4 million) in 1971 and sharply increased to 3,310.3 billion *won* in 1976. This trend continued, and it was 7,187.1 billion *won* in 1979.

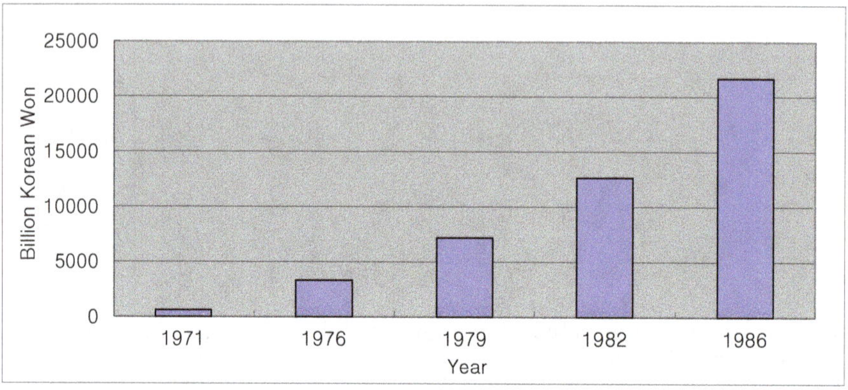

FIGURE 2.5 *Trends of retail sales (nominal term: billion Korean* won). SOURCE: SK, WHOLESALE AND RETAIL TRADE CENSUS (1971, 1976, 1979, 1982), WHOLESALE AND RETAIL TRADE CENSUS WITH THE OVERALL ESTABLISHMENT STATISTICS (1986).

3.2.2 The Increase in Population and Families

In general, industrialization is accompanied by the change of family composition and a concentration of population in urban areas, which are the pre-conditions for development of the retail industry. Korea was no exception to this process. The rapid industrialization which accompanied economic growth went side by side. The average rate of population increase was 2.8 per cent per annum from 1970 to 1975 and 1.6 per cent between 1975 and 1980. The average number of household members declined from 5.2 persons in 1970 to 5.0 in 1975 and to 4.5 in 1980. The total number of households rose from 5.6 million in 1970 to 6.6 million in 1975, and to 8 million in 1980 (SK, Population and Housing Census, annual). This is closely related to the change in family composition. Table 2.3 shows the decline of three and over four generations' households.

In particular, the decline of three generation households was quite considerable in the 1970s. In contrast, both one person and one generation households increased gradually from 1970 to 1985. With this, what should be noted is the level of urbanization because concentrated population is a significant factor for development of the retail industry. The percentage of the urban population in the total population increased by about 10 per centage points from 39.7 per cent in 1970 to 47.9 per cent in 1975 and to 57 per cent in 1980. This means an increase in the number of households in urban areas as purchasing units.

According to Figure 2.6, the number of households was smaller in urban areas than in non-urban areas. This was slightly reversed in 1975 when the number of households was 3,331,000 in urban areas but 3,316,000 in non-urban areas.

TABLE 2.3 *Trend of generations in household (%)*

	1970	1975	1980	1985*
One person households		4.2	4.8	6.9
One generation**	6.8	6.7	8.3	9.6
Two generations	70	68.9	68.5	67
Three generations	22.1	19.2	16.5	14.4
Over four generations	1.1	0.9	0.5	0.4

* The sum of figures in each year has been a bit under 100 since 1980 because non-relative households, which consist of members of non-blood relationship, have been classified as a separate item.
**One generation: household which consists of members of the same generation, like a married couple without children.
Source: SK, Population and Housing Census, annual

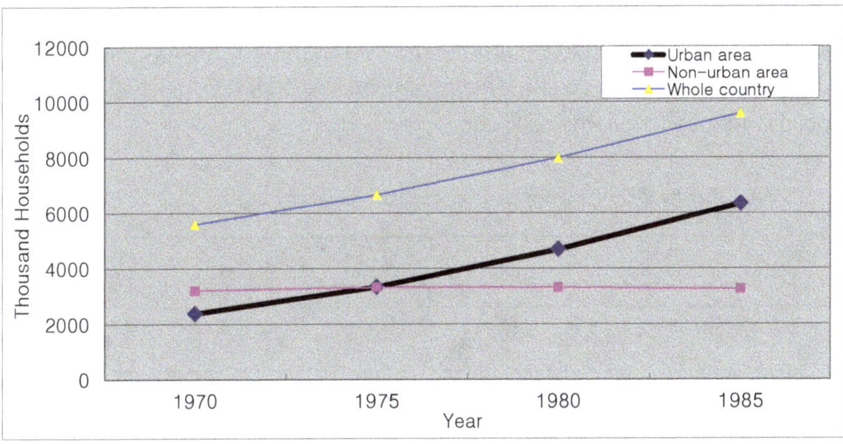

FIGURE 2.6 *Number of households (urban area: administrative districts authorised by the government to call themselves by the name of city as administrative districts where their number of population are over 50,000. 'Administrative district' means that population density is not a significant criterion).* SOURCE: SK, POPULATION AND HOUSING CENSUS, ANNUAL.

By 1980, the former was 4.7 million but the latter was 3.3 million. This may be solid evidence that urbanization as a significant condition for development of the retail industry, was rapidly progressing in the 1970s. This is borne out by the increase in the number of large cities. There were just eighteen cities of over 100,000 population in 1970, their number increased to twenty-eight in 1975, including six cities over 500,000. In 1980, the number of such cities rose to thirty-four, including four cities with a population of over one million. The population of Seoul was around 5.5 million people, which was 17.6 per cent of the total population of the country in 1970. By 1980, the population of Seoul was 8.4 million (22.3 per cent of the national total). In general, the concentration of the population in big cities continued (SK, Population and Housing Census, annual).

3.3 *The Aggravation of Distribution Inequality*

3.3.1 Inequality of Income

Because of the official survey's lack of data on income distribution, research on income distribution was scarce during the 1970s. Most of the existing studies concerning income distribution used the survey of urban households and the survey of agricultural households for its calculations before 1980. However, limited samples meant that the surveys were not enough to show the precise situation of income distribution. To cope with this, researchers tried to calculate income distribution using separate surveys or other economic data. As Table 2.4 shows, Ju Hakjung (1979) calculated Gini Coefficients in 1965, 1970 and 1976 through estimation of income of non-labour forces contained in existing data. EPB produced Gini Coefficients in 1980 and 1985 on the basis of the social statistics survey in each year.

TABLE 2.4 *Trends of the Gini coefficient in the whole country*

	1965	1970	1976	1980	1985
Gini*	0.344	0.332	0.391	0.389	0.345

* Gini are the results from Ju Hakjung (1979) and Economic Planning Board (EPB 1987, 1990).
Source: as cited in Choe Gwang and Hyeon Jingwon (1996: 23)

Table 2.4, shows that the income distribution was aggravated in the 1970s. This is understood to be closely related to rapid industrialization in the period. In fact, most of the research in this field has underscored rapid industrialization with heavy chemical industry as an important reason. The various kinds of support of this industry, such as taxation supports and credit rationing, led to imbalance between economic sectors and between regions and consequently resulted in income inequality. The high inflation of around 20 per cent annually also contributed to the aggravation of income distribution (Hyeon Jingwon 1996: 24; I Jeongu and Hwang Seonghyeon 1998: 161).

3.3.2 Inequality of Wealth

In general, it can be said that the main types of assets are financial assets and land. However, land is more likely to be important in less developed countries because their financial markets are also less developed. The Korean financial market in the 1970s was undeveloped due to the backwardness in the economy. All the commercial banks were owned by the government as a tool to support industry, and financial goods were hardly developed except for traditional deposits. The stock market was merely a titular institution for a few gamblers. As a result, land was the main asset in Korea in the 1970s (Son Jaeyeong 1991: 61). The problem in research concerning wealth, however, is that there is little data relating to the distribution of the ownership of land. An official survey was carried out for the first time in 1986, before the enforcement of the public concept of land ownership. This enforcement consisted of strong regulation on the ownership of the land. Therefore, its distribution before 1986 cannot be shown precisely. Nevertheless, I will try to combine the scattered data concerning land to calculate inequality of wealth in the 1970s. For this purpose, I focuses on the trends in increase in the price of land because the value of land as a form of wealth depends on its price. It is inevitable that the rise of land prices is concentrated mainly in urban and industrial areas, because of the difference of demand between agricultural and urban areas. Therefore, it can be said broadly that the higher the increase in land prices, the worse the situation of wealth equality. It is also highly possible that the greater the speed of industrialization, the greater the speed of exacerbation in wealth inequality of land. This implies a discrepancy between urban and agricultural areas. If a large number of people in an agricultural area move into an urban area within a short time frame, then wealth inequality is likely to be aggravated rapidly.

In fact, those conditions that will exacerbate wealth inequality can be seen to apply to the Korean case in the 1970s. The Korean government began its official survey of land prices from 1974 because the rise of land prices became one of the most serious social problems with rapid industrialization.[12]

Figure 2.7 shows the trend of the rate of increase of land prices by region between 1975 and 1985. As it indicates, land prices were led by the big cities during the period. It shows that there was a huge gap in the rate of increase by region, in the period when prices increased rapidly. In 1978, the rate of increase in land prices in big cities was nearly 60 per cent while that in the counties was only 6.3 per cent. The gap in land prices between regions can be more clearly shown in terms of the cumulative rate of increase.

---

12 The government published the annual rate of change of land prices until 1986 and, after that, carried out a quarterly survey.

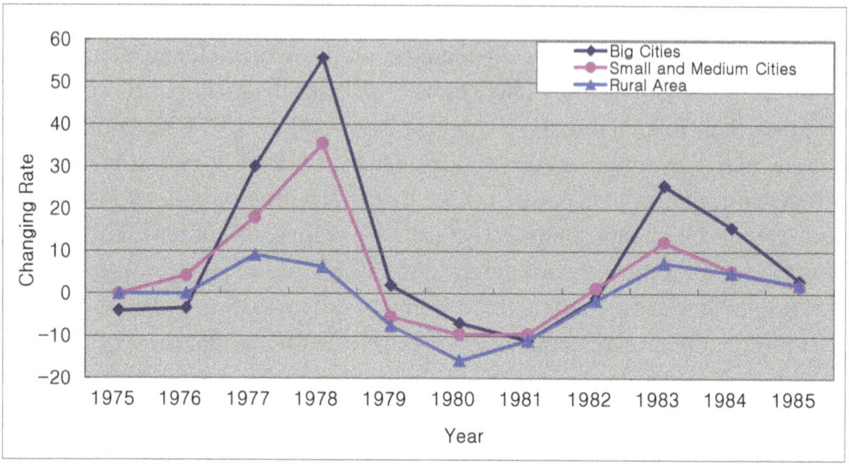

FIGURE 2.7 *Trends of land prices (real term calculated by the author through the* GDP *deflator based on 100 at 2000).* SOURCE: MINISTRY OF CONSTRUCTION-TRANSPORTATION (MOCT), SURVEY OF LAND PRICES, ANNUAL.

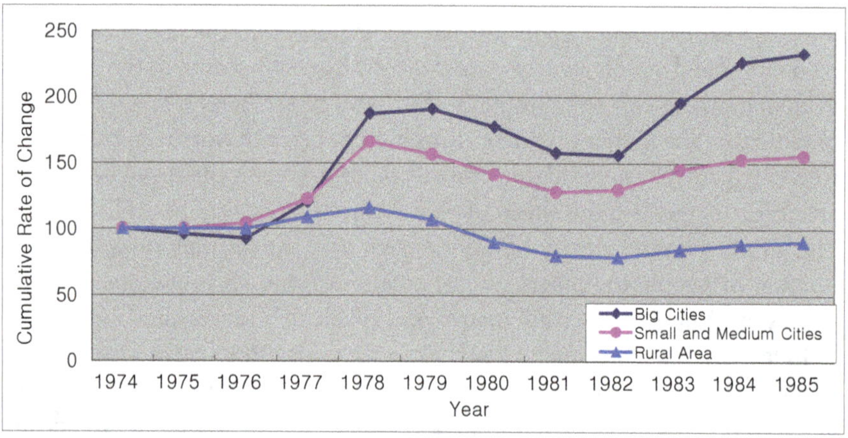

FIGURE 2.8 *Index of real land prices (1974=100) (real term calculated by the author through the* GDP *deflator based on 100 at 2000).* SOURCE: MOCT, SURVEY OF LAND PRICES, ANNUAL.

When the starting points of all the regions are fixed as 100 in 1974 in Figure 2.8, the cumulative rate of increase of land prices in the big cities was over 233.28 per cent between 1974 and 1985. In contrast to this, that of the counties was at a minus level (90.3 per cent). As we have seen earlier, if the huge gap in land prices before 1974 is considered in relation to this discrepancy, it can be seen that the gap in land value between these regions was constantly increasing throughout the 1970s. These trends may be closely related to rapid industrialization and urbanization which make the value of land different by means of demand and city land is the main factor that influences the change of land prices (Bak Heonju et al. 2000: 32). It is worth emphasizing that urbanization is likely to expand the gap in land wealth between original residents and migrants from outside the city because most of the migrants are jobseekers. In this respect, the speed of urbanization from the 1960s in Korea is important. The rate of urbanization in Korea was 28 per cent in 1960 and it increased to 39.6 per cent in 1970. Its expansion in the 1970s was the fastest in decades since the 1960s with a rise of 17.3 percentage points to 57 per cent in 1980. It rose to 65.4 per cent in 1985 (SK, Population and Housing Census, annual). This implies that the difference of land wealth among people probably increased at a greater speed in the 1970s. Even if it is impossible to know the precise situation of land wealth within the period, we can presume that the distribution of land was not good at that time because the Gini Coefficient of land was calculated as 0.86. Among corporations alone it was recorded as 0.96 in the early 1990s (Hyeon Jingwon 1996: 266–267). In this respect, the situation of inequality in the Korean economy was already likely to have been well-established in terms of the distribution of land as wealth in the 1970s.

4 Backwardness of the Retail Industry in the 1970s

4.1 *An Overview of the Distribution Industry*

The state of the distribution industry had improved in the amount of sales through the 1970s even though there had been barriers in the path of improvement in terms of both the number of employees per company, and the legal status of companies. Given such limitations, it can be said that there was hardly any structural change in the distribution industry in the 1970s, while at the same time there was huge development in terms of an increase in quantity accompanied by rapid economic growth.[13]

According to Table 2.5, the value of total sales in the distribution industry increased by about ten times during the 1970s. In particular, the rate of increase in the retail industry was much greater than that of the wholesale industry in general, being about eleven times over the same period. Another interesting

13 The survey of wholesale and retail trade in the 1960s and 1970s was a type of census and so is regarded as less consistent according to administrative ability and technology surveys at that time. In particular, the items concerning sales were estimated to be less accurate due to the limitations of interviews. Therefore, the comparison between censuses has to be used in a limited way, focusing on rough trends, for example.

TABLE 2.5 *Annual sales in the distribution industry*

	Annual sales by the industry			
	1968	1971	1976	1979
Wholesale* (million *won*)	297,659	454,937	2,448,662	3,851,343
Retail** (million *won*)	243,404	607,958	3,310,255	7,187,050
Total (million *won*)	541,063	1,062,895	5,758,918	11,038,393

* Wholesale means a business in which goods are sold in large quantities to retailers or other wholesalers for resale (*Jo-sa-gae-yo* (Outline of the Survey), annual).
** Retail means a business which sells goods to an end consumer (*Jo-sa-gae-yo* (Outline of the Survey), annual)
Source: SK, Commerce Census (1968), Wholesale and Retail Trade Census (1971, 1976, 1979)

thing was an increase in the importance of the retail sector in the distribution industry. This can be shown through the percentage of sales in both industries compared to total sales of the distribution industry. The phenomenon of a reversal in the amount of sales between both sectors in the early 1970s was closely related to a change in statistical methodology. Foreign trade, which accounted for about 25 per cent of sales in the wholesale trade, was excluded in the survey in 1971. Nevertheless, the decreasing trend in sales of the wholesale sector during the 1970s was clear. The percentage of sales of the wholesale sector in the total sales of the distribution industry decreased to just 34.9 per cent in 1979 from over 40 per cent in previous surveys. This meant that the Korean economy attached too much importance to the production sector, even in the distribution industry, because a large part of the sales in the wholesale sector of the distribution industry was composed of raw materials, such as metallic minerals, building materials, etc. Accordingly, the fact that the percentage of the wholesale sector in total sales had decreased since the late 1970s could be a result of the fact that the concept of consumption was taken, for the first time, as being useful in the Korean economy in the late 1970s.

Table 2.6 shows that the distribution industry had also developed in terms of the number of companies[14] in the 1970s. The number of companies in-

14 The companies surveyed are retailers which had actually operated for more than three months at the same place before the indicated date for the survey (SK, *Jo-sa-gae-yo*

TABLE 2.6 *Number of companies in the distribution industry*

	Number of companies				Ratio of composition (%)			
	1968	1971	1976	1979	1968	1971	1976	1979
Wholesale	13,939	17,471	20,260	23,835	5.0	5.2	4.9	5.3
Retail	264,100	320,471	393,651	422,012	95.0	94.8	95.1	94.7
Total	278,039	337,942	413,911	445,847	100.0	100.0	100.0	100.0

Source: SK, Commerce Census (1968), Wholesale and Retail Trade Census (1971, 1976, 1979)

TABLE 2.7 *Annual sales per company and per employee in the industry (million* won)

	Per company				Per employee			
	1968	1971	1976	1979	1968	1971	1976	1979
Wholesale	21.3	26.0	120.9	161.6	4.5	7.0	26.1	33.0
Retail	0.9	1.9	8.4	17.0	0.5	1.1	4.8	9.4

Source: SK, Commerce Census (1968), Wholesale and Retail Trade Census (1971, 1976, 1979)

TABLE 2.8 *Legal status of the business*

	Wholesale (ratio in total wholesale number, %)		Retail (ratio in total retailing number, %)	
	Corporate Bodies	Personal Businesses	Corporate Bodies	Personal Businesses
1968	920 (6.6 %)	13,019 (93.4 %)	349 (0.1 %)	263,751 (99.9 %)
1971	337 (1.9 %)	17,134 (98.1 %)	359 (0.1 %)	320,112 (99.9 %)
1976	2,556 (12.6 %)	17,704 (87.4 %)	1772 (0.5 %)	391,879 (99.5 %)
1979	1,862 (7.8 %)	21,973 (92.2 %)	2,961 (0.7 %)	419,051 (99.3 %)

Source: SK, Commerce Census (1968), Wholesale and Retail Trade Census (1971, 1976, 1979)

creased to about 446,000 in 1979 from 278,000 in 1968, and in particular the number of retail companies was 422,000 in 1979, an increase of 59.8 per cent

(Outline of the Survey), annual). This means that the census covers actual retailers beyond legal registration.

over the period. However, the trend of increase slowed down towards the late 1970s.

According to Table 2.7, the sales per company and per employee had risen dramatically as the increasing trend in the number of companies and employees had slowed down in the 1970s, while the amount of sales in the distribution industry had increased rapidly over the same period. In the case of the retail industry, the annual sales per company rose about eighteen times between 1968 and 1979 and a rate of increase of annual sales per employee also recorded a similar figure for the same period.

This might mean that the internal economic environment for development around the retail industry had improved in the 1970s, even though the important conditions for its modernization were insufficient in terms of its internal structure, such as the composition of the labour force and the legal type of business, which we will examine in the next part.

First, the percentage of corporate bodies in the distribution industry was quite low. According to Table 2.8, in the case of the wholesale industry, even though the percentage was over 10 per cent in the survey in 1976, it fell back to less than 10 per cent in the survey in 1979.

The retail industry was even worse than the wholesale one. While its sales grew rapidly, the percentage of corporate bodies never exceeded 1 per cent in the 1970s. This might mean that the retail industry was severely limited in its ability to grow into a large-scale modernized retailing institution in terms of, especially, finance, even though it was not impossible to have large-scale retail institutions of the personal business type.

Such a tendency can be confirmed through the percentage of companies according to the number of their employees. As we can see in Table 2.9, in the case of the retail industry, the percentage of companies with two or fewer employees was nearly 90 per cent for the whole of the 1970s, while the percentage of those with ten or more employees was never over 0.5 per cent for the same period. Even though the number of employees per company in the wholesale industry was more than that in the retail industry, the ratio of companies with ten or more employees was never over 10 per cent for the whole of the 1970s. This was a reason why small businesses were pointed out as one of the most important characteristics of the Korean retail industry.

Another characteristic of the Korean retail industry was that business was at subsistence level, rather than for profit as a usual business. This may explain the high ratio of family workers to the total number of workers in the retail industry.

Table 2.10 shows that the percentage of family workers to the total in retail was over 80 per cent throughout the 1970s, while the number of regular

TABLE 2.9 *Percentage of companies by number of employees*

	Wholesale				Retail			
	1968	1971	1976	1979	1968	1971	1976	1979
1~2	42.2	44.7	48.2	38.1	87.7	87.3	89.3	89.9
3~4	36.1	37.0	29.4	32.7	11.0	10.9	8.9	8.2
5~9	15.4	14.3	14.3	21.1	1.2	1.6	1.4	1.5
Over 10	6.3	4.0	8.1	8.1	0.1	0.2	0.4	0.4
Total	100.0	100.0	100.0	100.0	100.0	100.0	100.0	100.0

Source: SK, Commerce Census (1968), Wholesale and Retail Trade Census (1971, 1976, 1979)

TABLE 2.10 *Composition of employees and type of employment*

	Wholesale			Retail		
	Family*	Regular employees	Temporary and daily workers	Family*	Regular employees	Temporary and daily workers
1968	19,725 (27.0)	46,745 (64.1)	6,548 (8.9)	393,972 (81.7)	62,890 (13.0)	25,410 (5.3)
1971	28,098 (43.1)	32,485 (49.8)	4,656 (7.1)	494,679 (85.1)	61,013 (10.5)	25,482 (4.4)
1979	33,387 (28.6)	76,132 (65.3)	7,090 (6.1)	645,086 (84.3)	112,352 (14.7)	7,742 (1.0)

Percentage in brackets. *Family means self-employed and unpaid family workers.
Source: SK, Commerce Census (1968), Wholesale and Retail Trade Census (1971, 1979)

employees was around 12 per cent in the same period. In particular, the fact that the percentage of family workers scarcely changed even though sales per company, as well as throughout the whole retail industry, increased rapidly, needs to be considered. This could be because retail companies' gains did not reach a high enough level to enable companies to pay employees normal wages. This was another reason why small and poor businesses were identified as one of the most important characteristics of the Korean retail industry. Unlike the retail industry, the wholesale industry came much closer to running businesses as enterprises when the percentage of regular employees reached 65 per cent in the 1970s. Additionally, despite the slump of the early 1970s, the increase in regular employees in the retail industry could be considered a sign of partial progress made by large-scale businesses as indicated by the rise in the percentage of companies having more than ten employees in the retail industry.

4.2 *The State of the Traditional Markets*

As we have seen, the percentage of big businesses in the retail industry was very small in the 1970s. This meant that the heart of the retail industry was the traditional market, where most of the SMSTRs were located, regardless of size. In general, the traditional market was classified into two types: the permanent market and the periodic market (Bucklin 1972).

As shown in Table 2.11, the number of periodic markets increased until the middle of the 1970s and then decreased, while the number of permanent markets increased continuously. The increase in periodic markets meant that there were a lot of non-commercial areas until the middle of the 1970s in Korea. The increase in permanent markets meant the continuous progress of urbanization in local areas, as, in many cases, the permanent markets were developed through the conversion of periodic markets (Jo Byeongchan 1993: 336). This phenomenon could be considered a uniquely Korean retail industry phenomenon, in that the number of periodic markets increased until the middle of the 1970s, when GNI per capita was over US$1,000 due to rapid industrialization. Moreover, periodic markets outnumbered permanent markets until the early 1980s, when GNI per capita reached nearly US$2,000. Additionally, according to Bucklin (1972), the fact that permanent markets, as a retail institution, increased in number until 1991, when GNI per capita was about US$7,000, might be considered unusual. It seems that these phenomena were related to rapid industrialization and unequal economic development strategy in terms of both industry and region since the middle of the 1960s. With such a strategy, it was inevitable that there would be huge discrimination between regions, as well as industries, in all aspects. In spite of rapid industrialization, the wider existence of periodic markets was an important factor in explaining such a phenomenon. The increase in periodic markets which were located mainly in agricultural areas (FKI 1967: 422) implied that the degree of commercialization was much lower when compared with the degree of economic development in the whole nation. Furthermore, it might be difficult to classify even the regions around periodic markets as areas to be commercialized, because one of the characteristics of markets is as a place for exchange between consumers (Hwang Myeongsu et al. 1992: 289–290) and people were actually exposed to the market only once every five days.

TABLE 2.11 *Change of the relationship between periodic and permanent markets*

Year	Number of periodic markets	Number of permanent markets
1970	994	260*
1975	1,018	492
1977	961	686
1979	925	766
1981	884	785
1983	866	1,118
1987	755	1,083
1988	752	1,099
1991	686	1,176
2000	491	696

*This figure is the number of permanent markets in 1968.
Source: KCCI, *A Comprehensive Bibliography of the Retailing and Wholesale Industry* (1992, 1995) as cited in Baek Insu (2003: 167); Institute of Korean Distribution Industry (2000: 5)

With this delay in commercialization, another characteristic of the Korean retail industry was the prosperity of the permanent market as a traditional retail institution. The permanent market, where a great number of independent retailers run their businesses with traditional methods such as haggling, is a place where the retail institutions are permanently clustered.

As a typical example of permanent markets, Figure 2.9 and 2.10 show one of the traditional markets in Anyang City, south of Seoul. Anyang Central Market (*An-yang jung-angsi-jang*) was established with 283 shops run by independent retailers in 1961. Developing rapidly, it had 1,151 shops in an area of 59,177 square metres, including some buildings in 2008. The shops in the market mostly deal with edible items, clothes and groceries <http://www.anyang.go.kr>. Figure 2.9 shows one of the main entrances, and Figure 2.10 the inside of the market just beyond the entrance. Figure 2.9 also indicates that there are a number of independent retailers outside of the market. On entering the market, one can see the main retailers, who deal with various kinds of items, on both sides of the wide corridor. Their shops are just partitioned by adjustable transparent sheeting even if they have a right to use their spaces permanently. Another group of independent retailers run shops just like stalls (*no-jeom*) in the middle of the corridor. Even if they are smaller and weaker than the main retailers in terms of stability and property rights, they also run their shops on a permanent basis.

FIGURE 2.9 *Anyang central market 1*

FIGURE 2.10 *Anyang central market 2*

Most goods here are purchased through haggling without price tags. Of course, this is a traditional market which has been continuously developed since establishment. Its shape would have been much smaller and less organized in the 1970s than it is today.

Even though the permanent market was also a typical retail institution in the pre-business era, according to Bucklin, it was the dominant retail institution in urban areas (Hwang Myeongsu et al. 1992: 311) until the period of industrial capitalism in Korea, and the number continuously increased until the early 1990s. This might imply that permanent markets absorbed a huge part of the mass-consumption which appeared in the industrialization stage. This is potentially related both to their competitive structure and to the various kinds of environments around them. Furthermore, as a result, their prosperity has a close relationship with the inactivity or development of the department store as a retail institution to meet mass-consumption. This is an important factor to be examined later.

4.3 *The Dominance of Manufacturing Companies in the Distribution Sector of the Domestic Market*

In the 1970s, when government policy was remarkably influential on the economy, the intention of the government to drive the manufacturing sector influenced the relationship between industries in the domestic market. In the distribution industry, this influence appeared as the dominance of manufacturing companies in terms of bargaining power. Even though the period of manufacturing dominance over the distribution industry appeared generally during the period of industrialization, it is regarded as an obstacle to the development of the distribution industry, because the innovation of distribution can be delayed (O Sejo and Bak Jinyong 2004: 106). However, in the absence of a proper network for the distribution industry in the 1970s in Korea, the manufacturing companies were not the only barrier to development of the industry. On the one hand, even if the companies constructed a distribution network solely for their sales they would have contributed to the establishment of a basic infrastructure for the industry; on the other hand, they would have oppressed the autonomous development of the distribution industry in the 1970s. Data limitations, however, mean the state of the distribution industry in the 1970s needs to be estimated from the 1991 survey. Generally, it seems that the conditions of the distribution industry in the 1970s were worse than in 1991. The policy report by the government, which was published in 1991, illustrated the relationship between the manufacturing and the distribution sectors.

According to Table 2.12, in 1990, in the case of the foods, 70 per cent of the goods produced by large companies were marketed in the supply channel

TABLE 2.12 *Pattern of distribution by items*

Items	Classification	Type controlled by manufacturer		Independent retailer	Others	Total
		Owned by manufacturer	Franchise			
Foods	Big Businesses	35.0	35.0	25.0	5.0	100
	SMSCs*	5.9	41.2	41.1	11.8	100
Cars	Big Businesses	100.0	0	0	0	100
Clothes	Luxurious Apparel	50.0	30.0	10.0	10.0	100
	Cotton Goods	7.5	0	84.7	7.8	100
Wooden goods	Big Businesses	0	69.2	23.1	7.7	100
	SMSCs	16.7	16.7	50.0	16.6	100
Electric and electronic appliances	Home appliances	40.0	50.0	10.0	0	100
	Others	4.0	57.0	4.0	35.0	100

*SMSCs: Small and Medium Size Companies. Unit: Ratio of sales volume.
Source: DTI, *the State and Policy Direction of the Distribution Industry*, 1991, as cited in Cha Sinheung (1995: 78)

controlled directly by manufacturing companies, while merely 25 per cent were managed by independent retailers. In this case, the manufacturing companies managed such a system through two types of outlets: one was the type of outlet owned by the companies (35 per cent) and another was the type of franchise completely controlled by the companies (35 per cent). Of course, the 25 per cent of independent retailers could not occupy an equal position in negotiations with manufacturing companies. In the case of clothes, two types of different phenomena were shown.

While sales of the luxurious and expensive apparel were mainly controlled by the producers (80 per cent), about 85 per cent of cotton goods, which fell into the category of cheap necessities of life, were sold by independent retailers. This related both to the small scale of the independent retailers and the producers' aim to maintain the luxurious image of their brand. A much stronger tendency for producers to lead in the sale of expensive goods appeared in industrial products. In the case of electric and electronic appliances, such as refrigerators and washing machines, 90 per cent of the sales were marketed directly by the manufacturing companies, and the sales of cars were completely managed by producers (100 per cent) (DTI, 1991).

The existence of an extensive network for sales by manufacturing companies was one of the most important characteristics of Korea's retail sector (An Gwangho and Jo Jaeun 2003: 75). According to Chandler (1999: 285–288), the merging of manufacturing companies with retail companies was a natural phenomenon in the development of mass-consumption because the manufacturing companies needed to establish a comprehensive plan which included distribution as well as production in response to mass-consumption. However, Korea's situation as a developing country was quite different. The dominance of the manufacturing sector had appeared before the stage of mass-consumption. Nevertheless, as the appearance of Chandler's merger had been natural in the development of mass-consumption in Western countries (where various types of distribution capital had existed in the process of the development of capitalism for a long time), it was natural for manufacturing companies to establish their own sales outlets or distribution networks in the context of 1970s Korea.[15] These outlets or networks were completely dependent on manufacturing companies as commercial agents because of distribution shortages, due to the extremely unequal development between the manufacturing and distribution sectors. In particular, in the case of high-priced durable goods, it might have been impossible for them to have been distributed only through small-scale retailers without the manufacturers' sales network. In this respect, it was also clear that the manufacturers' sales networks contributed to the development of the Korean distribution industry by playing an important part in the early period of its economic development. However, due to the limitations placed on their origins, it could not be expected that they would develop autonomously as distribution capital which, sometimes, could not but conflict with manufacturing capital. For example, it was not possible that manufacturing companies would give distribution organizations – which in effect functioned as branches for their sales – a chance to make huge profits. Furthermore, the manufacturers controlled independent retailers through their own or completely dependent organizations, thus avoiding direct trade with them. This meant that the organizations could not be

15 'Own sales organizations' means a manufacturing company's branches for sales where most of the employees in the branches work for the manufacturing company, while the 'completely dependent distribution network' are legally independent organizations whose employees work for the distribution company. In fact, most of them were established through various kinds of support by the manufacturing company and only sell goods produced by a single company.

developed autonomously even if they were in a more profitable position than that of independent retailers. According to a survey measuring sales by type of shop in the wholesale industry in 1979, the proportion of manufacturers' own sales organizations, or completely dependent distribution networks, was 52.3 per cent, while that of independent wholesalers was merely 40.9 per cent. This meant that over half of the wholesale sector was entirely managed by the manufacturers. The manner and amount of trade in the rest of the sector could also be controlled because of the small scale of the wholesalers (KCCI 1985: 87).

In the case of the retail industry, the hostile circumstances affecting their relationship with the manufacturing sector were the same as those affecting their relationship with the wholesale industry, but were on the whole more severe. In general, retailers purchased goods in three ways: from a wholesaler, from the manufacturers' own organizations, or from networks closely affiliated with the manufacturers and which functioned as both wholesaler and retailer with price discrimination. Aside from wholesalers, retailers usually preferred to purchase goods directly from manufacturers at wholesale prices, because in this way the goods cost less than if purchased from a network affiliated with the manufacturer. However, most manufacturers did not permit direct sales to normal retailers, but made them purchase goods through the affiliated networks. In reacting against this practice, the Korea Super-chain Association (KOSCA),[16] which was established in 1975 with government support for the expansion of the supermarket chain, suggested changes to the government in 1977. These included: the institutional establishment of direct trade with manufacturers, the cost of transport to be paid by the manufacturer, the correction of unilateral contracts decided by manufacturers, and the prohibition of the ability of manufacturers to refuse to trade with supermarkets. However, the practices scarcely changed because of the reluctance of manufacturers to comply with the suggestions without continuous government pressure (KOSCA 1995: 44, 51, 70). Additionally, the Association wanted a discount of 5 per cent in the purchase price from the Haitai Confectionary and Foods Company and Tong Yang Confectionary (now the Orion Group) as oligopolistic companies in the confectionary industry in 1976, but this demand was not accepted (KOSCA 1995: 41). On the contrary, in the case of manufacturers' commercial agents, they could use credits from the manufacturer as a measure of settlement, instead of taking as their goal the amount of sales from the manufacturer. If even supermarkets which had been established due to government policy did not occupy an equal trading position with manufacturers in the 1970s, there was little hope for the status of other independent retailers.

16 The Korea Super-chain Association changed its name to the Korea Chainstores Association (KOCA) in 1999.

In sum, the relationship between manufacturers and retailers was unfair, which was a very serious factor in obstructing the development of the retail industry. It was difficult for retailers to make a profit under such conditions. In this respect it could be said that the dominance of manufacturers in the distribution industry had a negative effect on the development of the retail industry even though its distribution network played an important role in the distribution industry in the 1970s.

5 Conclusion

This chapter has looked at the environmental factors as well as the situation of the retail industry in the 1970s. It is clear that there was a lag of development between the retail industry and other economic factors. For example, the rapid economic growth in the 1970s provided good conditions for the development of the retail industry. There was a rapid increase in GNI per capita in accordance with economic growth. The changes of social indexes such as population and family were remarkable with the rapid urbanization in the 1970s. Nevertheless, there was hardly any change in the structure of the retail industry even if the industry grew in terms of the amount of sales. In particular, it seems very unusual that there were seldom any big retailers even in big cities such as Seoul and Busan with a population of over 1 million. The only shops for end-users were traditional retailers at permanent markets even in big cities. These saw some progress in commercialization because of successful industrialization. Accordingly, this unbalanced backwardness of the retail industry may imply that there was a particular reason for the backwardness of the retail industry in the 1970s.

Another consequence of this market structure is that the Korean consumer market was not stratified in the 1970s. As will be seen, while there were just two department store companies serving as a luxurious retail format in Seoul, the amount of their sales was extremely trivial and unstable in the 1970s. In contrast, the permanent market grew quite rapidly. Thus, the period of the 1970s can be called the era of the traditional market. This implies that most people purchased goods from traditional retailers in everyday life whatever the size of the purchases. This uniformity of consumption also looks unnatural, appearing like unbalanced backwardness within the retail industry, when set against the fast increases in income that rapidly expanded the income gap in the 1970s. In particular, it appears unusual that similar patterns of consumption continued even in big cities such as Seoul and Busan. Accordingly, this phenomenon can be presumed to be the result of some other factor. However, most existing studies on the Korean retail industry argue that economic conditions were not mature enough for a new type of retailer to emerge in the 1970s, and that the eventual materialization and rapid development of the sector were the result of more economic development in the 1980s. In this respect, my view is different from existing studies in terms of its perception of the economic situation in the 1970s. The reason why I examined the various developments of economic conditions in this chapter is to question existing studies. Furthermore, I will argue that the emergence of the new retail format and its rapid growth since the 1980s stems to a huge extent from the backward and unstratified situation of the retail industry in the 1970s. This is regarded as an inherently historical approach. An unusual situation cannot emerge without a corresponding particular historical context. In this respect, if the unusual situation of the 1970s is well examined, it would look normal under the conditions present within that particular context. Thus, in the next chapter, I will trace the behaviour of three actors which significantly influenced the formation of the retail industry, namely: the government, the consumer and the retailer.

CHAPTER 3

Consumption Repression, Frugal Consumers and Passive Retail Industry in Rapid Economic Growth in the 1970s

1 Introduction

The Korean economy, which had begun to recover in the 1960s, experienced high economic growth continuously during the 1970s, even if there were occasional serious recessions. The average annual growth rate in the 1970s was over 8 per cent and in the case of 1976, it was over 10 per cent (BOK, National Accounts, annual). It is said that Korea's economic growth was led by industrial policy and investment for exports, or a good combination of the market system and the state (Amsden 1989; Wade 1990; World Bank 1993; Rodrik 1995). At any rate, the Korean government did play an important role in economic growth in terms of both allocations of resources, and provision of a market. The government had been able to act as the provider of capital because for a long time it had been the main borrower of foreign capital. At that time the Korean government preferred loans from abroad as a source of capital rather than direct foreign investment. Even when companies tried to borrow from abroad, they needed the government's permission because it was impossible to borrow without a guarantee from the bank, which the government owned (Cole and Bak Yeongcheol 1984: 72–76). The government also held full power over internal capital through its hold over the banking system. Moreover, it frequently encouraged savings at the national level. One such example was the government presentation of a national prize for savings on the establishment of 'Savings Day' in 1963, which became an annual event. The winner became a hero or heroine as his/her indomitable story concerning savings became known to the Korean people. This greatly influenced the saving habits of younger Koreans and had a significant role in the continuous high rate of savings (*Jo-seon-il-bo* 26 September 1970, 23 January 1972a, 26 October 1973b). In fact, the government had almost complete control over the collection and use of capital. Under such conditions, the Korean government made a drive towards economic growth through, mainly, industrial policy. As some scholars (White and Wade 1988; Rodrik 1995, etc.) pointed out, it consistently placed an emphasis on production and exports through investment in the manufacturing sector, even though there was a transition from light industry in the early period of

 | DOI 10.1163/9789004274228_004

development, to heavy and chemical industries. The government made use of its immense power to direct capital towards these industries. The 'Five-Year Plan for Economic Development', started in 1962, began the implementation of a policy that lasted twenty years.

Such a tendency in the policies followed by the Korean government meant that the consumption and retailing sectors were neglected in terms of supporting policy. Instead, they were aggressively repressed as an obstacle to economic growth even in the 1970s. The government sometimes displayed the attitude that consumption was harmful for economic growth and encouraged people to view frugality as a virtue. Furthermore, it often criticised the consumption of imported goods, and periodically punished people for importing and consuming foreign goods regardless of whether it was legal or not (*Jo-seon-il-bo* 6 June 1974a, 12 June 1974b, 30 May 1975a, etc.). In this social situation, prosperity in the retail industry was difficult to attain because most people showed temperate behaviour towards consumption. The government had an unfriendly attitude towards the retail industry, which it saw as bolstering consumption and getting excessive profit. It also regarded the industry not as an important sector contributing to economic growth but as merely a tool to make the economy function. Accordingly, the government did not place a great deal of weight on the development of the retail industry, even if it sometimes tried to improve and stabilize the distribution network. In particular, even in the case of its rare support, it is clear that the government was giving preferential treatment to the protection and improvement of traditional retailers, and ignoring the development of a modern retail industry for the 1970s.

As a result, during the period of rapid economic growth in the 1970s the prosperity of the manufacturing sector coexisted alongside the relative backwardness of the retail sector; there was even a tendency to argue that the former was necessarily accompanied by the latter, particularly in terms of raising capital.[1] Therefore, the retail industry could hardly be expected to develop in an environment where government intervention was disadvantageous to its development, irrespective of whether the economic environment was receptive or not. Furthermore, the role of government was not just one among various factors to influence the development of an industry at that time. As has been pointed out, the Korean government exercised its power by controlling matters of life and death for industry in general in the 1970s, and so that period in the Korean economy could be called the period of policy dominance. In this

1 Some scholars pointed out that the repression of the industries concerning the consumption sector by the Korean government was one of the key factors to boost the Korean economy (Jones and SaKong 1980; White and Wade 1988).

respect, the underdevelopment and backwardness of the retail industry in the 1970s was crucially influenced by the political environment.

2 The Repression of Consumption

2.1 *Consumption Repression in Economic Policy*

There were a number of policies to repress consumption in the 1970s. First of all, one of the most important institutions which influenced the behaviour of consumption was the taxation system. The consumption tax was one of the most significant influences on consumption because it was highly possible that the tax rate was directly connected with the rise in prices. The consumption tax in Korea was composed mainly of items such as value added tax, special excise tax and liquor tax. Of these, value added tax[2] and the special excise tax,[3] which were introduced at the end of 1976 accounted for over 80 per cent of total internal indirect tax revenues. For example, thus in 1978, the revenue from value added tax was 838.9 billion *won*, amounting to 60.7 per cent of total internal indirect tax revenues. Special excise tax revenues were 327 billion *won*, making up 23.6 per cent of its total revenue. In 1979, the revenue from value added tax was 1087.8 billion *won*, amounting to 58.1 per cent of total internal indirect tax revenues. Special excise tax revenues were 484.5 billion *won*, providing 25.9 per cent of its total revenues (MOF 1982: 44–45). The ratio of indirect tax has been over 60 per cent of total internal tax since the introduction of value added tax in Korea. Consequently, the portion of the value added and the special excise taxes have been remarkably large within the taxation system, as the former's portion in total internal tax has been around 40 per cent and the latter's has generated around 14 per cent. Such a change in the taxation system would have influenced the atmosphere of consumption through inflation. The consumer price index (CPI) rose gradually after the imposition of the value added tax. While the increasing rate of the CPI was moderate in the third quar-

2 The value added tax was introduced for the simplification of the taxation system and acceleration of exports and investment, etc. (Committee of Finance in National Assembly (Gug-hoe jae-mu-wi-won-hoe) 1976: 5). In fact, it was estimated that tax exemption for manufacturing companies under the system of the value added tax was easier than before thanks to the simplification of taxation without duplication of tax.

3 The value added tax in Korea was imposed on all items as a single tax rate of 10 per cent and the special excise tax on some more luxurious goods was simultaneously introduced in order to both weaken its regressive character and repress consumption of luxuries. Accordingly, the rate of the special excise tax was quite high between 10 per cent and 160 per cent even though it decreased gradually through several revisions (Gim Chang 1994: 30–33).

ter of 1977 when the tax was introduced, it became stiffer after that (BOK, Consumer Price Indexes, annual). Psychological pressure or uncertainty from the new consumption tax also greatly influenced the consumption environment. This can be seen from the following examples. First, the institution of value added tax was to be enforced from the beginning of the 1977 but its enforcement was delayed for six months. The rate of taxation was also reduced to 10 per cent from the planned 13 per cent. Another aspect of conflict was the collective closing down of about seven hundred shops, as a form of tax resistance in Pyounghwa Market in October 1977, one of the biggest traditional markets in Korea (*Jo-seon-il-bo* 14 October 1977a, 16 October 1977b). Such a situation reflects the degree to which the social atmosphere worsened around the period of the enforcement of the value added tax. It also had a major effect on the amount of consumption. As we have seen earlier in the SK annual surveys, the rate of increase of annual sales within the retail industry dropped to half its previous level, at 39 per cent between 1976 and 1979, compared with that of 88.9 per cent between 1971 and 1976, even though the period between 1976 and 1978 constituted the biggest boom of the 1970s. In particular, in the case of electronic goods subject to the special excise tax, there was also a report that Korean consumers paid two or three times more tax than those in Taiwan, and ten or fifteen times more than the level paid in Japan[4] (Gim Chang 1994: 51–52). Banks also exercised consumption repression by limiting the number of loans to households. The government hardly permitted loans to households and strongly induced long-term savings with the incentive of higher interest rates. In fact, most households just had savings but had no right to loans at all in the 1970s. Thus most households never expected loans from banks and used the private money market where much higher interest rates were levied if they needed money. Finance for consumption was unthinkable in the 1970s (Cole and Bak Yeongcheol 1984: 166–167)

Second, the strong control on imports was another important device to repress consumption. The Korean government carried out the liberalization of imports in 1978 following rapid growth in the 1970s. The importation of a number of items including consumer goods as well as capital goods, which were illegal to import until then, were now allowed, and the rate of import liberalization increased to 60.7 per cent in 1978 from 52.7 per cent[5] in 1977.

4 Even though it was highly possible that this analysis was exaggerated because it was produced by the electronic industry in August 1992, it meant that the special excise tax was seen as a burden even to manufacturers in Korea, and not just consumers.

5 This refers to the ratio of items which can be automatically imported without any permission in items of Standard International Trade Classification (SITC).

With this, the government introduced an 'Import Watch System' to discourage and regulate the amount of imports. It also enforced a 'System of Advance Notice on Import Items' (*Su-ib ye-si-je*) to mitigate damage to the domestic industry resulting from imports. Despite such controls, the rate and the amount of import liberalization increased rapidly. It rose to 68.6 per cent in 1979, and reached 74.7 per cent in 1982 (Sim Otaek 1986: 26–27). Accordingly, with consumers preferring foreign goods, department stores had experienced a small boom in sales as they established a separate counter for imported goods (Shinsegae 1987: 156). However, the process of import liberalization was not smooth. Because of foreign exchange problems, the schedule would be delayed occasionally and consumption goods in particular, often became the object of government regulation. For example, the government controlled its imports through huge increases in the rate of emergency tariffs, and limitations of both the amount and the number of cases imported (Gim Deokjung 1984: 36). As a consequence of the measures, the liberalization rate of consumption goods was much lower than for other goods. For instance, the rate for processed foods was only 29.1 per cent and for durable goods and non-durables were just 49.8 per cent, and 53.9 per cent respectively, even in 1982. In contrast, rates for building materials and machinery were each 96.2 per cent and 59.9 per cent at the same time[6] (Ibid: 23).

Finally, the government sometimes imposed specific measure to repress consumption. One was the prohibition of the gift voucher system, which was enforced in December 1975. The gift-voucher had a fairly significant history in Korea. The 'Law of the Gift Voucher' (*Sangpumgwon-beob*) was enacted in 1961 and through amendment in 1971 and 1973, its use expanded rapidly. In the case of Shinsegae Department Store, the proportion of these vouchers in total sales was over 50 per cent in the autumn, the period of the traditional harvest festival [*chu-seog*] and near year-end, which was the high season (Shinsegae 1987: 140).

The prohibition had an especially severe impact on the department store because about 35 per cent of its sales were generated by such vouchers (Shinsegae Department Store 1987: 140). As we have seen, the period around 1975 was when the Korean economy was driven by heavy investment in HCI under

6 In particular, mass media such as newspapers and broadcasters criticised the phenomenon of increasing imports of consumption goods as social laxity whenever the problem of balance of payments deficit was highlighted in the 1970s and 1980s. In response to such criticism, the government often published regulations on imports of consumption goods. As the government also blamed wealthy people for such a phenomenon, it seemed that it focused on tightening the reins in terms of the social atmosphere.

government encouragement, but the economy was in recession in the aftermath of the oil shock in 1973. In this situation, the government wanted to tighten its control over the social environment in order to convert economic recession into recovery. It seems that the reason why the gift voucher was targeted was closely related to its character as a kind of unregistered security. In general, the gift voucher was bought for a third party as a present. In this process, a retailer who issued the voucher was only reimbursed when it was exchanged for goods. Thus, it was a kind of private finance which was not operated by any financial institute (Gim Seongcheon 2000: 16). This was contrary to the government's measures at that time which were intended to limit loans concerning consumption and the retail industry. The government believed that gift vouchers promoted excessive consumption because they were like an unexpected bonus and could only be used to purchase goods. Thus the government prohibited the gift voucher, as it was believed to encourage consumption and to hinder economic recovery (Gim Seongcheon 2000: 17). In addition, it seemed that the government intended to warn the rich by banning the gift voucher because it was believed to be largely circulated by the wealthy. Therefore, as a key measure for suppressing its circulation and usage, the government also branded it as a device for bribery (Gim Seongcheon 2000: 17). This clampdown on gift vouchers sent shockwaves through the department store industry. After one year it pleaded with the government for the gift voucher's reinstatement, but its plea was rejected point-blank and it was not until the end of 1993 that the gift vouchers were again allowed. That is to say, a kind of security which was invented to stimulate consumption in the capitalist system was banned for twenty years in Korea.

2.2 *Consumption Repression in Social Policy*

'Why can't I spend my money as I wish in Korea? Korea is not a normal country at all in the capitalist system.'[7]

In fact, it seemed that Korea was not an ordinary country, where production and consumption were naturally interdependent, in terms of economic circulation. The Korean government urged that capital, whether domestic or foreign, should be wholly concentrated on production. In this regard, Krugman's argument (1994) that the rapid economic growth of East Asia resulted from a

7 This is a comment frequently heard by the writer from news sources as a journalist in the late 1980s. In particular, wealthy people, such as people over the level of director of a company or owner of a medium-sized company, strongly expressed such views.

huge sacrifice of consumption and leisure by the people, is meaningful, even though there appears to be another serious problem with his argument.[8]

However, it was not easy to control consumption in a private area under the system of a market economy. The repression of consumption would have been impossible without a convergence between social regulation and the people's spontaneity. The Saemaul Movement (*Sae-ma-eul-un-dong*),[9] which stemmed from President Park's idea at a provincial governors' meeting in 1970, was one of the most important campaigns for social control in the 1970s. While in the beginning it was a campaign to develop rural districts, gradually it changed into a campaign for spiritual reform as it expanded to various types of organizations in Korean society, with the establishment of company and urban organizations for the Saemaul Movement. Eventually, it became one of the biggest organizations composed of both government and people in Korea (Moore 1984–1985: 586–590). Its three main tenets were diligence, self-help and cooperation based on 'Let's be rich', one of the most popular slogans in Korea in the 1970s. Accordingly, the actual practice of the movement was mainly focused on increased production and income brought about through consistent frugality and cooperation. In fact, the regional headquarters leading the movement often held conferences to announce successes and the best examples were publicised at conferences held by larger regions. Finally, the best examples in the whole country were announced at conferences at nationwide level. Moreover, the Korean government enacted a law[10] to award merit to outstanding Saemaul men or women.

Supporting only villages which showed a desire to improve their circumstances, the government stimulated others and helped them to participate in

---

8 This related to the controversy initiated by Young (1994, 1995), by Kim and Lau (1994) and by Krugman (1994) when they said that the economic growth of East Asia, including Korea, depended very little on Total Factor Productivity (TFP). One of their points of view was that this growth resulted not from an increase in productivity, but from the amount of investment. However, what the present work wants to emphasize is not whether or not their analysis of the lack of productivity in economic growth should be admitted, but that it was clear that there was concentration on investment through constraints on consumption. For reference, Sarel (1997) emphasized the increasing rate of productivity in Asian countries.

9 *Sae-ma-eul* means new village.

10 The Saemaul Movement had two levels of award; the 'Order of Saemaul Service Merit' (*sae-ma-eul-hun-jang*) and the Saemaul Service Medal (*sae-ma-eul-po-jang*), and an upper level, with five types of prize. This was one of the twelve most important prizes given by the nation to a person of merit (MOLEG, the 'Law of Citation of Merit' (*sanghun-beob*), 2008).

the movement (Davis 2004: 131). In terms of such a strategy, a famous example is that the government gave an additional five hundred sacks of cement and one ton of iron frames only to self-help villages after it had given 335 sacks of cement each to 33,267 villages throughout the whole country in 1971 when the movement began (Naver Encyclopaedia <http://naver.com>). In this process, the Saemaul Movement rapidly spread throughout the whole country as the government developed five distinct branches of the urban movement; the Factory Movement, the Movement of Office Workers, the School Movement, the Movement of Service Groups and the Movement in Residential Areas (Davis 2004: 142). In this atmosphere, there was even a period in the 1970s when the Saemual signature tune written by President Park was one of the most popular songs in the country.[11]

The establishment of the 'Day of Savings' was also deeply related to the social policy which encouraged frugality and savings. This was established in 1964 by presidential decree with the goal of inculcating the importance of saving upon the Korean people and then was re-established in 1973. President Park stressed that people had to consider savings before consumption (*Jo-seon-il-bo* 26 September 1970) and Prime Minister Kim Jong-pil also stated that domestic money commensurate with the amount people could save should be invested (*Jo-seon-il-bo* 26 October 1973b). The Day of Savings was also the day when the national savings' champion was announced and became 'King/Queen of Savings of the Year'. Whenever it was announced, newspapers usually carried a special interview. Most of the narratives were preter-human. For example, a female worker who lived at absolute poverty level saved over half her income, or a shoeblack who travelled to a bank to deposit his savings without ever missing a day even though he sometimes had to skip a meal. In response to this, as President Park gave an unplanned gift of money to him, his contribution to savings was awarded high merit (*Jo-seon-il-bo* 23 January 1972a). Accordingly, these stories were the focal point of attention for people in the days following such announcements, and, naturally, the winners became paragons of ordinary people's lives.[12]

11 Apart from their achievements, it was a fact that the Saemaul Movement was criticised because of the political implication that it was highly possible that President Park established the movement to avoid a serious political crisis in the early 1970s. Actually, it became clear later on that the movement had a strong orientation.

12 Such an atmosphere has weakened remarkably since the 1990s. However, a press release by the Bank of Korea (BOK) in 2002 showed that strong encouragement for frugality has been carried on even in the twenty-first century. The document suggested sensible consumption, life savings and a contribution to the spread of savings as the criteria of the

The government paid particular attention to the importance of educating children in school about frugality. With such a goal, education supervisory institutes informed each school of the goals of diligence and frugality, and most primary and secondary schools had no alternative but to follow the direction of these institutes, which had the power to appoint and dismiss. A document concerning the savings award revealed how much direction there was. The document, which recorded communications between the supervisory institute and an individual school, contained the following meritorious deeds of the school. First, the school which emphasized education about diligence and frugality took the campaign for saving energy and tap water to the classroom, and enforced the movement for the recycling of used school supplies, such as uniforms, sports clothes and reference books, to the lower class students. Secondly, it also implemented a movement to spare and repair the school facilities, including desks and chairs. Thirdly, the school collected and sold 5,000 kilogrammes of recyclable goods, such as cans, bottles, used paper and scrap iron, to the recycling institute. Fourthly, the school taught the importance of diligence and frugality in all subjects and stressed the conservation of school supplies, self-restraint regarding unnecessary eatables such as sweets and the importance of saving continuously. Finally, it strongly encouraged each student to have a bankbook and established a school bank which would take deposits at any time. Additionally, it established a clerk in charge of checking the savings of each class and so the monthly savings in the school doubled, compared with those of the previous year (JOE[13] 1997). In such an atmosphere, it was natural that parents as well as students came to think of frugality and savings as two of the most important virtues in their lives.

The social atmosphere of parsimony was strengthened in many ways. One was the movement for the banishment of foreign goods as a form of over-consumption. Examples of the banishment of foreign goods are too manifold to enumerate. In the middle of the 1970s, the government declared penalties against an official if his/her family members were caught using foreign goods (*Jo-seon-il-bo* 6 June 1974a). Furthermore, the government directly initiated a campaign against such goods. The Ministry of Health and Social Affairs announced a boycott of foreign goods in the middle of the June 1974 (*Jo-seon-il-bo* 12 June 1974b). While it was a fact that the movement for the banishment of

award. The press release stated that 412 people received prizes in 2002, including ordinary people, students and teachers (BOK 2002).

13 I could not find a document from the 1970s, but the 1990s document suggests how serious the situation was in the 1970s with respect to diligence and frugality, because it was clear that by the 1990s such an atmosphere had conspicuously weakened.

over-consumption was led by the government, the establishment of the 'Citizen's Action for the Expulsion of Over-consumption' (CAEO) (*gwa-so-bi-chu-bang beomgug-min-un-dongbon-bu*) as a non-governmental organization in 1996 showed how strong people's loyalty to the movement has been. Soon after its establishment, the CAEO become an influential NGO and top leaders in the main religious circles took part in the organization.[14] The CAEO, which decided on a thrifty life style and reform of luxurious consumption as a general principle, tried to conduct a campaign, hold symposia and produce an educational programme to disseminate its principles <http://cceo.or.kr>. Even though a number of the policies enforced by the previous authoritarian government were denied after liberalization in the 1980s, the establishment and activity of the CAEO as a pure non-governmental organization could be considered an example of such dissemination because of the degree to which people assimilated the government's ethos of clamping down on consumption.

With such varied policies for the inducement of repression on consumption, another important sign of success was the imposition of serious penalties against over-consumption and the consumption of luxury goods, as a means of strengthening its policy (*Jo-seon-il-bo* 30 July 1972b, 30 May 1975a, etc.). The Korean government often carried out tax investigations on companies or people, and the result was promulgated in newspapers and broadcasts during the 1970s and 1980s.[15] Most investigations were carried out because of matters such as tax evasion. However, usually most companies being investigated initially thought they were being scrutinised because of other non-tax related problems because most companies experienced tax problems due to the lack of structure in the taxation system (*Jo-seon-il-bo* 24 May 1973a). In any case, when companies discovered they were being investigated, it was common for companies to simply pay the penalty demanded. Politics was believed to be another important reason for an investigation to take place. Companies or individuals who took part in activities supporting an opposition group or party against Park's regime were inevitably the subject of greater scrutiny. Most opposition politicians, including the later president, Kim Dae Jung, winner of a Nobel Peace Prize in 2000, said that no person or company was able to support them officially, and those that did barely survived. Another reason was related

14 Koreans had established a comprehensive civil government through a presidential election in 1992 as part of meaningful progress towards liberalization which began in the mid-1980s. As a cause and result of this, the retreat of the state occurred rapidly in the 1990s, and the number of NGOs related to public rights and interests increased from about 1,000 in the 1980s to over 3,500 in the 1990s (*Si-min-ui sin-mun* 2003).

15 Companies considered a tax investigation as a step towards bankruptcy.

to people's attitude towards their lives, particularly, their consumption. For instance, it was said that consuming foreign luxury goods openly was tantamount to giving up a business. In other words, the consumption of foreign luxury goods catalysed government investigations (*Jo-seon-il-bo* 6 July 1975b, 3 June 1979a, etc.). Thus, there was an atmosphere which encouraged property owners as well as businessmen to abstain from consuming luxury goods.

Even now, this kind of atmosphere has hardly changed. Whenever a feature article concerning notable people from different social spheres is published in a newspaper, their frugal private life is one of the most important topics that must be mentioned in the article. For example, one of the previous presidents of the BOK was famous for the fact that his private car was one of the smallest cars ever produced in Korea even though he had achieved a lot by being in office after the financial crisis of 1997 (*Han-gyeo-le 21* 14 March 2002). An anecdote told of Jeong Juyeong (Chung Juyung), who was founder and chairman of Hyundai group, one of the largest *chaebol* in Korea, was that he mended his own shoes throughout his whole life. He was very famous as a paragon for ordinary people as well as successful businessmen (*Jo-seon-il-bo* 14 April 2005a).

In this social atmosphere, it seemed that Korean consumption behaviour was limited by social pressure to conform, whether it was on a conscious or unconscious level. Curbing consumption, and the ethos of consumption equality, affected communal relations to a greater and greater extent. Of course, this effect was an unintended consequence, because the goal of government policy was probably initially to prohibit the waste of foreign exchange rather than to affect communal sensibilities with respect to consumption. The government's focus on limiting foreign exchange was because earning US dollars was regarded as the goal of exports, and the only way to raise funds to import advanced machinery for economic growth. However, as time went by, it would also be natural that wealthy people complained, 'I do not know the reason why I cannot consume my own money at my own discretion.'

3 Consumption Repression on the Retail Industry

3.1 *General Government Policy on the Retail Industry in the 1970s*

As mentioned, one of the most important factors leading to industrialization was government policy in the 1970s. Assessing government policy is thus one key way of establishing the reason for the backwardness of the Korean retail industry despite progress in the socio-economic environment.

3.1.1 Characteristics of Government Policy – Regulation Rather than Support

One of the most important policy aspirations concerning the retail industry in the 1970s was price stability, even if the policy was changed somewhat in the middle of the decade.[16] This aspiration demonstrates that, in fact, most policies regarding the retail industry related to the prohibition of unfair profits, for example the limitation of margins and the enforcement of the price tag system. The tendency to prioritise stability of prices was inevitable for a government which thought that lower wages were necessary for capital accumulation in view of the low level of technology, and so the majority of the capital available had to be concentrated on investment for economic growth. This system of lower wages was impossible without stability of prices particularly for the necessities of life, including food.[17]

Even in positive policies for support of the retail industry, the government would mainly focus on lukewarm goals to mitigate the gap between the industrial and retail sectors, otherwise, it could become an obstacle to economic growth. This meant that to the Korean government at that period, the retail industry was just a supplementary factor, rather than one of the leading factors for economic growth. Such a characteristic of the policy had continued since the 1960s. In fact, the 'Law of the Market' was also established to stabilize prices because the government believed that price instability resulted mostly from the disorder of the retail and distribution systems. The government intended to reduce the disorder of the retail system through a law which defined the market and contained regulations covering it (KCCI 1999: 44). The government aim had been reflected in the 'Five Year Plan for the Modernization of the Distribution System', which began its policy concerning the retail industry in the 1970s. This plan, published in February 1969, was enacted between 1970 and 1974. First of all it focused on making retailers, particularly small- and medium-size operators, form chains, claiming that this would provide them with stability. The policy was to control the unregulated retailers, because it was believed that they were the center of the chaos and unfair trading practices in the retail system. Secondly, it emphasized that a merchants' association was needed (Hwang Myeongsu et al. 1992: 307). This meant that the government felt the

16 It is said that the period between 1962 and 1973 was the dawn of the retail industry and the period between 1974 and 1979 was the stage of understanding in the sector (Im Jongwon 1989: 217).

17 Relating to the price of food, some scholars (Gim Cheolho 1992: 162–163) insist that economic growth in Korea was a process of exploitation of the agricultural areas by the urban areas in that the government strictly suppressed the price of grain.

necessity for a window to facilitate order within, and consultation with, the retail industry. In fact, industry associations are sometimes used as conduits for orders or consultations in the relationship between the government and industry in the Korean economy. From the point of view of the government, associations seem to be a very efficient method of passing their intentions to the industry. The Federation of Korean Industries (FKI), which is the biggest and the most representative institute of associations concerning industries, was also established in 1961 by a government 'suggestion' that was, in fact, an order (FKI 2001: 207). Therefore, the government's intention was understood to be to manage the processes of the retail industry, whether the type of intervention was direct or indirect. The Korean government had established many industrial associations in individual industries since the 1960s, such as the Korea Federation of Textile Industries (KOFOTI), the Korea Iron and Steel Association (KOSA) and so forth. At the same time, the Korean government designated former high government officials as chiefs in those organizations. Most of the organizations functioned as both interest institutions for their respective industries and a window for government control. This format changed from 1980, as the chairman has been appointed from the ranks of CEOs of main companies. However, having a former high government official as the vice chairman has had a considerable effect on management of the institute even now <http://www.kofoti.or.kr>; *Fashion Insight* 25 February 2002). Other associations such as the KOSA and the Korea Automobile Manufacturers Association (KAMA) are in a similar situation to the KOFOTI (<http://www.kosa.or.kr>; <http://www.kama.or.kr>; *Gyo-tong-il-bo* 8 May 2008).

Thirdly, the government indicated its support for improving the existing markets and building new buildings such as retailing centers (Hwang Myeong-su et al. 1992: 307). Under the basic plan, the government continuously announced concrete policies. The government decided to invest 3 billion *won* on the modernization of markets, in particular, on the expansion of wholesale markets, in 1970. Under the influence of such policies, the Dongdaemoon Shopping Street, which worked in the wholesale as well as the retail market sectors, was built in 1970. Subsequently direct sale stores belonging to small- and medium-size manufacturers opened in the Dongdaemoon Shopping Street in 1971 and the government announced a plan for the modernization of about 1,500 markets in 1972. The opening of small and medium size manufacturers' direct sale stores was understood as a policy with dual goals as follows: first, the manufacturers were provided with markets; and secondly, consumers were provided with cheap goods (Shinsegae Department Store 1987: A Chronological Table of Retail Policies; DTI 1970, 1972). In this way, the government played the role of coordinator between providers and consumers to enable the circulation of domestic goods. The government had confirmed three principles for their policies covering the retail sector in a plan, which had been established in 1973, as follows: the enlargement of individual retail institutions; to establish chains of retailers: and the modernization of traditional markets (Hwang Myeongsu et al. 1992; A Chronological Table of the Retail Industry, DTI 1973). The government's efforts for the modernization of the retail sector were developed in the 'Law for the Stimulation of the Modernisation of the Distribution Industry' (*Yu-tongsan-eob geun-dae-hwa chog-jin-beob*) in 1980. However, despite the title of the law, its first goal was the protection of consumers and achieving price stability, not the development of the retail industry (MOLEG 1980).

As we have seen, one of the most important characteristics of the retail policies of the 1970s was the fact that they focused mainly on price stability.[18] The government implemented consecutive measures for stability in the retail industry at the time of the first oil shock in 1973. The price tag system was enforced in Seoul and Busan, the second largest city in South Korea, in 1973, and the improvement of the distribution industry was emphasized in the 'Comprehensive Measures for the Stability of Prices' (*Jonghab-mul-ga-an-jeongdae-chaeg*) in 1974. In particular, the attitude of the government towards the retail industry was well illustrated in the presidential 'Emergency Measures for Stability of People's Livlihood' which was proclaimed to aid economic stabilization on 14 January 1974. The government basically denied the role of the retail industry by legally banning an increase in the price of main goods such as necessities. It decided their prices and announced that selling at a rate higher than the prices decided was regarded as illegal trade, and unfair profits would be strictly punished (MOLEG, Article 5 of the Presidential Emergency Measures, 1974). It seemed that the government thought the rise in prices was caused, to a certain extent, by the retail sector together with the price jump in raw materials such as oil. Accordingly, the government enforced a 'System for the Standardisation of Retail Margins' (*Pyo-jun-yu-tongma-jin-je*) in the same year, and published various kinds of measures for the improvement of the retail structure. These included an increase in the number of small- and medium-size manufacturers' direct sale stores, and the expansion of the number of chain stores in the big business sector. What is interesting here, as will be

18 What was more, such a tendency continued through the 1980s. Introducing a 'Law for the Promotion of the Wholesale and Retail Industry' to replace the 'Law of the Market' in 1986, the DTI stressed price stability, rather than the development of the industry, as a remarkable achievement in the previous year in the 1987 'White Paper of Trade and Industry' (DTI 1987: 408).

examined next, is that changes appeared in policy relating to stores formed into chains before and after the first oil shock. Before the oil shock, policy focused on voluntary chains of existing small and medium stores, after the shock it began to emphasize the establishment of big direct management chain companies in order to stabilize prices. The government recommended to existing big retailers such as Shinsegae and Midopa Department Stores that they should take part in chain store business of the supermarket type. The government recommendation, was more accurately like an order, given the nature of the relationship between government and private companies during the period of policy dominance. Even though the government's strong desire for price stability made the stores participate in the super-chain business, most of them were not confident of success because they thought that consumers' perception of such stores was very low (Shinsegae Department Store 1987: 120). In fact, the chain stores were not successful and most of them withdrew from the business.

Even in the late 1970s, most policies concerning the retail industry were implemented as part of measures for price stability, including the strengthening of the regulation against unfair trade (June 1976) and the expansion of the compulsory price tag system (February 1979). This tendency became stronger with the enforcement of value added tax (VAT) in 1977. The government, confronted with a shortage in tax revenue, especially since the development of the HCI in the early 1970s, introduced VAT at the end of 1976, despite strong resistance, following an aggregate income tax in 1974. The government strengthened regulations concerning price stability at the same time as the introduction of VAT, including the imposition of price ceilings on monopoly and oligopoly items, and a system of compulsory assignment of consumer prices. Even though these measures meant regulating the manufacturers as well, the main target was retailers who were already inferior to the manufacturer in their trade relationship. After the introduction of VAT, most retailers, particularly traditional retailers, received a double shock: on the one hand a relatively larger burden diverted from the manufacturer with the strict regulation of prices; on the other hand, a decrease in sales which stemmed from the increase in prices between retailer and consumer. Even if the Korean economy had experienced an unprecedented boom between 1976 and 1978, the extreme slowdown of the annual rate of increase in retail sales between 1976 and 1979 was closely related to the introduction of VAT. While the annual average increase rate of GDP between 1976 and 1979 was around 3 percentage points higher than that of the first half of the 1970s, that of retail sales was much more moderate at about half that level. The establishment of the 'Law for the Stimulation of the Modernisation of the Distribution Industry' in 1978 occurred in response to an earnest request by the KCCI under such desperate circumstances. In it the government proposed various measures to support the retail industry, including measures for the development of the distribution industry (February 1979) and the expansion of financial support (May 1979). Additionally, for the first time, the government established the position of director in charge of the distribution industry in the Economic Planning Board (EPB), which initiated a plan of economic development in April 1979, and eventually decided to establish the 'Law for the Stimulation of the Modernisation of the Distribution Industry' (*Yu-tongsan-eob geun-dae-hwa chog-jin-beob*) in September 1979 (Shinsegae Department Store 1987: A Chronological Table of Retail Policies).

3.1.2 The Introduction of the Supermarket as a Retail Institution – Just Means for Price Stability

One of the most important projects on which the government laid emphasis concerning the retail industry in the 1970s was the establishment of supermarket chains. It seemed that the government, which regarded the chaos in the retail system as one of the most important reasons for price instability, thought that if the retail network was well constructed, price stabilization could be realized. To achieve this goal, it urged the introduction of the supermarket chain as a component of the retail institution. Such a plan appeared clearly in the 'Five Year Plan for the Modernization of the Distribution System' (*Yu-tong geun-dae-hwa 5gae-nyeon gye-hoeg*) with which government policy relating to the retail industry in the 1970s began. The plan for the improvement of the network of the wholesale and retail sectors, in particular, focused on forming the retailers into chains like the supermarkets.

In this process the government was unwilling to make use of existing big retail institutions, such as department store companies, to develop chains in the early period of the plan, even though it professed to support the development and modernization of the retail system. This attitude was very different from policies towards the manufacturing sector, where the focus was on the development of big business. It seemed to be closely related to the protection of small- and medium-sized traditional retailers (SMSTRS), which made up over 90 per cent of the whole retail industry, rather than modernization of the retail industry. The government treated the retail industry as being different from the main pillars of its economic policy, which acted as a driving-force for economic growth. From the government viewpoint, the voluntary chain was emphasized more than branches of big business which enabled direct management. As a part of such a policy, the government established the 'Saemaul Super chain' as a model for such an organization in June 1971. This was an incorporated body supported by the DTI and began with ten member shops with strong support from the government.[19] Even though it was launched under relatively favourable conditions due to government support, it was difficult to make a profit due to shortages of both goods and management expertise. In particular, as prices soared owing to the 1973 oil shock, the environment around the supermarket became worse and worse with serious shortages of goods and hoarding by consumers. As a result, the first trial of chains of SMSTRs by the government failed as the Saemaul chain became insolvent in 1974 (KCCI and CKER 1977: 70).

After the failure, as mentioned earlier, an aspect of the policy affecting the retail industry was changed from just SMSTRs to include big business. The government withdrew its direct intervention and instead appointed private companies which could manage a superchain. For the first time, seven companies, including Shinsegae Store, Je-il Superchain, Lucky Chain, Midopa Chain, and Hannam Chain, were appointed as superchains in April 1974. The method of forming the chains was also changed. While the 'Saemaeul Superchain' was composed of voluntary members' shops and operated with a membership fee, new companies organized chains mainly as branches under direct management with some voluntary member chains. Moreover, the President's Special Order, which contained regulations covering the appointment of the private superchains, said that every appointed company should establish fifty stores to provide the necessities of life under stable conditions (Baek Insu 2003: 37). Instead, the Special Order emphasized that 'the Superchain companies would be permitted to be established as independent corporations'; it made it clear that their managerial autonomy would be guaranteed as much as possible, including permission for exceptions to the 'Law of the Fair Trade' concerning the price and amount of trade. Such a measure showed that the government was desperate to maintain supply of essential goods, even though permission for managerial autonomy was one of the incentives for constructing a distribution network though private companies. Moreover, the government published criteria covering the minimum size of shops and stressed the importance of the ability of the organization to expand. This could be considered as a change in retail policy to centers composed of big shops modernized from SMSTRs. In particular, the change of policy became clearer when the government opened the way for financial support to the companies appointed as superchains, as it excluded them from the existing financial limitations (Baek Insu 2003: 38).

19 The government's particular support for the superchain could be seen in the fact that the First Lady cut the tape on the opening of 'The Sukyo Supermarket', the first member shop <http://firstplus.co.kr>.

However, strictly speaking, it would be more accurate to argue that government policy concerning the retail industry began to show two contradictory directions after the Special Order in that protection and support to SMSTRS was strengthened simultaneously, rather than just being a change in the tendency of retail policy. In fact, the government published 'Special Criteria for Chain Businesses' (*Teug-byeol-yeon-swae-hwa-sa-eob-gi-jun*) in November 1974 following their goal of preventing huge unemployment that would result from the bankruptcy of many of the SMSTRS. Moreover, the government made it clear in the 'Special Criteria for Chain Businesses Created through the Organization of Small- and Medium-Sized Retailers' (*Jungso-sang-in jo-jig-ui teug-byeol yeon-swae-hwa sa-eob-e gwan-han gi-jun* – February 1975) that the policy goal was the expansion of the organization of the SMSTRS (EPB 1976: 158–159). In this atmosphere, various kinds of SMSTRS organizations were established, including the 'Korean Council for the Chain Businesses of Small and Medium Sized Retailers' in 1977 and the 'Korean Cooperative Association of Supermarkets' in 1978. As the number of regional cooperative associations increased, organizations for SMSTRS expanded across the country and the number of chain members increased to 28,819 in 1979 from 18,482 in 1975 (KCCI 1985: 138)

As has been seen, it was clear that the Korean government intended to improve the structure of the retail industry and made an effort to do so. In particular, it is worth noting that the government tried to introduce supermarket chains directly as a specific retail institution, on top of their general support for the industry. However, this was different from their other supportive policies, particularly when compared to their support for the manufacturing sector, in that the government's concern was in socio-economic stabilization rather than just the development of the retail industry. As a result of this basic attitude, policies concerning the retail industry could not but wander around both the goal of price stability and protection of the SMTSRS. Additionally, it also seemed that the actual circumstances in the retail industry concerning industrial structure and consumer behaviour were not very friendly to the transplantation of supermarkets, as imported institutions, in the early period of their introduction.[20] Accordingly, a unique type of 'Korean' supermarket, which was not self-service, spread nationwide,[21] and thus for a while the supermarket was

20 In fact, in the case of the Shinsegae Stores owned by the Shinsegae Department Store, all the shops were closed for periods of between eight and nineteen months (Shinsegae 1987: 126).

21 The supermarket, as an innovative retail institution, was first established by Michael J. Cullen in the US in the 1930s when the US economy was suffering greatly due to the Great Depression. Cullen achieved a great success with discount prices through the adaptation

understood to be just a replacement of the signboard of the existing 'mom and pop' stores. Such a modification might also be related to both the traditional practice of trade being accompanied by negotiation and communication between buyer and seller, and the small size of most supermarkets resulted from the participation of existing poor retailers rather than newly established modernized retailers.

3.2 *Disincentive to Management of the Distribution Company*

The government had various tools to support industry including finance and taxation. In particular, because the Korean government had owned banks in the 1970s, it took control of finance. Thus its actions were some of the most important factors affecting the fate of industry. In this respect, the retail industry was placed in a disadvantageous position. First of all, the retail industry was placed in a different position from the manufacturing industry in terms of taxation support. In the case of the Regulation Law on Tax Reduction and Exemption in 1965, there was no tax reduction or exemption clauses for the distribution industry while there were a lot of such clauses for the manufacturing industry. Relating to a transfer income tax, a small- and medium-size company could benefit from tax reductions and exemptions but retailers and wholesalers were not included in the category of small- and medium-sized companies. The distribution industry suffered from almost the same disadvantage for corporation tax, acquisition tax and property tax. In particular, facilities of the distribution industry also came under a special excise tax which was imposed on luxuries (MOLEG 1965; Jeon Huijae 1980: 76–79). For example, even when retailers purchased a refrigerator, a freezer and gasoline as company facilities or utilities, they had to pay a special excise tax in the same way that consumers did, unlike a manufacturer. A special excise tax was a high rate between 40 per cent in the case of a refrigerator and 160 per cent in the case of gasoline even though the rate decreased over time. This meant that companies in the distribution industry had to assume much higher running costs, compared with manufacturing companies. This made it difficult for retailers to develop their companies and furthermore, for investors to be attracted to the retail industry. With the taxation system, differences in direct financial support between the manufacturing and the distribution industry could be illustrated through the money loaned by the banks to industries. The difference between industries concerning bank loans is a very important factor with which to examine government motiva-

to self-service and mass purchasing. After that, self-service was one of the most important distinctions of the supermarket (Yu Gijun 2004: 154).

tions, because the government's key instrument of control over the Korean economy has been its control over banks (Koo 1994: 173).

Table 3.1 shows that the amount of loans given to the retail and wholesale industry proportionate to the total amount of loans by banks, was hardly over 10 per cent in the 1970s. Such a tendency had become stronger and stronger from 1972 when the government pushed HCI as a key factor for economic growth. Its proportion, which at its height, recorded 10.9 per cent in 1971 decreased to 6.5 per cent in 1974. After that, even if the proportion increased a little, it did not reach two-digit percentage figures in the 1970s. The bias was more severe in terms of the facility fund loans for capital investment. The ratio of facility fund of the retail and wholesale industry to total loans by banks was only 0.3 per cent in 1971 and at most was 3.1 per cent in 1978.

With discrimination of the support through the taxation system above, this meant that the Korean government had no intention of developing the retail and wholesale sectors as an industry. On the contrary, manufacturing industry's total loans increased dramatically in the 1970s. While manufacturing loans amounted to 49.5 per cent of total loans in 1971, their number rose to 60 per cent in the mid-1970s and maintained almost the same level even after the 1970s. The interesting thing about this was the changeover of facility fund ratios between the manufacturing, agricultural, and fishery industries. The largest ratio of facility funds was the agricultural and fishery industries until 1972 which amounted to 40.8 per cent, compared with 28.4 per cent for the manufacturing industry. However, their ratios were reversed afterwards, and the ratio of the manufacturing industry rose to 40 per cent. This was understood as a result of both the stagnation of the primary industry, rapid movements in population within the agricultural area in the 1970s, and intensive investment in the HCI as well. To summarize, it seemed that the ratio of the retail and wholesale industries in total loans and facility funds was far too low, while their value in total industries had consituted around 20 per cent of GDP in the 1970s. This meant that most in the distribution industry used their own money in conjunction with family money or the private money market. Such an unbalanced phenomenon could only appear under artificial conditions created by government policy.

With the imbalance in the amount of loans, the more serious problem to the distribution industry, as I Byeonggi's work shows in Table 3.2, was the big difference in loan conditions such as interest rates, according to the type of loan provided. Export finance and facility funds by KDB were representative forms of policy finance which, in fact, were loaned with the permission of the government, and thus at the prime rate of interest.

TABLE 3.1 *Money loaned by the banks to industries*

	Items	Wholesale, retail, food and lodging industry (ratio of the industry in all industries, %)	Manufacturing industry (ratio of the industry in all industries, %)	Agricultural and fishery industry (ratio of the industry in all Industries, %)	All industries
1971	Total amount	94,605 (10.9%)	428,497 (49.5%)	125,986 (14.6%)	865,034 (100%)
	Loan for facility*	321 (0.3%)	31,461 (29.2%)	40,549 (37.7%)	107,563 (100%)
1972	Total amount	91,747 (8.15%)	590,052 (52.4%)	160,264 (14.2%)	1,125,582 (100%)
	Loan for facility	1,193 (0.6%)	53,339 (28.4%)	76,760 (40.8%)	188,117 (100%)
1973	Total amount	108,232 (7.3%)	849,501 (56.9%)	201,715 (13.5%)	1,492,794 (100%)
	Loan for facility	4,070 (1.4%)	102,027 (35.8%)	91,754 (32.2%)	284,908 (100%)
1974	Total amount	150,273 (6.5%)	1,402,458 (60.9%)	262,241 (11.4%)	2,303,869 (100%)
	Loan for facility	6,864 (1.8%)	148,369 (38.3%)	117,872 (30.4%)	387,587 (100%)
1975	Total amount	190,734 (6.9%)	1,660,355 (60.3%)	303,283 (11.0%)	2,751,616 (100%)
	Loan for facility	7,967 (1.6%)	191,947 (37.6%)	154,881 (30.3%)	510,399 (100%)
1976	Total amount	259,369 (7.4%)	2,133,606 (60.6%)	383,811 (10.9%)	3,522,072 (100%)
	Loan for facility	13,533 (2.0%)	270,498 (40.7%)	193,201 (28.1%)	686,908 (100%)
1977	Total amount	343,233 (7.7%)	2,663,063 (59.8%)	508,352 (11.4%)	4,451,279 (100%)
	Loan for facility	26,625 (2.9%)	364,398 (39.7%)	253,003 (27.5%)	918,572 (100%)
1978	Total amount	550,461 (8.7%)	3,597,685 (57.1%)	658,419 (10.4%)	6,302,483 (100%)
	Loan for facility	41,273 (3.1%)	499,069 (37.7%)	336,540 (25.4%)	1,323,559 (100%)
1979	Total amount	554,286 (7.9%)	3,993,580 (56.6%)	824,890 (11.7%)	7,058,097 (100%)
	Loan for facility	44,660 (3.0%)	547,589 (36.9%)	393,683 (26.5%)	1,483,727 (100%)

Unit: million Korean *won*
*The loan for facility can be used for investment only in capital goods such as machinery. This kind of loan has usually been a bigger amount than the traditional loans towards company operations, but its requirements and regulations have also been stricter than loans for company operations.
Source: BOK, Monthly Bulletin, February and July 1979 as cited in Jeon Huijae (1980: 23)

TABLE 3.2 *Difference of annual interest rate between policy and general finance*

		1970	1975	1980	1985	1990
Return of Corporate Bond (A)		24.6	20.1	30.1	14.2	16.5
Interest rate of the Private Money Market (B)		50.8	41.3	45.0	24.0	18.8
Interest rate of Export Financing (C)		6.0	9.0	15.0	10.0	10.0
Interest rate of Facility Fund by KDB* (D)		12.0	12.0	20.0	12.0	12.0
Difference of Interest rate between policy and general finance	A – C	18.6	11.1	15.1	4.2	6.5
	A – D	12.6	8.1	15.0	2.0	4.5
	B – C	44.8	32.3	30.0	14.0	8.8
	B – D	38.8	29.3	25.0	12.0	6.8

* KDB: The Korea Development Bank
Source: I Byeonggi 1998: 46

The returns of corporate bonds were almost the same as normal interest rates applied to general finance by financial companies. Even in the case of the manufacturing sector, it was estimated that many companies used the private money market because the Korean economy suffered from a chronic demand for money in this period of development. Nevertheless, as we have seen above, the manufacturing sector's demand for money was covered to some extent by banks. However, the retail and wholesale industrie were driven to use the private money market because they were not the recipients of preferential rate loans, either for policy or general finance. As a result, most retail and wholesale companies were said to use the private money market. As we can see from the table, the interest rate of the private money market was nearly ten times higher in the maximum case than that of policy finance. Retail and wholesale companies could not expect export finance because their business was unrelated to the export industry. In the case of money for facilities which manufacturing companies mainly used, its interest rate (by KDB) was only about one-quarter of the private money market's interest rate. While the gap in interest rates narrowed over the 1970s, the interest rate of the private money market was over two times that of the KDB even in 1980. This aggravated the management of existing distribution companies and simultaneously had a remarkably bad effect on investment incentives in the distribution industry.

4 Collective Behaviour of Frugal Consumers in the 1970s

The remaining research required to prove consumption repression is an examination of how people have responded collectively to government policies. Of course, it is believed that its policy was implemented very well during the period characterized by backwardness in the retail industry, as we have seen in the previous chapter. Nevertheless it is also important to examine how the policy influenced people's consumption behaviour in everyday life, because this collective behaviour could be another factor influencing the backwardness of the retail industry. Furthermore, the analysis of collective consumption behaviour is meaningful research because collective habits crucially influence subsequent collective behaviour. This then leads to changes in institutional structure. It could also be argued that this is both a consequence of the policy and simultaneously a reason for the backwardness of the retail industry.

For this reason, we will examine income, expenditure and the average propensity to consume (APC) as a variable of consumption collective behaviour. In general, the change in income could be considered a basic indicator of the change in consumption, which is a main component of expenditure. APC, which is denoted as a ratio of consumption expenditure in income, means the average propensity to consume in a society where data is being collected. Therefore, the general characteristics concerning the consumption behaviour of society can be understood through the trends and shape of APC.

APC will be examined on the basis of its general characteristics in accordance with the Keynesian absolute income hypothesis as follows:

1. The APC shows a tendency to decrease gradually according to the rise in income, because the increment in consumption is usually smaller than that of income: (APC > MPC).
2. The APC usually rises in recessions but it diminishes in boom periods, because consumption is a very stable economic factor, and thus the decrease in consumption is smaller than that of income in recessions, while the incremental increase in consumption is usually smaller than that of income in boom periods (Jeong Unchan 1985: 240–243).

APC, however, cannot show any individual characteristics because it is an aggregate concept. It also cannot divide consumption into quantity and quality because it is calculated simply as the total price value of consumption. In spite of these problems, it may be useful to examine comprehensive attitudes towards consumption in a society. In particular, if we are to undertake an international country comparison, the comprehensive attitude towards consumption in a given society could be explored, and its characteristics interpreted. For instance, if the level of APC in a country is even lower than other countries with the same level of income, it could be understood that the consumption attitude of that society is more passive than others, for whatever reason.

Periodic analysis of trends in a society is also helpful for an examination of its consumption changes and characteristics over time. For example, as we shall see in the following sections, if the rate of increase of consumption is continuously lower than that of income regardless of the business cycle, then there may be a tangible or intangible institutional apparatus present which is intended to repress consumption. In particular, if such trends are continued for a considerable time, it should become clearer that the apparatus plays a role. Additionally, if the trends are not seen in another period, we can conclude that it no longer plays a role in the society, whether the government represses consumption or not. In this respect, periodic analysis of APC serves as a tool that can be used to explore the relationship between a policy and consumption behaviour.

Analysis of the Korean case will be carried out by comparing other countries' APCs with that of Korea. Korea will be compared to various categories of countries such as developing and developed groups of countries. This will be performed at the level of national accounts for the same criterion of comparison. Following this work, this research will contain two different categories of data of both income and expenditure in internal analysis of Korea: The National Accounts and the Salary and Wage Earners' Households in urban areas (SWEHS). National Accounts can show whole consumption trends in the national economy and the SWEHS can demonstrate that the characteristics of urban areas are more sensitive to consumption. This is, on the other hand, an attempt to see the difference in accordance with income classes. Even though the urban households are contained in the National Accounts, generally the level of income of the former is higher than that of the latter. In particular, the Korean case is a good example of this, in that the uneven industrial strategy based on heavy chemical industry was implemented mainly in urban areas after the 1970s. Therefore, although there is no data on this type of subset of income and expenditure, such as quintile data, broadly the difference between higher and lower classes in terms of income and expenditure could be analyzed through these two types of data.

4.1 *Collective Behaviour of Frugal Consumers in Internal Comparison*

First of all, we need to know the extent of passive consumption attitudes in the Korean economy during the 1970s, through a comparison with other countries.

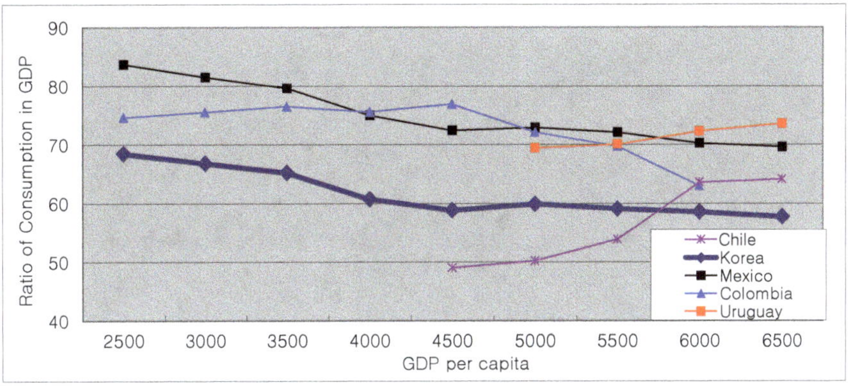

FIGURE 3.1 *APCs of Korea and Latin American countries at each income level.* SOURCE: PWT 6.2.

For comparison, this section uses 'Penn World Tables Version 6.2 (PWT 6.2)'. The comparison of APC is carried out in accordance with level of income, which is the factor most influencing consumption. Here, APC is defined as the consumption share of real GDP[22] in each year in a national economy. According to PWT 6.2, of these definitions, Korea's GDP per capita was US$ 2,621.31 in 1970, US$ 3,458.24 in 1975, US$ 4,556.59 in 1980 and US$ 6,193.52 in 1985. Accordingly, comparison work is carried out at the level of GDP per capita between around 2,500 and 6,000 US dollars.

Figure 3.1 shows that during the 1970s-early 1980s Korea's APC was much lower than that of Latin American countries at equivalent income levels. There is a continuous gap in APC of over 10 percentage points between Korea and Mexico while their trends were similar in income level between 2,500 and 6,500 US dollars. The APC of Colombia was also even higher than Korea's for the whole period of income. What is interesting for both countries is the widening APC gap at lower levels of income. Furthermore, the fact that the economic growth rate has been considerably moderated, with the decline of APC since the late 1970s, when GDP per capita was around US$ 4,500, may imply that the role of consumption was quite important in Colombian economic growth. According to Figure 3.1, it can be considered that the importance of consumption in the early period of economic growth was fairly similar to Uruguay and Chile as well. The Chilean APC which recorded 48.96 at a level of US$ 4,500, rose to

22 In PWT, 'real' means 'Purchasing Power Parity (PPP) converted' instead of 'in constant price' (Alan Heston, Robert Summers and Bettina Aten, Penn World Table Version 6.2, Center for International Comparisons of Production, Income and Prices at the University of Pennsylvania, September 2006).

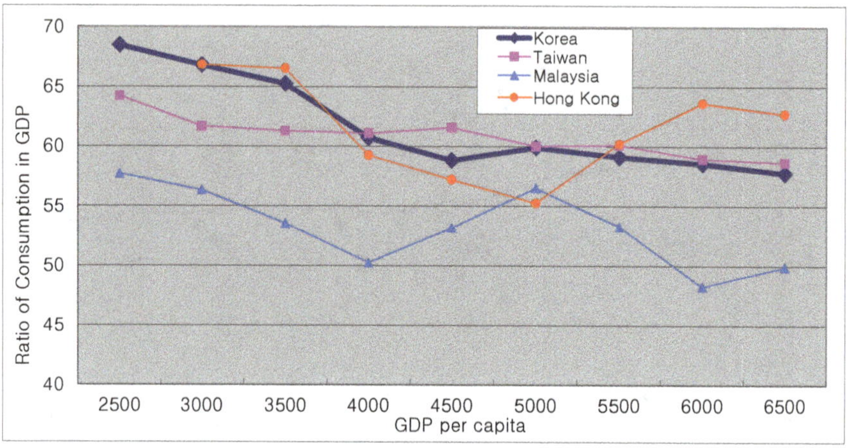

FIGURE 3.2 *APCs of Korea and Asian developing countries at each income level.* SOURCE: PWT 6.2.

63.59 at an income of US$ 6,000. The Uruguayan APC also shows a similar trend to Chile's despite its more moderate increase. In contrast, the Korean case is completely different because rapid economic growth was achieved even while the APC was decreasing in the early period of development. In other words, consumption had less of an impact on economic growth in Korea than in Latin American countries. This, we can assume, is related to various factors, including development strategy such as export-led or import substitution. However, this is not the main concern here. What is important is that the APCs of most Latin American countries are substantially higher than Korea's APC at the same level of income. This implies that Korean consumers were much more frugal in terms of consumption for the same level of income than Latin American developing countries.

According to Figure 3.2, the overall level of APCs of Asian developing countries was much lower than that of Latin American countries. This shows that people in Asian developing countries consumed more frugally than Latin Americans, and broadly illustrates that the contribution of consumption to economic growth was smaller in the former than in the latter. Here, what should be noted is the trend of the Korean APC. Its level was the highest at the income level of US$ 2,500 among Asian countries shown in the Figure, but its rate of decline was the fastest as the income level rose. In particular, comparison between Korea and Taiwan as 'Asian Tigers' leads us to believe that the consumption environment was quite harsh in the 1970s in Korea. At the income level of US$ 2,500 in circa 1970 in Korea, the Korean APC was higher at 68.43, than the Taiwanese one at 64.18. However, due to the rapid decline of the

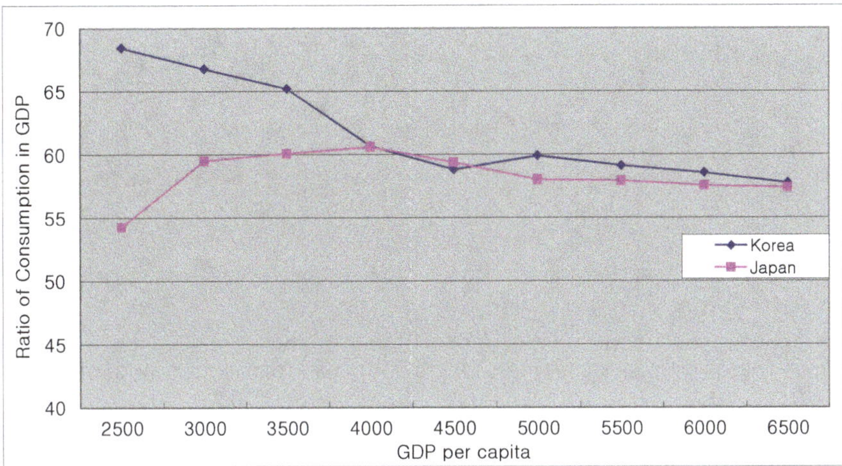

FIGURE 3.3 *APCs of Korea and Japan at each income level.* SOURCE: PWT 6.2.

Korean APC, this situation was reversed from the 1977 Korea income level of US$ 4,000. The situation was even more dramatic because the Taiwanese APC had diminished as well from US$ 2,500 US dollars. This may imply that there had been unusual repression on consumption for the period in Korea.

It is also worth comparing Korea and Japan. Even if it is generally known that Korean development strategy is similar to the Japanese strategy, their attitudes in terms of consumption were quite different in terms of income level of between US$ 2,500 and US$ 4,500. This income level was reached between 1950 and 1960 in Japan and between 1970 and 1980 in Korea. These periods were very important stages in both countries in that they were the starting point and springboard for successful economic growth.

Figure 3.3 shows that the shape of Japanese APC, which increased during the period, is consistent with research on Japanese economic growth which argues that Japanese rapid economic growth after the Second World War was based on the expansion of domestic consumption (Partner 1999; Synodinos 2001: 238; Yoshikawa 2003). In contrast to this, the shape of the Korean APC which decreased rapidly during the period implies that the driving force of economic growth was not domestic demand in the period. On the other hand, consumers had a passive approach to consumption whether on a relative or absolute basis despite rapid increases in income.

4.2 *Collective Behaviour of Frugal Consumers in the National Accounts*

The peculiar frugality of Koreans in the earlier period of development can be shown through international comparison. With this, periodic comparisons are

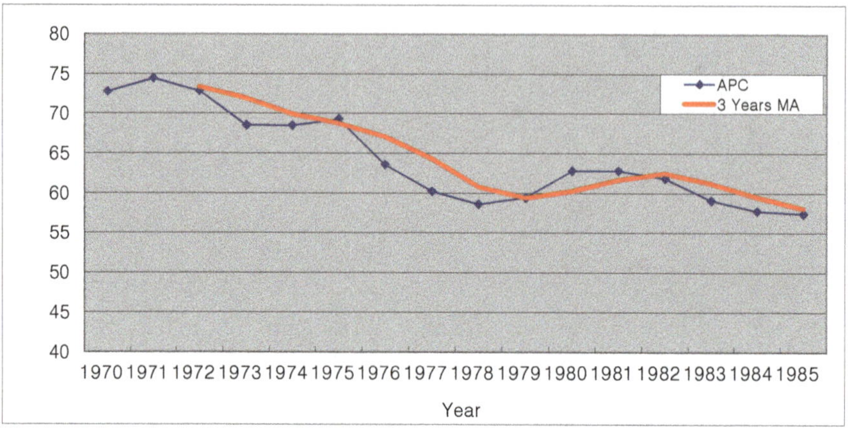

FIGURE 3.4 *Trends of APC (APC: PFCE/GNDI; GNDI: Gross National Disposable Income; PFCE: Private Final Consumption Expenditure).* SOURCE: BOK, NATIONAL ACCOUNTS, ANNUAL.

needed in order to know periodic differences in Korea. Therefore, given that a scrupulous comparison will be carried out in the next few chapters, this section will look at the APC and its basic characteristics in the 1970s.

First, the collective behaviour of frugal consumers is shown through APC trends in the National Accounts produced by the Bank of Korea. As an original definition, the APC is here defined as the ratio of Private Final Consumption Expenditure (PFCE) in Gross National Disposable Income (GNDI).

Broadly the trend of the APC in Figure 3.4 is similar to that of the APC as the ratio of consumption in GDP which we saw in the previous section even if its absolute level is not the same because of a difference in parameters. Figure 3.4 indicates that the Korean APC decreased rapidly in line with increases in income in the 1970s. The APC, which recorded 74.4 in 1971, declined to 58.6 in 1978 but increased to 62.8 in 1981 because of a serious recession. After that, it again diminished to 57.4 in 1985. This curve, however, does not give information about changes in consumption proportionate to business cycles. It is necessary to disaggregate the APC into the changing rates of GNDI ($\dot{I}_n$) and PFCE ($\dot{C}_n$) to perceive more clearly the relationship between income and consumption under business cycle conditions.

In Figure 3.5, $\dot{I}_n$ can be considered as a proxy of the business cycle because it is a figure based on GDP. It is clear from the three year moving average of real $\dot{C}_n$ and $\dot{I}_n$ that $\dot{I}_n$ was higher than $\dot{C}_n$ over almost the entire period of the 1970s, regardless of the business cycle. In the boom period, $\dot{I}_n$ was over $\dot{C}_n$ and even in recession, $\dot{I}_n$ was also mostly over $\dot{C}_n$. This implies that the trend of the Korean APC was completely different from general characteristics of the APC which

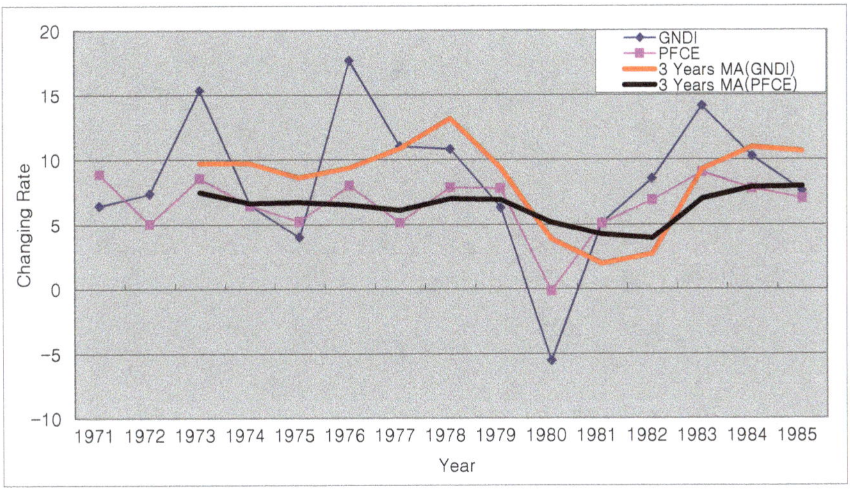

FIGURE 3.5 *Trends of GNDI and PFCE (GNDI: changing rate of Gross National Disposable Income ($\dot{I}n$); PFCE: changing rate of Private Final Consumption Expenditure ($\dot{C}n$); Real term based on 100 at 2000).* SOURCE: BOK, NATIONAL ACCOUNTS, ANNUAL.

usually rises in recessions as mentioned earlier. This suggests the possibility that there was an institutional apparatus which was intended to repress consumption in the Korean economy, because it was different from a general characteristic of consumption where the change of consumption is relatively slower than income proportionate to business cycles. At the same time, this implies that consumption hardly played a role as a stabilizing factor for the business cycle. This analysis is consistent with the general interpretation that the business cycle in the Korean economy depended mainly on the export and investment situation and not on domestic consumption in the 1970s (Rodrik 1995; Yu Cheolgyu 1992). This pattern of the curve was similar to that of the 1980s, but the gap between them was smaller. As we shall see, this kind of change shows characteristics of the 1980s as a transition period for economic liberalization, from the state to the market. In contrast, an exception appears at the end of the 1970s, when the political system was shattered by the assassination of President Park and a serious economic crisis took place. It was the first time that the changing rate of GDP recorded a minus figure since the establishment of the economic development plan in the early 1960s.

In this respect, if it is considered that it was a very unusual incident, the trends of the APC in the 1970s and at least by the mid-1980s show that the policy of consumption repression penetrated throughout the actual life of people in the Korean economy. Figure 3.6, which shows the trends of the gap of both

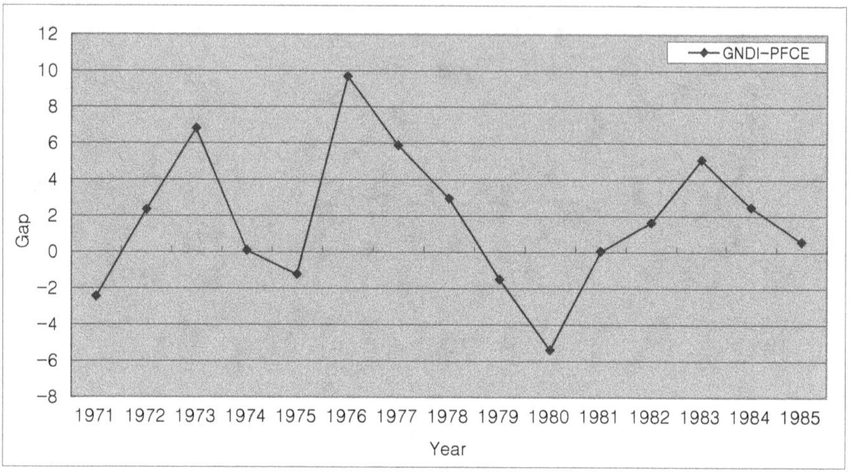

FIGURE 3.6 *Trends of the gap between GNDI and PFCE (GNDI: changing rate of Gross National Disposable Income ($\dot{I}n$); PFCE: changing rate of Private Final Consumption Expenditure ($\dot{C}n$)).* SOURCE: BOK, NATIONAL ACCOUNTS, ANNUAL.

curves ($\dot{I}_n - \dot{C}_n$) from 1971 to 1985, may be useful for comparison of frugality between periods and between regions. Years over zero mean $\dot{I}_n > \dot{C}_n$ but those below zero mean $\dot{I}_n < \dot{C}_n$. Likewise, APC rises in the period of $\dot{I}_n < \dot{C}_n$ but APC declines in the period of $\dot{I}_n > \dot{C}_n$. In other words, the higher the figure is, the bigger the gap and so the more frugal the consumer is. It can be presumed from the graph that the gap between $\dot{I}_n$ and $\dot{C}_n$ was bigger in the 1970s than in the 1980s. This means that consumers were more frugal in the 1970s than in the 1980s. However, this comparative work between periods will be looked at more substantively in the following chapter, which deals with the next period.

4.3 *Collective Behaviour of Frugal Consumers in Urban Labour Households*

Data relating to 'Salary and Wage Earners' Households' in urban area (SWEHS), which has been surveyed monthly since 1963, is the most important data for discovering the change in the ability to consume. The survey covers over 4,000 households that have family members of more than two people in the whole country. This includes most items concerning income and expenditure. As mentioned earlier, this data, compared with the data from the National Accounts, has the advantage that the characteristics of the higher income group can be explored because the average level of income of urban labour households is much higher than that of the whole country. Moreover, a more sensitive response to the environment concerning consumption should be shown because urban areas are more commercialized than non-urban areas.

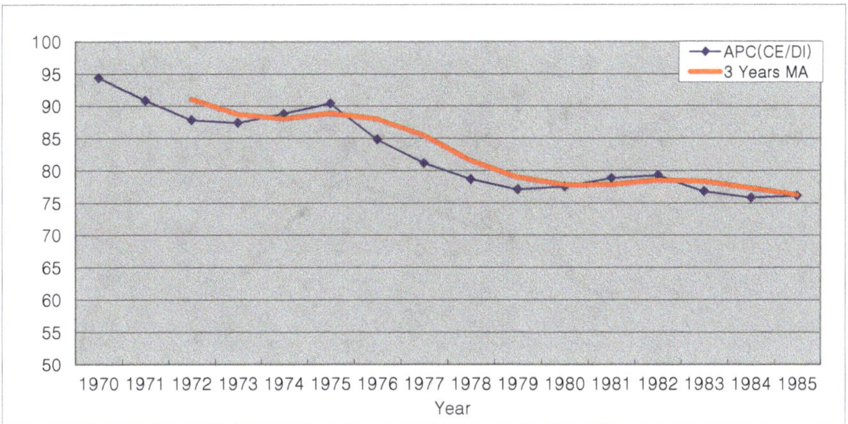

FIGURE 3.7 *Trends of APC in SWEHS (APC: CE/DI; DI: Disposable Income; CE: Consumption Expenditure).* SOURCE: SK, MONTHLY INCOME AND EXPENDITURE PER URBAN HOUSEHOLD, ANNUAL.

As has been seen in the National Accounts, signs of consumption repression will also be shown through the APC of SWEHS, which is denoted as a share of consumption expenditure in disposable income of the household.[23] Figure 3.7 shows that, like the APC of the National Accounts, the Korean APC of urban labour households decreased rapidly in line with increases in income in the 1970s. The APC which recorded 94.38 in 1970 declined to 77.09 in 1979 but increased to 79.27 in 1982 because of the serious recession.

After that, it again diminished to 75.81 in 1984. Like the APC of the National Accounts, this curve, however, does not give information about changes in consumption related to business cycles. It is necessary to disaggregate this APC into the rates of change of DI ($\dot{I}_u$) and CE ($\dot{C}_u$) to more clearly view the relationship between income and consumption under business cycle conditions.

In Figure 3.8, $\dot{I}_u$ can be considered a proxy of business cycles because it is a figure based on GDP. It is clear from the three year moving average of real $\dot{I}_u$ and $\dot{C}_u$ that $\dot{I}_u$ was higher than $\dot{C}_u$, regardless of the business cycle, except in 1974 and 1975. Not to mention that $\dot{I}_u$ was over $\dot{C}_u$ in the boom period, $\dot{I}_u$ was

23 The level of APC of SWEHS is higher than that calculated from the National Account. This is stemmed mainly from difference of statistical criteria between both. In particular, one of the most significant differences is that the disposable income of SWEHS is after tax whereas GNDI of the National Account is before tax. Due to this, the level of APC of SWEHS is necessarily higher as proportional as the denominator is smaller. However, here, this is not a problem because what we need to notice is not gap of their levels but periodic difference of consumption attitude in their own curves.

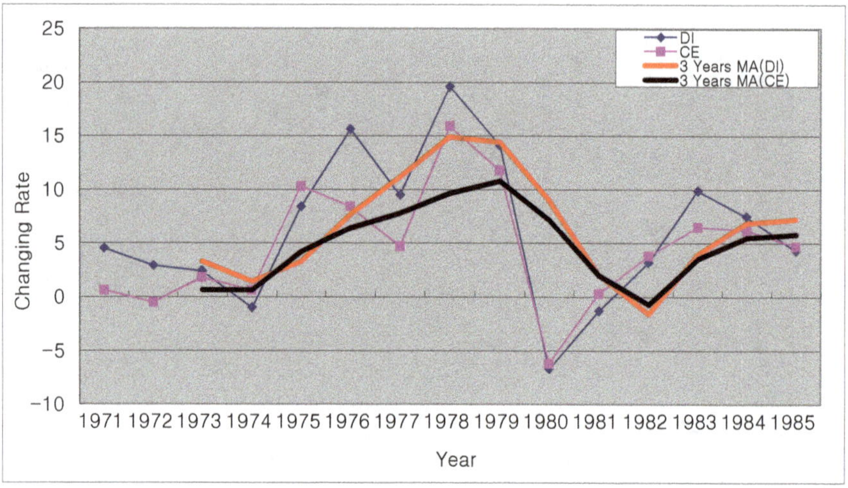

FIGURE 3.8 *Trends of DI and CE in urban households (DI: changing rate of Disposable Income ($\dot{I}u$); CE: changing rate of Consumption Expenditure ($\dot{C}u$) (real term calculated by the Consumer Price Index (CPI) based on 100 at 2005).* SOURCE: SK, MONTHLY INCOME AND EXPENDITURE PER URBAN HOUSEHOLD, ANNUAL.

also mostly over $\dot{C}_u$, even in the period of recession. This implies that the trend of the Korean APC was completely different from the general characteristics of the APC which usually rises in recessions as mentioned earlier. From this pattern of the curve, it can be seen that these were the environments shaping strong consumption repression even in urban areas in the 1970s. The pattern demonstrates a sign of change since the 1980s, even though this was not clear. As we shall see, this shows the characteristics of the 1980s as a transition period for economic liberalization, from the state to the market.

Like the APC of the National Accounts, Figure 3.9, which shows the trends in the gap of both curves ($\dot{I}_u - \dot{C}_u$) from 1971 to 1985, provides a useful comparison of frugality between periods.

Years over zero mean $\dot{I}_u > \dot{C}_u$ but those below zero mean $\dot{I}_u < \dot{C}_u$. Likewise, the APC rises in the period of $\dot{I}_u < \dot{C}_u$ but the APC declines in the period of $\dot{I}_u > \dot{C}_u$. In other words, the higher the figure is, the bigger their gap is and so the more frugal the consumer is. Figure 3.9, accordingly, shows more clearly that consumers were more frugal in the 1970s than in the 1980s. Again, this comparative work between periods will be carried out in the next chapter.

As we have seen, two kinds of curves in Figure 3.10 denote gaps of ($\dot{I} - \dot{C}$) in urban areas and the whole country. Figure 3.10 may be useful to compare differences in consumption attitude between urban and non-urban areas in the same period as a means of knowing the evolutionary pattern of the retail

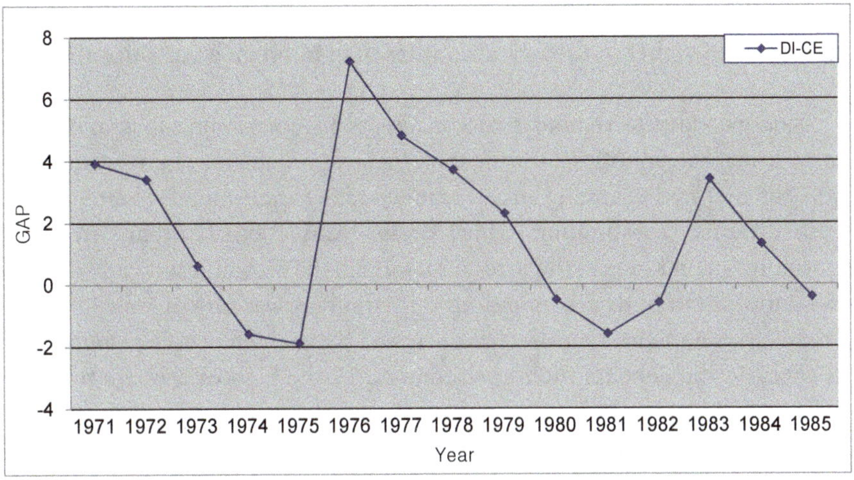

FIGURE 3.9 *Trends of the gap between DI and CE in urban households (DI: changing rate of Disposable Income (İu); CE: changing rate of Consumption Expenditure (Ċu)).* SOURCE: SK, MONTHLY INCOME AND EXPENDITURE PER URBAN HOUSEHOLD, ANNUAL.

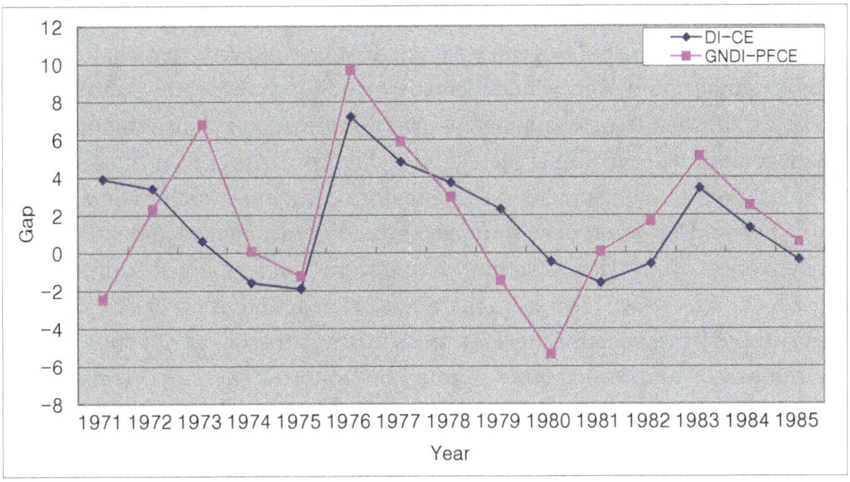

FIGURE 3.10 *Differences in consumption between urban and non urban areas (DI: changing rate of Disposable Income in urban labour households (İu); CE: changing rate of Consumption Expenditure in urban labour households (Ċu); GNDI: changing rate of Gross National Disposable Income (İn); PFCE: changing rate of Private Final Consumption Expenditure (Ċn)).* SOURCE: SK, MONTHLY INCOME AND EXPENDITURE PER URBAN HOUSEHOLD, ANNUAL, BOK, NATIONAL ACCOUNTS, ANNUAL.

format. According to the figure, there was a tendency for the gap in the figure to have been higher in the whole country than in urban areas since the early 1970s.

Thus we can understand that consumers in non-urban areas adopted a more frugal consumption attitude than those in urban areas in the same period. This may be because of urban characteristics that promoted a receptiveness towards consumption. Thus, on a relative basis, urban areas led consumption in Korea in the 1970s even though the prevailing attitude towards consumption in both urban and non-urban areas was one of frugality. Such urban characteristics also affected the speed with which people responded to changes in the consumption environment. In the case of the boom period from 1976, consumption increased relatively earlier in urban areas and expanded more moderately afterwards. However consumption began to increase later in non-urban areas but then expanded more sharply.

5 The Limitation of Department Stores

Even by the mid-1970s, the department store industry as an example of a modern retail phenomenon, was scarcely different from that of the 1960s. At the end of the 1960s, the Shinsegae Department Store followed a typical form with direct management. The Midopa Department Store, which was established in 1964, established a new management structure in 1973, introducing direct management like the Shinsegae Department Store. Apart from these two examples, even though some department store companies such as *Si-dae-baeg-hwa-jeom* and *Ga-go-pa-baeg-hwa-jeom*, which were managed under the letting system, were built, they became bankrupt and were merged <http://stock.koscom.co.kr>. As we have seen, there was no clear definition of a department store in the 1970s because the 'Law of the Market'of 1961 did not state specific definitions of the various types of retail institutions. These problems continued until 1981, when an amended 'Law for the Market' was enacted. Therefore, in an extreme case, it was not impossible for a 'mom and pop' store to be launched with the designation of department store.[24] In this respect, it could be said that there were just two department store companies, Shinsegae and Midopa, in Korea during most of the 1970s. Such a situation changed in 1979

24 Of course, as mentioned, because the image of the department store as a luxurious shop remained in people's memory, such an extreme case was not in fact meaningful. However, in the case of a big shopping place, discrimination between a typical department store and an imitation one was not easy.

when the Japan-based Lotte Group,[25] built the Lotte Department Store in Seoul and the situation in the department store industry developed into a fierce contest between the three (*Jo-seon-il-bo* 6 July 1979b, 18 December 1979c). Even if there was acute competition between the three stores, it was impossible to expect that the department store industry as a whole had an important role in the retail industry in such a situation. Because there is no precise data concerning department stores' sales in the 1970s, we can obtain rough estimates through survey data on big retailers in the 'Census on the Wholesale and Retail Trade' by SK. There were only ten retail companies with more than fifty employees out of 320,471 retail companies in 1971, and their proportion of the total sales of the retail industry was 0.6 per cent. Even though the sales per company were much higher than those of the smaller companies in the numbers of employees, the percentage of sales in the whole retail industry was virtually unnoticeable. In data of 1979, because the statistical methodology changed in 1976, the retail companies were classified into two types of stores: general retailers, and general merchandise stores (GMSs), which meant department stores and supermarkets. According to this classification, there were only twenty-four GMSs with more than twenty employees out of the total of 422,012 retail companies and their percentage of sales was 0.2 per cent (SK, Wholesale and Retail Trade Census 1979). What this rough data tells us is that the proportion of department stores in the whole retail industry had been small throughout the 1970s.

Despite the rapid increases in the retail industry in the late 1970s, the strategy of only taking the luxury end of accounts was one reason why the industry did not develop. The Shinsegae Department Store usually utilized a strategy of concentrating on higher-priced luxury goods, rather than the mass sale of medium-priced reliable goods. For example, through technical cooperation with a foreign company, it introduced new technology to mature various kinds of meat, and emphasized the difference between its meat and others. In the case of fruit, it selected farms which would produce fruits under a special contract only for its own store and used such a process as a selling point (Shinsegae Department Store 1987: 152–153). It was inevitable that the price of goods in the Shinsegae Department Store was higher than those of other retailers, particularly, the traditional markets. Such practices showed up more clearly in the field of apparel. In 1973, the Shinsegae Department Store concluded a contract for technology with McGregor, a famous clothing company in the US, to be the

25 Although the Lotte Group was a Japanese conglomerate, the Lotte Department Store could be built despite the prohibition of foreign investment in the retail industry because Sin Gyeokho, its founder and chairman, was a Korean resident in Japan.

first to introduce the technology and brand to Korea. It then sold the various kinds of brand clothing at about twice the price as the same kinds of clothes of other brands. For example, in the case of jackets, the price for a McGregor jacket was 8,000 *won*, while other brands were 3,000–4,000 *won* (Ibid: 133–136). It also concluded an alliance covering technology with the French company of Pierre Cardin in 1978 and strengthened its reputation for stocking luxury goods. Because of these strategies, people were likely to perceive it as a retail institution with extremely high prices although its goods were reliable. From this, it seemed that the department store was used mainly by a small number of wealthy people in Seoul,[26] and its strategy strengthened such a tendency in the 1970s. This trend differed from that which followed in the 1980s.

With respect to the inactivity of department stores, it was possible that investment in the retail industry was a low priority for the manufacturing conglomerates, *chaebol*, which were only able to invest large amounts of capital in large retailers to meet mass-consumption, irrespective of whether it was a department store. First, this was related to the fact that the government focused its support on the manufacturing sector. The interest rate offered for financial support to the manufacturing sector was preferential to that of the retail industry. There is no reason why any company would give up their investments in a profitable field to invest in a relatively unprofitable one. Moreover, the fact that investment in the retail sector could have been understood as resistance to government policy would have been a serious burden to *chaebol*. This was dangerous behaviour in the period of policy dominance because it made it possible for the government to exclude the disobedient *chaebol* from favourable support. Additionally, the fact that *chaebol* could be blamed for depriving the poor of the means of making a living was not negligible, because this public atmosphere was able to stimulate a response from the government.[27] In addition, the existence of the manufacturers' distribution network played an important role in the decline of motivation for investment in the retail industry. Because manufacturers were in a dominant position and controlled the distribution sector, and therefore the manufacturers' profits were not affected

26 In fact, this kind of situation was very similar to what happened in Japan around 1910 as the early period of the department store format. At the start, Japanese department stores targeted the upper and upper-middle classes (Hirano 1999: 380). As mentioned earlier, this seems to be a similarity among countries which imported this retail format, despite time differences.

27 This factor was not important in the 1970s because the proportion of department stores was so small. However, since the middle of the 1980s, this has become a big social issue around the department store industry and thus the government regulated it strongly through fair trade policies and a licence system for the establishment of new outlets.

by retailers' behaviour, manufacturers did not feel any real necessity to establish large general retailers themselves. In sum, while there were many barriers for manufacturers to surmount in order to enter the retail industry, they possessed a safety device to protect them from the effects of unsatisfactory sales.

There was a third point regarding the inactivity of department stores; the competitiveness of traditional markets in the mass market was an important factor when examined in conjunction with the stores' strategy of stocking luxury goods. According to Okubo, first of all, it is possible to find in a Korean traditional market everything any consumer might want to buy, and thus one stop shopping might be possible. In addition, one of the most important reasons why the traditional market attracted people was related to the competitiveness of its prices, compared with department stores. Generally, the price of goods in the traditional market was much lower than the normal price, while the quality was more or less the same. Okubo pointed out the uniqueness of the purchasing process in the traditional market as key, stating the prices there were at least 20 per cent lower than normal prices. First, the traditional retailers usually purchased slightly flawed goods, which the manufacturer could not sell through the normal marketing process, below cost. Second, they purchased goods which manufacturers sold cheaply for cash payment when they faced cash flow difficulties. Third, they purchased goods which department stores had failed to sell at cut prices. Thus, the traditional market was a terminal for goods deviating from the normal distribution process (Okubo 1991: 52).

In conclusion, under such circumstances, the role of department stores in the 1970s could not help being limited and their prosperity was dependent on a change in the internal and external conditions around the department store structure.

6 Conclusion

As we have seen, the department store industry in the 1970s experienced an economic and social environment that was conducive to its development. The increase of income and fast urbanization following rapid economic growth, was a key factor, and the change in the family structure was an advantageous condition for the industry. However, it only accounted for a small portion of the growth in the Korean retail industry within the period. The policy environment was the most important factor. The authoritarian Korean government in the 1970s, concentrated on the investment of all of its resources in the manufacturing sector, particularly the HCI, and had ignored the role of the retail industry for promoting economic growth. The government regarded the industry as a supplementary factor for mere economic circulation, rather than a basic factor for economic growth. Consequently, while it gave various kinds of incentives to the manufacturing sector, it created disadvantageous conditions for the retail industry in terms of finance and taxes. As a consequence, the *chaebol,* which were the only entities to possess sufficient capital necessary for investing in modernizing the retail industry, were not incentivised to do so. This is because, on the one hand, the *chaebol* had various opportunities to make profits from the manufacturing sector with support from the government. On the other hand, they did not wish to be discriminated against by the government and were constrained by the government's preferential support for the manufacturing sector.

Apart from this policy, the government's focus on the manufacturing sector, was a type of general repression of consumption. It suppressed the increase of consumption through the taxation system with measures such as value added tax, and special excise taxes. It used various kinds of restrictions such as import prohibition and a very high rate of emergency tariff in order to control consumption of luxury goods from abroad. It also imposed extraordinary measures for the repression of consumption such as a ban on gift-vouchers, which were a long-established feature in Korea. Such high-handed policies had a particular motive: to repress consumption of luxury goods. Alongside these measures, the government regulated the social atmosphere with the intention of repressing consumption through several kinds of social policies. They included the strong encouragement of frugality and severe punishment against overconsumption. These policies had several attendant effects unlike the selective industrial policy described above, in that they had an effect on the pattern of the behaviour of a great number of unspecified people, and moreover it was highly possible that it contributed to the formation of a particular kind of social ethos. Of course, it was clear that the policy goal was to concentrate capital within the manufacturing sector, by lowering the general level of consumption in the 1970s. In this respect, the policy was remarkably successful. However, from a socio-economic perspective, its effect was deeper and more long-term. The social psychology of low inequality in Korea as an environmental factor friendly to economic growth was maintained as a mechanism of consumption repression.

As we have seen, the level of income inequality in Korea was worse in the 1970s. Nevertheless, the reason why social conflict around distribution was relatively unnoticeable can be ascertained through the pattern of consumption.[28] In general, people might feel discrimination from income inequality at

28 Most existing studies (Haggard, Rodrik, Wade, etc.) concerning this have emphasized mainly the extreme control of the labour market by government and the initial condition

the stage of consumption rather than that of income, because consumption manifests material inequalities more clearly. Thus even in the case of a society characterized by high inequality of income, the social psychology of equality could be influential if consumption were controlled uniformly. Such a condition in the 1970s, particularly, was the opposite of the retail format exhibited by the department store which created its own image through marketing luxury goods.

However, it is incorrect to say that no positive policies were directed at the retail industry in the 1970s. Such government policy was, however, unsuccessful in its bid to develop the retail sector as an industry. At that time, the government focused mainly on the stability of prices and consumer protection. It tried to construct a retail network for price stability through the introduction of the supermarket chain in the early 1970s. Despite its efforts, the introduction was not successful because of lukewarm government support compared with the support extended to the manufacturing sector, and a hostile retail environment such as the shortage of goods in the early 1970s. In particular, the fact that the SMSTRs were the main object of retail policy at that time shows that government policy was social rather than economic in nature. The premature emphasis on consumer protection also reflected the government's view of the retail industry. Of course, even though consumer protection was not premature, it could be said that the building blocks necessary for supporting such a policy within the retail industry were lacking. This is because there was little focus on the role of the manufacturer for providing consumer protection, and this situation prevailed even in the 1990s.

Given this environment, it seemed impossible for the retail industry, and the department store in particular, to develop. And yet, even with such conditions, the retail industry achieved some increase in sales, without a change in quality, proportionate to an increase in income following rapid economic growth in the 1970s. Even though sales of the retail industry grew in such conditions along with an increase in the number of companies for the same period, structural changes such as the appearance of large retailers and the change in relationship between manufacturer and retailer scarcely took place in the

---

of equality relating to relatively successful land reform. However, it could not be expected that social conflict around distribution had been managed through only suppression for at least twenty years of rapid economic growth without minimum social agreement. It was also unrealistic that such an initial condition should remain unchanged for the period. Nevertheless, it was a fact that the social conflict around distribution weakened and it was also clear that Korea has shown a strong tendency of egalitarianism even thereafter. If so, another factor through which such a tendency can be explained has to be examined.

retail market. Of course, such a result was related to both the marketing strategy of department stores as existing large retailers, concentrating on luxury goods, and the competitiveness of the traditional market as a cluster of SMSTRs in which one-stop shopping was possible for popular goods.

CHAPTER 4

Modernizing, Stratifying Retail Industry and Rapid Economic Growth since the 1980s: The Golden Age of the Department Store Industry I

1 Introduction

The period of the 1980s in Korea began disastrously in both economic and political terms. The Korean economy had already shown signs of serious recession since early 1979 due to over-investment in HCI and to make matters worse, it had received a severe shock as a result of the second oil crisis. As a consequence of the extreme instability which occurred after the assassination of President Park in October 1979, the military, led by General (later President) Chun Doo Hwan, seized power in 1979–80. The result was that the Korean economic growth rate dropped to 6.8 per cent in 1979 from 9.3 per cent in 1978 and it even recorded minus 1.5 per cent in 1980, for the first time since the establishment of the economic development plan. Such a dark start, resulting from past economic policies, led to expectations that policies in the future would be different in terms of content and method. First of all, Chun's regime had to concentrate on economic matters in order to recover from the severe recession and furthermore it desperately needed to resolve these problems because the process of grasping power lacked legitimacy. For the same reason, it was also inevitable that the regime would take, on one hand, resolute measures against the causes of the problem, but, on the other hand, it would make a gesture towards a policy of appeasement in order to change the government's image. The representative measures to achieve this goal were the 'Measure of Rearrangement of Investment in HCI' (*Junghwa-hag-gong-eob-tu-ja-jo-jeongjo-chi*) as a gesture of toughness towards *chaebol*, and the 'Monopoly Regulation and Fair Trade Act' (*Dog-jeomgyu-je mich gongjeonggeo-lae-e gwan-han beob-lyul*). The establishment of a separate Korea Fair Trade Commission in 1981 was a soft measure which worked for the benefit of the consumer and strengthened the market function. The name of the fifth 'Five-Year Plan for Economic Development' in 1982 was changed to the fifth 'Five-Year Plan for Economic and Social Development' and, for the first time, the stability of prices was referred to as an important goal of the plan[1] (Gang Gwangha 2000: 87–89). In this atmosphere,

---

1 In fact, the change of the meaning in the name of the plan is more dramatic in Korean than in English. In Korean, the word for Development in its name has been called *bal-jeon* since

 DOI 10.1163/9789004274228_005

liberal measures such as the privatization of banks and the expansion of economic openness were enforced.

Apart from the internal situation, it was in the 1980s, with the appearance of neo-liberal governments such as those of Ronald Reagan in the US and Margaret Thatcher in the UK, that the retreat of the state gradually became one of the most important international trends. This tendency became stronger and stronger with the end of the Cold War at the end of the 1980s. In the process of liberalization at the international level, Korea was also affected to a remarkable extent. In particular, the social movement against the authoritarianism of the state was hugely influenced by this international situation, because of the similar goal of weakening of the state, despite considerable differences between the ideological positions of both movements. Accordingly, the Korean government was in a very difficult situation in which, on one hand, the social movement was pushing it to retreat in the name of democracy and social liberalization, and, on the other hand, the capitalists were pushing it to obtain liberalization of the market from the government in the late 1980s. The circumstance of the international economy also required the changing of the Korean economy. First of all, US trade policy was changed to one of aggressive intervention to open even the markets of developing countries, because of the US fiscal and trade deficits. Especially after September 1985, when the 'Plaza Accord' was signed, the US heavily coerced Korea to open its market due to the dramatic increase of exports thanks to the strong Japanese Yen.

With these changes, the size of the domestic consumption market expanded rapidly since the 1980s. This resulted from a dramatic increase in income, while the Korean economy grew rapidly, recording an annual average growth rate of over 10.5 per cent between 1986 and 1988. Meanwhile, the size of population had also increased from 36 million in 1980 to 42 million in 1990 (SK, Population and Housing Census, annual). These new environments changed the pillars of Korean society from those of the state, production and protection into those of the market, consumption and economic liberalization. In this process, consumption and the retail industry, which had been repressed, met a period of explosive development in both qualitative and quantitative respects from the 1980s. In social-political terms, the establishment of the first civilian government since President Park Chung Hee, the 1993 Kim Young Sam admin-

the fifth plan of 1982 whereas it had been called *gae-bal* before then. While *gae-bal* is a word focused just on economic growth, *bal-jeon* is a more comprehensive word meaning advance and improvement of the whole society. Thus this change of the name implied that the contents of the plan altered dramatically as well and they were actually carried out (Gang Gwangha 2000: 87).

istration,[2] had a huge affect on the trend towards social-economic liberalization and deregulation. In fact, liberalization of various policies, already in progress under the previous Roh Tae Woo administration (1988–93) was spurred on by the Kim administration. In particular, the decision to join the Organization for Economic Cooperation and Development (OECD) in 1996 was considered a representative symbol of liberalization. This change evoked a much friendlier consumption atmosphere in contrast to social oppression occasioned by the government's support for production in the 1970s. With this change of policy, people could consider the expansion of consumption as a form of victory against the authoritarianism of the regime. This was particularly the case regardless of its economic effects, because the repression of consumption was understood as a form of the repression of human rights, rather than as a strategy of economic development by an authoritarian regime. With the increase in income, the social conditions for consumption had begun to develop perception along such lines. Consequently, the change of policy and the needs of the time are linked to the beginning of an era of explosive consumption. This chapter will show the characteristics of the burgeoning Korean retail industry, particularly in terms of its structure; the Korean retail industry has modernized and stratified since the 1980s. It pays especial attention to the rapid growth of the department store industry as a model of the only modern retailer, compared with traditional retailers. In addition, it examines how this rapid growth is quite a distinct phenomenon in the history of the retail industry.

2 Overview of Rapid Economic Growth since the 1980s: General Economic Policy and Rapid Economic Growth

2.1 *General Economic Policy and Rapid Economic Growth*

As mentioned, the situation of the Korean economy was very dismal at the beginning of the 1980s. President Chun, who achieved political power through violence, had to concentrate on economic recovery through reform of the economic structure so as to justify his grasp of power. Economic policy in Chun's period was characterized by retrenchment and stabilization policy. This was adopted because the reason for the severe recession in the early 1980s was regarded as duplication and over-investment in HCI. The first policy was the 'Measure of Rearrangement of Investment in HCI' in 1981. The government

2 The administration of President Kim Young-sam is called *mun-min-jeongbu* which means *mun* [the pen] against the sword and *min* [civil] against soldiers.

forced *chaebol* to rearrange their speciality and investment in HCI in order to avoid further duplication of investment. For example, in the case of the motor industry, the government ordered that only KIA Motors could produce commercial vehicles and other companies, such as the Hyundai Motor Company and the Daewoo Motor Company were not allowed to produce them. The regulation on *chaebol* also corresponded to the public sentiment which was opposed to the overwhelming position of *chaebol*. Thus the government could obtain two good results through its adoption of this policy, namely both the effect of stabilization, in terms of the economic aspect, and the effect of offsetting doubt over imbalanced socio-political support for *chaebol*. Even though the *chaebol* resisted this policy as much as they could, they consequently had to accept it because of both the dominant power of government and a sense of responsibility for the economic recession amongst the public.[3] Of course, their resistance could be understood as one of their strategies to induce benefits, in that they got various kinds of support from the government in the process of this measure.

The 'Monopoly Regulation and Fair Trade Act' can be considered as a symbolic action in which the government demonstrated the orientation of its economic policy. This meant that a discretionary regulation of government was changed into a general one through the legal process, and the market function was emphasized. It could also be said that it was the first law to enact the original meaning of the Fair Trade Act, in that players in the market opposed to competition were regulated comprehensively in terms of fairness of trade. On the other hand, the previous 'Law of Price Stabilisation and Fair Trade' focused mainly on price stability. In this respect, even though it was a policy which announced the beginning of economic liberalization, it was also understood as one of the ways to regulate *chaebol* and thus they desperately resisted the introduction of the law[4] (FKI 2001: 427). In fact, the economic stabilization policy was different from the growth policy through government intervention and thus it was natural that *chaebol*, which had depended on support from the government as an object of the growth policy, felt uneasy. To the wider public, however, this policy seemed like a progressive move towards autonomy in the

3 According to an order of the government, the FKI, which was an association of *chaebol*, established 'The Committee for the Rearrangement of Subsidiaries' in its organization and suggested ways of rearrangement, including merging and abolition, sale, and liquidation (FKI 2001: 431). The fact that *chaebol* suggested measures to deny their own property rights might reflect the oppressive atmosphere of that time.

4 It could be understood as a similar situation to that of the Japanese case in which the US military government led by General MacArthur tried to dismantle the *zaibatsu* by strengthening the rule of fair trade after the end of the Second World War.

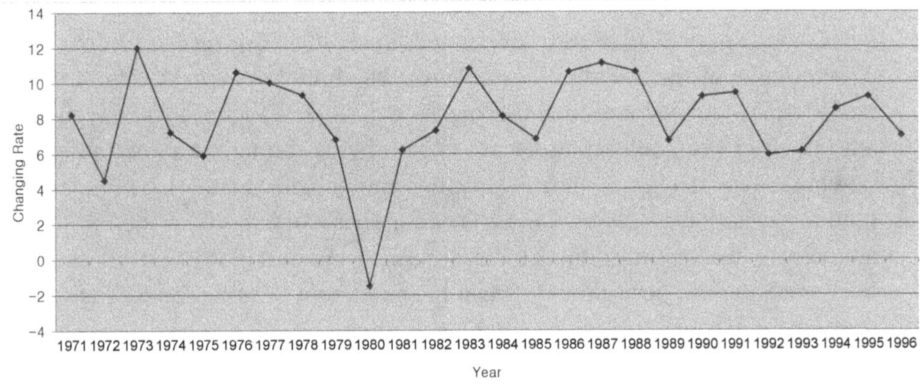

FIGURE 4.1 *Trend of GDP growth (real term).* SOURCE: BOK, NATIONAL ACCOUNTS, ANNUAL.

market, instead of the previous system which was understood as a corrupt relationship between government and business.[5] The balance between growth and welfare or between manufacturer and consumer, instead of concentration on growth and manufacturing was suggested.

As part of the same trend, the government tried to introduce the privatization of commercial banks in 1982. Even though the power of governance of the banks was not turned over to the private sector right away, at that time, the policy seemed to contribute hugely to the change in economic policy towards liberalization. In the course of these policies, the Korean economy began to recover. The annual economic growth rate was 7.3 per cent in 1982, 10.8 per cent in 1983 and 8.1 per cent in 1984. In particular, the rate of increase of consumer prices, which had recorded annual increases of over 15 per cent during the 1970s, and 21.4 per cent in 1981, diminished dramatically to 7.2 per cent in 1982. It subsequently recorded 2.3 per cent in 1984, and 3.4 per cent in 1983 (BOK, the National Accounts, annual).

5 Of course, it is too much to say that a few policies adopted in the early 1980s meant a complete changeover in the tendency of the government policy because the government did not abandon the attitude of intervention even after that time. However, it was clear that there was a signal of change in the direction of policies as a reaction to the economic failure at the end of the 1970s. Furthermore, this tendency could not help becoming stronger and stronger gradually over the 1980s with the change in the relationship of power between government and business, because *chaebol* wanted their autonomy in the market rather than government intervention according to the development of the market system.

The Korean economy, which showed a rapid recovery in the first half of the 1980s, had experienced an extreme boom[6] since 1986. This resulted from the phenomenon of the so-called 'Three Lows' which meant depreciation of the US dollar, low interest rates and the low price of oil. The Korean economy took advantage of the booming atmosphere worldwide through the low interest rate and price of oil and, particularly, the appreciation of the Japanese Yen (and depreciation of the US dollar) for an increase of exports to the US. The annual rate of economic growth increased to 10.6 per cent in 1986 and consecutively recorded 11.1 per cent in 1987, and 10.6 per cent in 1988. The balance on the current account had been in the black since 1986, for the first time since the development plan, and the amount by which it was in the black reached US $ 14.2 billion in 1988. Nevertheless, the stabilization of prices had also not been disrupted during the same period.

However, the rule of the business cycle from boom to depression did not make an exception the Korean economy. The fantastic boom had finished in three years and, due to the appreciation of the Korean *won* and severe industrial strife, the rate of increase of exports decreased drastically to 2.8 per cent in 1989 from 28.4 per cent in 1988 and the growth rate of the Korean economy also abruptly diminished to 6.7 per cent in 1989. After that, the economic growth rate again recovered to 9.2 per cent in 1990 and 9.4 per cent in 1991. Suffering under the burden of the sharp rise in house prices since the end of the 1980s, the Korean economy somehow maintained its economic growth. As Korean exports increased, stronger protectionism on the part of the developed countries, including the US, was indicated as one of the important factors in its depression. The balance on the current account was reversed into a deficit of US $ 2.2 billion in 1990. This figure of balance of payments was greatly affected by a rapid increase of imports in consumer goods due to the opening of the domestic market.

2.2 *The Change of Socio-economic Environments*

2.2.1 The Increase in Income and Expenditure

It was natural that income increased rapidly because economic growth was sharp and in the same manner it was also inevitable that the amount of expenditure followed the speed of increase in income in the 1980s. Furthermore, the increase in expenditure was higher than that of income in the 1980s, unlike

---

6 The boom of the late 1980s was called the best period of prosperity since *dan-gun*, the progenitor of Korean history. Thereafter, a few scholars, who from a progressive perspective criticised the developmental plan through exports as dependency development, even changed their view to agreement with the economic policy.

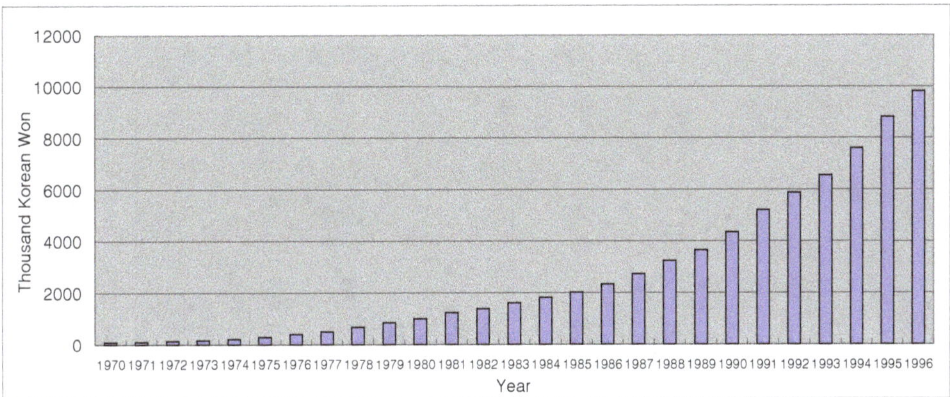

FIGURE 4.2 *Trend of GNI per Capita (Nominal Term of GNI per Capita: thousand Korean* won). SOURCE: BOK, NATIONAL ACCOUNTS, ANNUAL.

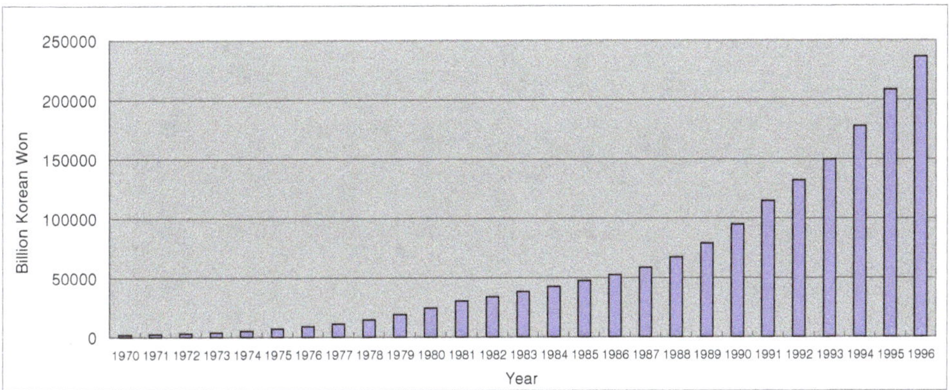

FIGURE 4.3 *Trend of consumption (nominal term of the Private Final Consumption Expenditure (PFCE: billion Korean* won). SOURCE: BOK, NATIONAL ACCOUNTS, ANNUAL.

that of the 1970s. This meant that the size of the domestic market grew more rapidly, compared with the 1970s, and to that extent its importance became greater and greater in the Korea economy. According to Figure 4.2, GNI per capita was 1 million Korean won (US $ 1,645) in 1980.

It took just five years for this to grow to more than 2 million *won* in 1985. It took just another five years for it to roughly double that amount at 4.4 million *won* in 1990, and again after five years, it had approximately doubled again at 8.8 million *won* in 1995. As a result, GNI per capita had increased to over eight times its 1980 value over the fifteen year period.

In line with the increase in GNI, private final consumption expenditure (PFCE) also rose rapidly. The PFCE, which was 24,250 billion *won* (US $ 39.89

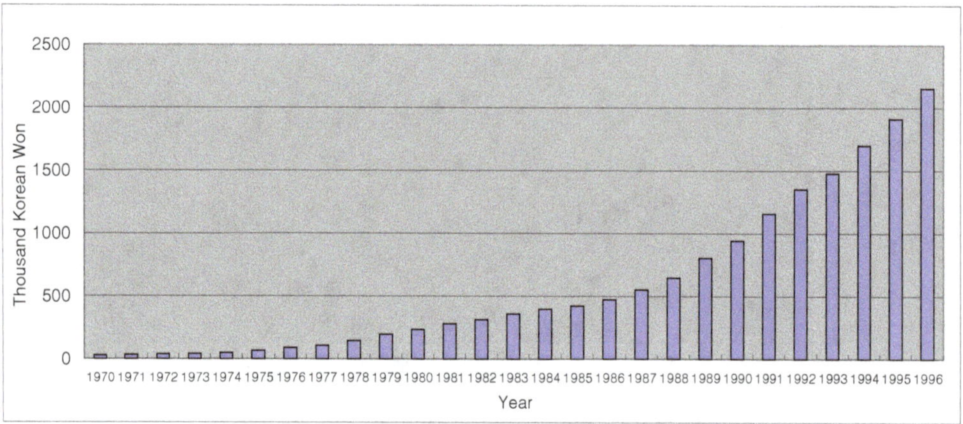

FIGURE 4.4 *Trend of income of urban labour household (nominal term: thousand Korean* won). SOURCE: SK, MONTHLY INCOME AND EXPENDITURE PER URBAN HOUSEHOLD, ANNUAL.

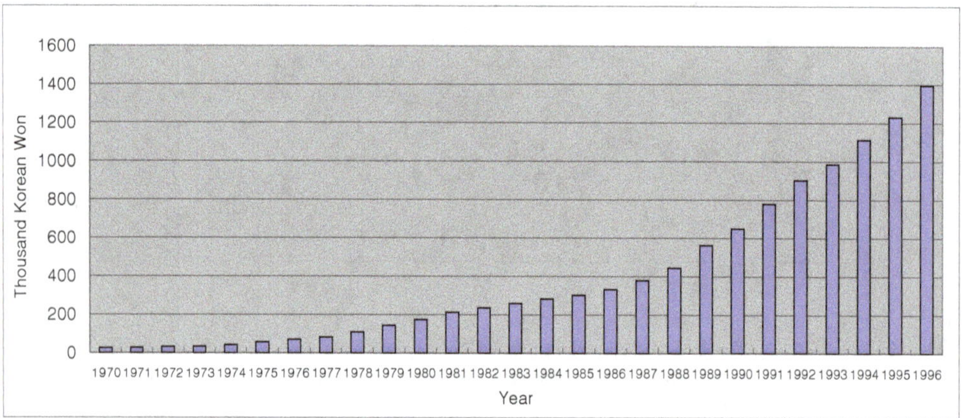

FIGURE 4.5 *Trend of consumption expenditure of urban labour household (nominal term: thousand Korean* won). SOURCE: SK, MONTHLY INCOME AND EXPENDITURE PER URBAN HOUSEHOLD, ANNUAL.

billion) in 1980, became 47,600 billion *won* in 1985. An increase of twice the amount in PFCE took just five years. An additional expansion of twice the amount also took just five years to reach 94,968 billion *won* in 1990, and again five years for two times that amount at 208,461.6 billion *won* in 1995. Like increments of GNI per capita, the amount of PFCE had expanded by about eight times over fifteen years.

According to Figure 4.4, monthly income of salary and wage earners households in urban areas (SWEHS) increased continuously as well. It was 234.1 thousand *won* (US $ 385) in 1980 and increased to 473.6 thousand *won* in 1986.

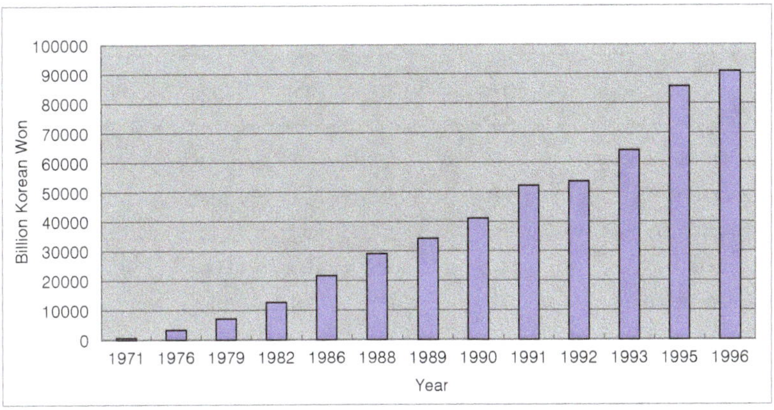

FIGURE 4.6 *Trends of retail sales (nominal term: billion Korean* won). SOURCE: SK, WHOLESALE AND RETAIL TRADE CENSUS (1971, 1976, 1979, 1982), WHOLESALE AND RETAIL TRADE CENSUS WITH THE OVERALL ESTABLISHMENT STATISTICS (1986, 1991), WHOLESALE AND RETAIL TRADE SURVEY (1988, 1989, 1990, 1992, 1993, 1995), WHOLESALE, RETAIL TRADE AND SERVICE INDUSTRY CENSUS (1996).

Monthly income which was 943.3 thousand *won* in 1990 rose to 1.9 million *won* in 1995.

Monthly consumption expenditure of the SWEHs also shows a similar shape to its monthly income in Figure 4.5. It was 174 thousand *won* (US $ 286.2) in 1980, 331.5 thousand *won* in 1986, 650 thousand *won* in 1990, and rose to 1.4 million *won* in 1996.

The expansion of consumption expenditure on the basis of increase in income was linked to the rise in sales within the retail industry. The total retail sales in Figure 4.6 were 12,655.5 billion *won* (US $ 17,292.5 million) in 1982 and increased to 29,036.5 billion *won* in 1988. Its growth trend was sluggish from 1991 and 1992 but rose to 64,093.2 billion *won* in 1993. After that, increasing continuously, it recorded 90,906.9 billion *won* in 1996.

2.2.2 Changes in Social Environments: Movements in Population and Urbanization

One of the most important things in the composition of the population for the retail industry was the change in the structure of the household; that is, a conspicuous decrease in the number of household members with an increase in the number of households, which meant the expansion of purchasing units. The average rate of increase in the population was around 1.5 per cent per annum from 1980 to 1990, when the whole population numbered 42.1 million. This rate of increase decreased sharply to 0.6 per cent per annum between 1990

TABLE 4.1 *Trend of generations in household (%)**

	1970	1975	1980	1985*	1990	1995
One person households**		4.2	4.8	6.9	9	12.7
One generation***	6.8	6.7	8.3	9.6	10.7	12.7
Two generations	70	68.9	68.5	67	66.3	63.3
Three generations	22.1	19.2	16.5	14.4	12.2	9.8
Over four generations	1.1	0.9	0.5	0.4	0.3	0.2

* The sum of figures in each year has been a bit under 100 since 1980 because non-relative households, which consist of members of non-blood relationship, have been classified as a separate item.
** One person households: household with just one member
*** One Generation: household which consists of members of the same generation, like a married couple without children.
Source: SK, Population and Housing Census, annual

and 1995 when the size of the whole population was 43.3 million. Under this condition, the average number of household members declined from 4.5 persons in 1980 to 3.7 persons in 1990 and to 3.3 persons in 1995. Accordingly, the total number of households rose from 8 million in 1980 to 11.4 million in 1990 and to 13 million in 1995 (SK, Population and Housing Census, annual). Such a change could be confirmed through the relative households classified by the number of generations.

According to Table 4.1, the proportion of one generation households in the total number of households was increasing continuously and so recorded 10.7 per cent in 1990 and 12.7 per cent in 1995. What is interesting is the rapid increase in one person households since the 1980s. Its ratio in total households had risen by around 2.5 times for fifteen years. In contrast to this, the ratio of three generation households diminished sharply to 9.8 per cent in 1995 from 16.5 per cent in 1980 and the ratio of over four generations was actually insignificant.

Big retail industries, additionally, need a population concentrated in urban areas as a pre-condition for development, as mentioned. With industrialization, this phenomenon progressed in the 1980s, just as it did in the 1970s. The percentage of the urban population in the total population rose from 57 per cent in 1980 to 74.7 per cent in 1990. Accordingly, the ratio of urbanization in Korea was almost the same as the developed countries, for example, 74 per cent in France, 75.2 per cent in the US, and 77.4 per cent in Japan in 1990 (SK 1995).

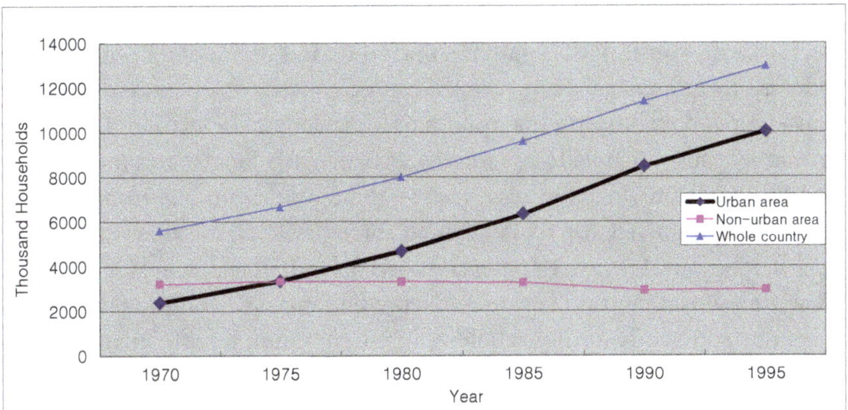

FIGURE 4.7 *Number of households.* SOURCE: SK, POPULATION AND HOUSING CENSUS, ANNUAL.

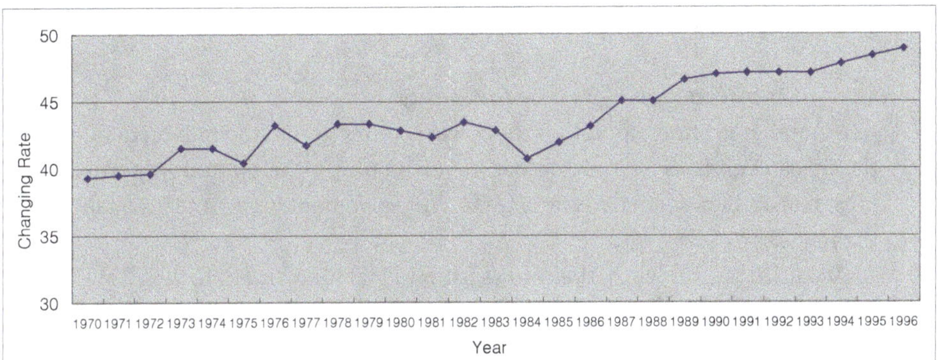

FIGURE 4.8 *Proportion of economically active females (the proportion = economically active female/all fifteen years old and over females).* SOURCE: SK, THE ECONOMICALLY ACTIVE POPULATION SURVEY, ANNUAL.

The regional distribution of households in Figure 4.7 shows the degree of urban concentration of households as a unit of purchase more clearly.

While the number of households in urban areas increased by over 80 per cent for ten years to 8.5 million in 1990, from 4.7 million in 1980, those in non-urban areas declined to 2.9 million in 1990, from 3.3 million in 1980. This was regarded as a phenomenon that accompanied the process of the movement of the population to urban areas from agricultural areas. This meant that most of the new households were concentrated in urban areas, and, to that extent, they were a basis for the development of the retail industry, and particularly of big retail companies.

The proportion of economically active females is also a remarkably influential factor on consumption patterns and so on the development of the retail industry. Its influence may be realized through, on the one hand, a decrease in household labour, and, on the other hand, an increase in income. The former inevitably causes people to use retailers, particularly food shops, increasingly, and the latter provides the resources enabling the rise in consumption. According to Figure 4.8, the female labour force participation rate was 42.8 per cent in 1980, but it rose to 47.0 per cent in 1990. A double income family due to female employment was likely to spend more money on eating out, and buying furniture and goods for household affairs than a non-double income family (Jeong Geonhwa 1998: 206). Therefore, even if the change in the figures was not large, the overall rise, particularly since the mid-1980s, was estimated to have a positive effect on the retail industry.

3 The State of Inequality since the 1980s

3.1 *The Reduction of Income Inequality*

In general, it is understood that there was a reduction in income inequality in the 1980s even if there is some controversy around the matter. In particular, most researchers agree that there was an improvement in income inequality in the 1990s.

According to Table 4.2, the results from Ju Hakjung and EPB, the Gini Coefficient which was aggravated by the end of the 1970s improved from the early 1980s. While the level of the Gini was around 0.39 in the late 1970s, it had improved to the level of 0.34 in the second half of the 1980s and to the level of 0.31 in the early 1990s.

The urban sector means both the urban labour households and the urban non-labour households and the latter is composed of businessmen and the self-employed. Due to limitations in the statistical data, here, the state of inequality in the urban sector is shown through data of labour households in the urban sector. According to Table 4.3, the Gini Coefficient in the urban sector improved from the figure of 0.311 in 1984 and 1985. In particular, its curve after 1989 indicates that the degree of improvement became clearer and clearer and it recorded 0.281 in 1993. Even if it rose after that year, it was not over 0.3 even in 1996 when it rose to 0.291. The ratio of the top (fifth) and bottom (first) levels of the income quintile show very similar trends to the Gini coefficient during the same period. The ratio which was 5.12 in 1985 declined to 4.35 in 1993. Its improvement was also particularly remarkable from 1989. It was 4.42 in 1995, but in common with the Gini it increased in 1996. Therefore, it can be said that

TABLE 4.2 *Trends of the Gini coefficient in the whole country*

	1970	1976	1980	1985	1988	1993
Gini	0.332	0.391	0.389	0.345	0.336	0.310

*Gini is the result from Ju Hakjung (1979) and Economic Planning Board (EPB, 1987, 1990).
Source: as cited in I Jeongu and Hwang Seonghyeon (1998: 159, 165)

TABLE 4.3 *Trends of the Gini coefficient in the urban sector*

Year	Gini coefficient
1982	0.309
1983	0.309
1984	0.311
1985	0.311
1986	0.307
1987	0.306
1988	0.302
1989	0.304
1990	0.295
1991	0.287
1992	0.284
1993	0.281
1994	0.284
1995	0.284
1996	0.291

Source: SK, Monthly Income and Expenditure per Urban Household, annual

income inequality in the urban sector has improved in the period between the mid-1980s and the mid-1990s.

In sum, the situation of inequality in terms of income became remarkably different from the middle of the 1980s, compared with the period of the 1970s. This may be a result, on the one hand, of rapid economic growth and, on the other hand, of an improvement in the rights of the labour class with the development of democracy since the middle of the 1980s.

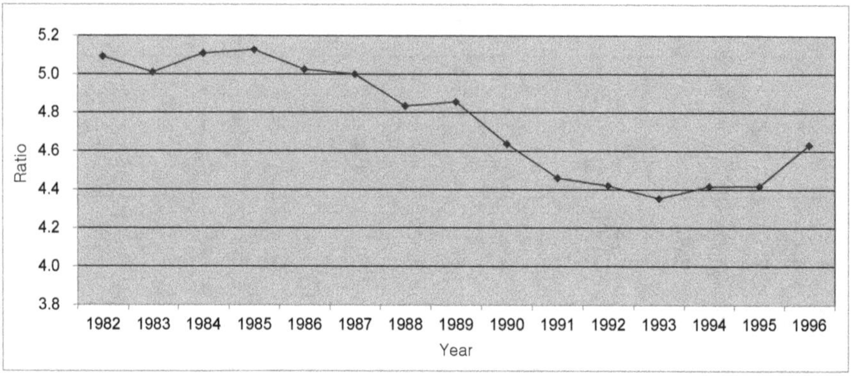

FIGURE 4.9 *Ratio of the top and bottom levels of the income quintile*). SOURCE: SK, MONTHLY INCOME AND EXPENDITURE PER URBAN HOUSEHOLD, ANNUAL.

3.2 *Inequality of Wealth*

As was mentioned in Chapter 2, the situation of land inequality as a form of wealth had deteriorated rapidly since the earlier period of economic development. As we shall see, it is likely that this situation hardly improved since the middle of the 1980s. However, the change in the financial market has to be considered in order to analyze the inequality of wealth in this period. Here, what should be noted is the difference in the financial market between the periods before and after the mid-1980s. The financial market, and particularly the stock market, developed very rapidly from the mid-1980s. The Korea Composite Stock Price Index (KOSPI) increased to 1007 on 1 April 1989 from 163 at the end of 1985. The size of the population which invested in stock rose to 19 million in 1989 from 0.8 million in 1985. It had increased twenty-four fold over four years (Securities Supervisory Board 1997: 622–623, 632). Its importance can also be seen by the fact that most newspapers have informed their readers of the stock market's whole price board every day since that time. This kind of change was deeply related both to the economic boom since 1986 and the privatization of state-run companies which sold most of their shares to ordinary people, who become involved in the stock market. Because of this change, in contrast to the 1970s, when land was only taken into account as a kind of wealth, financial assets should be considered as one of the main kinds of wealth from the mid-1980s.

First, what should be noted is the change in environment influencing trends in land prices between the periods before and after the mid-1980s.

Figure 4.10, shows that even if the increasing rate of land prices in urban areas was broadly higher than in the countryside, the convergence of these trends became clearer and clearer with relative stability since the mid-1980s.

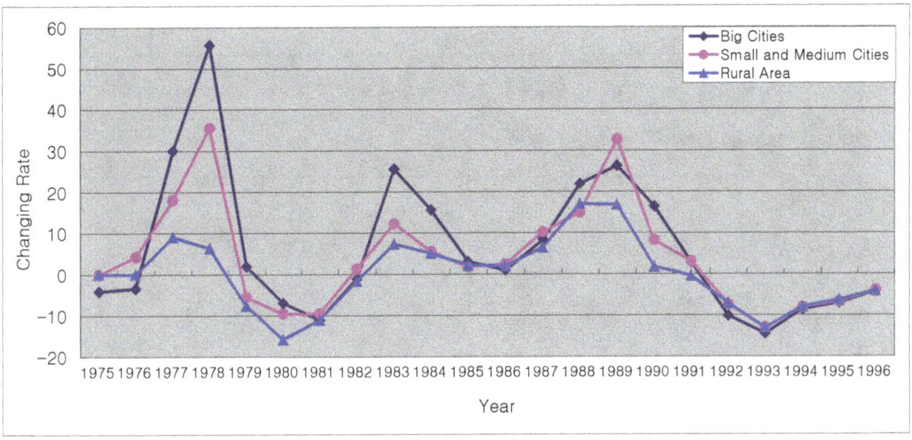

FIGURE 4.10 *Trends of land prices (real term calculated by the author through the GDP deflator since 1970, based on 100 at 2000).* SOURCE: MOCT, SURVEY OF LAND PRICES, ANNUAL.

This kind of phenomenon is closely associated with the expansion of urbanization to previously non-urban areas. The rate of urbanization, which means the proportion of the population living in urban areas compared with the total population, was 65.4 per cent in 1985 and rose to 78.8 per cent in 1995 as the speed of urbanization was decreasing (SK, Population and Housing Census, annual). This implies that people were concentrated in both small- and medium-sized cities and counties in the period characterized by a relatively high degree of urbanization. In contrast, people were mainly concentrated in big cities in the period typifying a low degree of urbanization. The relative moderation of the rate of increase in land prices may also be regarded as a result of such phenomena since the mid-1980s. Thus, the distribution of landownership in terms of size became an important factor as a criterion of land inequality from that time, unlike the 1970s, when the rate of increase in land prices was more important because of the regional gap in the rate of increase. According to the survey of the distribution of landownership which was carried out, for the first time in 1986, its inequality was already considered to be seriously uneven as is shown in Table 4.4. The top 5 per cent of the total population owned 65.2 per cent of all privately owned lands and the top 10 per cent owned 76.9 per cent in 1986. The ratio of lands owned by the highest 20 per cent of the population was 87.7 per cent at the same time. In contrast, only 2 per cent of all the privately owned lands belonged to the lowest half of the population (I Jinsun 1993: 113)

TABLE 4.4 *Distribution of privately owned lands*

The ratio in population	Cumulative owned size of lands (year, %)	
	1986	2005
Top (1%)		51.5
Top (~2%)		65.3
Top (~5%)	65.2	82.7
Top ~10%	76.9	91.4
Top ~20%	87.7	93.4
Top ~30%	93.1	

Source: I Jinsun 1993: 113; MOGAHA, 'The State of Distribution of Individual Landownership-In Owned Size' (Gae-in-byeol-to-ji-so-yu-bun-po-hyeon-hwang-myeon-jeog-gi-jun), 2006

This serious level of inequality in land is unlikely to have improved even after this period. Due to data limitations, it can only be estimated through the second survey on the distribution of landownership which was carried out by the Ministry of Government Administration and Home Affairs (MOGAHA) in 2005.

Table 4.4, shows that the top 2 per cent of the total population owned 65.3 per cent of privately owned lands in 2005, which was equivalent to the size of the lands owned by the top 5 per cent of the population in 1986. The top 5 per cent owned over 80 per cent of privately owned lands in 2005. The figure of 93.4 per cent which indicated the ratio of the size of the lands owned by the top 20 per cent in 2005 was almost the same as the figure of 93.1 per cent, the ratio owned by the top 30 per cent in 1986. Due to the limitations in the data, the precise picture of land distribution is difficult to draw in the period between 1980 and 1996. Moreover, given that a serious economic crisis took place in 1997, it is more difficult to estimate the situation in the period between 1980 and 1996 by using the results of 2005. Nevertheless, if the trends of the period before and after 1986 are considered, at least it cannot be said that the inequality of landownership improved during that period. In particular, Hyun's analysis that the Gini Coefficient of land was 0.86 in 1993 implies that the situation of inequality in landownership was never sound during the period of the 1990s in the Korean economy (Hyeon Jingwon 1996: 266).

Research on the distribution of financial assets has also not been a popular topic in studies of the Korean economy. Because the taxation system for financial assets was not well documented during the 1990s, it was not even easy to

TABLE 4.5 *Gini coefficient of financial assets*

	Year	Gini of financial assets
Kwon	1988	0.770
Daewoo Economic Institute (DEI)	1993	0.767
	1994	0.724
	1995	0.656

Source: Kwon 1992; DEI 1993–1995, as cited in I Jeongu and Hwang Seonghyeon (1998: 182–187)

calculate the size of the financial assets owned. Faced with this problem, most researchers who tried to estimate its distribution did so through special surveys using their own methods, thus producing individually distinct results. Nevertheless, there were usually affinities in the various research results when measuring the degree of inequality in financial assets relative to income; almost all such results measured the degree of inequality in financial assets as being much higher than that of income.

Table 4.5 shows that the inequality of financial assets as wealth was quite high, with a Gini coefficient of around 0.7, even if it was lower than the Gini coefficient of landownership. Here, what should be noted is the trend during the period of the 1990s. The survey by DEI shows that its inequality decreased gradually during the period, even though its absolute level was still high. This can be understood as a combination of a decline in income inequality, with the rapid development of the financial market since the end of the 1980s. In other words, as people increased their ownership of financial assets with the development of the stock market, the Gini coefficient of financial assets gradually decreased.

In sum, it cannot be said that the situation of wealth inequality had been sound in the Korean economy since the mid-1980s. Broadly speaking, it hardly improved at all during this period. In particular, it is likely that inequality of landownership was exacerbated after the mid-1980s. In contrast, income inequality was improved to a large extent during the same period and this is related to a slight improvement in financial assets during this period. As will be seen, the relative abundance resulting from this change will provide the financial resources for consumption expansion while socio-economic liberalization will provide its institutional background.

4 Stratifying Retail Industry in Expansion of the Retail Industry: Modern Department Store *vs.* Traditional Market

4.1 *The State of the Retail Industry and the Traditional Market*

According to Table 4.6, the total sales of the retail industry have continuously increased since the early 1980s. They were 12,655 billion Korean *won* (US $ 17,292.5 million) in 1982 but rose to 21,673 billion *won* in 1986. At 90,906.84 billion *won* in 1996, it was approximately 4.2 times the level of 1986.

Table 4.7 shows that the number of retail shops continuously increased during the 1980s, from 542 thousand in 1982 to 710 thousand in 1990. Annual sales per shop also continuously increased during the same period in accordance with a rapid increase in total retail sales.

The sales of 23.3 million Korean *won* per shop in 1982, rose to 57.9 million Korean *won* in 1990. This tendency did not change in the 1990s. However, the fact that the number of retail shops increased continuously intimates a possibility that the structure of a small business as a general characteristic of the Korean retail industry continued. In this respect, the fact that the number of retail shops first decreased in 1996 to 738 thousand, from 771 thousand in 1995, is significant. Even if its decrease was not huge, this suggests that structural change was taking place in the retail industry around that period.

According to Table 4.8, the average number of employees per retail shop (two people) hardly changed from the early 1980s. Basically this shows that the size of the retail shop had not grown from the 1970s. This also explains that most retail shops were managed as family businesses. Apart from this, annual sales per employee had grown in accordance with an increase in total sales. Therefore, the overall Korean retail industry was still made up of small businesses even from the 1980s although the volume of sales grew rapidly with fast economic growth.

This situation can be directly linked to the state of the traditional market because a large portion of the retail industry in terms of sales was still covered by the traditional market. The following Table 4.9, repeated from Chapter 2, explains such a situation although precise analysis is difficult due to limitations in the data.

According to Table 4.9, the number of permanent markets, which form the center of the traditional market, increased from 785 in 1981 to 1,176 in 1991. It was not until the 1990s that the number of traditional markets began to decrease, even if their number for the year 2000 cannot accurately explain this trend. The state of the traditional market seems to be related to the decrease in the number of the retail shops as we have seen in Table 4.7. In general, traditional markets in Korea were located along streets in the city center, or villages,

TABLE 4.6 *Annual sales by the retail industry*

	1979	1982	1986	1988	1990	1992	1995	1996
Annual sales	7,187.1	12,655.5	21,673.8	29,036.5	41,108.1	53,624.6	85,760.7	90,906.8

Unit: billion Korean *won*.
Source: SK, Wholesale and Retail Trade Census (1979, 1982), Wholesale and Retail Trade Census with the Overall Establishment Statistics (1986), Wholesale and Retail Trade Survey (1988, 1990, 1992, 1995), Wholesale, Retail Trade and Service Industry Census (1996)

TABLE 4.7 *Number of the retail shops and sales per shop*

	1982	1986	1988	1990	1992	1995	1996
Number of retail shops	542,458	637,762	673,552	709,888	737,667	771,019	738,063
Annual sales per shop*	23.3	34	43.1	57.9	72.7	111.2	123.2

* Unit: million Korean *won*.
Source: SK, Wholesale and Retail Trade Census (1982), Wholesale and Retail Trade Census with the Overall Establishment Statistics (1986), Wholesale and Retail Trade Survey (1988, 1990, 1992, 1995), Wholesale, Retail Trade and Service Industry Census (1996)

and varied in length from a few metres to kilometres. Okubo sketched the simple structure of the traditional market present around the late 1980s as follows. In the case of the Namdaemun Market, one of the largest traditional markets, there were a lot of buildings along both sides of the main street in the market, and many big street stalls were located consecutively on the ground floors of buildings. These stalls displayed various kinds of goods. Apart from this, there were various lunchrooms densely clustered along the middle of the main street and they also sold the ingredients of the food which they were selling. The total length of Namdaemun Market amounted to several kilometres and its huge size was remarkable. It was always too crowded to walk between the stalls (Okubo 1991: 51–52). Even though other traditional markets were smaller in terms of their length and scale, the structure and shape of the market was similar to Namdaemun. According to a survey by KCCI in 1981, the average number of shops per permanent market was 154 (Jo Gwansu 1981: 257). These investigations and surveys show that each traditional retailer in the Korean traditional

TABLE 4.8 *Number of employees and their performance per retail shop*

	1982	1986	1988	1990	1992	1995	1996
Number of employees per shop	1.7	1.9	1.9	1.9	1.9	2.1	2.1
Annual sales per employee*	13.4	17.7	22.6	30.2	37.7	53.6	58.6

* Unit: million Korean *won*.
Source: SK, Wholesale and Retail Trade Census (1982), Wholesale and Retail Trade Census with the Overall Establishment Statistics (1986), Wholesale and Retail Trade Survey (1988, 1990, 1992, 1995), Wholesale, Retail Trade and Service Industry Census (1996)

TABLE 4.9 *Number of traditional markets since the 1980s*

Year	Number of periodic markets	Number of permanent markets
1979	925	766
1981	884	785
1983	866	1,118
1987	755	1,083
1988	752	1,099
1991	686	1,176
2000	491	696

Source: KCCI, A Comprehensive Bibliography of the Retailing and Wholesale Industry (1992, 1995) as cited in Baek Insu (2003: 167); Institute of Korean Distribution Industry (2000: 5)

market might be a small business. The situation of the traditional market has deteriorated since then. The survey of the Institute of Korean Distribution Industry (IKDI) illustrates plainly such stagnation of the traditional market. According to its survey in 2000, the ratio of the traditional markets which were composed of less than 100 shops was 67.8 per cent of the entire traditional market and the ratio of those with 101–200 shops was 19 per cent. In contrast, the traditional market of more than 400 shops was just 5.2 per cent (IKDI 2000: 31). It pointed out that 77 per cent of the whole traditional market was sluggish but that only 26.2 per cent had refurbishment plans (IKDI 2000: 24, 27). It also explained that 825 traditional markets (69.5 per cent) had no parking places on offer, and, furthermore, a large number of them did not draw customers due to the uneven ground of the market (IKDI: 71–72).

4.2 *The Change of the Status of the Department Store Industry*

4.2.1 Obtaining of Legal Status of the Department Store Industry

In contrast to the traditional market, from the 1980s, the department store industry began to distinguish itself from the general retail industry in terms of management and thus its position in the retail industry. Eventually its legal status also changed, although it was not until the early 1980s that the department store was legally defined as a retail institution even though in practice it had long existed as a purveyor of luxury goods. The significance of this was that the new legal definition reflected socio-political acknowledgement. In 1982, when the department store was defined for the first time in Korea in the the 'Appended Chart No. 1 of the Enforcement Decree of the Market Law' (*Si-jang-beob si-haenglyeong byeol-pyo1*), it was described as a large retail store organized into departments offering a variety of merchandise for comprehensive buying by consumers, and operated mainly through direct management of over 50 per cent of total departments. It also laid down the minimum size of department store building: over 5,000 square metres in Seoul, and 3,500 square metres outside Seoul. Additionally, the size of store had to be over 60 per cent of the whole building, and some facilities relating to sanitary and consumer protection, etc. also had to be provided (Appended Chart No. 2 of the Enforcement Decree of the Market Law 1982). In 1987, the regulation concerning the size of the building in which the department store operated, was eliminated, and instead, the size of the store was defined as over 3,000 square metres in Seoul and over 2,000 square metres elsewhere. The clause stipulating over 50 per cent of direct management in total departments was retained. However, a clause that over 5 per cent of total employees had to possess certificates of expertise in sales was newly added, and the facilities regulation grew more stringent, stipulating four to ten items. For example, parking lots, a facility for cultural events, and a broadcasting system for consumers in the building, etc. was added in the 'Enforcement Decree of the Market Law of 1987'. In 1991, the regulation concerning the size of the store was amended to 3,000 square metres for the whole country including Seoul, although the clauses relating to the ratio of direct management and facilities remained the same (Appended Chart No. 2 of the Enforcement of Decree of the Law for Promotion of Whole and Retail Industry 1991).

Thus, the definition of the department store in Korea was not organic, but was instead dictated by various aspects of regulation. In fact, generally its definition was focused on the characteristic of the department store in terms of both the industrial classification and marketing in a way similar to the US and Japan. On the other hand, it was defined with the goal of promoting the department store industry in Korea (Okubo 1993: 15–17). For instance, such goals were shown through the regulation of the minimum size of the shop and the building in which the department store was stationed. It could also be shown through the fact that there was a strong regulation concerning facilities even though the shop needed to be mindful of the need for such facilities before regulation, in order to raise turnover. In particular, the strict regulation relating to the proportion of direct management in total departments was unique. While direct management or the letting system is one of the strategies which could be chosen by its own management, the department store had to provide at least 50 per cent of the direct management in total departments in Korea. This guidance reflected the government's goal of shaping the retail industry, including management economies of scale. The Korean government chose the department store in the period of structural change within the retail industry as a representative institution to modernize the retail industry in terms of management and marketing. Even though the number of department stores rose and keen competition emerged between them in the late 1980s, size regulation became stronger. The government raised the minimum criteria of shop size to 4,000 square metres for the whole country in 1995, although there was no change in the rule requiring over 50 per cent of direct management at that time (Appended Chart No. 2 of the Enforcement of Decree of the Law for Promotion of Wholesale and Retail Industry 1995).

4.2.2 Rapid Growth of the Department Store

As mentioned, the ratio of the department store industry in total retail sales was trivial in the 1970s. However, the status of the department store industry in the retail market changed from around the mid-1980s. This situation can be shown through the ratio of the department store industry in total retail sales since the mid-1980s.

It was not until 1986 that the department store industry first obtained separate status among various retail formats in the retail industry in the official statistics, even if its legal name was defined in 1982. Thus, it took a few years for the department store industry to be a statistically meaningful body after obtaining legal status. This is evidence of the change in the status of the department store industry. According to Figure 4.11, the ratio of the department store industry in total retail sales was just 4.3 per cent in 1986. This was not a trivial performance, given that its ratio in total retail sales was presumed even under 0.2 per cent in 1979. However, after that, its performance was more remarkable as the ratio increased to 8.7 per cent in 1992, and it expanded to 13.6 per cent in 1997. In particular, the legal definition concerning the size of the store was

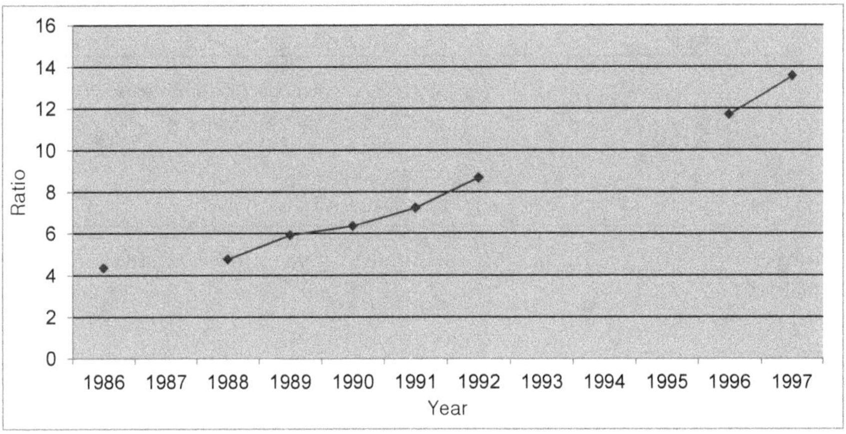

FIGURE 4.11 *The Ratio of the department store industry in value of total retail sales (absence of data is due to the fact that there was no survey or no inclusion of the department store in the survey that year).* SOURCE: SK, WHOLESALE AND RETAIL TRADE CENSUS WITH THE OVERALL ESTABLISHMENT STATISTICS (1986, 1991), WHOLESALE AND RETAIL TRADE SURVEY (1988, 1989, 1990, 1992, 1997), WHOLESALE, RETAIL TRADE AND SERVICE INDUSTRY CENSUS (1996).

strengthened in 1987 and 1991 respectively. This demonstrated that its ratio increased even more rapidly than official statistics observe. The number of department store shops had also increased rapidly during the period. As mentioned, whereas there were just two or three department stores in Korea in 1970, the number of department store shops rose to ninety-seven in 1986. Even though the number decreased to sixty due to the more stringent legal criteria in size in 1988 and 1991, it increased again to ninety-one in 1992, and to 120 in 1996 (SK, Wholesale and Retail Trade Census with the Overall Establishment Statistics, 1986; Wholesale and Retail Trade Survey, 1992; Wholesale, Retail Trade and Service Industry Census, 1996).

The remarkable growth of the department store can be better assessed through comparison of department store shops with shops belonging to other parts of the retail industry.

According to Table 4.10, sales per department store shop were 9,699.9 million Korean *won* (US$ 11 million) but sales per retail shop excluding the department store industry amounted to just 32.5 million Korean *won* (US$ 36.9 thousand). The gap in sales size between both was already quite big as the former was about 300 times as large as the latter. What should be noted here is the gap in growth after that. Sales per department store shop grew an average 25.5 per cent per annum in real terms during the period between 1986 and 1991, while sales per retail shop grew just 8.4 per cent per annum in the same period.

TABLE 4.10 *Comparison of per shop sales between the separtment store and the rest*

	1986	1991	1996	Average rate of increase per annum** (%)	
				1986–1991	1991–1996
Sales* per department store	9,699.9	41,903.8	88,502.6	25.5	10.2
Sales* per retailer excluding the department store industry	32.5	67.5	108.8	8.4	4.4

* Sales are a nominal term by sources. Unit: million Korean *won.*
** Average rate of increase per annum is a real term produced by the author through CPI based on 100 at 2005.
Source: SK, Wholesale and Retail Trade Census with the Overall Establishment Statistics (1986, 1991), Wholesale, Retail Trade and Service Industry Census (1996)

This propensity hardly changed even in the first half of the 1990s as 10.2 per cent of the former was much higher than 4.4 per cent of the latter. As a result of this, the gap in sales size per shop expanded to over 800 times in 1996. The number of employees per department store shop also increased to 744 people in 1996 from 217 in 1986 while that of most traditional retailers remained at around two people.

This rapid development of the department store industry and its distinction can briefly be shown by comparison with the British department store industry. As one of the modern retailing formats including co-operatives and multiples (chain stores), the department store format which was known to emerge around the middle of the nineteenth century in Britain, competed with other modern retail formats in achieving market share in the mass market (Fraser 1981: 130). In this process, it adopted the strategy of low prices through volume purchasing which could be competitive against other types of modern retailers, in this way they were called 'price cutters' and 'under cutters' (Jefferys 1954: 20). However, they gradually focused on the middle-class as their main customers. This tendency entailed a change towards better services, amenities, including restaurants, and luxurious decor even if they did not give up the strategy of low prices. They offered rest-rooms and writing-rooms for the exhausted lady. Goods were delivered, carefully wrapped and could be exchanged if they were later considered unsatisfactory (Fraser 1981: 130–131). Thus, according to Jefferys' estimation, even if the British department store industry continued to develop, its share in total UK retail sales was at most 5–6 per cent in the 1950s. The rest was composed of sales by multiples (18–20 per cent), co-operatives (10–12 per cent) and other retailers (around 65 per cent) including traditional retailers (Jefferys 1954: 61). In contrast to this, the Korean department store industry developed much more rapidly from under 1 per cent of the total retail sales at the end of the 1970s, and its share in the retail market eventually increased to over 13 per cent for about fifteen years. Korean department stores thus absorbed a large number of consumers who were likely to be multiples' and the co-operative's customers in the UK. In other words, this suggests that the category of customers shopping at department stores is wider in Korea than in the UK.

4.2.3 Emergence of Conflict with Traditional Retailers

As we have shown, the traditional market played the main role in the retail market in the 1970s and the the department store share was remarkably trivial even in the early 1980s. This meant that there was little conflict between the department store and traditional retailers in the 1970s. The department store provided just a few wealthy people with limited goods, while traditional retailers provided most people with essential goods. Thus it could be called a peaceful period in terms of the horizontal competition between the retail formats. However, the development of the department store industry broke such a stable situation. Under conditions of asymmetric development among retail formats as competitors, conflict to assume market share was bound to crystallize between them. The phase of the conflict between them was not interactive but one-sided because of the difference in managerial development and financial ability. The department store swept everything before it, but traditional retailers found such change nearly impossible to deal with. This situation made it inevitable for the government to intervene aggressively to slow the pace of change in the retail market, even though it had the goal of modernizing the retail industry through the development of big business. Various regulations affecting the retail industry were closely related to the change in status of the department store within the retail industry. In fact, the clear regulation of the department store was directly connected to the protection of small- and medium-size traditional retailers (SMSTRs). One of the representative policies for the protection on SMSTRs was articles which contained stringent restrictions against the establishment of new retail institution. These restrictions were contained in articles 6 and 15 of the 'Law for the Promotion of the Wholesale and Retail Industry' of 1986, the basic law concerning the retail industry.

Another regulation affected the big retailers and restricted their operations with respect to operation times and holidays, etc. (Article 16 of the 'Law for the Promotion of the Wholesale and Retail Industry', 1986). These laws arose as a result of the increased conflict between big and small retailers, thus complaints from the latter (KCCI 1999: 46).

The Fair Trade Act protected SMSTRs. The Korea Fair Trade Commission (KFTC) restricted the period within which bargain sales were offered by department stores to just ten days each and four times a year by means of the 'Working Standards for Discount Sales' in 1981, and subsequently, regulated sales with gifts by department stores in 1982. It also strengthened the regulation of discount sales by department stores in prohibiting excessive periods of discount sales and the painted expression of prices. (Shinsegae Department Store 1987: A Chronological Table of Retail Policies; KFTC 1983). Furthermore, the KFTC began a regular investigation on the unfair trade of department stores every year from 1986 (KCA 1990). Even if the investigation was basically a policy for the protection of consumers, it was somewhat in line with the regulations applied to the department store industry. As we can see, most of the regulations were closely related to the popularization strategy of the department store, not the differentiation strategy in luxuries. In other words, these regulations came about because the market share of the department store industry in the retail market expanded rapidly from the 1980s.

In sum, the development of retail formats has been different even if the whole retail industry has grown rapidly since the 1980s. While most traditional retailers retained their existing management structure, such as their small size and family run operation despite an increase in sales, the department store industry developed into the modern type of retail format with the rapid growth in sales. In this situation, this gap was directly linked to an increase in sales portion of department stores within the retail industry, and this produced conflicts between retail formats. Consequently, various kinds of regulations were brought to bear on the big retailers from the 1980s, reflecting the huge gap between the department store and the traditional retailer.

5 Conclusion

This chapter has examined the circumstances of, and the situation of, the retail industry during the period between the 1980s and the mid-1990s. While the retail industry in the 1970s was unusually backward, its state since the 1980s might be considered a process of normalization because the modern retail format has developed rapidly. Just as the modern retail format grew in the process of industrialization in developed countries, so the department store as a modern retail format was rapidly developed in the Korean economy from the 1980s. Total retail sales grew as much as 8.8 per cent per annum in real terms between 1986 and 1996. Sales of the department store industry increased as much as 20.2 per cent per annum while that of the traditional market was about 8 per cent per annum in the same period. Thus the gap in growth between the department store and the traditional retailer became ever bigger even if the latter still took a much larger share of the consumption market. Thus the market share of the department store industry in total retail sales increased to about 12 per cent in 1996 from 4.3 per cent in 1986 (SK, Wholesale and Retail Trade Census with the Overall Establishment Statistics 1986; Wholesale, Retail Trade and Service Industry Census 1996).

This type of development made the position of the Korean department store industry distinct from that of other countries. For instance, in terms of market share in total retail sales, the department store in the UK was at most 5–6 per cent in the 1950s even if it had developed from the middle of the nineteenth century. Its speed of growth was very different as well. The market share of the department store industry increased by about three times in just ten years in Korea, while in the UK it took forty-fifty years to grow from about 2 per cent in the 1910s to about 6 per cent in the 1950s (Jefferys 1954: 61). In this respect, it is clear that the department store was the only leading hitter of the Korean retail industry since the 1980s, and thus the period can be called the golden age of the department store industry.

Rapid development of the department store industry resulted in a different situation from the 1970s in the Korean consumer market. That was the beginning of the stratification in consumption. As we have seen earlier, the Korean consumer market was uniform in the traditional market in the 1970s even if it grew quantitatively. There were some department stores at that time but their role in the consumer market was very trivial under the condition of consumption repression in various aspects. This situation branded the 1970s as the age of backwardness in the retail industry, or of the traditional retailer. However, the equivalent situation in terms of consumer market repression was broken by the rise of the department store industry. This kind of change is unlikely to have had an effect on the consumer market alone. It is highly possible that the stratification of consumption impacts on the social psychology of equality and makes society unstable. However, it seems that economic environments such as the increase in income resulting from high economic growth, were very useful for mitigating possible social tension. What is more, income inequality which had been exacerbated since the 1970s was considerably improved and this meant the purchasing power generally increased at each income level.

Thus consumption of most people expanded considerably, regardless of income level, quite apart from the stratification of the consumption market in the period between the mid-1980s and the 1990s. The strategy of the department store, which will be examined in the next chapter, also played an important role in this result.

CHAPTER 5

Consumption Liberalization, Aggressive Consumers and Active Retail Industry in Rapid Economic Growth since the 1980s

1 Introduction

This chapter deals with the period between the early 1980s and the mid-1990s and concentrates on an analysis of the causes of the effects that were explained in the previous chapter. Like Chapter 3, this analysis will be carried out in terms of three actors, i.e. government, consumers and retailers, by which the retail industry is crucially influenced. This chapter shows that the changes in their behaviour resulted in the remarkable changes seen in the retail industry since the 1980s.

Government policy will be examined first. The change in policy can be represented in terms of consumption liberalization. It includes socio-economic policies as well as actual policies directed at the retail industry. Even if the period since the 1980s is called the period of the change from the state to the market in Korea, government policy was still influential. In particular, the government's industrial policy was an important factor for the development of industry because it was related to legal support in terms of taxation and protection. In this respect, an analysis of laws and regulations over time is useful for uncovering the political situation relating to consumption and the retail industry. Another subjective factor needed to actualise the development of the retail industry was consumers. Their attitude to consumption was one of the most influential factors for the retail industry. As we have seen in Chapter 4, conditions such as socio-economic environment, the level of income and the composition of the population surrounding consumption were rapidly creating favourable circumstances for consumption in the 1980s. These encouraging factors, in fact, seemed to contribute to the change in consumption in terms of both the quantitative and the qualitative aspects. However, the actual change in the retail industry is unlikely to be explained only by the change in environment. In other words, its concrete structure can be different in countries with similar conditions. This is the reason why we should examine subjective factors. In this respect, an analysis of consumer behaviour is likely to be very significant for the era of mass consumption which occurred from the 1980s. Thus this chapter will examine how consumers responded to these changes with

 | DOI 10.1163/9789004274228_006

altered consumption attitudes. There is no need to dwell upon the importance of the retail industry itself for the development of consumption and the retail industry. Here, we will focus on the department store as one of the representative modern retail institutions, and on what strategic changes the department store underwent in responding to changes in the policy and modified consumer attitudes. This will also be linked to the analysis of the absence of the appearance of the other retail formats for mass consumption such as supermarkets and general merchandise stores as a distinct phenomenon in the Korean economy. Outside Korea, in general the department store was initially one of the representative retail institutions for mass consumption, but it changed its position to retail luxury goods after competition with, and the defeat of, other institutions for mass consumption, such as supermarkets and discount stores. In Korea, however, the department store was a luxury retail outlet from the time of its original appearance as an imported institution in the earlier period of industrialization, and it became a dominant institute for mass consumption with the expansion of the consumer market in the 1980s. In other words, the development process of the department store format in Korea was different from that of its general type, particularly in the developed Western countries. A similar phenomenon appeared from the early period of the 1900s in Japan, as a late developing country which imported the department store (Larke 1994: 175–177; Ikeo 1997: 150–151; Young 1999: 57–59). In this respect, the popularization of department stores seems to be regarded as a common phenomenon occurring in countries which import it, such as late developing countries. However, there is also a considerable difference in the process of retail evolution between such countries. While, in Japan, the retail institution of the general merchandise store (GMS) emerged and fiercely competed with the department stores in the era of mass consumption since the 1950s, in Korea, there was no competitor to share the mass consumption market even in the era of mass consumption since the mid-1980s. This phenomenon can be understood as a result of a unique synthesis of both the strategy of the department stores, which tried to raise their market share, and the attitude of consumers, who responded to the existing socio-economic environment at that time. Moreover, as we will examine in the next chapter, the difference might be presumed to influence the behaviour of consumers in the future and so the strategy of a newly established retail institution in Korea, such as the discount store for mass consumption in the 1990s.

2 The Change of the Political Environment

2.1 *The Retreat of the State and Liberalization*

Even though the beginning of the 1980s in Korea was characterized by a much more dismal atmosphere than the period at the time of the coup in the early 1960s, it is ironic that this was the period when the retreat of the state and the process of liberalization progressed more rapidly than at any period in the past. This phenomenon, particularly, became clearer in the second half of the 1980s, with the dramatic boom of the Korean economy. In this regard, the Korean government was regarded as being on a different trajectory in the late 1980s to that of the 1970s. The state as an authoritarian entity, on the one hand, transferred its authority to impose its political power to people, and the state as a regulatory entity, on the other hand, gave the initiative of economic growth to the market and the private sector gradually. The retreat of the tides of authoritarianism and the weakening of regulation became increasingly clearer in all fields of Korean society, and proportionate to the speed with which this occurred, consumption repression was also liberalized.

2.2 *The Emergence of Change in Economic Policy*

As mentioned, the 'Monopoly Regulation and Fair Trade Act (MRFTA)' which was enacted at the end of 1980 was a sign of the change of economic policy towards the market. This tendency was expressed clearly in the aim of the establishment by law:

> As the pillar of economic leadership was transferred to the private sector from the government gradually, through fair competition of private companies ... (MOLEG, The Reason of Establishment of MRFTA, 1980)

Even though the meaning of the announcement did not often coincide completely with reality, it was clear that such an announcement by the government had significance concerning the direction of policy in the future. In particular, it was worthy of notice because the announcement of the government was connected with other policies such as the expansion of import liberalization and the privatization of commercial banks. 'The Korea Fair Trade Commission (KFTC)' on the basis of MRFTA was newly created as an internal organization of EPB in 1981 with a chairman at the level of deputy secretary.[1] After that, the

1 Before KFTC, fair trade policy was operated at the level of a division under the Price Policy Bureau in EPB. Therefore, fair trade policy was operated mainly from the viewpoint of price policy and the authority of the policy was also very limited. In this regard, the establishment

KFTC as a department to create a competitive market environment concentrated on promoting fair competition in the market by banning the abuse of market dominant positions, cartels and various other unfair trade activities. Especially, focusing on the regulation of market dominant firms, the KFTC was raised as a representative supervisor of *chaebols* in the market.

The privatization of commercial banks could also be considered an extraordinary policy. It was hardly possible, following its previous trajectory, that the government would release the banks because the bank owned by the state was one of the major tools used by the government to manage private companies and maintain leadership of economic policy. However, the government privatized four major commercial banks – Hanil, Korea First, Seoul Trust, and Cho Hung Bank – between 1981 and 1983.[2] In this process, the government put a strong limitation on shares owned, stipulating that they were not to exceed 5 per cent per corporate body or person, and limiting each person's ownership to 5,000 shares in order to retain the public character of the banking system. The government also imposed rigid public responsibilities concerning overall management, including the development of financial goods and loans by banks. Therefore, the privatization of the banks in the early 1980s did not mean the actual privatization of the financial sector. Despite this, such an action of the government was considered sufficient to express a different attitude from earlier government positions. Even though economic liberalization was not achieved right away with such policies, it could be said that the basic framework for it had been arranged (Song Daehui 1994: 46–47). However, it did not take long for the rush of privatization to occur. The government published the grand plan of privatization in 1987. The plan pointed out eleven companies including POSCO, Korea Electric Power Corporation (KEPCO), Korea Bank (KB).[3] Even though not all companies among those listed were privatized in the late 1980s, privatization subsequently became the dominant discourse in Korea with little controversy.[4]

---

of KFTC in 1981 could be considered an extraordinary measure. After that, KFTC was separated from EPB as an independent organization from 1994 and the level of chairman rose to a secretary from 1996.

2 This was understood as a beginning of the rush to privatization which took place in the 1980s.

3 These have been the largest companies within their industries in Korea.

4 The rush to privatize was influenced largely by international trends, including privatization in Eastern European countries which were in the process of transition, and in Latin American countries which were recovering from 'the lost ten years in the 1980s' after the financial crisis. Due to such trends worldwide, there was a strong social atmosphere in Korea which made it impossible for developing countries to enter into the advanced economy without privatization.

The expansion of import liberalization came into effect in this atmosphere. The government, which emphasized price stabilization, tried to expand imports to resolve the problem in market mechanisms. By doing so, the rate of import liberalization rose to 93.6 per cent in 1987 from 69.87 per cent in 1980 and 97.2 per cent in 1991 (Gim Uyeong et al. 2005: 37). The system of indication for imports was introduced both to ease the impact from imports, and to confirm the will of the government for imports. As mentioned, in this process, a number of foreign consumer goods were also imported, even if the rate of liberalization was lower than that of industrial goods. In particular, diffusion of foreign goods stimulated consumers and thus was closely related to the rapid development of the department store industry with an increase in income in the 1980s.

In the second half of the 1980s as the Korean economy faced a boom period, liberalization policy gathered strength. The sixth 'Five-Year Plan for Economic and Social Development', which began in 1987, suggested advances in the economic system and institutions, and an improvement in the quality of life as its goal, and stressed the promotion of the market economic system and the rearrangement of the role of government as a policy task (Gang Gwangha 2000: 99–114). In particular, before the Seoul Olympic Games in 1988, the government needed to make the atmosphere of Seoul more affluent and lively. From the fact that President Rho Tae Woo, who took office in 1988, stressed justice of distribution concerning economic matters in an inaugural address, the change of situation could be conjectured (No Taeu dae-tonglyeong, 1988a). Furthermore, Rho announced a 'Declaration of Democracy for the Economy' which gave priority to distribution for the development of democracy on the first anniversary of the 6.29 Declaration[5] (I Janggyu et al. 1995: 41). The atmosphere at that time was illustrated through a quotation from a civil servant as follows:

> The conversation even among departments of economics was hardly possible without contents of equality and welfare. Economic policy was just treatment to resolve social conflict which had accumulated in the authoritarianism period. (Ibid: 41).

5 The civil movement in June 1987 resulted in the 6.29 (29 June) Declaration and is sometimes called the the June revolution. In the declaration, Rho accepted a direct vote system for the presidential election, as proposed by the people. Soon afterwards, around 3,000 cases of industrial conflicts occuured in July and August 1987. This figure was over ten times that of the previous year (Yu Jongil 1998: 123–124). This was interpreted as a reaction to coercive oppression of the labour sector, which was committed under the justification of economic recovery in the first half of the 1980s.

Controversy centring on the independence of the central bank was also suggested by the process of economic democracy as the authoritarian state retreated in the second half of 1987. In fact, because the Bank of Korea was completely subordinated to the government, being called 'a branch of the Ministry of Finance', it was accepted as a necessary requirement for the development of democracy regardless of the aim and efficiency of financial policy in the country. While the independence of the central bank was not realized despite acute conflict for some years afterwards, its status with the government rose, and this conflict was interpreted as typical of the phenomena which occur in the process of the state retreating (*Jo-seon-il-bo* 26 March 1992; I Janggyu et al. 1995: 174–176). The chairman of the National Agricultural Cooperative Federation (NACF) was no different from a subsidiary agency of the government, and had advocated independent management of the NACF away from government control (I Janggyu et al. 1995: 64–67). Of course, this target was not realized immediately, but later the NACF did gain considerable autonomy.

2.3 *The Change of Social Policy*

One symbolic early event which showed that the state was retreating from intervention in everyday life, was when in 1982, the curfew which had been maintained for thirty-five years, was finally lifted. The curfew, which prohibited people from leaving their homes after midnight, began during the US military government's administration immediately following Korea's independence from Japanese occupation. This measure was criticised as one of a number of measures which were used to control people during that period. Thus, the military government led by President Chun chose to remove this curfew as a gesture towards relaxing the social atmosphere, and in so doing softened the public's perception of a draconian government. Before and after the lifting of the curfew there were a number of other such events. The government removed the crackdown on long hair in men and the wearing of miniskirts by women, and allowed the uniforms and hairstyles of secondary students to change from their rigid army-style. The government additionally tried to establish professional baseball teams, and weakened regulations against eroticism in various types of journal and film. Therefore such policies were criticised and branded the 3 Ss (Sports, Screen and Sex) to divert people's attention away from political matters at that time, and, in doing so, they created a social atmosphere quite unlike that of the past (*Yonhap News Agency* 18 May 2005a). The beginning of TV broadcasting in colour in 1980 also greatly influenced changes in the social atmosphere.[6] It was inevitable that a sense of colour became more

6 It was a widely accepted opinion that this event attempted both to soften the social atmosphere and to compete with the regime in North Korea which broadcast colour TV from the middle of the 1970s, regardless of its degree of diffusion.

pronounced in society than it had been in the era of the black and white TV. In fact, some people in the field of advertising felt that Korean tastes for fashion and design were rapidly developed and diversified after colour television broadcasting began. Furthermore, we can presume that the change in the colour environment in society had an effect on social psychology by gradually changing consumer attitudes. In this respect, the change in the APC was closely related to the change in the environment around consumption. Permission to travel abroad, which took place in the early 1980s, was also one of the important catalysts for social liberalization. Foreign travel had been prohibited in the name of thrift for foreign exchange purposes, and the strengthening of social discipline during the regime of President Park. Only a few senior civil servants, businessmen and some academics could get permission to travel from the government. In these circumstances, as part of the liberalization of foreign travel the government first issued a passport for foreign travel in 1983. This was an extraordinary measure, even though there were rigid limitations and the liberalization applied only to people over fifty years old. Liberalisation was an irreversible movement. Limitations on foreign travel steadily reduced thereafter, with the age reduced to forty-five years in 1987, forty in January 1988, and to thirty in July 1988. Finally, in 1989, the government lifted all regulations applicable to the age of people travelling, and the frequency of foreign travel (Gim Jeongman 1990: 29–31).

As we have seen, the events concerning liberalization in the 1980s were closely related to the mode of everyday life. In particular, they were connected with the change in the consumption environment and thus they inevitably caused changes in attitudes towards consumption.

3 The Beginning and the Expansion of Consumer Finance

As we have seen in Chapter 3, the repression of bank loans to households was one of the most important tools used to suppress consumption in the 1970s. In particular, bank loans for consumption were nearly unthinkable forms of behaviour for households and consumers. In fact, as we have seen, households were unable to apply for bank loans for consumption, since they had a duty to save their money for production. In this respect, the liberalization of consumer finance in the 1980s may have been one of the most decisive changes to influence the expansion of consumption.

The liberalization of consumer finance began with the use of the credit card. The history of the credit card in Korea goes back to the 1960s. The first credit card was introduced in 1969 by the Shinsegae Department Store. Shin-

TABLE 5.1 *Trends of credit card lending*

Year	1983	1985	1987	1989	1991	1993	1995
For purchases*	87.5 (50.17)	212.5 (45.77)	846.9 (41.79)	3,421.6 (42.07)	6,397.4 (50.04)	12,379.3 (45.92)	25,151.7 (48.76)
For cash*	86.9 (49.83)	251.8 (54.23)	1,179.8 (58. 21)	4,711.8 (57.93)	6,387.8 (49.96)	14,580.4 (54.08)	26,430 (51.24)
Total*	174.4	464.3	2,026.7	8,133.4	12,785.2	26,959.7	51,581.7
Indexes**	100	266.2	1,162.1	4,663.7	7,331.0	15,458.5	29,576.7

*Unit: billion Korean *won* (ratio in total credit lending, %)
**Indexes calculated by the author, based on 100 at 1983
Source: Credit Finance Association (CFA), Current Situation of Credit Card Lending, annual

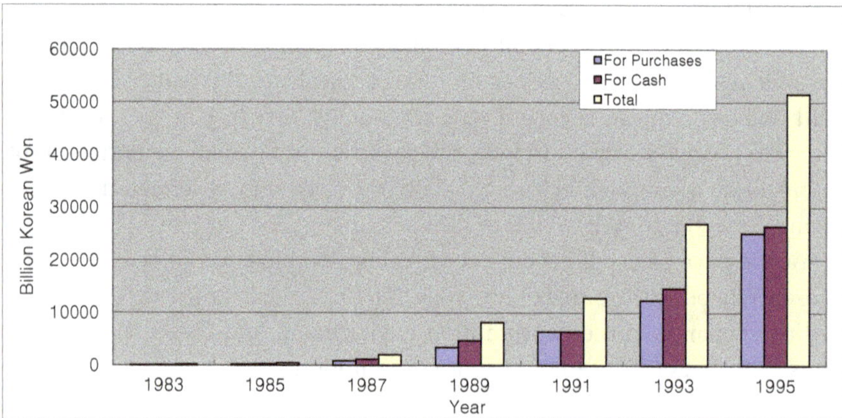

FIGURE 5.1 *Trends of credit card lending (unit: billion Korean* won*).* SOURCE: CFA, CURRENT SITUATION OF CREDIT CARD LENDING, ANNUAL.

segae issued it only to employees of Samsung, its mother company (Shinsegae Department Store 1987: 108–109). After that, the Midopa Department Store (1974) and the Lotte Department Store (1979) followed suit. Around the end of the 1970s, some credit card companies were established but this was far from leading to the popularization of the credit card as a financial institution (Seo Geunu 1997: 71). A basis for the popularization of the credit card took place in 1982 when five of the main commercial banks, i.e. the Choheung Bank, the Commercial Bank of Korea, the Korea First Bank, the Hanil Bank and the Seoul Trust Bank established a joint credit card company. This company was called BC Card and the number of banks affiliated to it had increased to thirteen by

1985 (Seo Geunu: 72). This trend in the financial market, of course, was linked to financial liberalization, such as the privatization of commercial banks in the early period of the 1980s, and led to a drastic increase in credit card lending.

According to Figure 5.1, the total amount of credit card lending was only some 170 billion *won* (US$ 224.6 million) in 1983. In particular, the amount of credit card purchases was merely 87 billion *won* at that time. However, such lending increased dramatically after that, and was over 2 trillion *won* in 1987, an eleven-fold increase in four years. The rate of increase continued to accelerate, to 25 trillion *won* in 1993, which meant it had increased 154 times in eleven years, and reached over 51 trillion *won* in 1995. Meanwhile, the amount of credit card purchases also increased sharply, from over 12 trillion *won* in 1993 to over 25 trillion *won* in 1995. The increase of credit card lending stands out when it is compared with the amount of retail sales.

The two kinds of indexes in Figure 5.2 based on 100 in 1986 are produced to compare the growth of credit card purchases with that of total retail sales. According to Table 5.2, the amount of total retail sales increased rapidly from 1986 to 1996. It rose over four times during the period.

This may imply that the expansion of consumption was vigorous in this period. Compared to consumption, it is no exaggeration to say that the increase of credit card purchases was explosive given that it increased about ninety times during the period between 1986 and 1996. This implies that the increase in consumption can, to a large extent, be attributed to credit card lending since

TABLE 5.2 *Trends of total retail sales and credit card purchases*

	1986	1988	1989	1990	1991	1993	1995	1996
Total retail sales* (Indexes)**	21,673.8 (100)	29,036.4 (134.0)	34,207.3 (157.8)	41,108 (189.7)	52,177.6 (240.7)	64,093.1 (295.7)	85,760.6 (395.7)	90,906.8 (419.4)
Credit card Purchases* (Indexes)**	375.7 (100)	1,996.7 (531.5)	3,421.6 (910.7)	5,045 (1,342.8)	6,397.4 (1,702.8)	12,379.3 (3,295.0)	25,151.7 (6,694.6)	32,624.3 (8,683.6)
The ratio of credit card purchases in total retail sales (%)	1.73	6.88	10.00	12.27	12.26	19.31	29.33	35.89

* Unit: billion Korean *won*.
** Indexes calculated by the author, based on 100 at 1986
Source: SK, CFA

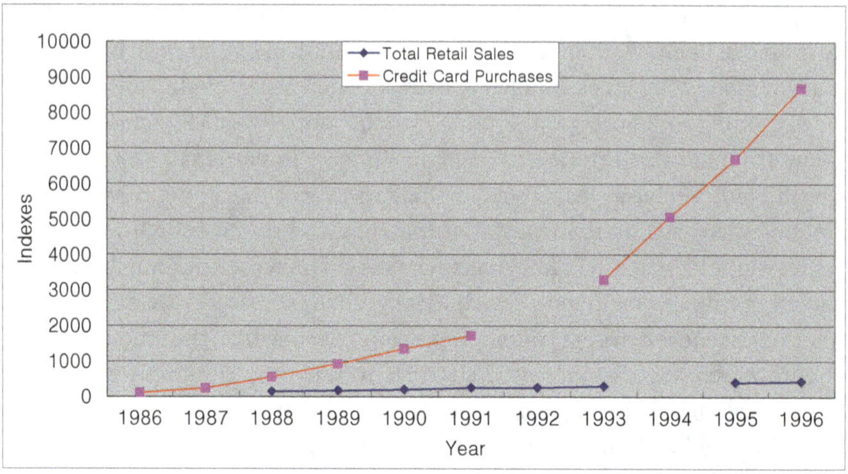

FIGURE 5.2 *Indexes of total retail sales and credit card purchases (indexes calculated by author, based on 100 in 1986).* SOURCE: SK, CFA.

the mid-1980s. Additionally, this could be crucial evidence that big modern retailers like department stores grew much more rapidly, compared with traditional retailers, because the machines for credit cards were mainly installed in such big retailers.

Reflecting this situation, Figure 5.3 illustrates that the ratio of credit card purchases in total retail sales sharply rose to 35.89 per cent in 1996 from only 1.73 per cent in 1986. Like the trend of credit card purchases, the curve of its ratio became remarkably steep from the early 1990s.

With credit card lending, bank loans to households were also an important factor influencing consumption because the household is the unit of consumption in a national economy. As mentioned earlier, households had almost no right to use bank loans in the 1970s. However, the situation changed with the progress in financial liberalization after the mid-1980s. Table 5.3 shows the trends of bank loans to all households since the early 1990s. The ratio of loans to households among total loans of commercial banks was just 7–8 per cent in the early 1990s, but it increased sharply to around 20 per cent in the middle of the 1990s.

The ratio of loans to firms among total loans of commercial banks decreased by over 10 per cent, to 75 per cent from 87 per cent during the same period. This trend can be shown more clearly by the table of these indexes.

Table 5.4 shows that the total amount of commercial bank loans increased gradually between 1990 and 1996 and reached over twice the 1990 level in 1995. However, the amount of commercial bank loans to households rose rapidly

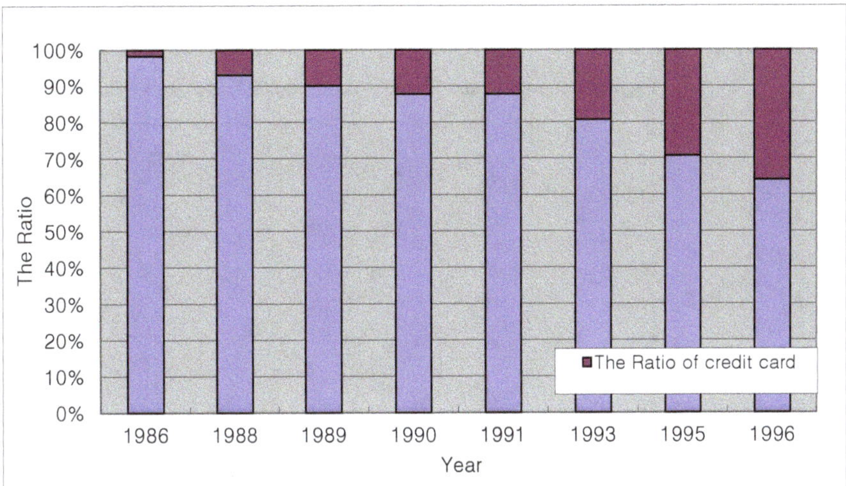

FIGURE 5.3 *Ratio of credit card purchases in total retail sales (ratio calculated by the author).* SOURCE: SK, CFA.

TABLE 5.3 *Trends of bank loans by commercial banks to households*

	Loans of all commercial banks		
	Total*	**Loans to firms (%)**	**Loans to households (%)**
1990	42,308	36,769 (86.9)	3,502 (8.3)
1991	50,440	44,668 (88.6)	3,888 (7.7)
1992	57,591	51,527 (89.5)	4,012 (7.0)
1993	62,513	55,060 (88.1)	5,454 (8.7)
1994	75,064	61,832 (82.4)	11,040 (14.7)
1995	97,242	74,871 (77.0)	17,011 (17.5)
1996	113,501	85,141 (75.0)	22,179 (19.5)

Unit: billion Korean *won*.
* Total loans of commercial banks are greater than the sum of loans to firms and to households because other types of loans are included.
Source: Financial Supervisory Service (FSS), Monthly Financial Statistics, 1999 (January), 2000 (January)

during the same period and had increased six-fold by 1996. Additionally, this situation also shows that the expansion of consumption has been led by credit card lending since the late 1980s. The amount of credit lending for purchases was already over 3.4 trillion *won* in 1989, while the amount of bank loans to

TABLE 5.4 *Indexes* of commercial bank loans to households*

	Total commercial bank loans	Commercial bank loans to households
1990	100	100
1991	119.2	111.0
1992	136.1	114.6
1993	147.8	155.7
1994	177.4	315.3
1995	229.8	485.8
1996	268.3	633.3

* Indexes calculated by the author, based on 100 in 1990
Source: FSS, Monthly Financial Statistics, 1999 (January), 2000 (January)

households was about 3.5 trillion *won* in 1990. Furthermore, if we consider that the amount of total credit card lending accounting for various kinds of consumption was over 8 trillion *won* in 1989, we can understand how important the role of credit cards in consumption had become.

4 Emergence of Mass Consumption

Generally speaking, mass consumption is defined as a phenomenon in which not a few individuals, nor a small upper class, but the majority of people enjoy the benefits of increased productivity and constantly expand their range of consumer goods. Even if there are a number of different opinions about the precise period in developed countries, broadly it is understood that most industrialized countries have gone through such a transformation since the Second World War (Matsuyama 2002: 1035–1036). Thus it is necessary to examine both the production and the consumption sectors in order to define a situation as being the stage of mass consumption. However, only the change in the consumption sector will be dealt with in this section[7] because the term mass consumption is used in the sense of the rapid expansion of consumption in accordance with economic growth.

7 Of course, a number of scholars who study Korean economic growth in terms of both production and consumption may consider the period since the middle of the 1980s as the stage of mass consumption, even if they do not use the same term (Yu Cheolgyu 1992).

The rapid change in the political environment for mass consumption was examined in the previous section. However, the political changes surrounding consumption need the cooperation of other subjects in order to achieve a system of mass consumption. One such subject is the consumer. Only when people consume actively in the liberalized economy (unlike in the previous period) can the liberalization of consumption become a reality in an economy. In this respect, the political situation can be regarded as just one environmental factor relating to consumption. So, how can the change of consumer behaviour be measured? In fact, in the previous section, we have already seen considerable evidence of such change through credit card purchases, and bank loans by commercial banks to households. We can presume that there has been a remarkable increase in consumption since the mid-1980s through this evidence. However, this evidence does not cover consumption as a whole. Thus, as with Chapter 3, this chapter uses the change in the average propensity to consume (APC) not only to see changes in whole consumption resulting from all sources, but also to see the impact of collective behaviour on consumption. Tracing its trends since the 1970s reveals the changes in consumer behaviour.

4.1 *International Comparison of the APC*

So far in this chapter we have seen a dramatic change in consumption attitudes before and after the mid-1980s in Korea. We can gauge the characteristics of such attitudes through comparison with other countries, using a similar methodology to that used in Chapter 3 in order to measure consumption repression in the 1970s. This chapter also uses 'Penn World Tables Version 6.2 (PWT 6.2)'. The comparison of APC is carried out in accordance with the level of income which is the most influential factor on consumption. Here, APC is defined as the consumption share of real GDP in each year in a national economy. The level of income for the period between the mid-1980s and the mid-1990s, namely, between US$ 6,000 and 14,000 is mainly taken into account in this section.

Even if there was a dramatic expansion of consumption from the mid-1980s in the Korean economy, the relative level of Korea's APC has not been high in comparison with the rest of the world even in this period. According to Figure 5.4, the Korean APC has been much lower than that of most Latin American countries regardless of income level. In particular, even in the period after income reached US$ 7,000, where Korea's consumption attitude was estimated to change, the Korean APC was still lower than those of most Latin American countries. Mexico's APC at the income level of US$ 7,000 is over 65 and rises to over 70 at the level of US$ 8,000.

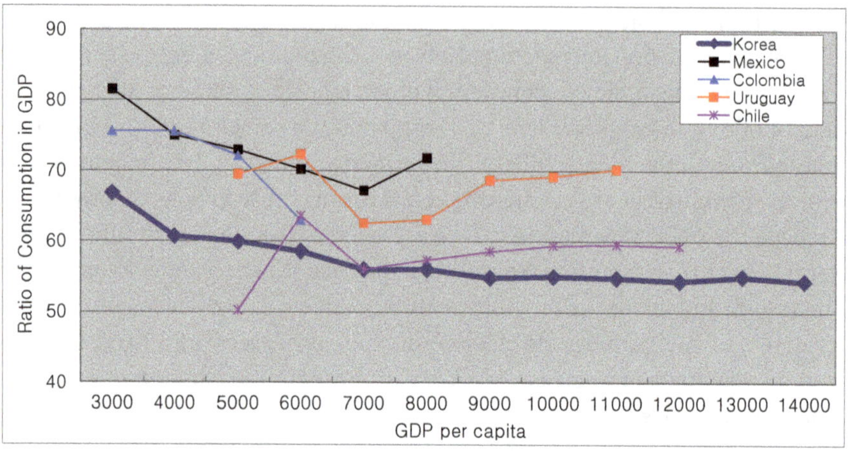

FIGURE 5.4 *APCs of Korea and Latin American countries at each income level (APCs calculated by the author from PWT 6.2).* SOURCE: PWT 6.2.

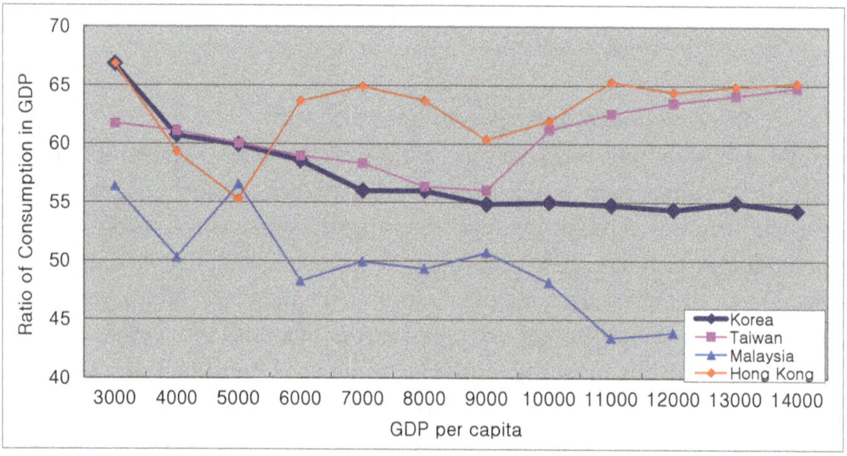

FIGURE 5.5 *APCs of Korea and Asian developing countries at each income level (APCs calculated by the author from PWT 6.2).* SOURCE: PWT 6.2.

Even Chile, one of the countries at a lower level of APC among the Latin American countries, shows a much higher level of APC than that of Korea.

Figure 5.5 shows that the overall level of APCs of Asian developing countries is much lower than those of Latin American countries regardless of income level.

However, as income increases, a change in consumption attitude occurs in the countries. Change in Taiwan is more dramatic than in Korea even when its income level is similar at around US$ 8,000. Presumably, this is closely related to rapid progress in socio-political democracy. First, the Taiwan government

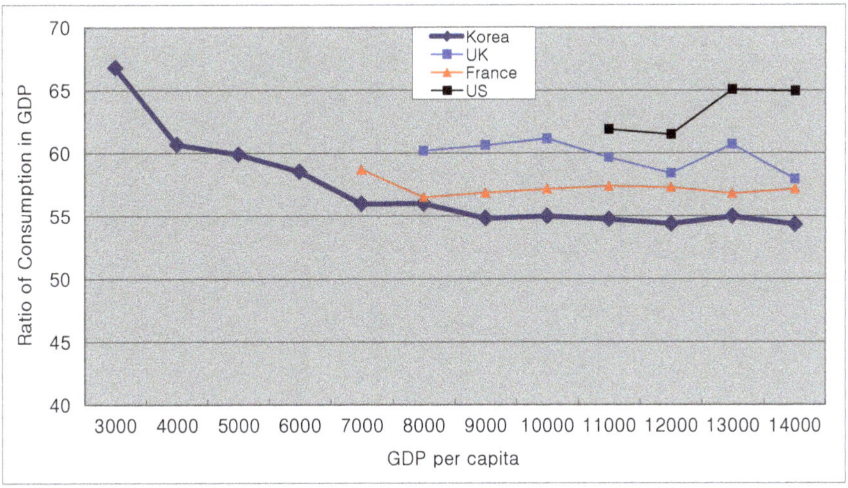

FIGURE 5.6 *APCs of Korea and the developed countries at each income level (APCs calculated by the author from PWT 6.2).* SOURCE: PWT 6.2.

encouraged economic liberalization from the mid-1980s. Following this change, its authoritarian character has been much weaker since the late 1980s, with some democratic policies, including the foundation of an opposition party, the abolition of martial law and the direct election of the country's leader (Sin Sangjin 2002: 161–163; Dent 2003: 469). This period exactly coincided with the income level of US$ 9,000 (1987) and US$ 10,000 (1989) when APC began to rise rapidly. These changes, which were very similar to the period since the 1980s in Korea, might imply the dismantling of the *Ancien Regime* in Taiwan and, as a result of this, they might also imply that the consumption attitude which was repressed by that regime also altered. Hong Kong may be in different trajectory from other Asian countries in that the APC increased conspicuously from its income level of US$ 5,000 in the mid-1960s, and rose again rapidly after US$ 9,000 in the mid-1970s. In contrast, the Malaysian APC curve declined sharply from its income point of around US$ 9,000 in the late 1990s. This was deeply related to the Asian financial crisis.

According to Figure 5.6, the general level of the Korean APC is lower than those of most developed countries, particularly Western countries, at each equivalent level of income. This implies that the relationship between domestic consumption and economic growth is relatively weaker in Korea than it is in Western countries. However, what is interesting is that the trend in Korea's APC is similar to those of countries at an income level between US$ 7,000 and US$ 14,000, despite their lower level. If it is considered that its curve decreased sharply before the income level of US$ 7,000, it is highly possible that the

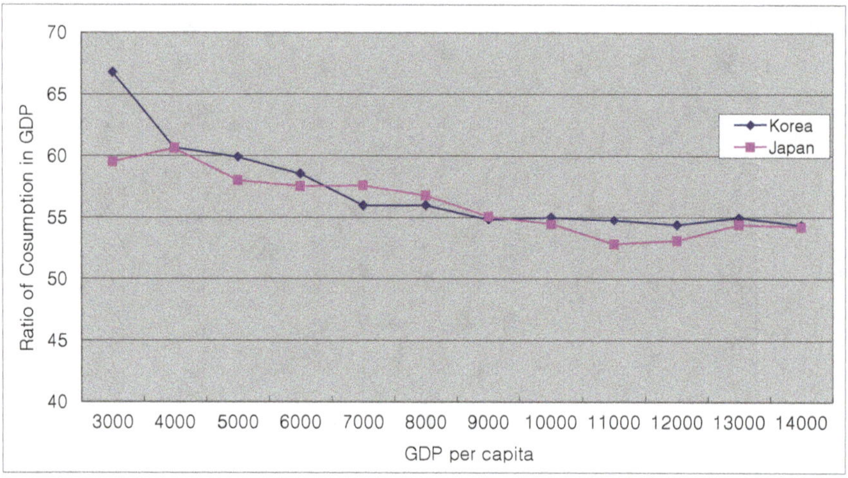

FIGURE 5.7 *APCs of Korea and Japan at each income level (APCs calculated by the author from PWT 6.2).* SOURCE: PWT 6.2.

change in consumption attitude took place between these two levels of income, and that the content of the change was one of relatively more enthusiastic consumption.

Figure 5.7 shows that the shape of the Korean APC is quite similar to the Japanese one in terms of both its level and trajectory from income level US$ 7,000. This implies that both nations' attitudes towards consumption and their consumption roles in the economy are similar. However, strictly speaking, the APCs of both countries are slightly reversed before and after US$ 9,000. While the Korean APC is lower than the Japanese APC before US$ 9,000, it is higher than the Japanese level after that level. What is interesting is that this happened at similar business cycle stages in both countries. The period in which GDP per capita was US$ 7,000–9,000 was the late 1980s in Korea, and the late 1960s in Japan when an extraordinary boom occurred in both countries. This period in which US$ 9,000–13,000 was generated was characterized by similar conditions in both countries in terms of relatively lower growth following the economic boom in the first half of the 1990s in Korea, and the 1970s in Japan. In this respect, there were considerable changes in consumption attitude in the Korean economy before and after the income level of US$ 9,000 in the early 1990s.

4.2 *The Result of the National Accounts*

This change in Korea's consumption attitude in the early 1990s has been shown through international comparison in the previous section. It is more clearly

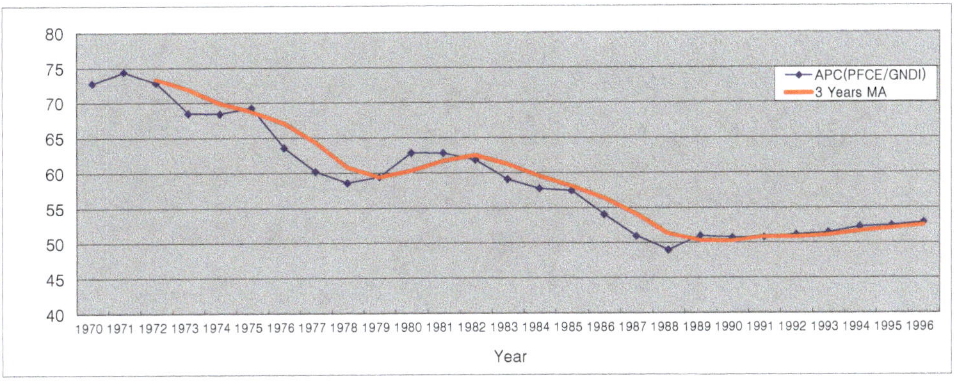

FIGURE 5.8 *Trends of APC (APC: PFCE/GNDI, calculated by the author from National Accounts; GNDI: Gross National Disposable Income; PFCE: Private Final Consumption Expenditure).* SOURCE: BOK, NATIONAL ACCOUNTS, ANNUAL.

shown through internal comparison of periodic APCs in Korean economy. This chapter will try to confirm the expansion of consumption since the late 1980s, following consumption repression in the 1970s, through the trends of APC in the National Accounts. As in Chapter 3, APC is, here, defined as the ratio of Private Final Consumption Expenditure (PFCE) in Gross National Disposable Income (GNDI).

From Figure 5.8, we can see that Korea's APC trend changed dramatically before and after 1989 when GDP per capita was US$ 8,700 US in PWT 6.2. At this point, the trend of the APC in Figure 5.8 is quite similar to that of the APC as a ratio of consumption in GDP, which we saw in the previous section. This trend in the APC means that Koreans had become much more avid consumers since 1989 for whatever reason. Figure 5.8, however, does not give information about changes in consumption with reference to business cycles. It is therefore necessary to disaggregate the APC into the rates of change of GNDI ($\dot{I}_n$) and PFCE ($\dot{C}_n$) to more clearly perceive the relationship between them.

In Figure 5.9, $\dot{I}_n$ can be considered as a proxy of the business cycle because it is a figure based on GDP. It is clear from the three year moving average of real $\dot{C}_n$ and $\dot{I}_n$ that $\dot{I}_n$ was higher than $\dot{C}_n$ by the late 1980s, regardless of the business cycle. Not to mention the fact that $\dot{C}_n$ was below $\dot{I}_n$ in the boom period, the former was also below the latter continuously, even in recession. However, the position of both curves of the three year moving average reversed since the late 1980s. Regardless of the business cycle, $\dot{C}_n$ was higher than $\dot{I}_n$. This can be interpreted as excessive consumption in accordance with the Keynesian absolute income hypothesis in Chapter 3 that $\dot{I}_n$ is higher than $\dot{C}_n$ in a boom period, but in general, their relationship is reversed during a recession. What is more, if it

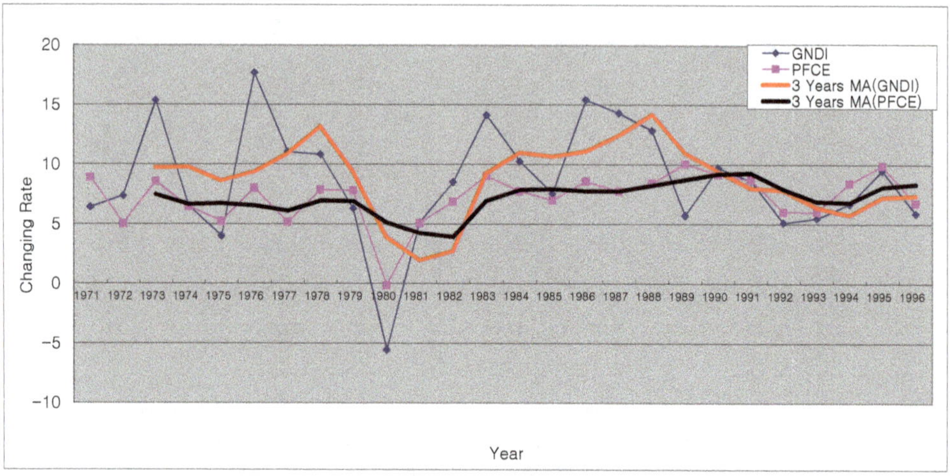

FIGURE 5.9 *Trends of* GNDI *and* PFCE (GNDI: *changing rate of Gross National Disposable Income* ($\dot{I}n$); PFCE: *changing rate of Private Final Consumption Expenditure* ($\dot{C}n$); *real term calculated by the author, based on 100 at 2000*). SOURCE: BOK, NATIONAL ACCOUNTS, ANNUAL.

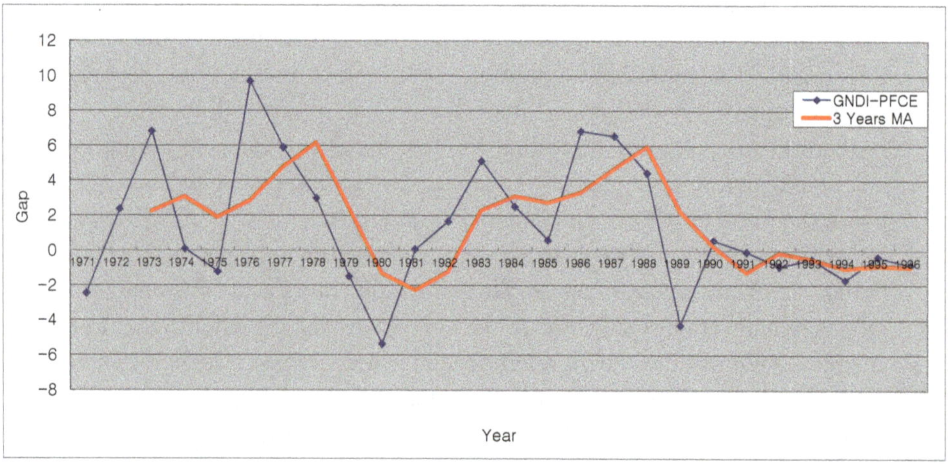

FIGURE 5.10 *Trends of the gap between* GNDI *and* PFCE (GNDI: *changing rate of Gross National Disposable Income* ($\dot{I}n$); PFCE: *changing rate of Private Final Consumption Expenditure* ($\dot{C}n$) (*real term calculated by the author, based on 100 at 2000*). SOURCE: BOK, NATIONAL ACCOUNTS, ANNUAL.

is considered that $\dot{I}_n$ was higher than $\dot{C}_n$ by the late 1980s, regardless of the business cycle, the change in their relationship since the late 1980s can be understood to be the result of radical changes in society's consumption attitudes. Therefore, Figure 5.9 supports the argument that there were key changes in consumer attitudes.

Figure 5.10 which shows trends in the gap between both curves ($\dot{I}_n - \dot{C}_n$) from 1971 to 1996 may be useful for comparing levels of frugality between periods and between regions. Years over zero mean $\dot{I}_n > \dot{C}_n$ but those below zero mean $\dot{I}_n < \dot{C}_n$. Likewise, APC rises in the period of $\dot{I}_n < \dot{C}_n$ but APC declines in the period of $\dot{I}_n > \dot{C}_n$. In other words, the lower the figure is, the smaller their gap is and so the more avid consumption is. It can be seen through the graph that the gap between $\dot{I}_n$ and $\dot{C}_n$ was smaller in the 1980s than in the 1970s. This means that overall consumption attitudes were more enthusiastic in the 1980s than in the 1970s. However, significant changes in consumption attitudes had taken place since 1989 when the real rate of increase of GDP per annum was 6.7 per cent. After that, the period of $\dot{I}_n < \dot{C}$ continued as consumption grew more aggressively.

How did this dramatic changeover happen? We need to draw additional comparisons to resolve this question. This can be carried out through understanding the chronological change in both GNDI and PFCE by looking at five yearly intervals. In particular, the boom period of the second half of the 1980s can be compared to the second half of the 1970s – that decade's equivalent boom period. In fact, when consumption attitudes are periodically compared in a society, business cycles between compared periods should correspond because there is a tendency for the ratio of consumption to income to be higher in a recession than a boom period. This is because the change in consumption is relatively slower than income with respect to business cycles. In this regard, both periods being compared show very similar curves in terms of the increase in GNDI, and the length of the boom period.

According to Figure 5.11, the real average rate of increase per annum of GNDI ($\dot{I}_n$) was 11.4 per cent in the second half of the 1970s and was 12.0 per cent in the same period in the 1980s. This can be said to be a boom period in terms of relative as well as absolute aspects. In contrast to $\dot{I}_n$, there is a difference in the real average rate of increase per annum of PFCE ($\dot{C}_n$) between both periods. The $\dot{C}_n$ was 7.2 per cent in the second half of the 1970s but was 8.7 per cent in the same period of the 1980s. Thus, the gap between $\dot{I}_n$ and $\dot{C}_n$ was 4.2 percentage points in the former period but was 3.3 percentage points in the latter one. This indicates that consumption attitudes were keener in the second half of the 1980s than they were in the second half of the 1970s. In other words, this implies that the difference in consumption attitudes between these two periods had already taken place by the mid-1980s. In particular, if we consider that the rate of increase of income in the 1980s was higher than that of the 1970s, we can presume that the change in consumption attitude between these two periods was more significant than that indicated. Thus, we can see that seeds of dramatic

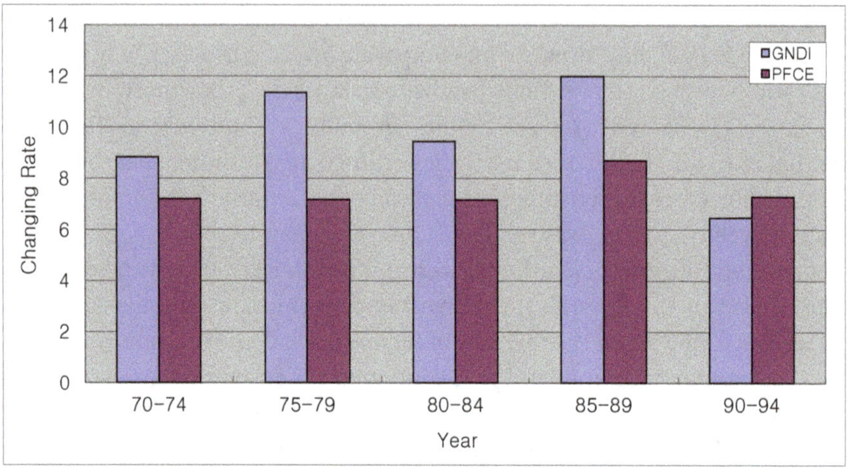

FIGURE 5.11 *Difference in consumption attitude between the 1970s and 1980s (GNDI: average rate of change per annum of Gross National Disposable Income ($\dot{I}n$); PFCE: average rate of change per annum of Private Final Consumption Expenditure ($\dot{C}n$) (real term calculated by the author, based on 100 at 2000).* SOURCE: BOK, NATIONAL ACCOUNTS, ANNUAL.

change in consumption attitudes in the first half of the 1990s, were, to an extent, already sown from the mid-1980s.

4.3 *The Results from Urban Labour Households*

As was mentioned in Chapter 3, this data is more useful than the data from the National Accounts in terms of analysis of higher income groups. Characteristics of the higher income group can be explored because the average level of income of urban labour households is much higher than that of the whole country. Moreover, a more sensitive response to the environment concerning consumption can be shown because of greater commercialization in urban rather than non-urban areas. As a result, the present section will analyze how the consumption attitudes of urban areas have already changed since the early 1980s ahead of that in the rest of the country. As the National Accounts reveal, signs of consumption repression and recovery are also shown through the APC of SWEHs which is denoted as share of consumption expenditure in the disposable income of the household.

From Figure 5.12, we can see that Korea's urban labour household APC trend is similar overall to the APC of National Accounts because the curve was more moderate in the 1980s than in the 1970s. While the former curve declined from 94.38 in 1970 to 77.09 in 1979 representing the gap between the peak and trough in the 1970s, the latter curve changed from 79.27 in 1982 to 73.56 in 1987 as the

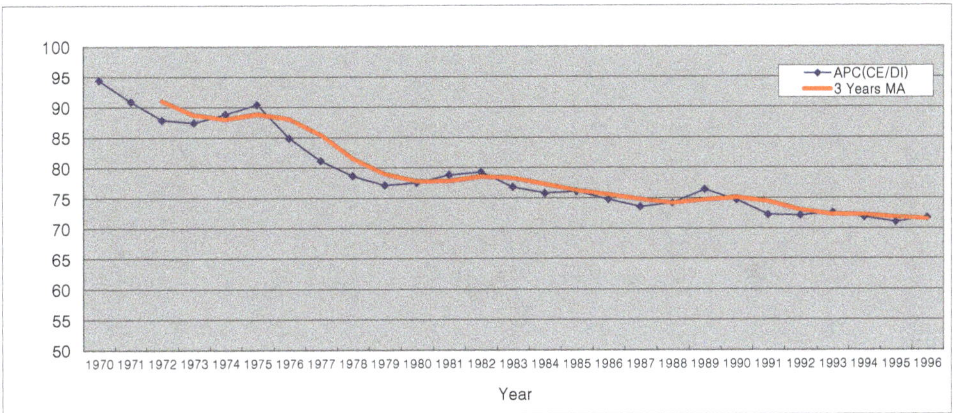

FIGURE 5.12 *Trends of* APC *in* SWEHS (APC*:* CE/DI*, calculated by the author from each monthly income and expenditure per urban household;* DI*: Disposable Income;* CE*: Consumption Expenditure*). SOURCE: SK, MONTHLY INCOME AND EXPENDITURE PER URBAN HOUSEHOLD, ANNUAL.

same gap and APC decreased to 71.03 in 1995 as the lowest level before the financial crisis in 1997. This APC trend indicates that Korean people's consumption attitude has become much more enthusiastic since the 1980s.

Like the APC of the National Accounts, this curve, however, does not give information about changes in consumption relative to business cycles. It may be necessary to disaggregate this APC into the rates of change of DI ($\dot{I}_u$) and CE ($\dot{C}_u$) to see more clearly the relationship between income and consumption under given business cycle conditions.

In Figure 5.13, $\dot{I}_u$ can be considered as a proxy of business cycles because it is a figure based on GDP. Like the APC of National Accounts, it is clear from the three year moving average of real $\dot{C}_u$ and $\dot{I}_{u,}$ that $\dot{I}_u$ was roughly higher than $\dot{C}_u$ by the late 1980s, regardless of the business cycle. However, the gap between both curves is even smaller in the 1980s, compared with that of the 1970s. In particular, what should be noted are the shapes of 1988 and 1989 when $\dot{C}_u$ was over $\dot{I}_u$ in spite of the period of economic boom. Accordingly, we can regard consumption in the 1980s as relatively more enthusiastic than that of the 1970s. Furthermore, we can argue that there was a remarkable boom in consumption in urban areas in the late 1980s. Additionally, this graph illustrates that consumption attitudes in urban areas changed more rapidly than those of non-urban areas because the decrease in gap between $\dot{I}_u$ and $\dot{C}_u$ in both the 1970s and the 1980s was more remarkable than that of non-urban areas in the same periods. As mentioned earlier, this trend reflects the more commercialized

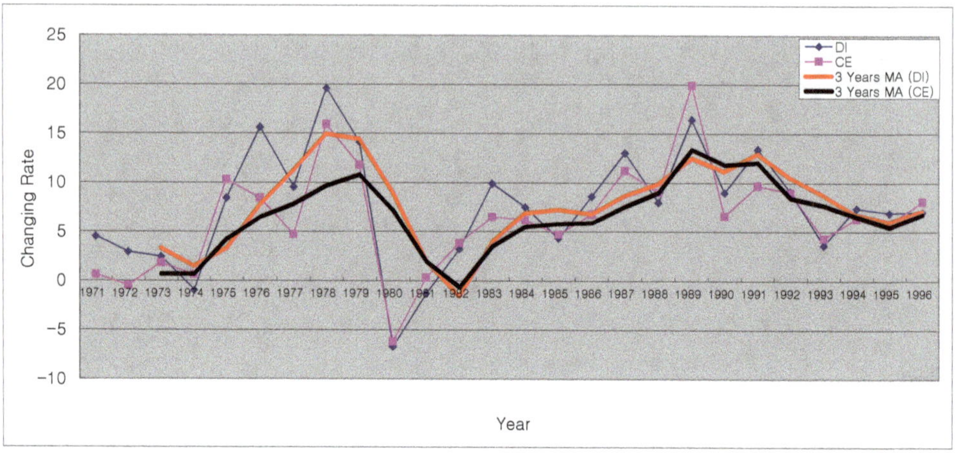

FIGURE 5.13 *Trends of* DI *and* CE *(*DI*: changing rate of Disposable Income ($\dot{I}u$);* CE*: changing rate of Consumption Expenditure ($\dot{C}u$); real term calculated by the author through the Consumer Price Index (*CPI*) based on 100 at 2005).* SOURCE: SK, MONTHLY INCOME AND EXPENDITURE PER URBAN HOUSEHOLD, ANNUAL.

character of urban areas and their sensitivity towards consumption, compared with the whole country.

Figure 5.14 which shows the trends in the gap of both curves ($\dot{I}_u - \dot{C}_u$) from 1971 to 1996, may be useful for comparison of the frugality between periods and between regions. Years over zero mean $\dot{I}_u > \dot{C}_u$ but those below zero mean $\dot{I}_u < \dot{C}_u$. Likewise, APC rises in the period of $\dot{I}_u < \dot{C}_u$ but APC declines in the period of $\dot{I}_u > \dot{C}_u$. In other words, the lower the figure is, the smaller their gap is and so the more avid the consumer is. Figure 5.14, accordingly, shows more clearly that consumption in the 1980s was relatively keener than that in the 1970s. In a manner similar to Figure 5.13, this shows that there was excessive consumption, and that $\dot{C}_u$ was over $\dot{I}_u$ in 1988 and 1989. In particular, unlike the graph of $\dot{I}_n - \dot{C}_n$ in Figure 5.10, consumption attitudes in urban areas entered a stable phase after a dramatic change around the beginning of the 1980s.

Basically, Figure 5.15 illustrates that the change in consumption attitude took place from the early 1980s in urban areas, whereas such change took place from the mid-1980s in the whole country. To understand this difference, the first half of the 1970s should be compared with the first half of the 1980s, as the period of relatively lower economic growth in each decade. The gap between $\dot{I}_u$ and $\dot{C}_u$ was 1.55 percentage points in the first half of the 1970s but was just 0.58 percentage points in the first half of the 1980s. Following this tendency, $\dot{C}_u$ was, in the end, over $\dot{I}_u$ in the second half of the 1980s and the focus on consumption was also maintained in the first half of the 1990s. This shows that

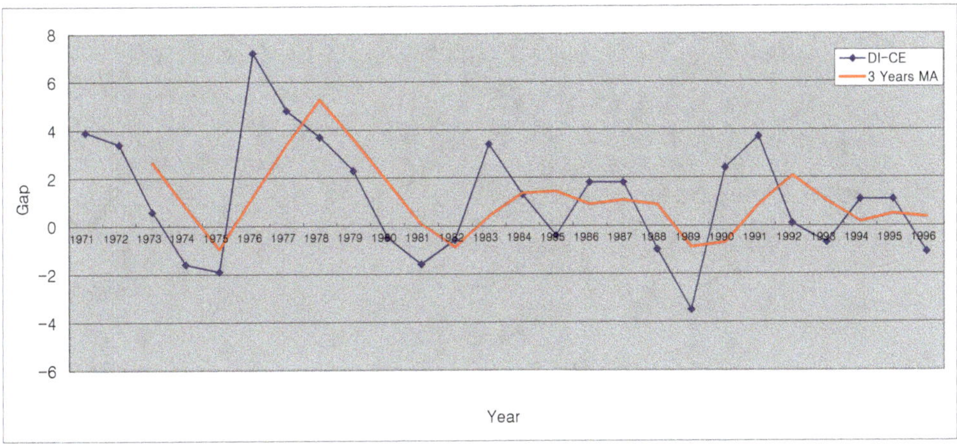

FIGURE 5.14 *Trends of the gap between* DI *and* CE *(*DI*: changing rate of Disposable Income ($\dot{I}u$);* CE*: changing rate of Consumption Expenditure ($\dot{C}u$) (real term calculated by the author through the Consumer Price Index (*CPI*) based on 100 at 2005).* SOURCE: SK, MONTHLY INCOME AND EXPENDITURE PER URBAN HOUSEHOLD, ANNUAL.

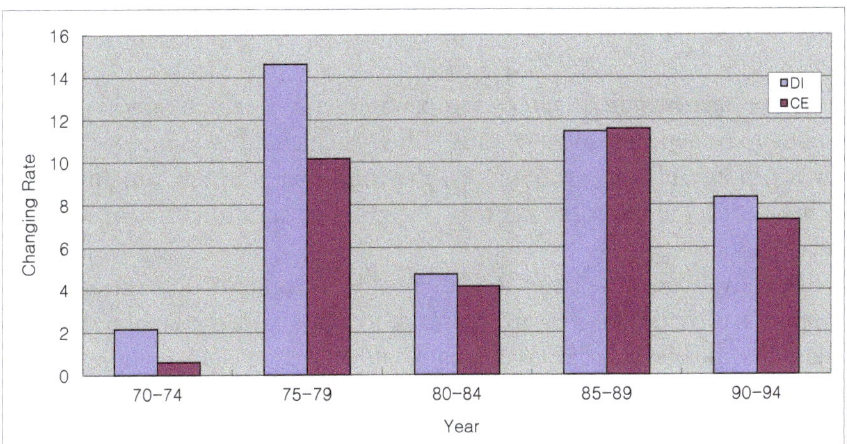

FIGURE 5.15 *Difference in consumption attitude between the 1970s and the 1980s in urban households (*DI*: average rate of change per annum of Disposable Income ($\dot{I}u$);* CE*: Average Rate of Change per annum of Consumption Expenditure ($\dot{C}u$) (real term calculated by the author through the Consumer Price Index (*CPI*) based on 100 at 2005).* SOURCE: SK, MONTHLY INCOME AND EXPENDITURE PER URBAN HOUSEHOLD, ANNUAL.

consumption attitudes in urban areas had already changed since the early 1980s. Thus, it can be said that the change in consumption attitudes in urban areas preceded any such changes in other areas.

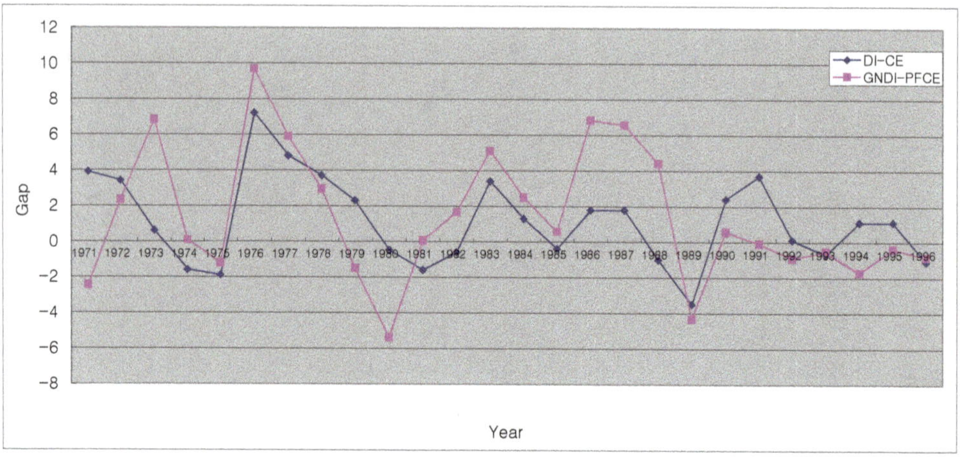

FIGURE 5.16 *Comparison of consumption attitude between urban and whole nation (DI: changing rate of Disposable Income in urban labour households ($\dot{I}u$); CE: changing rate of Consumption expenditure in urban labour households ($\dot{C}u$); GNDI: changing rate of Gross National Disposable Income ($\dot{I}n$); PFCE: changing rate of Private Final Consumption Expenditure ($\dot{C}n$)).* SOURCE: SK, MONTHLY INCOME AND EXPENDITURE PER URBAN HOUSEHOLD, ANNUAL, BOK, NATIONAL ACCOUNTS, ANNUAL.

As we have seen in Chapter 3, two kinds of curves denote gaps of ($\dot{I} - \dot{C}$) in urban areas and the whole country. Thus, the higher the figure is, the larger their gap is, and so the more frugal the consumer is in the same period. In other words, the lower the figure is, the more enthusiastic the consumption attitude is.

The advantage of Figure 5.16 is to be able to compare differences in consumption attitude between urban areas and non-urban areas within the same period, while previous graphs compared differences in consumption attitudes between periods in the same area. Figure 5.16 shows a dramatic reversal in the region which led consumption trends between the 1980s and the 1990s. The urban area took the initiative of consumption in the 1980s regardless of the business cycle but its role in consumption had been completely replaced by the country as a whole since 1989. This is evidence that the urban area responded to the atmosphere of consumption liberalization prior to non-urban areas. In particular, the difference between the first and the second half of the 1980s in both areas is pretty impressive. Although $\dot{I}_u$ was much higher in the second half of the 1980s than its first half, the gap between $\dot{I}_u$ and $\dot{C}_u$ in the second half of the 1980s decreased remarkably in urban areas. As we have seen earlier, this implies that consumption increased at an unusual rate during the period, in terms of the general relationship between $\dot{I}_u$ and $\dot{C}_u$ in the change of economic growth. In contrast to this, the curve for the whole country illustrates that the gap between $\dot{I}_n$ and $\dot{C}_n$ increased in the second half of the 1980s, compared with the first half of the decade. This looks more natural than the change in the urban areas. However, an unusual shape of the curve emerged in non-urban areas from the end of the 1980s. What is more, as the figure of ($\dot{I}_n$ – $\dot{C}_n$) continued at a level below zero, $\dot{C}_n$ was just over $\dot{I}_n$ during a considerable part of the 1990s. Thus, the change in consumption attitudes in non-urban areas in the 1990s was even more remarkable than that of urban areas in the second half of the 1980s.

Thus, following consumption repression in the 1970s, Korean consumption grew massively from the early 1980s with various kinds of policies geared towards consumption liberalization. However, changes were region-specific initially. The winds of change first blew in urban areas, and by the second half of the 1980s consumption was in full stride. This kind of change had a knock on effect on other areas, and, in fact, change was more pronounced in non-urban areas. In such locations changes in consumption attitudes first appeared from the mid-1980s but by the first half of the 1990s, the whole country had undergone radical changes in consumption attitude.

5 The Change of Strategy by the Department Store Industry

The last of the three subjects which is crucial for development of the retail industry, and which thus needs to be dealt with in this chapter, is the retail industry itself. The main aspect of department stores' management strategy was to make the stores increasingly popular. To this end, the department store lowered its position as a luxury retail institution as the period of mass consumption kicked in. This is different from general retail development where mass retailers such as the multiples, the supermarkets and the general merchandise stores become dominant in the period of mass consumption. For a considerable time, during the period of mass consumption, a remarkable growth of the department store co-existed with the slow progress of traditional markets while other modern retailers remained absent from the market. This trend helps to explain the distinctiveness of development trends in the Korean retail industry.

5.1 *Multiple Outlets Strategy of Department Stores*

As we have seen earlier, with economic growth and the beginning of liberalization, some new department stores had been established in the old and new city centers and some sub-center areas of Seoul, the capital city of Korea, since the early 1980s. Existing big department store companies responded to the appearance of new companies by having multiple branches in the sub-center areas. Here, this strategy is examined by analyzing the three biggest department store companies in Korea. Table 5.5 shows that the Shinsegae Department Store, owned by Samsung, established its first branch in Yeongdeungpo, a representative sub-center and residential area in Seoul. It subsequently added the Dongbang Plaza in Seoul's city center in 1984. Except for Dongbang Plaza, all the branches established in Seoul since the mid-1980s have been located both in sub-centers and in residential areas.

The Mi-a and Cheon-ho districts, which were big traditional suburban residential areas, were revamped at that time as the population was growing in conjunction with the rapid expansion of the capital. Yeongdongpo was newly developed as a residential district in the south of Seoul from the late 1970s. Thus, Shinsegae Department Store Company's new strategy of establishing multiple branches was a means of creating a popular store for necessities rather than that of luxury fashion goods. In contrast, we shall see in the next chapter, the branches which were established in the city centers of some provincial cities from the mid-1990s were the result of a further strategy to dominate local markets. Lotte's strategy was not different from Shinsegae's. Lotte, which established its own headquarters in the center of Seoul in 1979, began to carry out its strategy of expansion both to sub-centers and to residential areas from the late 1980s. Jamsil (1988), Cheonglyangli (1994) and Gwan-ag (1997) are also big suburban residential areas. What is interesting is that the first provincial branch of Lotte (Bu-san Main Store) was built in the same year as the first of the Shinsegae stores (Gwangju Store), even if their locations were different. This suggests that big department store companies were expanding their branches into the provincial cities even in the mid-1990s.

The Hyundai Department Store, which was the last of the big three to enter the market, adopted a rather different strategy. It built its own headquarters in 1985, when other existing competitors were already pushing the strategy of creating multiple branches. Accordingly, it decided to establish its headquarters in a new city center in the south of Seoul.[8] After that, the Hyundai Department

8 Seoul, the capital city of South Korea, is broadly divided into the north and the south along the Han River. The north of the city where Joseon Dynasty set up the capital in 1393 is the original center of Seoul. In contrast, the south of the city has been developed since the end of the 1970s as rapid economic growth led to the growth of the capital city. The south side of the river was at first developed as a dormitory town for the north. However, it has now become another center of Seoul in its own right. As a result of rapid development, the area has become a much more splendid and richer place than the northern area since the middle of the 1980s.

TABLE 5.5 *Trend of the multi-branches strategy in the main department store companies*

Company name	Name of the shop	Year of foundation	City	Location
Shinsegae Department Store	Shinsegae Department Store (Headquarters)	1963	Seoul	City Center
	Shinsegae Yeoungdeungpo Store	1984	Seoul	Sub-Center
	Dongbang Plaza*	1984	Seoul	City Center
	Shinsegae Mia Store	1988	Seoul	Sub-Center
	Shinsegae Chunho Store*	1992	Seoul	Sub-Center
	Shinsegae Youngdong Store*	1993	Seoul	Sub-Center
	Shinsegae GwangJu Store	1995	Gwangju Metropolitan City	City Center
	Shinsegae Incheon Store	1997	Incheon Metropolitan City	City Center
Lotte Department Store	Lotte Department Store (Headquarters)	1979	Seoul	City Center
	Lotte Chamsil Store	1988	Seoul	Sub-Center
	Lotte Yeoungdeungpo Store	1991	Seoul	Sub-Center
	Lotte Cheongnyangri Store	1994	Seoul	Sub-Center
	Lotte Busan Main Store	1995	Busan Metropolitan City	City Center
	Lotte Gwanak Store	1997	Seoul	Sub-Center
Hyundai Department Store	Hyundai Department Store (Headquarters)	1985	Seoul	Sub-Center (New City Center)
	Hyundai Trade Centre Store	1988	Seoul	Sub-Center
	Hyundai Banpo Leisure Town	1988	Seoul	Sub-Center
	Hyundai Bupyong Store*	1991	Incheon Metropolitan City	Sub-Center
	Hyundai Busan Store	1995	Busan Metropolitan City	City Center
	Hyundai Chunho Store	1997	Seoul	Sub-Center

* Shops which were closed within a few years of their establishment.
Source: <http://about.shinsegae.com/company/COHistoryV.asp>, <http://dpt.lotteshopping.com/shopping/company/history.jsp>, <http://www.ehyundai.com/home/ir/ir_history.jsp>.

Store expanded its branches mainly around the south. It made inroads into provincial cities at the same time as both its competitors in the mid-1990s. Before that, it established its first provincial branch, Hyundai Bu-pyeong Store at In-cheon in 1991. This was different from the other provincial branches because the Bu-pyeong district is a dormitory town for Seoul. It was clear that the strategy of the main department stores, which had been to serve as purveyors of luxury fashion goods, changed to becoming popular purveyors of staples from the mid-1980s. It is also evident that this strategy was carried out through the management of multiple branches, unlike the previous example of a single outlet. In this respect, it is no exaggeration to say that most department stores in Korea since the mid-1980s have been general merchandise stores, albeit they were labelled department stores. In particular, this is evident through comparison of market share of the department store industry with other countries. As mentioned in the previous chapter, its share in the total retail sales in the UK was at most as much as 5–6 per cent in the 1950s. As with other modern retail formats carrying staple goods, the market share of multiples was 18–20 per cent and co-operatives was 10–12 per cent at the same time (Jefferys 1954: 61). The market share of department stores in the UK, rather, showed a decreasing tendency after that time. It was 5.1 per cent in 1961 and declined to 4.9 per cent in 1970 (Hill 1974: 28).

In contrast to this, the market share of American department stores, which carried price lines primarily in the medium range around the year 1920, was estimated to be one sixth in 1948 (Robert 1963: 40–41). This indicates that the department store industry in the US still covered the medium range of the consumer market to a large extent. This also corresponded with the view that the success of the discount store format from around 1950 was to a substantial degree at the expense of the department store industry in the US (Kibarian 1960–1961: 203). What we can presume through this comparison is, on the one hand, that the consumer market was likely to be less diversified in the US than in the UK, and on the other hand, that the department store in the US had played a role in popular retail formats for mass consumption at least until the innovation of discount store formats. In this respect, it appears normal that, since the 1980s, the department store industry in Korea played a similar role to that of the general merchandise store for mass consumption, rather than the luxurious retail format for the rich given the less diversified consumer market.

Ab-gu-jeongdong, where the Hyundai Department Store has its headquarters, is the center of the southern area.

5.2 *The Change in the Assortment of Goods*

The change in the department store format due to the strategy of popularization is linked to the change in the assortment of goods available. In general, the change of the department store towards luxuries can be explained, on the one hand, through the expansion of fashion goods such as apparel, and on the other hand, through the reduction of necessities in its turnover. In this regard, the ratio of foodstuffs in the turnover of the department store was a crucial criterion for the change towards popularization because foodstuffs are among the most important necessities. What is more, the use of the criterion of foodstuffs explains the strategic change in department stores, in that there was no modern retailer for foodstuffs in Korea at that time. This demonstrates a considerable difference between the department stores of the UK and Korea. In general, department stores hardly deal with groceries in the UK because modern multiple shops and co-operatives specializing in foodstuffs developed in tandem with the beginning of the department stores in the 1850s (Jefferys 1954; Fraser 1981; Alexander and Akehurst 1999; Purvis 1999). In contrast, groceries have been carried mainly by traditional retailers in Korea because there had been no big retailers specializing in foodstuffs. Due to this historical condition, unlike the UK case, Korea's department stores dealt with some foodstuffs of high quality for high income people even before the 1980s. This is related to the historical characteristics of retailers. Thus, what this chapter takes into account is the extent to which the ratio of foodstuffs changed from the mid-1980s relative to the conditions characterizing Korean department store goods.

According to existing research, the ratio of foodstuffs in total turnover rose in most newly established department stores in the sub-centers after the mid-1980s, compared with those in the city center. This research used as its basic criteria that 45 per cent of sales were accounted for by apparel, and 10 per cent by foodstuffs. In other words, in those outlets in which foodstuff sales were strengthened, the proportion of apparel in total sales was under 45 per cent, and simultaneously the ratio of foodstuffs was over 10 per cent (type B). In contrast to this, the pre-existing type of retailers before sales of foodstuffs were increased had a ratio of apparel in their total sales of over 45 per cent (type A). These criteria are to some extent arbitrary, but it is clear that, according to this research, the ratio of foodstuffs amongst goods in department stores rose before and after the mid-1980s. For example, in the case of the Shinsegae Department Store, unlike the existing headquarters in the center which carried apparel (type A), all six branches established in Seoul since the foundation of the Yeoungdeungpo Store in 1984, were classified into outlets in which kinds of foodstuff were strengthened, constituting type B goods. In particular, the Dongbang Plaza concentrated further on purveying foodstuffs despite its location in the city center. The Lotte Department Store had a slightly different strategy from Shinsegae in that it managed the Lotte Chamsil Store and the Lotte Yeoungdeungpo Store as type A entities. However, it also adopted the altered strategy (type B) in the Lotte Cheongnyangri Store in 1994. The Hyundai Department Store established its headquarters as type B in format because its location was at the center of a new residential area. Instead it managed the Hyundai Trade Centre Store in 1988 as a type A outlet because it was located at an important traffic junction in a large newly developed area of southern Seoul. However, it adopted the strategy of type B again in the Hyundai Bupyong Store in 1991. Apart from these companies, the New Core Department Store, which was established in a new residential area of Seoul in 1985, managed most branches as type B and the Hanshin Core, which was established in 1988, adopted the strategy of the type B in most of its branches as well (Baek Insu 2004: 174–176).

This change of strategy was inevitably reflected in the purchasing behaviour of consumers. According to a survey by the Shinsegae Department Store in 1984 after the establishment of the Shinsegae Yeongdeungpo Store,[9] the outlet in the sub-center took sales of foodstuffs as well as of apparel to a large extent away from other retailers.

What we need to take into account in the two tables, Table 5.6 and Table 5.7, are the changes in the pattern of purchases of foodstuffs and apparel in accordance with the existence of big retailers in the sub-center. Before the establishment of the department store in the sub-center, most people (60 per cent) frequented a kind of neighbourhood mom and pop store to buy foodstuffs. As the second most popular shop, 23.9 per cent of respondents used a kind of small- and medium-size retailer in the sub-center which belonged to the traditional permanent markets. The big retailer in the city center, in other words, the department store, was used by only 6.5 per cent of respondents for purchasing foodstuffs. In contrast, 48.3 per cent of respondents said that they bought some kind of apparel in city center big retailers and 31.7 per cent of them used a small and medium size retailer in the center in order to buy apparel. This implies that 80 per cent of respondents used retailers in the city center to purchase some kind of apparel. In sum, over half the respondents bought apparel at retailers in the city center, but chose to buy foodstuffs from

9 This survey was carried out in November 1984, six months after the establishment of the Shinsegae Yeongdeungpo Store as the first branch in which the strategy of type B was adopted in the sub-center. 252 people were interviewed for this survey but only the answers from 230 people were analyzed because 22 respondents had never used the department store or did not give proper answers. (Jo Jinsang 1985: 95)

TABLE 5.6 *Shopping before the establishment of the department store in the sub-center*

	City center		Small and medium size retailer in the sub-center	Mom and pop store in the neighbourhood	Others	Total
	Big retailer	Small and medium size retailer				
Food stuff (%)	6.5	9.6	23.9	60.0	0.0	100
Household goods (%)	14.8	13.0	24.8	47.4	0.0	100
Apparel (%)	48.3	31.7	15.7	3.9	0.4	100

TABLE 5.7 *Shopping after the establishment of the department store in the sub-center*

	City center		Sub-center		Mom and pop store in neighbourhood	Others	Total
	Big retailer	Small and medium size retailer	Big retailer*	Small and medium size retailer			
Food stuff (%)	0.0	8.3	43.0	12.6	36.1	0.0	100
Household goods (%)	0.9	10.9	33.9	17.8	36.5	0.0	100
Apparel (%)	5.7	14.3	73.0	6.1	0.9	0.0	100

* A big retailer in the sub-center actually means a department store which has been newly established.

Source: Jo Jinsang (1985: 95)

within their neighbourhoods. The establishment of big retailers in the sub-center sharply altered the purchasing behaviour of consumers. First, big retailers in the sub-center assumed the dominant market share of apparel, drawing demand away from retailers in the city center. In fact, 73 per cent of respondents said that they bought apparel at big retailers in the sub-center. The case of foodstuffs also shows a great change. Newly established big retailers in the sub-center were the most popular places even for foodstuffs as 43 per cent of respondents used them to buy some kind of foodstuff. As a result of this, the market share of mom and pop stores in foodstuffs dramatically decreased to

36.1 per cent from 60 per cent before the establishment of the sub-center big retailers. In summary, the sub-center big retailer, in this case the department store, became a purchasing center for both apparel and foodstuffs, unlike a department store in the city center. Consequently, this shows, in terms of the purchasing behaviour of consumers, that the department store in the sub-center strengthened sales of foodstuffs, compared to its counterparts in the city center. It also implies that the assortment of goods carried changed from luxury goods to popular staples, and such stores also pursued the strategy of establishing multiple outlets.

6 Conclusion

This chapter has examined the reasons for the rapid expansion of consumption and the growth of the department store industry since the 1980s in terms of three actors, i.e. government, consumers and the retail industry. The economic policies of the government had been liberalized and deregulated, particularly with respect to consumption, during the process of democratization from the 1980s. General economic policy showed a tendency to transfer gradually from state driven to market driven and from production to balance between production and consumption. Social policy which was in a strongly restricted atmosphere also changed as shown by the liberalization of foreign travel, and the lifting of curfews. In this way, policy in the retail industry changed gradually from a repressive position to an attitude of support. One determining policy which resulted in the expansion of consumption was the start of consumer finance. With the increase in income in the 1980s, this provided Korean consumers with plenty of resources for consumption. On the other hand, social psychology relating to democratization should be considered as well. At that time, the expansion of consumption rights seemed to be understood as part of democratic rights. This is because concentration on the production sector, which is the other side of the coin of consumption repression, overlapped with unfair support for entrepreneurs by the authoritarian regime. In other words, the authoritarian regime appeared, on the one hand, to unfairly drive the economy by concentrating on production rather than consumption. On the other hand, it seemed like a dictator by absolutely preferring the rich to the poor. Because of this, consumption can be linked to the fruits of democratization. In this situation, people became much more progressive in relation to consumption. Along with this historical environment, the retail industry, particularly the department store, grew rapidly as the only modern retail institution to exist at that time.

Here, what needs to be taken into account in terms of evolution of the retail institution is that the expansion of the consumption market was gradually linked to stratification of the market according to the level of income. This is a general phenomenon to be shown in the development of the consumption market and the retail industry. For example, in most developed countries, the emergence of mass consumption was linked to a new type of retailer which was consistent with the newly emerging situation. The rapid growth of the department store industry and the increase in conflict between the department store and the traditional market since the 1980s, shows that such a phenomenon took place even in Korea. However, the Korean case shows its uniqueness in terms of the evolutionary process of the department store industry. In general, the department store format emerged with the emergence of mass consumption, and targeted mass consumers first, but eventually positioned itself in the luxury goods market with the emergence of competitors such as multiples (the UK), the discount store format (the US) and the general merchandise store (Japan). Even if such changes took place at different times in each country, the trajectory of development of the department store industry was very similar. In this respect, most of the theories of retail evolution suggest that a retailer transferring itself from the lower market to the upper one constitutes the general path of retail evolution.

In contrast to the general path, the Korean department store format which had already long existed as a luxury retailer, repositioned its status in the retail market through its popularization strategy from the 1980s. This can be explained by the absence of other modern retailers, such as the supermarket and the general merchandise store, which are generally considered as more appropriate types of store for mass consumption. This characteristic seems to be a result of strategic choices made by the department store. This, however, cannot be understood as resulting only from the strategy of the department store. Rather, the strategy of the department store is likely to be closely related to the preferences of consumers, because a retailer usually adopts a strategy that is consistent with consumers' preferences in order to maximize its own profits. Otherwise, some new department store companies would have established other types of retail institutions in order to raise their own market share. However, there was hardly any such differentiation at that time. From this, it can be presumed that Korean consumers have a strong preference for upmarket retailers regardless of levels of income. It is also highly possible that the consumption repression, despite increases in income in the 1970s, increased the gap between income and consumption, and consequently a number of consumers had high purchasing power within department stores when consumption was liberalized. As was analyzed in the previous section, the drastic decrease in the gap or reversal between DI and CE since the 1980s would appear to support this argument. With the presence of such consumers the strategy of popularization by the department store was very useful for creating an explosive expansion of its market. In summary, the Korean department store, like the discount store, was a uniquely Korean entity in the period of mass consumption. As will be examined, this kind of characteristic will also be seen in the much more stratified process of the retail market since the mid-1990s.

CHAPTER 6

The Stratified Retail Industry and the Sign of Relatively Low Economic Growth since the Middle of the 1990s: The Golden Age of the Department Store Industry II

1 Introduction

The department store industry which had enjoyed its heyday with an explosive increase in turnover could not avoid the fate of a short sunny day which lasted as long as its rapid growth. The tendency of the consumer market towards stratification since the 1990s has been strengthened by the rise of discount stores as a new kind of retail institution targeting the mass consumption market. On the one hand, the heyday of the department stores, which had led mass consumption as representative modern retailers, had already passed after fifteen years, and on the other hand, the department store as a luxurious retail format returned to its original status in the hierarchy of retail institutions.

It was the financial crisis of 1997 that was at the center of this structural change. Even if the Korean economy had already changed since the mid-1990s, the financial crisis, which the Korean economy had not experienced before, had created the momentum necessary for changing the whole structure of the Korean economy. Broadly speaking, the marketization of the Korean economy has been driven forward much more speedily than before and simultaneously the retreat of the state and the process of deregulation have become clearer and clearer since that time, according to the requirements of the International Monetary Fund (IMF) which was the fire fighter that had to deal with the crisis. Despite the structural reforms of the IMF however, the Korean economy has fluctuated considerably and has even shown signs of lower economic growth than it showed before the crisis. In this process, one of the most dramatically restructured fields was that of industrial relations, as the structural reforms were believed to exacerbate the instability of employment and thus to be linked to rising income inequality (Choe Jinseok and Gim Yeongdeok 2007; Jeon Byeongyu 2007; I Jeongu and I Seongrim 2001, etc.). In fact, the amount of non-regular employment has risen remarkably and the Gini Coefficient has been exacerbated as well since the crisis. As a result of this, the problem of polarization in income has become the biggest social issue in Korea. Thus, a number of social conflicts have developed around this issue. What is worse,

 | DOI 10.1163/9789004274228_007

the relatively lower economic growth since the crisis has not contributed to resolving this kind of social problem. Rather, this situation triggered a severe controversy around what should be prioritized in both economic growth and redistribution.

On the other hand, this was directly connected with the stratification of consumption which the Korean economy had hardly experienced before. Due to strong consumption repression, Korean consumers were in an unstratified condition of consumption until around the mid-1980s, in spite of the huge income gap. Even after the liberalization of consumption was rapidly carried out since the 1980s, liberalization did not seem to be directly linked to the differentiation of consumption until the mid-1990s. This was a result of a combination of factors; the decrease in income differentiation as part of the economic environment, avid consumption as a form of consumer behaviour, and both the popularization strategy of the department store and the absence of another retailer for mass consumption as characterizing the structure of the retail industry. In contrast, the expansion of the income gap after the crisis has caused consumption differentiation under the condition of consumption liberalization. Unlike the 1970s, without conditions of consumption repression, it was natural for the income gap to be linked to consumption differentiation. In this situation, change in the retail industry was inevitable. The retail industry, which already faced a crucial change of momentum with the complete opening of the domestic market in 1996, has been drawn into a much fiercer whirlpool since the crisis. Dramatic changes, such as the moderation of the department store, the rise of the discount store and the collapse of traditional retailers resulted from this situation. The fastest of these changes in terms of sales growth was the change in the retail format of the discount store and its amount of sales which, in the end, exceeded that of the department store industry in 2003. The type of discount store which has emerged since the mid-1990s seemed to provide an alternative for consumers who felt some burden in shopping at department stores, and who were dissatisfied with the prices and service of the traditional retailer. The department store, on the other hand, had to accept a rearrangement of its position in the retail industry with a decrease (or at best, a much more moderate increase) in its market share. Apart from the short heyday of the department store format as one of the characteristics of the Korean retail industry, the situation needs to be examined through the theory of retail evolution. The competition and interaction between the department store and the discount store implies that conflict theory is one of the theories of retail evolution that can be applied to the Korean retail industry[1]

1 Of course, the conflict theory can be applied to the situation in which the department stores compete with the traditional retailers. However, generally their relationship does not seem to

(O Sejo and Sekine Takasi 2002: 141). Conflict theory claims that conflict and competition among retailers are the driving forces in retail evolution. The struggle to be better fitted for survival in the market decides both the direction of, and the extent of, retail evolution (Brown 1987). In this respect, the structure of the Korean retail industry in which two different types of modern retailers exist and compete might be consistent with the claims of the conflict theory.

However, what requires caution in the Korean situation is the character of ownership and thus the governance of the main retail companies. The oligopolistic character of the Korean economy due to the existence of the *chaebol* should be considered in the case of the retail industry as well. Most of the main retailers, such as the department stores and the discount stores are owned by *chaebol*. For example, the Shinsegae Department Store Company owns E-mart as a discount store division and the Lotte Department Store Company has Lotte Mart as its discount store division; they are all the main competitors in each type of mass retailer. Due to the comprehensive structure of ownership, two different types of retailers in the same company might mainly be in a co-operative relationship rather than in a survival game, although there is internal competition to some extent within the same company. In this regard, they can be instruments which carry out the strategy of price differentiation in order to maximize the profits of the big retail companies under the condition of a differentiated consumer market. In other words, they can be components of an asset portfolio at the level of the comprehensive retail company. This implies that the main driving force for their evolution may not be conflict but cooperation with each other in accordance with the situation of the consumer market.

This chapter examines the concrete situation of the economic environment since the mid-1990s in light of these factors and explores the change of factors relating to consumption such as income distribution. It looks at the response of retailers to these circumstances and thus the emerging situation in the retail industry. The strategic change of the department store and explosive growth of the discount store format is documented. This chapter will not examine the issue of theoretical adaptation because this would require a different kind of analysis. Instead, the next chapter will tackle further theoretical issues.

---

be an example of the conflict theory because the department store as a modern retailer tends to take over the market one-sidedly from the traditional retailers. This tendency also seems to be related to the huge differences between both in terms of the scale and scope of their operations.

2 The Financial Crisis and Lower Economic Growth since the Mid-1990s

2.1 *The Financial Crisis and Its Socio-economic Impacts*

It is not an exaggeration to say that the financial crisis of 1997 was one of the most important turning points in Korean economic history. The shock from the crisis resulted in the lowest record of economic growth in its history. From the beginning of the crisis in 1997 until 2000, nine of the biggest thirty *chaebol,* including the Daewoo Group – which was the third largest in terms of asset size among the *chaebol* – faced the crisis of bankruptcy (*Jo-seon-il-bo* 2 June 2000). The myth that the *chaebol* were too big to fail was destroyed. As we have seen earlier, some of the *chaebol* already faced a serious crisis in the early 1980s. The Korean government resolved this problem, on the one hand, through the rationalization of their industries, in which the *chaebols* had to pay part of the cost and, on the other hand, through financial support which provided them with an opportunity for survival. However, the financial crisis in the late 1990s was completely different. The government had no omnipotent power which could resolve the crisis of the firms. This was related both to the size of the bankruptcy and to the decreasing power of the government since liberalization. It was impossible for the government to prevent avalanches of bankruptcies and instead the government changed its own role to the disposal of the bankrupted. In the meantime, some of the main commercial banks, which had won public confidence at the level of the state, also faced a similar crisis to the *chaebol.* Some of them were bankrupted and others underwent enforced mergers. In the course of this process, investment in the financial market, including the ownership of banks, was completely opened to foreigners. In other words, financial liberalization and the opening of the market, which was gradually carried out in planned stages, were enforced as a solution during the crisis (Chang et al. 1998: 735–746). As a result of this, the Korean people were seriously wounded in their self-confidence at the national level, which had originally stemmed from the highly successful history of their late industrialization. Instead of avoiding the dishonour of a moratorium, the debt relief imposed by the IMF was unavoidable. 3 December 1997, when both the Korean government and the IMF signed the debt relief with an agreement on its various conditions, was generally called 'The Day of National Disgrace' (*Jo-seon-il-bo* 4 December 1997a, etc.). Some of the media used expressions like the loss of economic sovereignty on this day and the IMF trusteeship was one of the more common expressions used to denote the period of the crisis (*Jo-seon-il-bo* 19 December 1997b). The fact that some of the senior bureaucrats involved in the crisis were convicted later on, was also deeply related to public sentiment, even if there was fierce controversy over the farirness of bringing them to trial. These examples permit us to see how Korean people understood the crisis.

Apart from such matters, what concerned people after the crisis was the change in everyday life. While matters of expectation and trust in the existing economic system affected people's opinions, the changes in everyday life directly influenced their physical and concrete existence. One of the most important changes was in the employment structure, which became remarkably vulnerable due to the crisis. This is because the employment structure as a source of income was one of the most basic factors in people's lives. The deeper the crisis became, the more unstable the employment structure became. Industrial relations since the crisis can be characterized by an expansion of labour flexibility. It was brought about by the deregulation of dismissal practices. Replacement labour in the event of strikes was now permitted through the requirements of the IMF (I Jongseon 2001: 179). Inevitably, the introduction of this kind of rapid change would incur resistance from the labour force, given the strong development of trade unions since the late 1980s. To alleviate the problem, the Korean government built an organization which created a social pact among the labour force, the capitalists and the government in the beginning of 1998. Although a compromise between the groups was quite difficult, the organization produced some successful outcomes. The representatives of the trade unions obtained strong labour rights, including 'the right to organize' the public sector labour force, as a trade off for an acceptance of the expansion of labour flexibility. This was the first social pact among the three parties in Korean history (I Jongseon: 180). However, the restructuring of the employment system was prior to the social pact. The government, on the one hand, had a passive attitude to the enforcement of some of the clauses of the social pact, which was not very consistent with the goal of restructuring. And the labour force, on the other hand, resisted the restructuring of the employment system (I Jongseon: 182). In this situation, it was inevitable that the number of strikes increased rapidly, from just 78 in 1997, to 129 in 1998, 198 in 1999, and 462 in 2004. (MOL, Annual Return of the Number of Strikes). Nevertheless, the policy of ignoring labour interests became the main stream in government policy and, as a result, employment instability steadily increased.

2.2 *Moderate Economic and Domestic Market Growth*

The vulnerable situation which resulted from the financial crisis was exacerbated due to relatively lower economic growth compared with the previous period. In turn, this might also be linked to lower economic growth at the next stage because of the increase in social conflict and the shrinking of consumption.

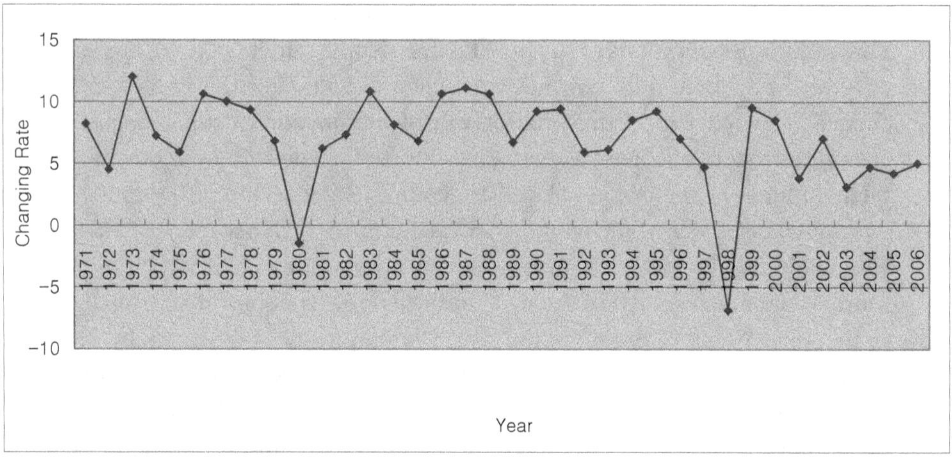

FIGURE 6.1 *Trends of economic growth rate (real term).* SOURCE: BOK, NATIONAL ACCOUNTS, ANNUAL.

The annual GDP growth rate sharply declined to 4.7 per cent in 1997 from 7 per cent in 1996, although the impact of the crisis had not yet spread towards the whole economy. However, the spread of the impact was fast. In 1998, the Korean economy recorded its worst annual rate of economic growth, minus 6.9 per cent, since the establishment of the development plan in the early 1960s. The growth rate in 1999 looked strong at 9.5 per cent because it was based on the much lower rate of the previous year. The recovering trend of the economy continued in 2000, as the economic growth rate recorded 8.5 per cent in that year. However, the aftershock of the crisis lasted much longer. The economic growth rate was sharply moderated in 2001 at 3.8 per cent. The rate of increase of GDP increased to 7 per cent in 2002, thanks to the policy of stimulating the economy, but it declined again to 3.1 per cent in 2003. Consecutively, recording 4.7 per cent in 2004, 4.2 per cent in 2005 and 5 per cent in 2006, the rate of increase of GDP did not show the robust trend of the previous period.

Figure 6.2 indicates that GNI per capita, which rose continuously to 10.63 million *won* (US$ 11,176) in 1997, declined to 10.29 million *won* in 1998, under the impact of the financial crisis. After that, it showed a rising curve again. However, the real rate of increase was much more moderate than in the previous period.

Figure 6.3 shows the conspicuous difference in the rate of increase of real GNI per capita before, during and after 1997. While the annual rates were mostly between 5 per cent and 10 per cent before 1997, most rates after 1997 have been between 0 per cent and 5 per cent.

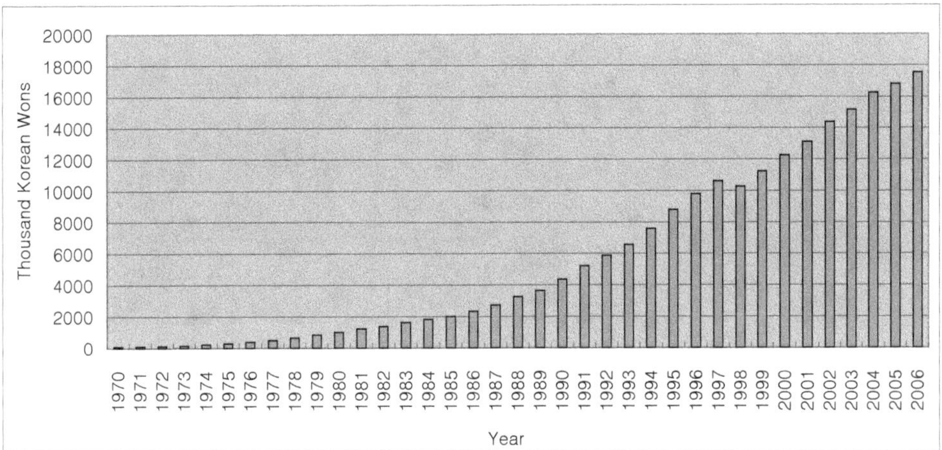

FIGURE 6.2 *Trends of income (nominal term of* GNI *per Capita: thousand Korean* won). SOURCE: BOK, NATIONAL ACCOUNTS, ANNUAL.

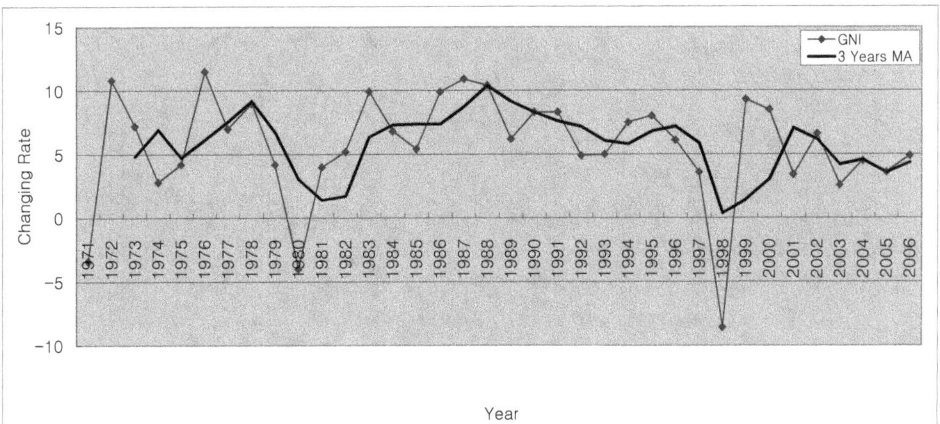

FIGURE 6.3 *Rate of increase of* GNI *per capita (real term).* SOURCE: BOK, NATIONAL ACCOUNTS, ANNUAL.

The average rate of increase of GNI per capita was 7.5 per cent per annum between 1986 and 1996, while it was just 3.7 per cent per annum between 1996 and 2006, which is under half that of the previous period. This moderation of the rate of increase in GNI per capita may imply that basic conditions for domestic consumption have exacerbated since the financial crisis.

According to Figure 6.4, the PFCE declined sharply in 1998 but increased rapidly again until 2002. However, its trend of increase has been slower since 2002.

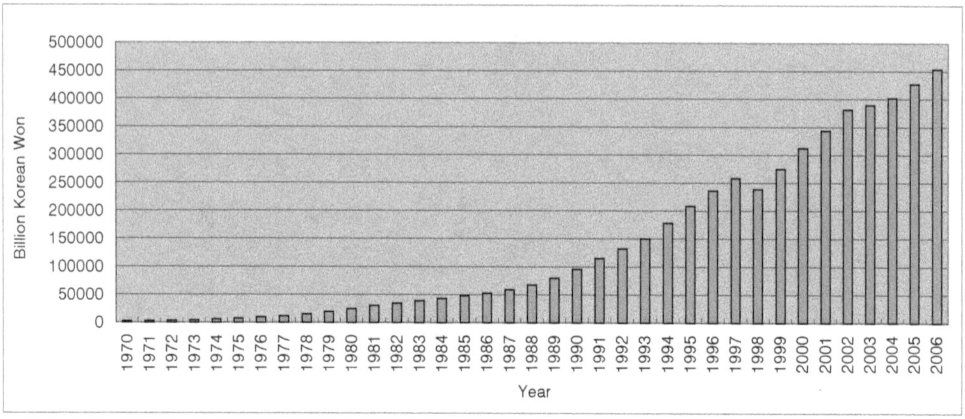

FIGURE 6.4 *Trend in Private Final Consumption Expenditure (nominal term of the Private Final Consumption Expenditure (PFCE): billion Korean* won). SOURCE: BOK, NATIONAL ACCOUNTS, ANNUAL.

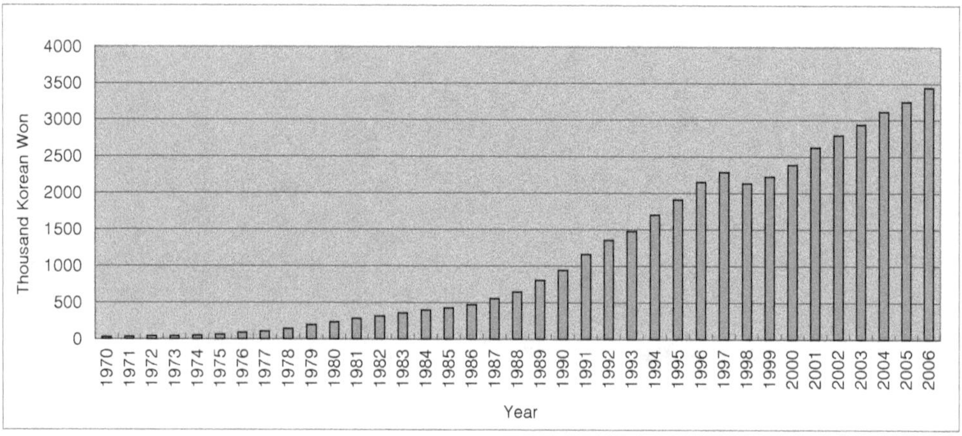

FIGURE 6.5 *Trend of income of urban labour households (nominal term: thousand Korean* won). SOURCE: SK, MONTHLY INCOME AND EXPENDITURE PER URBAN HOUSEHOLD, ANNUAL.

We can see in Figure 6.5 that the monthly income of Salary and Wage Earners' Households in urban area (SWEHS) declined to 2.1 million *won* (US$ 1,524.7) in 1998 due to the impact of the financial crisis. Even though the decrease in income looks like recovery afterwards, its real rate of increase was much more moderate than in the previous period.

In Figure 6.6, the monthly consumption expenditure of the SWEHS also shows a similar curve to its monthly income. It was 1.45 million *won* (US$ 1,528.5) in 1997 and decreased to 1.3 million *won* (US$ 927.7) in 1998. After that,

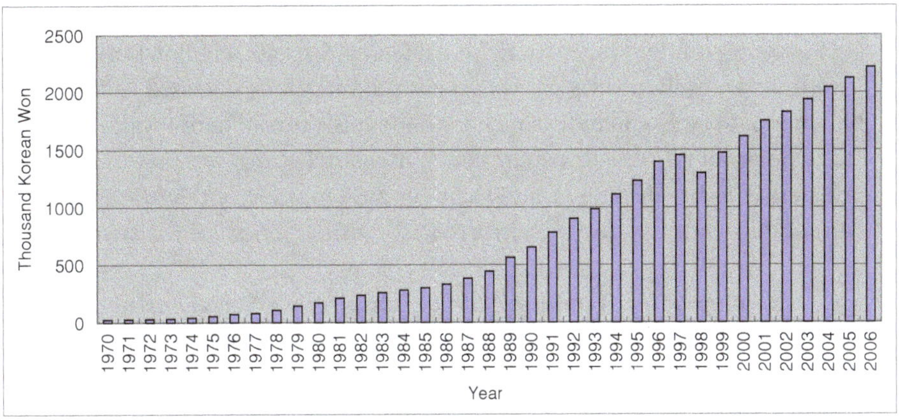

FIGURE 6.6 *Trend of consumption expenditure of urban labour households (nominal term: thousand Korean* won). SOURCE: SK, MONTHLY INCOME AND EXPENDITURE PER URBAN HOUSEHOLD, ANNUAL.

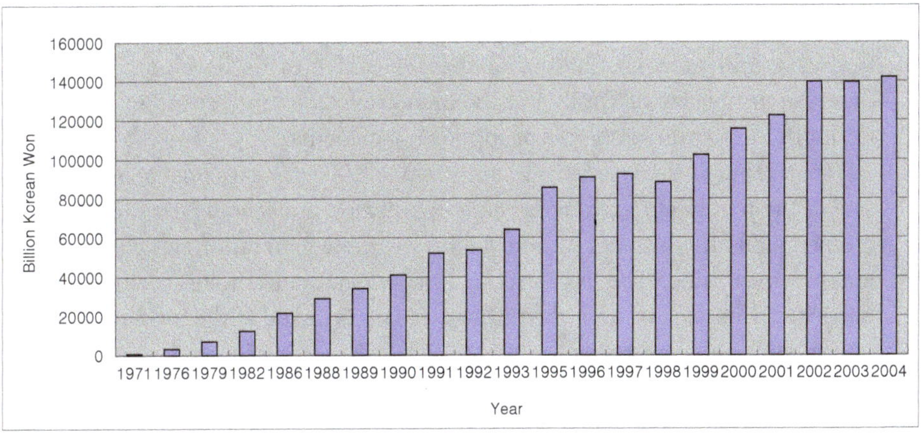

FIGURE 6.7 *Trends of retail sales (nominal term: billion Korean* won). SOURCE: SK, WHOLESALE AND RETAIL TRADE CENSUS (1971, 1976, 1979, 1982), WHOLESALE AND RETAIL TRADE CENSUS WITH THE OVERALL ESTABLISHMENT STATISTICS (1986, 1991), WHOLESALE AND RETAIL TRADE SURVEY (1988, 1989, 1990, 1992, 1993, 1995, 1997, 1998, 1999, 2000, 2002, 2003, 2004), WHOLESALE, RETAIL TRADE AND SERVICE INDUSTRY CENSUS (1996, 2001).

its real rate of increase was also much more moderate than in the previous period.

The total amount of retail sales is one of the most important factors which can indicate the size of the domestic consumption market. Figure 6.7 shows that this was also critically affected by the financial crisis.

The total amount of retail sales, which recorded 90,906.9 billion Korean *won* (US$ 112,968.3 million) in 1996, slightly increased to 92,561.4 billion Korean *won* (US$ 97,325.9 million) in 1997. However, it dramatically declined to 88,400.9 billion *won* in 1998, when the shock from the crisis spread nationwide. Thanks to the policy of boosting consumption, it increased again after that time. Nevertheless, another decline of retail sales in 2003 may imply that the situation surrounding consumption has exacerbated considerably since the crisis.

2.3 *Change of the Population and Urbanization as Social Environments*

Social environments such as population and urbanization around the retail industry have maintained a harmonious influence on its development as in the previous period. The ratio of the population which lived in urban areas increased to 78.8 per cent of the whole population in 1995 and to 80 per cent in 2000, growing to 81.5 per cent in 2005. The whole population increased to 47.3 million in 2005 from 44.6 million in 1995 (SK, Population and Housing Census, annual). Population conditions became much more conducive to the development of the retail industry. The direction of the change in the family composition as a unit of consumption has been positive to its development. The decrease in the size of family but the increase in the number of families, for example, are significant pieces of supporting evidence.

What Table 6.1 shows us consistently since the 1970s is the decrease in the size of the family. One generation and one person households have firmly increased while the number of households over one generation has clearly decreased over time. The increase in one person households seems to be particularly noticeable after the mid-1990s. This is linked to the increase in the number of total households.

Figure 6.8 shows that the total number of households was 11.4 million in 1990, 13 million in 1995, 14.3 million in 2000, and 15.9 million in 2005. Most increments in the number of households were generated by those households concentrated in urban areas. Thus, of the 1.4 million increase in the number of households between 1995 and 2000 1.2 million were households in urban areas and a mere 0.2 million households in rural areas.

The increase in economically active females is also a remarkably influential factor on consumption patterns, and so on the development of the retail industry, as was pointed out in Chapter 4.

Its proportion, which had risen since the mid-1980s, was 49.8 per cent in 1997 but sharply declined to 47.1 per cent in 1998 due to the financial crisis. After that, however, it increased gradually to 50.2 per cent in 2006.

TABLE 6.1 *Trend of generations in household* (%)

	1970	1975	1980	1985	1990	1995	2000	2005
One person households**		4.2	4.8	6.9	9	12.7	15.5	20
One generation***	6.8	6.7	8.3	9.6	10.7	12.7	14.2	16.2
Two generations	70	68.9	68.5	67	66.3	63.3	60.8	55.4
Three generations	22.1	19.2	16.5	14.4	12.2	9.8	8.2	6.9
Over four generations	1.1	0.9	0.5	0.4	0.3	0.2	0.2	0.1

* The sum of figures in each year has been a bit under 100 since 1980 because non-relative households, which consist of members of non-blood relationship, have been classified as a separate item.
** One person households: household with just one member.
*** One Generation: household which consists of members of the same generation, like a married couple without children.
Source: SK, Population and Housing Census, annual

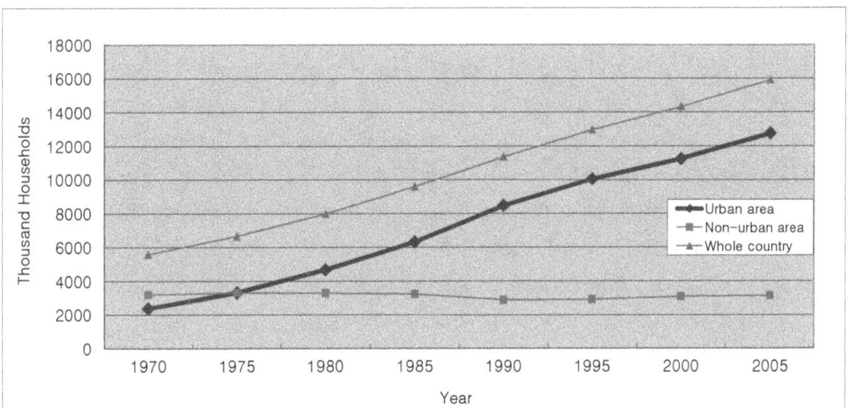

FIGURE 6.8 *Number of households.* SOURCE: SK, POPULATION AND HOUSING CENSUS, ANNUAL.

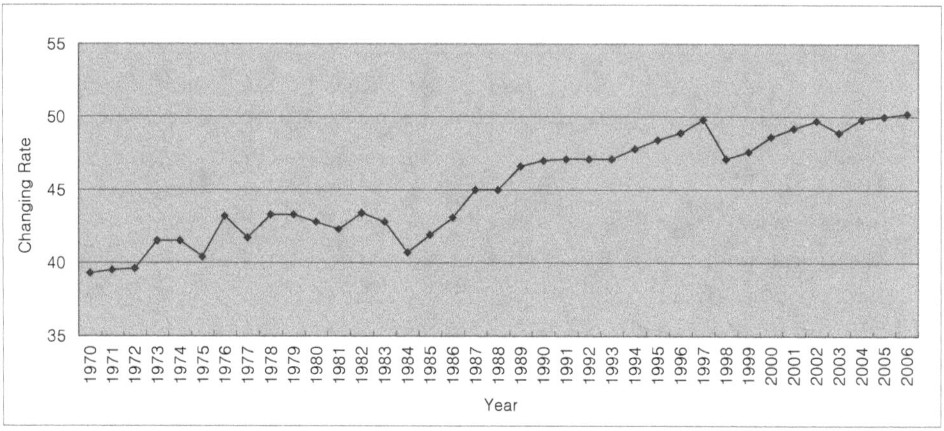

FIGURE 6.9 *Proportion of economically active females (the proportion = economically active female/all females fifteen years old and over).* SOURCE: SK, ECONOMICALLY ACTIVE POPULATION SURVEY, ANNUAL.

3 The Aggravation of Inequality and the Shrinking of Consumption

In general, it is highly possible that the aggravation of inequality is linked to the shrinking of consumption in the national economy. This is because of a more equal, higher APC. This view explains developments during the period from the mid-1980s to the mid-1990s in the Korean economy, when consumption was characterized by rapid expansion as income distribution improved. In contrast, the situation surrounding consumption after this period is likely to tell the opposite story. This can be explained by the shrinking of consumption as income distribution worsened following the financial crisis. This change in consumption had a considerable effect on the retail industry. Furthermore, it was a cause of the emergence of a new retail format, and a factor which encouraged a new trajectory for the retail evolution.

3.1 *The Aggravation of Inequality*

The problem of inequality has become more serious since the mid-1990s. The financial crisis considerably worsened this situation. One detrimental factor resulting from the crisis was the instability of the employment system and the increase in unemployment. For example, while the average unemployment rate per annum was 2.7 per cent from 1985 to 1996, it has increased to over 4 per cent since 1997 (SK, Economically Active Population Survey, annual). Inequality of wealth, which usually includes real estate and financial assets, was also worsening with the rapid increase in the price of houses. This change in the economic situation was a critical factor for the differentiation of the consumption market under the conditions of consumption liberalization.

3.1.1 Inequality of Income

A more serious problem for consumption was the aggravation of income inequality since the financial crisis. This is because the distribution of current income as a form of purchasing power is more influential on consumption in the short term than the amount of wealth, which cannot necessarily be liquidated. In fact, as we have seen earlier, consumption was progressive under the conditions of improvement of income inequality between the mid-1980s and the mid-1990s, although wealth inequality was hardly improved during the period.

Table 6.2 shows the trend of the income Gini Coefficient of labour households in the urban sector. As it shows, their Gini has been exacerbated since the financial crisis in 1997. The level of Gini was around 0.285 before the crisis, but it rose to over 0.310 after the crisis. There is a tendency for the income data of the urban labour force to be relatively less uneven than those of other categories, such as for the self-employed and income for the whole country. This is because the urban labour force works under more similar conditions in terms of workplace and pay schemes, etc. compared with other categories such as self-employment and income for the whole country.

In fact, as the figures since 2003 in Table 6.2 show, the Gini of nationwide households, which has been officially published since 2003, has been higher than that of urban labour households. In this respect, the Ginis of nationwide households before 2003 can be expected to be higher than those of urban labour households that have been published. According to research by I Jeongu and I Seongrim, the Gini Coefficient of nationwide households recorded 0.384 in 1998 as it rose rapidly after the financial crisis, while that of urban labour households was 0.303 at the same time (I Jeongu and I Seongrim 2001: 93–94).

Apart from the Gini Coefficient, the ratio of the top to the bottom quintile of income is also an important indicator of inequality. According to Figure 6.10, the ratio of the top (fifth) to the bottom (first) quintile of income rose sharply from the level of 4.4 before the financial crisis to the level of 5.4 just after the crisis. This high level has continued long past the crisis.

In other words, the income gap shows a completely different level before and after the crisis. Just like the Gini, the ratio for nationwide households was worse than that of the urban sector. It was 7.23 in 2003, and rose to 7.64 in 2006.

TABLE 6.2 *Trend of Gini coefficients*

Year	Gini coefficient (urban sector)	Gini coefficient (nationwide)
1986	0.307	
1987	0.306	
1988	0.302	
1989	0.304	
1990	0.295	
1991	0.287	
1992	0.284	
1993	0.281	
1994	0.284	
1995	0.284	
1996	0.291	
1997	0.283	
1998	0.316	
1999	0.320	
2000	0.317	
2001	0.319	
2002	0.312	
2003	0.306	0.341
2004	0.31	0.344
2005	0.31	0.348
2006	0.31	0.351

Source: SK, Monthly Income and Expenditure per Urban Household, annual

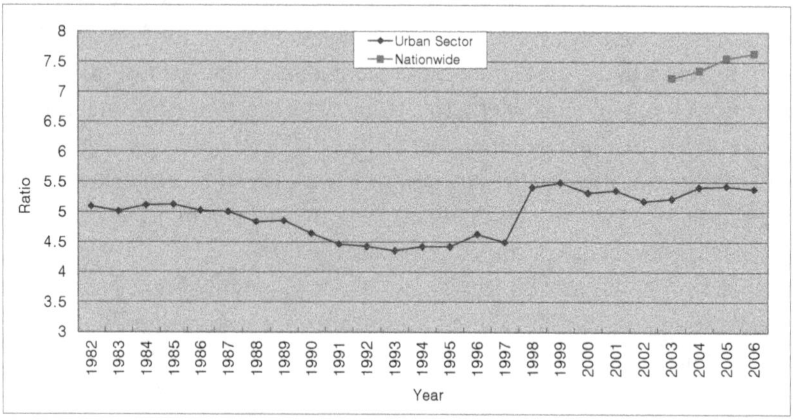

FIGURE 6.10 *Trend of the income gap: the top to the bottom quintile*). SOURCE: SK, MONTHLY INCOME AND EXPENDITURE PER URBAN HOUSEHOLD, ANNUAL.

3.1.2 Inequality of Wealth

We have already seen that inequality of wealth in terms of land has worsened since the 1970s. To examine this phenomenon, we have concentrated on the extremely uneven rate of increase in prices between urban and rural areas in accordance with the rapid industrialization and economic growth of the 1970s, and on the extremely uneven distribution of land ownership since the mid-1980s. With the development of the financial market, the gap between financial assets was also identified as an important factor contributing to the inequality of wealth since the mid-1980s. Consequently, wealth inequality has continuously worsened during the 1980s, whereas income inequality improved during the same period. Basically, the situation surrounding the inequality of wealth since the mid-1990s is almost the same as the situation since the mid-1980s. However, the gap in wealth has become bigger and bigger. This can also be shown through the huge gap in the rate of increase in house prices.

Figure 6.11 shows the trend of land prices since the mid-1970s. According to the figure, the regional gap in the rate of increase of land prices decreases among big cities, small and medium cities and counties over time. Figure 6.12 illustrates the indexes of the rate of increase in land prices in regions which are calculated by the criterion of 100 at 1995.

As the graph shows, there is nearly no difference in the rate of increase in land prices in the various regions. Rather, there is even a tendency for the rate of increase in big cities to be lower than that in other regions. Of course, this does not mean that land values have converged towards similar levels amongst regions since 1995, because there was already a huge existing gap. However, it is evident that the difference in the rate of increase amongst regions has not been a crucial factor in aggravating the inequality of land wealth, at least since the mid-1990s.

The distribution of land ownership is what counts. Because of the lack of data on land distribution, this chapter makes use of the same data used in Chapter 4. Table 6.3 illustrates the cumulative size of lands owned by the population in just two years, 1986 and 2005. According to the table, the situation in 1986 already seems to be serious, in that just 5 per cent of the total population owned 65.2 per cent of the total private land, but the situation deteriorated over the following twenty years.

Just 1 per cent of the population owned over 50 per cent of total private land in 2005 and the share of 5 per cent of the population expanded to around 83 per cent in the same period. With this, what should be noted concerning the matter of inequality, is the change in house prices, particularly since the late 1990s. Figure 6.13 shows the trends of house prices in the whole nation and in Seoul. Clearly, Seoul has led the rate of increase of house prices, particularly

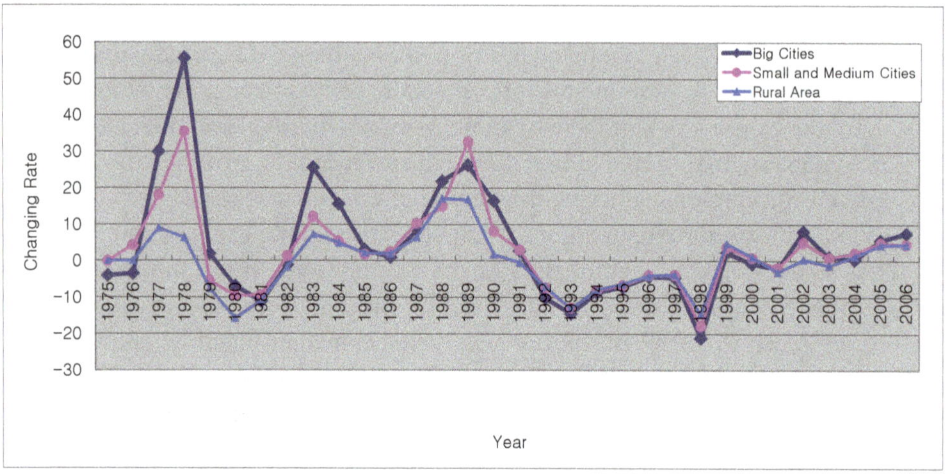

FIGURE 6.11 *Trend of land prices (real term calculated by the author through* GDP *deflator based on 100 at 2000).* SOURCE: MOCT, SURVEY OF LAND PRICES, ANNUAL.

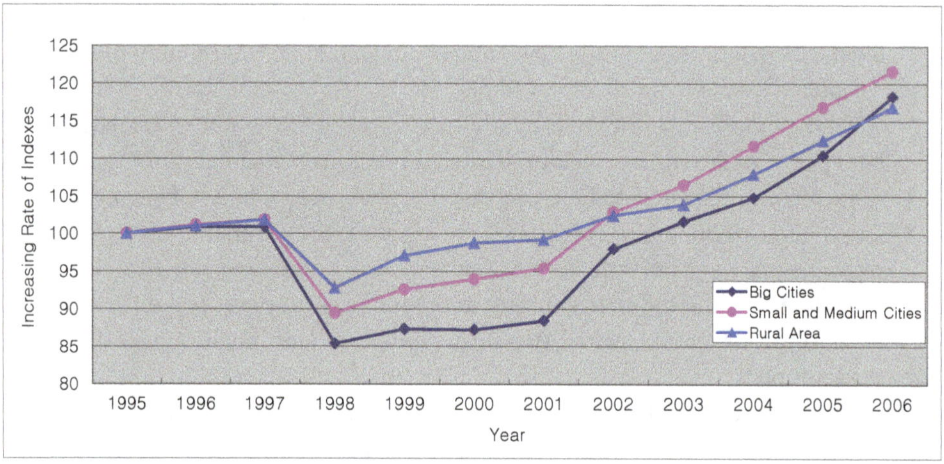

FIGURE 6.12 *Indexes of land prices in regions since 1995 (Indexes calculated by the author, based on 100 at 1995).* SOURCE: MOCT, SURVEY OF LAND PRICES, ANNUAL.

since the end of the 1990s. This is a phenomenon which is especially worth taking into account because the metropolitan area of Seoul is a place where the concentration of the population is much higher, given that as much as 50 per cent of the whole population is living there.

Thus, this implies that wealth inequality has expanded through the gap in house prices between Seoul and other areas. Then, how was the situation in Seoul in relation to house prices? What we need to do in order to grasp this

TABLE 6.3 *Distribution of privately owned lands*

The ratio of the population	1986	2005
Top 1 %		51.5
Top ~2 %		65.3
Top ~5 %	65.2	82.7
Top ~10 %	76.9	91.4
Top ~20 %	87.7	93.4
Top ~30 %	93.1	

Source: I Jinsun 1993: 113; MOGAHA, Gae-in-byeol-to-ji-so-yu-bun-po-hyeon-hwang-myeon-jeog-gi-jun [State of Distribution of Individual Landownership-By Owned Size], 2005

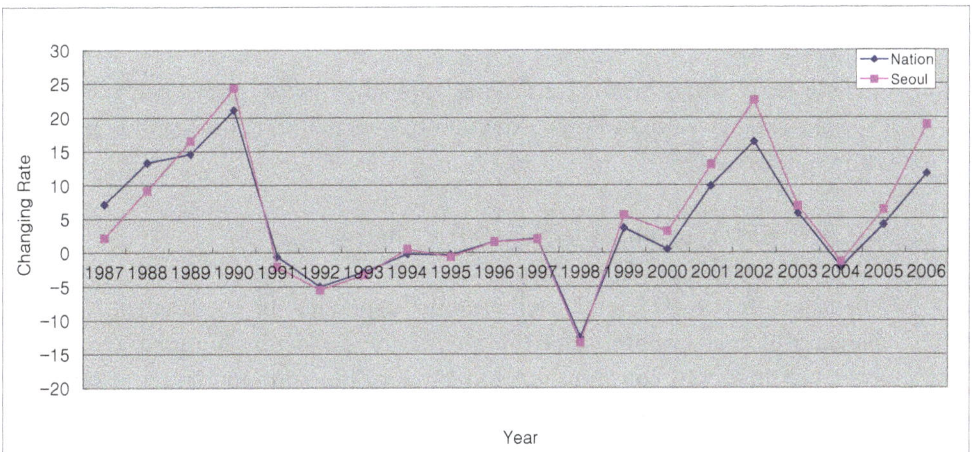

FIGURE 6.13 *Trends of house prices (real term calculated by the author, based on 100 at 2003).* SOURCE: MOCT, SURVEY OF HOUSE PRICES, ANNUAL.

situation is to trace the difference in the rate of increase of house prices between north and south of the river in Seoul.

Figure 6.14 shows the trends in the areas to the north and the south of the Han River. According to the figure, the south of river, which began to be developed at the end of the 1970s, has generally led the rise in house prices since the late 1980s. This trend has been more conspicuous since the late 1990s. In fact, this has been one of the most serious social issues, and has been instrumental

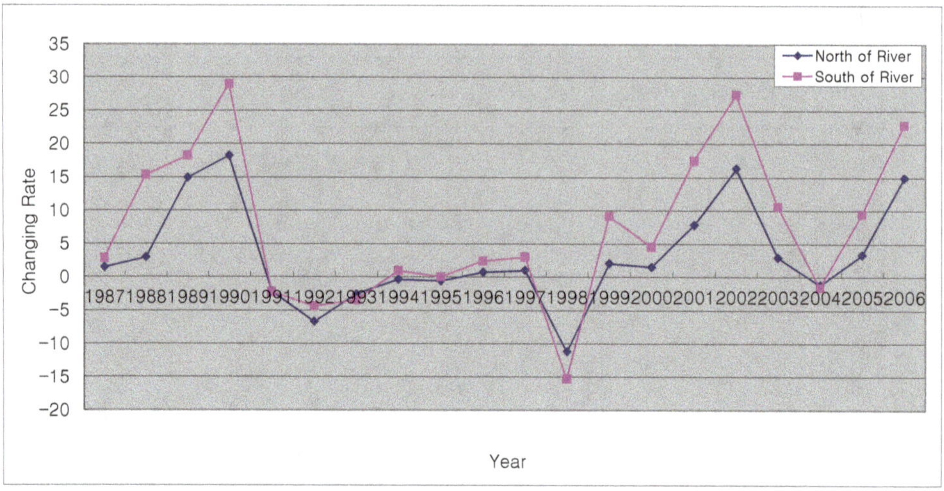

FIGURE 6.14 *Difference in house prices between regions in Seoul (real term calculated by the author, based on 100 at 2003).* SOURCE: MOCT, SURVEY OF HOUSE PRICES, ANNUAL.

in some fairly strong regulations being applied to house prices and trade.[2] Thus, the gap in wealth has been expanding through differences in house prices in Seoul as well.

3.2 *Shrinking of and Differentiation of Consumption*

3.2.1 Shrinking of Consumption

When consumption is liberalized it becomes dependent on income. Thus, the character of consumption since the financial crisis can be summed up as a general shrinking of consumption and greater differentiation in accordance with income levels. This change in consumption is linked to a more competitive environment for the retail industry and thus is likely to force the industry to try new strategies or to innovate. Shrinking consumption will be shown nationwide and through the urban sector.

As Figure 6.15 shows the rate of increase of both income and consumption has slowed down sharply since the mid-1990s. In particular, shrinking consumption was more serious than that of income in the second half of the 1990s, which is essentially a consequence of the financial crisis. What should be noted here is that consumption decreased more sharply than income despite the serious economic recession. This suggests that consumers were greatly

2 The Korean government imposed thirty or so special policies for cooling house prices since 2003 (*Younhap News Agency* 31 August 2005b).

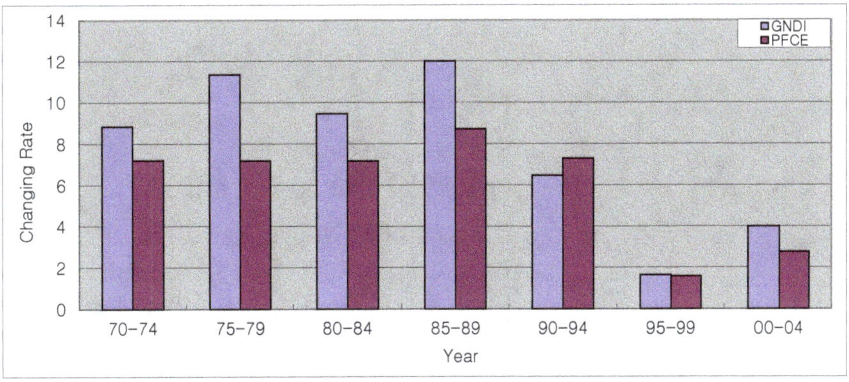

FIGURE 6.15 *Trends of income and consumption (GNDI: average rate of change per annum of Gross National Disposable Income (İn); PFCE: Average Rate of Change per annum of Private Final Consumption Expenditure (Ċn) (real term calculated by the author, based on 100 at 2000).* SOURCE: BOK, NATIONAL ACCOUNTS, ANNUAL.

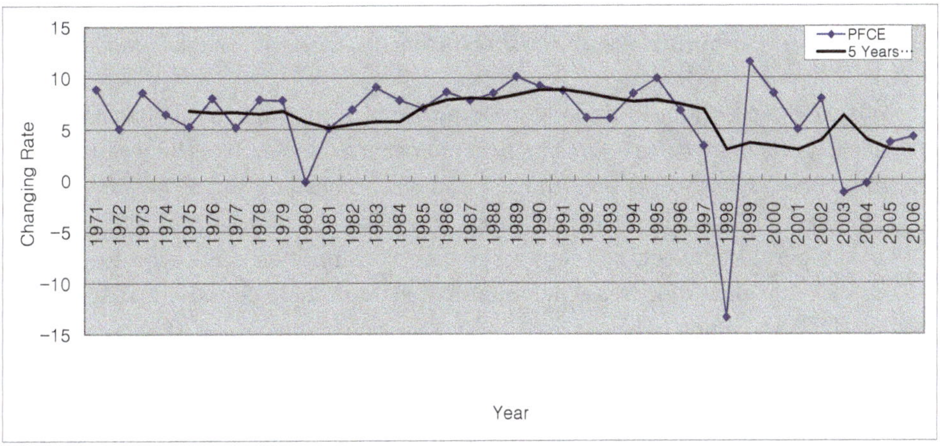

FIGURE 6.16 *Rate of increase of PFCE (PFCE: changing rate of Private Final Consumption Expenditure (Ċn); real term calculated by the author, based on 100 at 2000.* SOURCE: BOK, NATIONAL ACCOUNTS, ANNUAL.

affected by the recession to the extent that they reined in their spending; thus, consumption attitudes became extremely conservative. This seems clear when comparing the trends in the first and second halves of the 1990s with the corresponding periods in the 1980s.

Figure 6.16 shows the trend in final consumption expenditure (PFCE) in real terms since the early 1970s. What we see is that the rate of increase in the curve of PFCE, has been remarkably moderate and unstable since the crisis. A

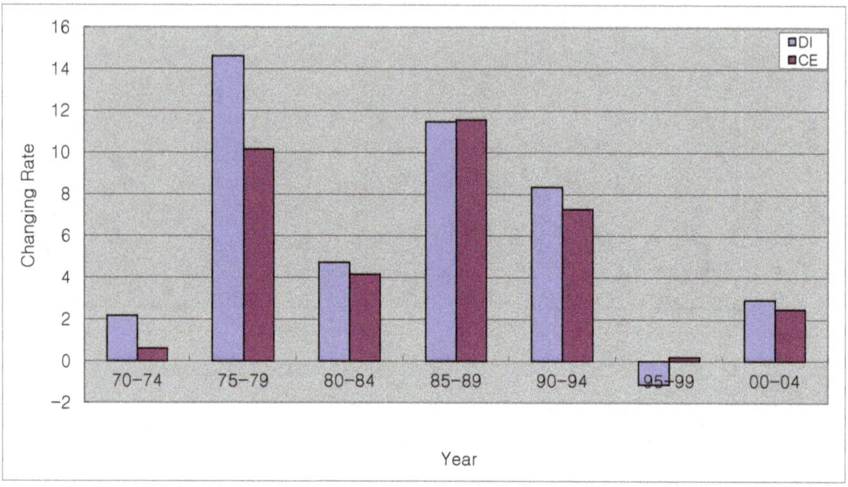

FIGURE 6.17 *Trends in income and consumption of urban labour households* (DI: *average rate of change per annum of Disposable Income* ($\dot{I}u$); CE: *Average Rate of Change per annum of Consumption Expenditure* ($\dot{C}u$) (*real term calculated by the author through the Consumer Price Index* (CPI) *based on 100 at 2005*). SOURCE: SK, MONTHLY INCOME AND EXPENDITURE PER URBAN HOUSEHOLD, ANNUAL.

decrease per annum in the real PFCE occurred thre times in 1998, 2003 and 2004. A rate of increase of under 5 per cent occurred seven times between 1997 and 2006. This is worse than in the 1970s when consumption repression was enforced. A decrease in PFCE occurred only once, the minus 0.2 of 1980, even in the period between 1971 and 1985 when consumption repression existed. The average rates of increase per annum of PFCE in these periods also support this fact. According to Figure 6.16, the average rate of increase of PFCE was 6.53 per cent per annum between 1970 and 1985 and it increased to 8.11 per cent per annum between 1986 and 1996. In contrast, between 1997 and 2006, it declined dramatically to just 2.6 per cent per annum. The rate of increase since the crisis is much lower than half that of the previous period.

Figure 6.17 shows that the economic situation in the urban sector was more unstable than that of the whole country in the second half of the 1990s. While the rate of increase of income at the national level declined sharply, the income of the urban sector decreased absolutely for the first time, since the 1970s, and consumption was also extremely sluggish in the period. Even after 2000, the situation of income and consumption was not better in the urban sector than in the whole country.

Figure 6.18 gives the trend in the rates of change of monthly consumption expenditure of working households in the urban sector since 1971. Real term is calculated by CPI with base of 100 in 2005. Broadly, the general shape of the

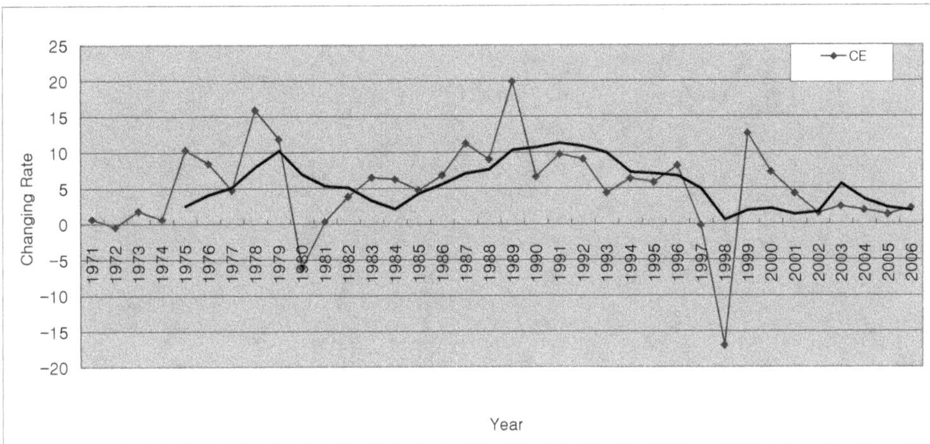

FIGURE 6.18 *Rate of increase of* CE *(*CE*: changing rate of Consumption Expenditure (*$\dot{C}u$*) (real term calculated by the author through the Consumer Price Index (*CPI*) based on 100 at 2005).* SOURCE: SK, MONTHLY INCOME AND EXPENDITURE PER URBAN HOUSEHOLD, ANNUAL.

figure is hardly different from the trend of PFCE in Figure 6.16. A small difference in both figures seems to be the degree of fluctuation of the rate of change in accordance with the business cycle. This figure shows more fluctuations than the figure of PFCE, presumably due to the urban sector which is more sensitive to the business cycle. What should be noted in Figure 6.18 is the consumption situation since the financial crisis. This illustrates the extremely moderate rate of increase of the consumption expenditure of labour households in the urban sector since the crisis.

This is clearer in the comparison of this period with others. According to Figure 6.18, the average rate of increase of CE was 4.46 per cent per annum between 1970 and 1985 and it increased to 8.89 per cent per annum between 1986 and 1996. In contrast, between 1997 and 2006, the average rate of increase of CE declined dramatically to just 1.51 per cent per annum. As a result, the average rate of increase of CE per annum since the crisis declined to a level of nearly one-sixth of that in the previous period. The shrinking of consumption in the urban sector was more dramatic than that of the whole country since the crisis, whereas the expansion of consumption in the urban sector was sharper than that of the whole country in the period of mass consumption.

3.2.2 Differentiation of Consumption

Here, we look at the differentiation of consumption through income quintile of working households in the urban sector. Figure 6.19 illustrates the ratios of

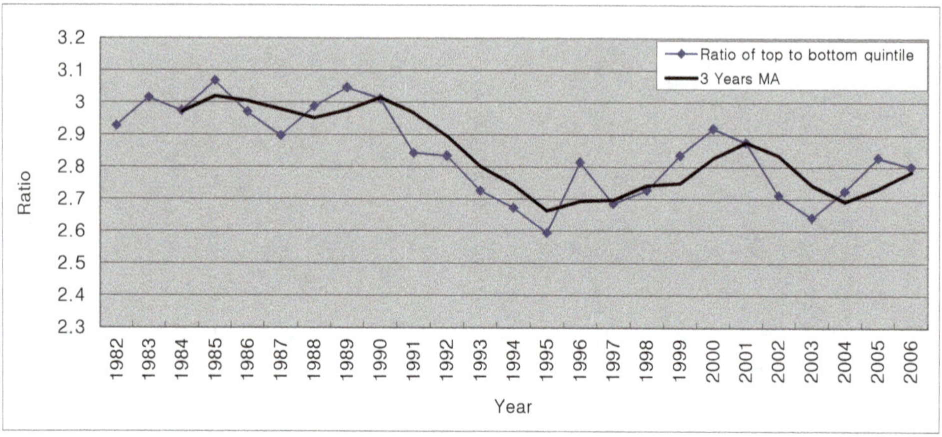

FIGURE 6.19 *Ratio of consumption: the top to the bottom quintile*). SOURCE: SK, MONTHLY INCOME AND EXPENDITURE PER URBAN HOUSEHOLD, ANNUAL.

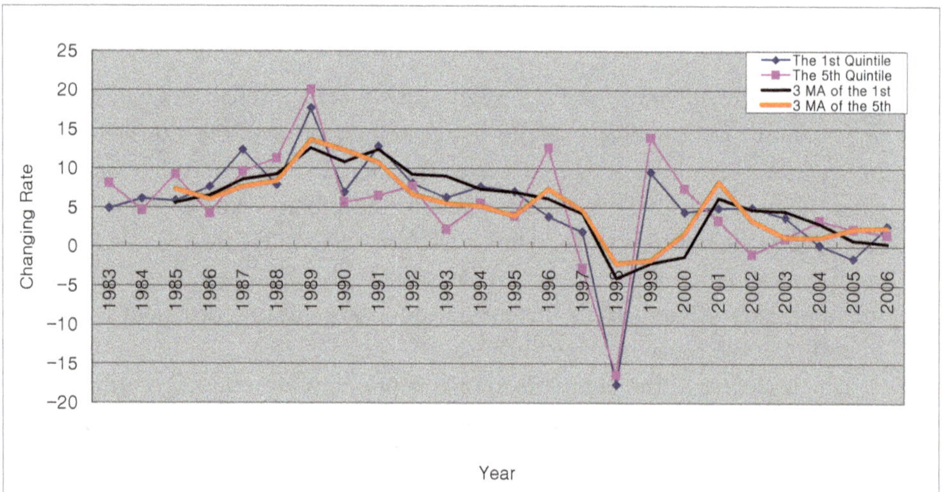

FIGURE 6.20 *Who was in the leading position of consumption? (real term calculated by the author through the Consumer Price Index (CPI) based on 100 at 2005)*. SOURCE: SK, MONTHLY INCOME AND EXPENDITURE PER URBAN HOUSEHOLD, ANNUAL.

consumption of the top (fifth) to the bottom (first) quintile of income in labour households in the urban sector since 1982. As is shown, broadly the ratio tends to decrease after the mid-1980s, and it particularly declines sharply from 1989 to 1995. As we have seen earlier, this is precisely consistent with the period of mass consumption.

However, since then, the tendency has reversed. This becomes especially clear from the financial crisis of 1997 to 2000. Thanks to the policy of boosting consumption, its differentiation had diminished by 2003, but it then shows a rising tendency. In sum, the differentiation of consumption has deepened since the crisis.

This is made clear by confirming who was in the leading position in the expansion of consumption. Figure 6.20 illustrates the trends of the changing rate of consumption expenditure and of its three years moving average in the first and the fifth quintiles.

What we can see in this figure is the clear exchange of the leading group in relation to consumption before and after the financial crisis. The rate of increase of consumption of the fifth quintile was overtaken by that of the first one before the crisis in the 1990s, but the relationship between them was reversed after the crisis. The fact that the first quintile initiated consumption before the crisis is linked to a decrease in differentiation of consumption between the rich and the poor in the period as we have seen in figure 6.19. However, the higher income group took the initiative in consumption among the income groups, and the gap between both widened since the crisis.

4 Return of the Department Stores to Luxury Goods with the Stratification of the Retail Industry

4.1 *Complete Opening and Its Effect*

The opening of the domestic market in the Korean economy began in 1981 when the government permitted the establishment of retail and wholesale shops of under 300 square metres, for just one operating category. After this, the limitation on the size of shops was expanded to 600 square metres in 1982, and the limitation on the number of traded items was also lifted in 1984. However, the number of foreign company shops which could be established was limited to just one (Gim Jundong et al. 2003: 65–66). The active opening of the domestic market began before and after the Uruguay Round which was a trade negotiation which lasted from 1986 to 1994. The Korean government announced that the domestic market was going to be opened in order to fulfil the Uruguay Round requirements and it announced a plan for a three-phased opening of the domestic market in 1988.

In the first stage, which began in 1989, the government permitted the import of technology from foreign retail companies and it deregulated the wholesale sector. Thanks to this, the existing big retailers imported technologies relating to the development of goods and to the operations of outlets from Japan, the

US and France (Choe Jangho et al. 1994: 7). During the second stage, which began in 1991, the government emphasized the opening of the retail sector. This allowed a foreign company that owned more than one shop to be able to build ten shops in the Korean domestic market. At the same time, the maximum size of shops that foreign companies could invest in was expanded to 1,000 square metres. The third stage began in 1993. The maximum size of shops was increased to 3,000 square metres and the number of shops to twenty. Following this, regulation of both the size of and the number of shops was completely lifted in 1996, and the establishment of discount stores by foreign companies has been permitted since then (KCCI 1999: 7–8). The discount store as a format that sells various goods at lower prices than other types of retailers, varies both in the assortment of goods it offers, and in the operation of the format. Thus, some researchers distinguish them according to their characteristics. In this respect, Walmart can be classified as a traditional discount store or US-type discount store which deals only with dry goods. Carrefour and Tesco (HomePlus in Korea) may be classified as hypermarket or European type discount stores which deal with both dry goods and foodstuffs. They can be regarded as a type of combination of the traditional discount dry goods store with the supermarket selling foodstuffs. If these two types of discount stores are classified in accordance with their range of goods, Costco, which operates shops by membership and is called a membership wholesale club, can be distinguished from them in terms of the operations of the shop (Seo Yonggu and An Yeonghyo 1999: 8–9; An Gwangho and Jo Jaeun 2003: 62–63; O Sejo and Bak Jinyong 2004: 94–102). The fact that all these types of retail format have been permitted since 1996 explains why the year 1996 has been called the beginning of a new period for the Korean distribution industry. However, the establishment of department stores by foreign companies was not permitted at that time to protect domestic companies. This protection, however, did not last long. As foreign investment was desperately needed after the financial crisis in 1997, this restriction was lifted from 1998 (Gim Jundong et al. 2003: 67)

Facing this dramatic change in the retailing environment, the government replaced a basic law affecting the distribution industry in order to rationalize the industry's management structure. For this the new 1997 law, 'Law for the Development of the Distribution Industry', focused on supporting the distribution industry. In particular, unlike the old laws, it concentrated on the deregulation of large rather than small retail institutions (MOLEG 1997). Before and after this change, foreign companies which entered the Korean domestic market were mainly concentrated in the field of discount stores, even if various types of foreign retail companies were expected to make inroads into the Korean domestic market (Gim Jundong et al. 2003: 70).

TABLE 6.4 *Number of established foreign discount stores*

	1996	1997	1998	1999	2000	2001	2002
Carrefour	3		3	5	9	2	3
Wal-Mart	2	2		1	1	3	6
HomePlus (Tesco)				1	5	7	7
Costco			1		1	1	

Source: KOSCA, *Yu-tong-eob-che yeon-gam* (The Yearbook of Retail Companies), annual

According to Table 6.4, the most aggressive foreign discount store company is Carrefour from France. Carrefour, which moved into the Korean domestic market in the first year of its opening, had been the largest discount store company among the foreign retail companies until it withdrew from the Korean market in 2006. Walmart, which is the largest retail company in the world, also aggressively moved into the Korean market but its performance was lower than that of Carrefour. HomePlus's penetration strategy was very different from these two companies; whereas Carrefour and Walmart directly invested with 100 per cent ownership from the beginning, HomePlus established a company as a joint venture with Samsung and gradually bought out Samsung. Under this strategy, it has further expanded the size of its investments over time. Costco's investment has been smaller than all of its foreign competitors, even if it also has been one of the most popular retailers among consumers. Investment from these foreign companies was a considerable factor in the discount store industry since their opening because the format of the discount store was not popular until then. In fact, the first discount store in Korea was built in 1993 in Chang-dong in Seoul by the Shinsegae Department Store (An Gwangho and Jo Jaeun 2003: 63). However, it is perhaps par for the course that this new format needed more time to gain popularity. In 1996, the total number of discount store shops was just thirty-four in Korea and thus the ratio of foreign companies already recorded 14.7 per cent in this field. As the ratio grew, it reached a level of 28.9 per cent in 2002 (KOSCA, *Yu-tong-eob-che yeon-gam* (The Yearbook of Retail Companies), annual). In particular, the period since the financial crisis has been a golden age for discount stores. The market opening and the influx of foreign discount stores created the momentum to enable people to get to thoroughly familiarise themselves with the format, which had previously been so unpopular. This is because the opening of the market and its effects constituted an important social issue at that time. What was more, the differentiation of income which had been deepening since the mid-1990s, required a new retail format for people who could not continue consuming luxuries.

4.2 *Rapid Growth of the Discount Store and the Stratification of the Retail Industry*

As mentioned, a picture of the retail industry since 1996 can be drawn as a conspicuous convulsion combined with a complete opening of the domestic market and the emergence of a new retail format throughout the serious economic crisis. In general, economic recession can be said to have created the momentum for the emergence of the new retail format because consumers become more sensitive to prices due to the fall in their income. In this regard, it is evident that the financial crisis following the market opening provided the momentum for structural change in the retail industry from the late 1990s in Korea. As a new retail format, discount stores have rapidly grown in this environment since the late 1990s. Figure 6.21 shows that total sales of discount stores in 1995 was 672.3 billion Korean *won* (US$ 0.87 billion), which was just some 6 per cent of total sales of department stores which amounted to 10,697.2 billion Korean *won* (US$ 13.87 billion).

Discount stores' total sales increased seven times over three years, as they generated 4,973.9 billion Korean *won* (US$ 3.56 billion) in 1998, and they eventually overtook department stores' sales of 17,252 billion Korean *won* (US$ 14.5 billion), by generating 19,509 billion Korean *won* (US$ 16.4 billion in 2003. Since that time, the gap between both has been steadily widening.

The gap in growth between these two retail formats is clearer from the indexes shown in Table 6.5 which are calculated from a base of 100 in 1995. The sales indexes of department stores have never been over 200 since 1995. Their highest index was 169.4 in 2006.

However, that of discount stores was twenty times bigger at 2,051.4 in 2001 and was over thirty-five times bigger at 3,789.6 in 2006. Whereas sales of department stores increased by just 1.8 per cent in 1997 and decreased by minus 9.8 per cent in 1998, due to the financial crisis, those of discount stores increased by 69.7 per cent in 1997 and by 56.8 per cent in 1998. Thus, the financial crisis was rather a good opportunity for the discount store. Even if the rate of increase of sales of discount stores has become more moderate over time, the increase in their total sales is still robust.

Figure 6.22 shows that the ratio of sales of discount stores in total retail sales has also undergone a dramatic change since 1995. It was just 0.78 per cent compared to 12.5 per cent for department stores in 1995. However, its growth has been very rapid since then. Like trends of sales, figures of its ratio in total retail

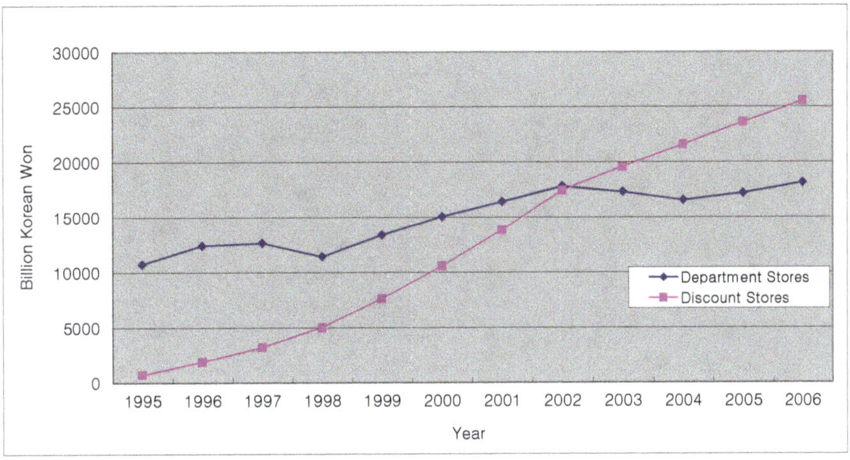

FIGURE 6.21 *Value of sales of department stores and discount stores (1. Sales of department stores in 1995, 1996 are calculated by the author through sales indexes by retail business type, based on 100 at 2000; 2. Sales of Discount Stores in 1995, 1996 and 1997 are calculated by the author through sales indexes by retail business type, based on 100 at 2000).* SOURCE: SK, CURRENT WHOLESALE AND RETAIL TRADE SURVEY, ANNUAL.

TABLE 6.5 *Indexes of value of sales in department stores and discount stores*

	Department stores	Discount stores
1995	100	100
1996	115.8	278.1
1997	117.9	471.9
1998	106.4	739.8
1999	124.6	1126.1
2000	140.3	1562.5
2001	153	2051.4
2002	166.3	2588.9
2003	161.3	2901.7
2004	154.3	3197
2005	160.4	3499.9
2006	169.4	3789.6

* Indexes are calculated by the author, based on 100 at 1995.
Source: SK, Current Wholesale and Retail Trade Survey, annual

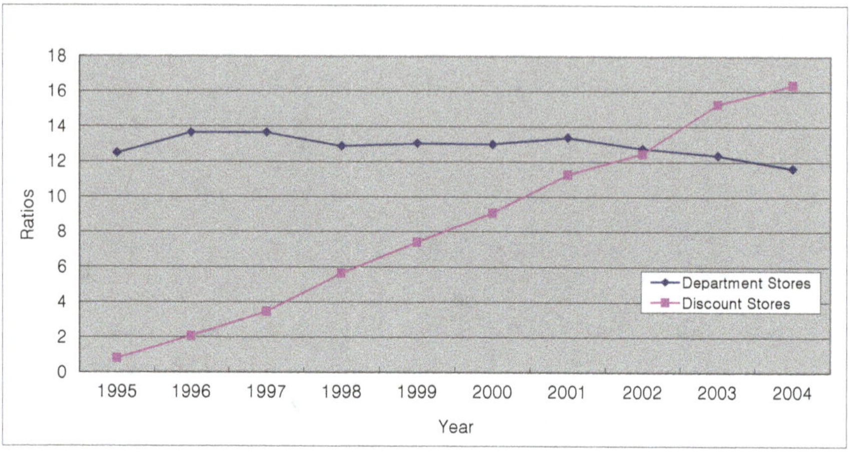

FIGURE 6.22 *Ratios of sales of both formats in total retail sales (1. Sales of department stores in 1995, 1996 are calculated by the author through sales indexes by retail business type; 2. Sales of discount stores in 1995, 1996 and 1997 are calculated by the author through sales indexes by retail business type).* SOURCE: SK, WHOLESALE AND RETAIL TRADE SURVEY (1995, 1997–2000, 2002–2004, ANNUAL), WHOLESALE, RETAIL TRADE AND SERVICE INDUSTRY CENSUS (1996, 2001), CURRENT WHOLESALE AND RETAIL TRADE SURVEY, ANNUAL.

sales before and after the financial crisis were quite impressive, as they increased without a pause while those of department stores declined or were sluggish.

The ratio increased to 5.6 per cent in 1998 from 2.1 per cent in 1996. This implies that sales of discount stores were still noticeably robust although sluggish sales were a general phenomenon in the retail industry, as well as in department stores. After the ratio increased rapidly again to 15.3 per cent in the recession of 2003, it has remained vigorous.

This emergence and rapid growth of the new retail format since the crisis was directly linked to the differentiation of the retail industry. In fact, it is clear that the department store industry was not ruined, although its stagnation was emphasized until now, compared with the rapid growth of the discount store industry. Its market share in whole retail sales was at the level of over 10 per cent even in 2004, even though it was lower than that of the discount stores. In this respect, it is highly possible that the growth of the discount stores demonstrated a reduction in market share of traditional retailers rather than department stores. In other words, this retail format, which grew more rapidly than the department store, emerged between the department store industry and traditional retailers, and appeared to take a market share away mainly from traditional retailers. The retail industry, which had been composed mostly of department stores and traditional retailers, thus changed to a tripartite structure. This can be considered a division within the modern retail sector, which was now composed of both department stores and discount stores whereas previously, since the 1970s, the modern retail sector had consisted of only the department store industry. Department stores had been the only modern retail format in existence even during the period of mass consumption because they moved from being a purveyor of luxury goods to one of popular goods. In this respect, the structure of the Korean retail industry had been unique because the emergence of mass consumption generally results in the differentiation of the consumption market with the emergence of proper retail formats for mass consumption such as supermarkets and general merchandise stores. The emergence of the discount store format thus implies that the structure of the Korean retail industry performed according to the general trajectory of the retail evolution. As an appropriate retail format for mass consumption emerged and grew during the economic crisis and the liberalization, the modern retail sector in Korea divided. As a result, the tripartite structure of the Korean retail industry took shape: the department store serving as an upmarket store; the discount store serving the middle market; the traditional market catering for the lower end of the marketplace.

4.3 *Back to Luxury for the Department Store*

4.3.1 Fierce Competition in the Existing Retail Market

Both the opening of the domestic market and the coming of the financial crisis have been directly linked to the emergence of the new retail format in the Korean market, and this has inevitably caused fierce competition in the mass retail market. It was clear that this change of situation contributed to the depressed growth of department stores, which had led the mass retail market since the emergence of mass consumption in the mid-1980s. While the Korean department stores had changed their strategy to one of adding lower prices and popular goods to their existing structure in order to obtain market share of the emerging mass consumption market since the mid-1980s, the basic strategy in developing the new retail format was that of lower prices and popular goods. In other words, it mirrored the situation in which department stores had to withdraw from the middle market. In fact, new retailers have been more competent than department stores in the mass consumption market. One key indicator of this is that the number of their outlets has increased more rapidly than those of department stores. The trends of the figures in Table 6.6 clearly show the differences between the discount store and the department store. Whereas the number of department store shops has been decreasing since 1998, the number of discount store shops has been increasing.

TABLE 6.6 *Number of outlets in department stores and discount stores*

	1996	1998	2000	2002
Department stores	106	116	101	86
Discount stores	40	87	123	233

Source: KCCI, Analysis of Current Retail Management, annual.

It is likely that the number of discount store shops outnumbered that of department store shops in 1999 and there were nearly three times the number compared to department stores in 2002. This is related to the faster establishment of relatively small shops by discount stores in residential areas. In fact, the average size of discount stores, which was 11,364 square metres in 2002, was about 30 per cent smaller than that of department stores which averaged 15,600.9 square metres in the same year (KCCI 2003: 28, 45). To that extent, investors seemed able to decide and carry out their projects quickly. Second, their range of goods is more fitted to the mass consumption market than those of department stores. This is evident with foodstuffs, which represent essential rather than luxury goods. While the ratio of foodstuffs among discount store goods is over 50 per cent in value of sales, that of department stores is just roughly 15 per cent, although there are periodic variations (KCCI 2003: 25, 44). Accordingly, the discount store format seems to have occupied a more favourable position than that of the department store for mass consumption in residential areas. Finally, one of the most important things which makes discount stores more competitive is price competitiveness. According to a survey by KCA in 1998, 74.1 per cent of 701 respondents indicated that the most important reason for consumers buying goods in discount stores was lower prices (KCA 1998: 21). In fact, the prices of goods on offer in discount stores, were analyzed as roughly 10 per cent lower than those of department stores (KCA 1998: 34).

The intense competitiveness of the retail market which emerged since the mid-1990s has provided a disadvantageous environment for department stores. This critical factor has driven department stores out of the mass market.

4.3.2 Emergence of New Markets for Luxuries

The expansion of the income gap is linked to the differentiation of consumption during liberalization when no consumption repression is present. After the financial crisis, the Korean socio-economic situation coincided with this condition. As we have seen, both the wealth and income gaps had expanded

TABLE 6.7 *The change of sales in the department stores*

	1995	1996	1997	1998	1999	2000	2001	2002
Apparel	42.7	46.2	44.4	44.2	46.6	49.1	53.9	55.3
Foodstuffs	20.9	18.4	22.3	21.4	21.1	15.7	18.6	15.1

Source: KCCI, Analysis of Current Retail Management, annual.

rapidly since the crisis. What is more, consumption liberalization from the mid-1980s had already become familiar to people. This environment provided a new market for luxuries for the department store industry. Although the market for luxuries was not absent before, this environmental change provided fresh opportunities for the department store industry which faced real difficulty in the existing middle market. Department stores began to change direction strategically in the mid-1990s as preparation for the liberalization of the domestic market; this change has sharpened since the late 1990s with the establishment of new shops specializing in globally luxurious brands such as Prada, Bally and Wedgwood (Gim Inho 2006: 114–115).

This change is shown in the ratio of apparel goods and foodstuffs to total sales of department stores. A survey by KCCI illustrates opposite trends for apparel and foodstuffs, as shown in Table 6.7.

The ratio of apparel to total sales rapidly increased from 42.7 per cent in 1995 to 55.3 per cent in 2002. In contrast to this, the ratio of foodstuffs to total sales decreased from 22.3 per cent in 1997, to 15.1 per cent in 2002. In particular, this change in the strategy has been conspicuous since the financial crisis. Thus, it can be presumed that the strategic change of the department stores has accelerated from the time of the crisis. This strategic change would not have been successful without new markets for luxuries. In this respect, it is likely that the better managerial performance of the department stores, which has been achieved since the late 1990s, can be understood as the successful adaptation to cater for new markets. The department stores' rate of margins shows that the ratio of income to expenses has improved since 2000. According to Figure 6.23, department stores' rates of margin maintained a level of 24 per cent until the mid-1990s when in 1998, it declined to 21.66 per cent due to the financial crisis.

However, the margin increased to 32.85 per cent in 2005, bouncing back again after that. In particular, the trend since 2001 seems to indicate that there has been a dramatic change in the management of department stores. This

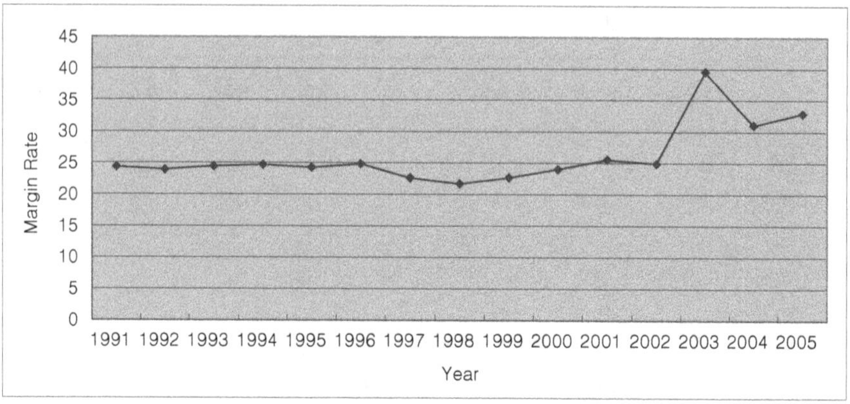

FIGURE 6.23 *Trend in department stores' rates of margin (rate of margin = (1-cost of sales/sales) * 100 which represents gross margin as a percentage of sales and so shows what a firm makes on its cost of sales, revealing productivity and efficiency).* SOURCE: BOK, FINANCIAL STATEMENT ANALYSIS, ANNUAL.

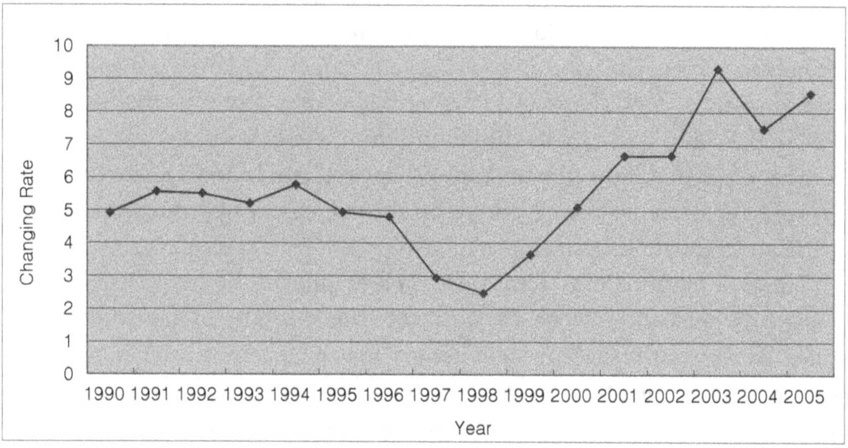

FIGURE 6.24 *Trend of ratio of operating income to sales of department stores.* SOURCE: BOK, FINANCIAL STATEMENT ANALYSIS, ANNUAL.

implies that their productivity and efficiency has been higher since the crisis. The trend in operating income to sales also shows a similar trend to the margin rates.

The ratio of operating income to sales increases when the rate of increase of operating income is higher than that of sales.

Figure 6.24 shows that the trend in the ratio of operating income to sales was maintained at the level of 5 per cent and 6 per cent until 1995, but diminished to less than half that level during the financial crisis. After that, the

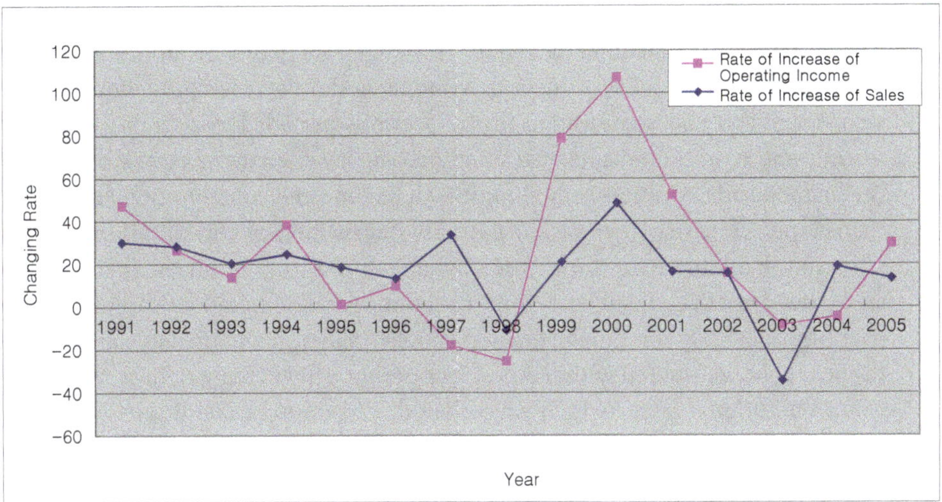

FIGURE 6.25 *Relationship between sales and operating income of department stores.* SOURCE: BOK, FINANCIAL STATEMENT ANALYSIS, ANNUAL.

change to over 7 per cent indicates that profit structure of department stores had improved.

Figure 6.25 allows the curve for the ratio of operating income to sales to be disaggregated into both rates of increase. Through this figure, it can be understood that there was a conspicuous change in the profit structure before and after the financial crisis. Put simply, there was an increase in income while sales were relatively sluggish. Thus, it can be presumed that department stores were returning to the market for luxuries which have a higher margin per unit than staple goods. This presumption is more convincing if changes – such as the fierce competition in the middle market and the relative stagnation of their market share in total retail sales – are considered.

5 Conclusion

The Korean economy changed drastically before and after the financial crisis. The economic growth rate slowed and social stability worsened because of instability in the employment system. The income gap became bigger. In addition, the consumer market became turbulent because of the complete opening of the domestic market just before the crisis. Needless to say, this structural change of the Korean economy catalysed change in the retail industry.

First, one of the most important factors which influenced the retail industry was the change in consumer behaviour resulting from poor consumption conditions. As we have seen, a thriving economy and a decrease in income gap were beneficial for consumption in the previous period. The situation since the mid-1990s presented a reverse situation. The lower economic growth from the financial crisis dramatically shrank both income and consumption. In particular, the decrease in income and extreme sluggishness of consumption took place in the urban sector during the second half of the 1990s for the first time since the 1970s. Even if such a serious economic recession gradually improved over time, basically the Korean economy looked sluggish and unstable around the year 2000, compared with the previous period. The increase in income gap was an additional factor which exacerbated consumption conditions. While the rich had money for excess consumption, the poor were short of money for consuming even basic necessities. In this respect, the consumption environment of the Korean economy has been bad since the financial crisis, and it made the Korean consumer market more competitive in terms of demand. In addition, participation of foreign retailers in the Korean market due to market liberalization, significantly increased competitiveness in the consumption market in terms of the number of players. Furthermore, consumers become more sensitive to price in the recession. Yet, at that time, there was no modern retail format in the existing retail structure to accommodate these developments. The only modern retail format was the department store, which had broadly catered for upmarket consumption and some mass consumption until then. This situation was a necessary and sufficient condition for retail innovation. In other words, the Korean consumer market can be said to have been receptive to retail innovation at that time. Consumer sensitivity to prices could be satisfied through the evolution of the discount store format. Now the department store which had expanded its marketing since the 1980s, stood at the crossroads, deciding whether to move upmarket or downmarket. This indicates that stratification of the Korean retail industry was an inevitable consequence of economic development. As we have seen, the Korean department store industry chose to move upmarket, which was its original position in the retail hierarchy. As it ended its short golden age, its role at the lower end of the market has been gradually taken over by the discount store format since the mid-1990s. Since then, the discount store has led the mass market with explosive growth.

CHAPTER 7

Distinctive Evolution of Korean Retailing: Theoretical Consideration and Contemporary Developments

1 Introduction

This study concludes by summing up the recent evolutionary pattern of the department store and discount store formats, and reappraising the application to the Korean case of the evolutionary theory of retail development. In that respect this chapter moves away from the structure of the previous chapters in focussing on analysis of the present shape of these formats rather than their historical evolution. Nevertheless, the conclusion retains the historical perspective, in as far as it analyzes the current situation, through identifying a causal relationship between present and past retail formats.

This chapter contends that the department store enjoyed only a short heyday, but that this phenomenon was the natural result of the evolution of Korean retail institutions. It can be said to be an integral and unavoidable part of Korea's retail evolution. It was the outcome of the range of interactions between the three 'actors' in retail development that have been described, namely the government, the retailers and the consumer. This will therefore also continue to influence retail evolution in the future. This in turn leads to a need to re-examine application of the conflict theory of retailing, which argues that competition between different retailing formats is integral to the development and evolution of retailing. As we have seen, the absence of any serious survival game between the department store and discount store formats in Korea, calls this accepted theory into question. The department store has compliantly withdrawn from its existing market, and the discount store has quietly replaced it. We therefore have a relationship of cooperation, rather than conflict, between the two. The short heyday of the department store is closely related to this cooperation and peaceful situation. In other words, conflict theory is of limited explanatory power in relation to Korea's retail evolution. I argue for a distinctive pattern of evolution resulting from the distinct ownership structure in the Korean retail industry, one of the three elements mentioned above.

Whatever the reason for this distinctive evolution, there is no doubt that it is likely to play a significant role at the next stage of Korea's retail development. The Korean department store format occupied a significant part of the mass

 | DOI 10.1163/9789004274228_008

consumption market from the beginning of the period of mass consumption starting in the mid-1980s. This suggests a pattern different from that found in many other economies, in which major changes in consumption pattern, such as the development of mass consumption, tend to give rise to an environment that generates new retail formats, such as the discount store and the general merchandise store. As a result of competition with these new retail formats, it is common for department stores to adopt the strategy of focussing on luxury goods. However, despite the rise of mass consumption in Korea, it appears that the emergence and development of new retail formats better suited to such consumption needed more time, and were somewhat delayed. The late development of these new retail formats is not simply a matter of delayed emergence, it has also generated a certain kind of path dependence. A number of other factors both inside and outside the retail industry responded in particular ways to the gap, in turn creating conditions that are likely to continue to mean that Korean retail development possesses certain distinctive characteristics. One result of this distinct evolution has been the luxurious discount store format identified here as the Korean-style discount store (KDS), which will be discussed in this final chapter. It will be shown how the Korean-style discount store interacts with a pattern of consumer behaviour that became accustomed to a high level of department store service since the start of the period of mass consumption, and has been shaped by a longstanding environment of equal or uniform consumption.

2 The Short Heyday of the Department Store

The year 2003 is understood in the Korean retail industry as the beginning of a new era. This is because the leading position in the mass retail format changed to the discount store from the department store, as the former exceeded the latter in sales (Hitoshi 2003: 37). The heyday of the department store finished at most around fifteen years after the period of mass consumption started in the mid-1980s. Even if there were department stores before the period of mass consumption, as has been seen earlier, they were negligible in terms of market share and influence on the retail industry. That was the era of the traditional market. However, the department store in its heyday in the period of mass consumption took the initiative in innovation and in the modernization of the retail industry. As the only modern retail format in Korea, its market share rose rapidly, although it did not exceed that of traditional retailers. Its growth rate was the highest among all retail formats. This continued for around fifteen years. The fact that the discount stores' sales exceeded that of the department stores, however, seems to imply that the leading position in the retail industry was transferred from the department store to the discount store, and that the former's heyday is over. What should be taken into account here is that the heyday was much shorter than those of other countries. For instance, the 'Golden Age' of the department store lasted until the First World War in most Western countries even if there were some local differences. Its turnover had remarkably expanded up to that period (Perkins and Freedman 1999: 124). Since the department store format had emerged and developed the middle of the nineteenth century, the 'Golden Age' of the department store lasted around seventy years in these countries.

Even in comparison with the Japanese case, which was similar to the Korean example, its character looks clear. The Japanese department stores' role as the leading retailer lasted for over fifty years. The first department store in Japan was the Mitsukoshi Department Store. The 'department store proclamation' was issued by Osuke Hibi, the first senior managing director, in 1904. After that, Matsuzakaya began the operation of a department store in 1910 and subsequently Matsuya (1919), Takashimaya (1919), and Daimaru (1920) followed them (Larke 1994: 172). They were just retailers of luxury goods previously, but with the emergence of mass consumption, mainly in the urban sector after the 1920s, they became popular shops for the masses. The turning point of this strategy was the period of the early 1920s. After the First World War, the Japanese economy boomed, and urbanization and the growth of salaries accelerated the process. This led department stores to expand their range of goods to meet the demands of their rapidly increasing customer base. Second, the growth of large cities produced a movement of the population into the suburbs. This was linked to the emergence of private railways which connected the city with the suburbs. In this process, private railway companies took part in housing developments around suburban terminals and the construction of what were called 'terminal department stores' (Ikeo 1997: 150–151). Examples of major terminal department stores are Odakyu, Keio and Tobu in Tokyo, Sotetsu in Yokohama, Meitetsu in Nagoya, and Kintetsu, Hanshin, Hankyu and Sanyo, all in the Kansai area. Traditional department stores responded to this change of circumstance by means of a strategy of expansion through the opening of new branches. For instance, Mitsukoshi built Shinjuku Store in 1929, Ginza Store in 1930, Takamatsu Store in 1931 and Sapporo Store in 1932. Inevitably, this accelerated the establishment of modern management based retailing as a large-scale business (Larke 1994: 185–190). This type of competition and strategy in the department store industry seems to be quite similar to the Korean case since the 1980s. Taking the initiative in retail innovation, the department store was the only modern retail format that expanded its operating area in both countries, although in different periods. The Japanese department store industry, which suffered from the military economy and strong regulation in the 1930s, faced its second period of rapid development after the Second World War. The momentum of the economic boom came with the Korean War between 1950 and 1953. Thereafter, the Japanese economy entered a period of long-term economic growth. Domestic consumption expanded rapidly with the 'Income Doubling Plan' in 1960 (Ishihara 1997: 106). This second development period of the department store, however, came out of fierce competition with another retail format, the Self-Service Discount Department Store (SSDDS), or the Japanese General Merchandise Store (GMS) (Ikeo 1997: 126–127). SSDDS which came later but achieved competitiveness, due to having lower prices than the department store, grew rapidly. For example, Daiei, the largest GMS, which was established in 1957, was ranked tenth in sales among Japanese retailers in 1963, and fifth in 1968. Continuing its rapid growth, it became the top retailer in terms of sales eventually in 1972, when it operated ninety outlets and the amount of its sales was recorded as 305.2 billion yen (Tatsuki 1995: 77–78). In this process, as the sales of the department store were exceeded by those of GMS in 1972, the department store handed over its leading position in the retail industry to GMS (Hitoshi 2003: 37). Consequently, even if there are considerable similarities between the Korean and the Japanese cases in the evolutionary process of the department store, the length of the heyday of the department store was quite different in the two instances.

3 The Limitation of the Conflict Theory in the Korean Retail Industry

3.1 *Two Different Formats under the Same Roof*

While the procedure of retail evolution in Korea has mainly corresponded to environmental theory since the 1970s, its procedure from the late 1990s would be more appropriate to conflict theory which argues that conflict between retail formats decisively influences the evolution of each retail format (Brown 1987). Both the emergence of the discount store as a new retail format and the change in the department store as a response to competition and as a result of conflict with the new retail format, seem to present a clear example of conflict theory. Some scholars also suggest the application of conflict theory to the evolution of Korean retail formats (O Sejo and Sekine Takasi 2002: 141). In fact, the existence of other competing retail formats is likely to be inevitably accompanied by a conflict between them and thus to be related to conflict theory. In this regard, the Korean case since the middle of the 1990s has not deviated from the general principles of the theory.

However, the Korean example seems to be different from other cases in respect to the emergence and developmental procedure of the new retail format. The emergence of a new retail format will usually assume the appearance of different ownership and organization from the existing dominant retail format, whether it is a newcomer or not to the retail industry. For example, Walmart in the US, Carrefour in France, Tesco in the UK and Daiei in Japan, which are the most representative discount store companies in each country, fit this pattern (see their web pages). They each began as one of several small companies among existing retailers, but have become leading retailers through many innovations. For example, Tesco was established by Jack Cohen in 1919 when he began to sell surplus groceries from a stall in the East End of London. The first store which was named Tesco, opened in 1929 and Tesco Stores (Holdings) Ltd floated on the Stock Exchange in 1947. It was 1956 when Tesco opened the first self-service supermarket in Maldon and afterwards it assumed its present shape with rapid growth <http://www.tescocorporate.com>. The history of Carrefour is not hugely different to that of Tesco. It was founded in 1959 and opened its first supermarket in 1960. It was 1963 when it took the name Carrefour and opened a new type of store called the hypermarket, offering food and non-food items within a floor area of 2,500 square metres. It established the first hypermarket outside France, in Belgium, ten years after its foundation in 1969, and was listed on the Paris Stock Exchange in 1970. Even if Carrefour grew more rapidly than Tesco through some mergers, it is clear that it has become the most dominant retailer through many innovations towards a new retail format <http://www.carrefour.com/cdc/group/history>.

In contrast, most of the Korean discount stores began as offshoots of big business from the start, owned by the existing dominant retail companies. For instance, E-Mart, which is the biggest discount store company in Korea, was established in 1993 by Shinsegae Department Store Company. Its market share is estimated as over 30 per cent of sales within the whole discount store industry. While its growth was relatively slow before the financial crisis in 1997, it became more rapid after the crisis with the change of socio-economic environment. It opened its tenth store in 1997, but established its first store outside Korea, at Shanghai in China in the same year, just four years after its establishment. This strategy, whereby it could aggressively make inroads into foreign markets from its early establishment, is likely to have been one that only big business could follow. Its growth became more rapid after the crisis, with an increase in investment. E-Mart opened its twentieth store in 1999, its fortieth in 2002, and its one-hundred-and-sixth in 2007. Meanwhile, it opened its seventh store in China as part of increasing its foreign investment <http://about.shinsegae.com/company>. Lotte-Mart which is the second biggest discount store chain in Korea also followed a similar path of development to that of E-Mart, even if its discount store business began later. It started its operation in 1998 with two stores established as a business division by Lotte Department Store Company. By 2001, it had built its twentieth nationwide store. It opened its thirty-fifth store in 2004, and by 2007, was operating fifty-seven stores <http://company.lottemart.com/company/history_2007.jsp>.

Accordingly, in Korea, the emergence of the discount store as a new retail format would imply, on the one hand, a kind of innovation in the retail industry and, on the other hand, a kind of business diversification by the existing dominant retail companies. They still have two different kinds of retail formats under the same roof, even if there is no lack of competition within each retail format.

3.2 The Conflict Theory under the Market Segmentation of the *Chaebol*

It is inevitable that this type of firm structure has had a huge effect on the shape of competition and conflict between different retail formats. Conflict between different ownerships and organizations in each retail format can occur around the survival of the organization, and consequently of the retail format. In contrast, conflict and competition between different retail formats under the same roof, are regulated by the principle of survival of the company, rather than of a particular retail format. In these circumstances, the determining factor for retail evolution is not conflict and competition between different types of retail formats, even if there is superficial conflict between them. Rather the crucial factor is cooperation for big businesses profit maximization. The reason why the application of the conflict theory should be limited in the Korean case is related to this ownership structure.

As we have seen, Korean income inequality has grown rapidly since the mid-1990s. In addition, consumption liberalization was likely to have already been sufficiently embedded in society. This means that the material and the social conditions necessary for upmarket trends were present. On the other hand, the shock and recession after the financial crisis strengthened the market need for lower priced goods. It was particularly inevitable that the expansion of the income gap and of unstable employment made consumption attitudes conservative, unlike the enthusiastic attitude in the past. A differentiated market would require a differentiated retail format. Therefore, a retail company that had taken both the middle and the upper market through the existing department store format, needed to accommodate the new developments. In this respect, the establishment of discount stores by existing big retailers can be understood as a response to the segmented market for profit maximization of the company and, in turn, the rapid growth of the discount store can be considered a good result from the positive strategy of market segmentation. In Korea, the fast retreat of, and the strategic change of, the department store are closely linked to this context. While the department store's return to supplying upmarket goods, constituted, on the one hand, a loss of a part of the market, it provided the opportunity, on the other hand, of being able to open up a new market with different kinds of retail formats. What is more, as seen in the previous chapter, the productivity and efficiency of the department store had considerably improved despite its sluggish turnover after the financial crisis. This implies that the strategy of market segmentation by the retail company was very successful. From the viewpoint of the retail format, evolution of the department store was not a result of conflict, but a result of cooperation with the discount store for the profit maximization of big businesses. Thus, it can be seen, that from the mid-1990s, conflict theory has only had limited application to the Korean case. Consequently, the short heyday of the department store format can be understood as being linked to the market segmentation strategy of big retail companies under such circumstances.

4 The Different Trajectory of Retail Evolution: The Korean-style Discount Store Format

4.1 *The Character of the Discount Store Format in Korea*

The character of the birth and development of the discount store is necessarily linked to the character of its management and its evolutionary trajectory. First of all, as we have seen earlier, the new retail format had to offer lower prices as a modernized mass retailer, which was different to the traditional market. This was a primary requirement of the segmented market before and after the crisis. The discount store format, in this respect, was indispensable in this socio-economic situation characterized by the income gap, embedded consumption liberalization and the economic crisis.

There are various kinds of discount store formats in the world, such as the discount store, the supercenter and the hypermarket. Among them, the Korean discount store format is considered similar to the hypermarket where the supermarket format for foodstuffs, and the discount store format for dry goods are mixed up (O Sejo and Bak Jinyong 2004: 107). According to the definition of the International Chamber of Commerce, 'the hypermarket is a retail establishment of a minimum sales area of 2,500 square metres selling mainly in self-service and at very competitive prices a wide range of food and non-food products with adequate parking facilities available'. But individual countries have slightly different definitions even if the above definition provides the basic concepts of the hypermarket format (Dawson 2002: 14–15). The hypermarket such as Tesco, Sainsbury's and Carrefour, is a format which combines the supermarket with the discount store. This kind of format developed in Europe, and has expanded rapidly in developing countries where the modern retail format is not diversified. In contrast, this format has not been successful in the US until now because the position of the supermarket format has been very strong among retail formats (O Sejo and Bak Jinyong 2004: 100–102). This implies that the Korean discount store is similar to Tesco and Carrefour as a type of hypermarket rather than Walmart as a type of original discount store. This difference seems to be deeply related to the historical structure of the retail industry and of consumption. For example, there was a supermarket chain which specialized in foodstuffs in the US when the discount store technology of dry goods was developed by Walmart around the 1940s. Thus, as its technology has spread, the supermarket format as the type of discount store format for foodstuffs has developed separately from the discount store for dry goods (Yokomori 2003: 193). Unlike this, the hypermarket format has developed in the UK and France as multiple chains which specialized in foodstuff and non-food items, but which adopted discount store technology and expanded their range of goods (Lyon et al. 2004: 30; Dawson 2002: 20–22). In this respect, it is natural that the discount store format has been closer to the hypermarket format in Korea, where modernized retailers did not have a specialized retail format for foodstuffs. Furthermore, the importance of edibles seems to be quite high in the Korean discount store format, which was established in order to take over the middle and necessity market shared by department store companies. In other words, it is not an exaggeration to say that the discount store aimed to take over the market for food provisions as a necessity market, while the department store assumed market dominance as a purveyor of luxury goods. This can be shown in the trends of goods for both the department store format and the discount store format. Table 7.1 shows the trends in the ratios of main items to sales in the department store and the discount store since 1995, when the discount store format began to constitute one of the retail formats.

According to Table 7.1, it was around 1997 that the change in these trends was clearly shown in the ratios of apparel and foodstuffs to department store sales. The ratio of foodstuffs decreased by 7.2 percentage points from 22.3 per cent in 1997 to 15.1 per cent in 2002, while that of apparel increased by 11.1 per centage points from 44.4 per cent in 1997 to 55.5 per cent in 2002. As we have seen earlier, basically this can be understood as evidence of the department store's move upmarket in accordance with the change in socio-economic

TABLE 7.1 *Ratio of each item to sales in both retail formats*

		1995	1996	1997	1998	1999	2000	2001	2002
Department Store	Apparel	42.7	46.2	44.4	44.2	46.6	49.1	53.9	55.3
	Foodstuff	20.9	18.4	22.3	21.4	21.1	15.7	18.6	15.1
Discount store	Foodstuff	50.9	54.3	52.8	56.8	57.6	58.6	54.6	49.7

Source: KCCI, Analysis of Current Retail Management, annual

conditions. Thus, Table 7.1 explains how the discount store format played a role in the department store's transition, as the discount store increased the ratio of foodstuffs in its sales. In particular, the discount store is expected to take over a considerable portion of the foodstuffs market owned by the department store, with its rapid growth since 1997. As we have seen earlier, this is closely related to the ownership structure of the Korean big retail company which has different types of retail formats in-house. As a result of this, the Korean discount store is much more similar to Tesco and Carrefour, as a type of hypermarket, rather than Walmart which is just a discount store. Apart from this, we can see a decreasing ratio of foodstuffs even in the discount format since 2001. This phenomenon is likely to be closely related to the character of the Korean-style discount store (KDS) which was a discount store similar in some respects to the department store. We will examine this in the next section.

4.2 *The Discount Store like the Department Store*

The Korean discount store's uniqueness is that it differs from the hypermarket, offering higher-class services normally associated with the department store. It can be understood as a new retail format which simultaneously combines a low cost, comprehensive range of goods with high-quality service (Choi 2003: 50–55). In fact, the discount store format as an innovative newcomer operates on the conceptual basis of the exchange of high services for low prices. This seems consistent with the retail wheel theory of McNair (1931, 1958, 1976, 1978). As a compensation for the sacrifice of high services like the department store, the consumer is to be given a lower price of goods. This is shown in the reduction of decoration and staff for consumer services in terms of its operations. It is also the reason why the discount format, in general, employs a warehouse system and self-service technology, compared with the luxurious decoration and face-to-face sales of the department store. In contrast to this, the KDS carries out face-to-face sales to a large extent, although it basically employs a self-service system. Most of the KDSs are also decorated with luxurious materials and an atmosphere which is similar to the department store (Im Yeonggyun et al. 2002: 55–56). Consequently, it is different even from the hypermarket format and, thus, it can be understood as a new retail format. This character has often been pointed out as a main factor in its competitiveness, as global winners withdraw from the Korean domestic market (O Seyeong and Gim Ilsan 2003: 216–217). For instance, Walmart which made inroads into the Korean domestic market in 1998 withdrew in 2006. Just before that, Carrefour also announced that it was withdrawing from the Korean market. The withdrawal of Carrefour, which had always been in second or third place among the Korean discount stores since the establishment of its Korean branch in 1996, was considered very surprising. Furthermore, its departure was doubly unusual given that its version of the discount store was quite similar to that of the KDS. Some scholars pointed out that the sluggish performance of foreign discount stores is related to the high services presented by the KDS, unlike Walmart and Carrefour (Gim Juheon 2005: 87–89; Im Yeonggyun et al. 2002 etc.).

This type of management seems to be closely related to the role of the department store as the first modern retail format in Korea. As we have seen, the period of mass consumption in Korea was dominated by the department store, which moved from a strategy of carrying luxury goods to popularization. With the increase in income and the decrease in the income gap, consumers in the middle market have enjoyed the department stores' high-quality services since the mid-1980s. This character of the retail format necessarily influences the development of consumers' tastes, although influences in the opposite direction are also true because each unavoidably depends on the other. What is more, customary preference, for whatever reason, does not easily change. Accordingly, consumers who were accustomed to the consumption pattern of the department store in the period of mass consumption might have had a tendency to maintain their attitude towards consumption for quite some time, even if some of the conditions surrounding their consumption and retail structures themselves had changed.

In addition to this, such a consumption attitude seems strengthened due to the condition of equal consumption for a long time, as we have seen earlier. Even if the department store as an existing retail format moves upmarket and a new retail format appears to cater for mass consumption, people in the mass market are unlikely to be satisfied with the new format if it provides considerably different circumstances of consumption from the previous one. This inference can be backed up by arguments about the same class identification through consumption. In research on the structure of consumption during the period from the mid-1980s to the early 1990s, Baek pointed out that the structure of consumption expenditure had converged in Korean society regardless of income level. He particularly emphasized that the main factor which made people claim the same class identification was consumption rather than income and wealth (Baek Ukin 1994: ii-iii, 125–126). The main thrust of Baek's research is different from the present work, in that it focussed on the structure of consumption at each income level. However, it is clear that people were quite sensitive to consumption and consumption patterns in terms of social equality from the mid-1980s. This view, which emphasizes consumption or a particular item of consumption as a criterion of same class identification, is consistently reflected in other research (Jo Donggi 2006; Jang Sehun 2006 etc.). Whatever your income level, if you think of yourself as middle-class, for example, you will wish to consume at a middle-class level. As a result, it is natural that the KDS, which is similar to the department store, was more successful than foreign discount stores which concentrated mainly on low prices, as Choi pointed out (2003: 50–55).

This initial condition seems to predict a future path for retail formats. Competition for luxury goods shops appears to accelerate in the Korean discount retail format. The Korea Economic Daily sketched a picture of the discount store industry which competed as a luxury shop (*Han-gug-gyeongje-sin-mun* 14 October 2002). A representative example is the success of Homeplus, which is late-comer to the discount format in Korea. Homeplus, which is owned by Tesco, had just two outlets in 1999. However, after growing very rapidly, it had sixty-two outlets in 2007 with the second biggest market share behind E-mart in the discount retail format. It comes into the spotlight because of its high performance as the biggest provider of sales per square metres with the most rapid growth rate of sales in the industry. This high performance is understood to be closely related to its strategy of being a luxury outlet with low prices (*Mae-il-gyeongje-sin-mun* 18 September 2007). In fact, this company aggressively stresses this marketing strategy claiming 'higher elegance than a department store, lower price than a discount store' in advertisements <http://corporate.homeplus.co.kr>. This pattern of competition among discount store companies has increased and is encouraging the development of even a discount store equivalent of the department store (*Jo-seon-il-bo* 27 September 2007). A director of sales promotion of a department store said, 'as the discount store becomes more and more luxurious, competition between the department store and the discount store is taking place in some goods' (*I-de-il-li* (*E-Daily*) 9 October 2007). Nevertheless, this does not mean that the discount store format changes to that of the department store in its goods and basic management skills. Thus in a bid to further differentiate itself, the department store has sought to boost its image of being much more comfortable and luxurious than the discount store (*I-de-il-li* (*E-Daily*) 9 October 2007).

In sum the KDS is different from the ordinary discount retail format in terms of its customer service and decoration of the shop. Instead, it is likely to be similar to the department store format. However, the fact that it offers low prices and self-service and mainly sells necessities like foodstuffs implies that it is basically a category of the discount store format. As mentioned, this character, which earlier made it competent when competing with foreign discount stores, was the result of a survival strategy in Korea's distinctive consumption environment, including consumption attitude. On the other hand, this can be said to be an evolutionary result in terms of the retail company; the department store in the city center as a luxury shop for the rich; the department store like the discount store in sub-city centers, reflecting a mixed department and discount store to cater for the mass market; and the discount store like the department store as a luxury shop carrying necessities for the mass market. Even if the direction of evolution heads downmarket, the character of the original format does not disappear due to the Korean distinctive context surrounding the retail industry. Consequently, the KDS, may be a creation of Korea's various retail industry and consumption conditions.

5 Conclusion

In general, fierce competition between existing and the emerging retail formats usually takes place in the early stages of retail innovation. Conflict theory, in particular among theories of retail evolution, pays attention to this competition and conflict between both formats as one of the determined factors of retail evolution. In this regard, much research has dealt with the pattern of conflict between the department store and the discount store (Gross 1964; Greenley and Shipley 1992 etc.). However, as we have seen, the relationship between both formats in Korea was very different from other cases because most main discount stores in Korea are managed as a business division of the department store company. In other words, both formats under the same roof are an instrument of market segmentation to maximize profits in a big retail company. Therefore, their relationship basically can constitute cooperation in the same company even if there is, sometimes, internal competition between both divisions. The direction and the speed of retail evolution would be determined not by conflict but by performance in market segmentation. So, conflict theory may have a limited value for examining the Korean retail evolution because of the nature of company ownership in Korea. On the other hand, this can also be said to be basically produced by the character of the consumption market because the market segmentation has been decided as a strategy for profit maximization of the company, under changeable consumption market conditions. The fact that the department store which has moved upmarket makes much better results than before implies that it has an accurate understanding of the consumption market, and thus its strategy is very successful.

Another characteristic of the Korean retail evolution is the emergence of a discount store similar in character to the department store, which is called the Korean style Discount Store. Of course, evolution of the KDS may primarily depend on the character of consumption attitudes. The period of mass consumption in Korea was initiated by the department store, and consumers in the middle market have enjoyed various services for consumers presented by the department store. Therefore, consumers who became accustomed to the marketing pattern of the department store in the period of mass consumption may not alter their consumption attitudes for some time. Put simply, consumers might expect a new retail format to be a modified department store in the mass market, even under the stratified consumption market conditions. Nevertheless, the reason why this is a result of the interaction between the retailer and the consumption market is shown by a comparison between the domestic and foreign retailers. Most foreign retailers did not change their original discount store format strategies to fit the context. As a result, the foreign type of discount store has not been a main format of the discount retailer. This demonstrates that foreign retailers did not properly penetrate the Korean market. In contrast, the domestic retailer had created the KDS which has particularly catered for Korean consumption attitudes. In this respect, the KDS, though seeming unique, is the result of successful interaction between the retailer and the consumer, and is the natural embodiment of Korean retail evolution, reflecting the Korean context and its particular conditions.

CHAPTER 8

Conclusion

This study began with a question about the department store: why was the golden age of the department store so short in Korea? This question has inevitably been linked to other questions: why was the leading role of the department store in the consumer market delayed, and why was its golden age quite explosive? These were the empirical research questions suggested in the hypotheses articulated in Chapter 1. Thus this study first of all embodies historical research on the retail industry with special reference to the Korean department store industry. It has examined the distinctiveness of the Korean retail evolution since the 1970s. The research inevitably also relates to theoretical concerns, because this newly examined situation can be comprehensively and systematically understood through making use of existing theories of retailing, and seeing how far the Korean situation is in line with what these theories would suggest. On the other hand, all existing theories are always dependent for their development on the examination of new situations. The research strategy has been to relate these existing theories to the Korean case along these lines. In addition, this study has sought to locate the evolution of retailing within the context of Korean economic growth and the consumption market. As another perspective on retail evolution it has also explored the relationship between the stratification of consumption and economic growth.

The methodology adopted in this study can be summarised with two themes: the adoption of a chronological approach; and a focus on tracing the behaviour and response of the three main 'actors' in retailing develeopment, namely the government, the consumer and the retailer. The chronological account showed that retailing development can be categorised into three distinct eras according to the degree of stratification in the consumer market: the period from the 1970s to the middle of the 1980s; the period of the mid-1980s to the mid-1990s, and the period since the middle of the 1990s. It was argued that the three elements in retailing development – government, retailer and consumer – were engaged in a process of mutual interaction, and hence shaped the way in which retailing developed. This focus has been the main concern of this work. Of course, that role could not have been carried out without the presence of particular socio-economic circumstances, which were fundamental in influencing the different 'actors'. However, in order to focus on the three subjects these socio-economic circumstances have largely been considered as given conditions.

 | DOI 10.1163/9789004274228_009

TABLE 8.1 *Epitome of the present research*

		From 70s to the mid-80s	From the mid-80s to the mid-90s	Since the mid-90s
Circumstances	Economic growth	High growth	High growth	Low growth
	Income distribution	Inequality	Equality	Inequality
	State of consumption	Equality	Equality	Inequality
Actors	Government (consumption and retail policies)	Repression	Beginning of Liberalization	Liberalization
	Consumer (consumption attitude)	Frugality	More consumption	Less consumption
	Industry (investment in the retail industry)	Avoidance of Investment	Beginning of investment	Expansion of investment
Results	Stratification of consumption market	Uniform market (traditional market)	Stratifying market (department store & traditional market)	Stratified market (department store & discount store & traditional market)
	Status of the department store	Backwardness	Explosive growth	Retardation
Theory	Theory of retail evolution	Political economy theory in the environment theory (policy factor)	Political economy theory (policy & market factors)	Political economy theory based on the combined theory; limitation of the conflict theory (market factor)

Table 8.1 gives a chronological summary of the changes in the main factors that have been considered in this study. What should first be noted in the 1970s is the fact that the consumption and retail industry were firmly repressed by the Korean government. While some scholars have argued about whether consumption was generally repressed in the 1970s in order to invest in the manufacturing sector, concrete examination of consumption repression, including the retail industry, has been carried out in this work. It has explored why investment in the retail industry was very difficult in the 1970s. Through an international comparison of APC, it also found that this policy was reflected in everyday life. A consequence of this situation was uniformity in the

consumption market which provided a decisive clue towards understanding the backwardness of the department store industry as a modern retail format in the 1970s. This research then made it clear that the emergence of the modern retail format was artificially delayed despite its potential development given various favourable socio-economic factors.

This finding is in contrast to most existing research, which attributes the backwardness of the retail industry to economic immaturity in the 1970s.

In the 1980s, the political situation altered rapidly and Korean society began to pursue liberalization and democratization. As authoritarian repression weakened, it triggered a strong reaction in Korea. With continuous economic growth, the imbalance between income and consumption increased and thus consumption expanded explosively from the middle of the 1980s. The main characteistic in this mass consumption era, was that the department store was the only modern retailer. However, my research questions why the standard retail format for mass consumption did not appear, in contrast with other countries at that time. In relation to this point, my research argues that its absence was the combined result of two actors' behaviours: the department store's strategic transition from a supplier of luxury merchandise to a supplier of necessities; and the enthusiastic consumption attitude of the Korean consumer reacting to social achievement of liberalization and their purchasing power, resulting from an imbalance between income and consumption. I established that consumption attitudes changed sharply (within the period), and that the urban sector in particular was much more sensitive to consumption in accordance with the change of situation. This analysis might provide the real reason for the explosive growth of the department store industry. However, this might not be naturally linked to the short heyday of the department store despite economic recession since the middle of the 1990s. Strong growth and bargaining power of a retail format in the market is generally likely to make its golden age longer; the Korean department store industry has been in such a place. In order to resolve this deadlock, I have examined the fact that the consumption market was stratifying under the condition of liberalization. It is inevitable that liberalization causes stratification of consumption in accordance with income levels, while it stimulates consumption in general by lifting constraints on consumption. Of course, what we looked at more clearly in the second period of this research was a general expansion of consumption rather than consumption stratification. Yet within this situation, the need for a retail format which could be appropriate to a stratifying market became more and more apparent, particularly since the 1997 financial crisis. What has been noted here is the oligopolistic character of the Korean economy because of the *chaebol*. Because of this structure, a new retail format for the stratified market has been established by the existing big businesses in Korea, even though in other countries such as the UK, Japan and the US, the process began as small businesses run by separate investors, and grew from there. Accordingly, the emergence of the new format can be understood as a diversification of management with in-house innovation in Korea, whilst the cases in other countries showed innovation in the retail industry. The department store and the new format under the same roof are just components of the company to maximize profits, and are a kind of portfolio of assets by big business. According to strategic decisions of the company, one of the retail formats can decrease or increase regardless of the life of the format. The Korean department store industry moved into the luxury market and in doing so gave up its share in the existing mass market. Yet retail big businesses had nothing to lose because the discount store as a new format rapidly expanded its share in the mass market, filling the void which the department store had left. Besides, the strategy of the department store has been successful in terms of rapid improvement of its productivity despite sluggish turnover. At this point, the department store industry preferred to move into the new luxury market which had emerged since the financial crisis than to be ousted from the mass market. Therefore, this research found the short golden age of the department store is closely related to the Korean *chaebol* system and found that the pattern of the retail evolution greatly depends on the ownership structure of the company.

Even if the department store had left the mass market, it left a strong imprint on consumers who had known the department store as the first modern retailer. The memory of the previous period would have influenced the present irrespective of differences in direction. Consumption repression in the 1970s unexpectedly provided the psychological reason and the material source of explosive consumption of the department store in the next period. If consumption repressed was an unpleasant memory, the next phase of enthusiastic consumption within the department store provided a much more positive period of history. This period had an important influence on shaping the discount store as a new retail format. What is more, this research shows that Korean consumers have lived under the condition of equal or uniform consumption for a long time; equality of consumption repression in the 1970s and equality of affluent consumption since the 1980s. It is highly possible that these historical experiences made consumers prefer the same retail format in the mass market as that of the department store even after the consumption market had been stratified. Korean consumers have forged a distinctive consumption attitude through particular experiences over a long period. One consequence of this is linked to the appearance of the KDS, which has provided both a low cost, comprehensive range of goods and also high quality services like the department store format. My analysis shows that the main reason why the KDS domestic discount retailer has been dominant despite serious worries as market liberalization began, was related to the character of Korean consumption attitudes. A particular type of competition which was formed among market contenders in the initial period due to a particular historical situation was self-fulfilling in the trajectory of path dependency. The KDS strengthened its characteristics through interaction with consumers formed by distinctive historical environments.

This research has paid attention to the usefulness of political economy theory as a divergent view within environment theory. With this it has considered the view of combined theory as a part of the theoretical framework, while assessing the Korean case using a chronological framework. As mentioned in the introductory chapter, political economy theory which was applied, in many cases, to importers of the modern retail format, has been established as having enormous explanatory power for Korean cases too. Despite rapid economic growth in the 1970s, the backwardness of the retail industry can be explained by viewing policy motivations as an environmental factor. This is a key finding, given that most existing research has ascribed the backwardness of the retail industry to economic immaturity at that time. I also looked at the second period of this research, from the mid-1980s to the mid-1990s, in terms of political economy theory. In contrast to the previous period, policy factors were combined with market factors relating to the economic policy of liberalization. I have argued that the inverse-evolution of the department store format, from luxuries to necessities, is not well understood without this theoretical approach I use. The department store adapted itself to keen consumption trends when the market liberalized. In contrast, the emergence of the discount store format and return of the department store format to luxuries since the middle of the 1990s, provides a possible application of different theories – such as the convergence view of environment theory, the cyclical and the conflict theories – to the Korean retail evolution. First, immediately following the emergence of the discount store, the similarities in the outward structure of the retail industry with that of developed countries is consistent with the convergence view. The operating system of the two formats in terms of price and service has been similar to the principle of the wheel of retailing as one of the main theories in cyclical theory. Coexistence of two different kinds of retail formats has meant that some scholars have attempted to apply conflict theory to the Korean retail evolution. I have examined the application of conflict theory and argued that the applicability of this theory is limited in reference to the Korean retail evolution. This is related to the distinctive ownership structure of the Korean *chaebol* which have owned both retail formats. Given that both retail formats operated under the same roof, the emergence of the discount store format and return of the department store format to luxuries was a result not of conflict between the two formats but of the strategic decision to segment the consumption market to match changing market circumstances. Thus, under this condition, the evolution of the retailer, particularly the department store, seems not to depend on competition and conflict, but on cooperation for profit maximization by big retail businesses. Thus, this change in the retail industry can be considered as a kind of business diversification, and in-house innovation which has been carried out by big businesses. In this respect, the application of conflict theory to the Korean case has limited value even though there is an element of competition between the formats. And, as liberalization has left a greater imprint on the market, intervention has weakened over time. Other evolutionary theories apart from political economy theory, are more likely to be applied to the Korean case because most of them have been produced in such market conditions. The explanatory power of the convergence view in environment theory, which decides the stages of development in the retail institution according to the level of industrialization, seems to have become more prominent than before. However, although the convergence view is outwardly correct to some extent, the political economy theory as a divergence view in environment theory still holds the key to the interpretation of its evolutionary path. The emergence of the KDS provides an example. The historical distinctiveness of the relationship between internal (retailer) and external (consumer) factors is likely to produce distinct results even in a similar macro-economic liberalized environment. Therefore, this study underscores especially the usefulness of political economy theory for an examination of the Korean case, although other theories such as the environment-cycle theory and environment-cycle-conflict theory are taken into account.

In addition, I have tried to suggest new perspectives on the relationship between consumption and economic growth, although this was not the main purpose of my research. I looked at consumption as a criterion of equality or inequality, and paid attention to consumption as a factor that had a huge effect on people's attitudes to prevailing economic systems. This differs in two respects from conventional views of the relationship between consumption and economic growth. Conventionally, consumption has been argued in terms of the character of the demand side in research on economic growth (Gilboy 1967; Murphy et al. 1989a, 1989b, etc.). Gilboy, Murphy and others have argued that consumption was one of the leading factors for successful industrialization. In contrast to this, my research sheds light on the fact that consumption intervened on the supply side of the human factor. It argued that people's participatory attitude to the existing system as one of the determining factors for economic growth depended on the state of consumption. Secondly, the research on the relationship between equality or inequality and economic growth usually makes use of the income factor as a criterion of the distribution state. Various empirical and theoretical researches by Rodrik (1994, 1999a, 1999b, 2000a, 2000b), Alesina (1994, 1996), Perotti (1993, 1996), Persson (1994), Barro (1991, 2000, 2001), Bertola (1993) and Croix and Doepke (2003) have shown that less income inequality is very positively linked to economic growth. Most of them pointed out that social conflict resulting from income inequality causes huge costs and retards economic growth. In comparison, this study stressed consumption inequality, instead of income inequality, as a cause for social conflict while it accepted the main idea of the negative correlation between inequality and economic growth. Consequently what this study argued, is that the state of consumption plays an important role on the supply side, because it can cause social conflict. In other words, if consumption is classless, society can be less conflictual, even if income inequality is high. Thus, people would be willing to support the prevailing economic system. This argument is that people are aware of inequality at the stage not of income, but of consumption, in which any income distinction is actualized and realized. However, differences between incomes can be considered as an index of inequality when income is directly linked to consumption in a normal economic situation, and where there is no repression or strong regulation of consumption markets. In the real world it is the discrepancy or non-discrepancy between income and consumption that matters. For instance, if strong repression is imposed on consumption for whatever reason, the normal pattern of relationship between income and consumption will not appear. If the gap between incomes does not lead to differences between people's consumption patterns, in terms of quality and quantity, people cannot perceive the seriousness of the inequality even if there is a huge distinction between their incomes. This view stemmed from the Korean economic situation since the 1970s. In particular, the socio-economic situation in the 1970s might require a new perspective given that the Korean economy achieved high economic growth despite strong consumption repression and rapidly exacerbating income inequality. Most scholars who agree with this view argue that possible forms of resistance to this unequal situation, like the organization of trade unions, were banned by the authoritarian state (Amsden 1989: 199, 206; Evans 1994: 220, etc.). However, this study raises two questions about this argument; can such repression be successful in the long run and can a successful economic performance be realized in a repressive situation in which people may have a passive and resistant attitude to the existing system? According to conventional theories on the relationship between consumption, equality or inequality and economic growth, worsening income inequality since the 1970s is likely to have limited the level of performance of the Korean economy. Thus this study assumed that there is a seriously missing point in the existing research about people's agreement to the existing system.

The disparity between income and consumption was, in fact, a by-product of consumption repression resulting from an industrial policy concentrating only on the manufacturing sector, rather than an intended policy. The effect of this by-product has weakened with the beginning of socio-economic liberalization since the mid-1980s. The discrepancy between income and consumption eventually waned and, on the other side, income inequality considerably improved since then. The Korean economy has continuously achieved good economic results since the mid-1980s thanks to affluent consumption under less stratified retail market conditions. However, after 1997 the financial crisis, the social conflict has increased with the emergence of the obviously stratified consumption market under great income inequality conditions similar to those of the 1970s. At the same time, consumption is rapidly shrinking and the Korean economy is exhibiting symptoms of relatively lower economic growth than before. Conventional theories seem to recover their explanatory power when examining Korean society from the mid-1980s. However, from the viewpoint of this study, the resumed usefuleness of conventional theories just implies that income can be used as a proxy of consumption. This is basically because the discrepancy between income and consumption disappears with liberalization. Consequently the consumption approach of this study can be said to have more consistent interpretive power than the income approach for understanding Korean economic development since the 1970s.

This study therefore suggests a more general theory that can be applied to other contexts. Such a theory may indeed be required because a number of developing countries are pushing economic growth as their main political agenda. Furthermore, if consumption policy (consumption repression) is used successfully, it could be considered a highly significant policy for continuous economic growth, whereas in the Korean case it was more of an unintended consequence. Such an extension of the findings of this study will require time, effort, consistent data and a large body of evidence, but can, perhaps, be a topic for research in the future.

CHAPTER 9

Epilogue: Korean Retailing since the 2000s

The Korean retailing sector has been continuously changing since the middle of the 2000s. Indeed, it is said that change is one of the main characteristics of the sector. On the one hand, such change occurs in line with the process of continuous change over time and, on the other hand, it occurs through a combination of existing conditions along with newly-emerging factors. In this final chapter we examine the impact of these newly-emerging factors – specifically the behaviour and interactions of the three principal actors: the consumer, the retailer and the government. The chapter concludes with an examination of the new research that is linked to these changes.

It is the socio-economic polarization that has taken place under conditions of low, long-term economic growth that is the most important issue that has faced Korea since the 2000s.

As we can see in figure 9.1, the economic growth rate in the 2000s has been between zero and five per cent, compared with between five and ten per cent in the 1990s. It may be seen as a structural shock when viewed in light of the fact that a higher growth rate had been sustained since the 1970s. Indexes of distribution such as the Gini coefficient have been considerably exacerbated since the financial crisis of 1997 (SK, Index of Income Distribution, annual).

A structural change like this is a basic and important condition which must influence the retailing sector because the three actors which condition it behave and interact on the basis of such a structure. In particular, income is the most determinant factor as far as consumption is concerned and consumption is the most significant element of the retail industry. Therefore, the social changes which impact income may be among the most pivotal factors in changing the retail industry.

As income inequality has continually increased, consumption has been affected and has shrunk since the middle of the 1990s. First of all, consumers in this period showed a more conservative attitude towards consumption than they had in the previous period because of an increase in unemployment and a decrease in income. They also became even more sensitive to prices due to their unstable income. Of course, people at the high–end of the income scale continued to enjoy luxury goods and, to that extent, they achieved satisfaction in the sense that they were able to celebrate their difference from ordinary people. It was natural that people should consume on the basis of their income

 | DOI 10.1163/9789004274228_010

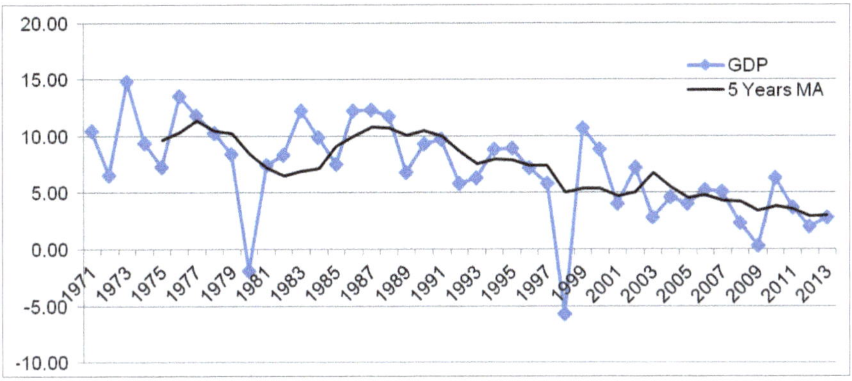

FIGURE 9.1 *The trend of economic growth* (GDP) (** real term*). SOURCE: BOK, NATIONAL ACCOUNTS, ANNUAL.

level when all repression on consumption had gone in the period of liberalization.

For the retailer, these changes could be both an opportunity to expand their market share and also involve a serious risk of losing their existing position in the retail industry. Therefore, it presents an opportunity for innovation and a period of strategic turning points. Korean retail companies were no exception in this kind of survival game. As has already been seen, the strategy of the department stores went back to when the luxury market began in the middle of the 1990s and gradually strengthened thereafter. The discount store format in the retail companies took over the mass market from the department store format. It can be said that this was an innovation by the retail companies which attempted to respond to the structural changes that have occurred since the middle of the 1990s. What they newly targeted in the 2000s was the more segmented mass market for necessities that was prompted by the conditions resulting from an unstable income. Even though Korean-style discount stores already played a leading role in the market, the pivotal aspect of the new strategy in the period of income polarization was diversification of the discount stores in terms of size and location through the segmentation of the mass market. However, it is inevitable that this kind of strategy caused social conflict surrounding the survival of small and medium-sized retailers. This was especially more problematic because it was during a period of long-term economic recession.

In this environment, a major controversy relating to the so-called SSMs (Super Supermarkets)[1] broke out in the late 2000s (Sin Gidong 2009: 11). While the

1 The term 'Super Supermarket' (SSM), which means small and medium sized stores for staple products owned by big retail companies, may be one of the expressions of a distinctive type

discount stores contended with the traditional markets in terms both of store size and of commercial area, the SSMs targeted the markets of the various small and medium-sized retailers that provided the corner shops of small towns and high streets. The number of SSMs was just 312 stores in 2006 but this rapidly increased to over 1,000 stores in 2011. The total sales of the industry rose to 6.1 trillion won from 2.3 trillion won during the same period (KOCA, *Monthly Retail Magazine*, each edition). A sharp growth in the number of the SSMs has been directly linked to the shrinking of the traditional supermarkets. According to a survey by the Korea Federation of Small and Medium-sized Businesses in 2013, 69.4 per cent of all respondents answered that there had been a decrease in sales after the establishment of an SSM within a distance of one kilometre. What was worse, 25.7 per cent answered that there had been a decrease in sales of over 30 per cent[2] (The Korea Federation of Small and Medium-sized Businesses 2013: 10). Social conflicts surrounding the arrival of new SSMs were expressed in frequent demonstrations throughout the country. Meanwhile, another type of Korean retail evolution was the emergence of lower price discount stores with stripped down décor and a reduced number of shop assistants. While the existing Korean-style discount stores resembled the department stores, the new ones which were first established in November 2010 are similar to the original discount store format, like warehouses in Western countries. They are run by big retail companies and their price level is 15~30 percent lower than that in the existing discount stores[3]. In terms of the retail hierarchy, these are located at a place between the existing discount stores and the traditional markets. With this development, it is understood that a new hierarchical structure of the Korean retail sector is being formed; this consists of the department stores – the Korean style discount stores – and the ware-

of Korean retail evolution. In general, supermarkets originated in the US as a retail format meaning big stores (chain) focused on food stuffs. However, as we have seen in chapter 3, the term 'supermarket' was introduced to the Korean people as refurbished 'mom and pop store's in the process of the 'Five Year Plan for the Modernization of the Distribution System' in the 1970s. Therefore, ironically, the supermarkets in Korea are not really 'super' but are usually small and poor. In this situation, big retail companies tried to expand their market share to small commercial areas of small towns and ordinary streets. They established smaller supermarkets than the existing discount stores but bigger ones than the existing supermarkets. Therefore, this new retail format is called SSM (super supermarket) in terms of the evolutionary shape of retail stores in the Korean context.

2 The Korea Federation of Small and Medium-sized Businesses surveyed about 300 supermarket stores which were located at a distance of one kilometre from an SSM in the period between 13th November and 25th November 2013.

3 <http://www.mt.co.kr/view/mtview.php?type=1&no=2013100915075696837&outlink=1>.

house discount stores – the traditional markets. Therefore, the traditional markets cannot avoid further pressure from the competition resulting from the new retail format. As we have seen, the segmentation of the Korean retail market is a one-sided shrinking process of the traditional markets and so the tension surrounding the possibility of the social conflict is becoming greater and greater as the economic recession persists over the long term.

Such dramatic changes in the retail markets are among the most significant factors in shaping the direction of government policy because it has to mitigate the problems affecting the market-place. However, legislation is likely to be a step behind reality because it reflects a reality that has already been revealed in general. As we have seen in chapter 6, 'the law for the development of the distribution industry', which was established in 1997, focused on the deregulation of large rather than small retailers (MOLEG 1997). Under the law, the rapid growth of the large retailers like the discount stores developed and the polarization of the Korean retail industry was increased. The Korean government had to change its policy direction to one of supporting the traditional markets and small and medium-sized retailers in the 2000s. First of all, it furnished a system to support them through several revisions to 'the law for the development of the distribution industry' which comprises the main legislation covering the retail industry. This was revised eleven times, including a complete revision in 2004 (MOLEG 2014). Apart from the law, 'the Act on special measures for the development of small and micro enterprises' (*So-gi-eop mit so-sang-gong-in ji-won-eul rwi-han teuk-byeol-jo-chi-beop*) is one of the main pieces of legal apparatus supporting the small retailers. While the act went unheeded around the year 1997, when it was established, it became a more and more important piece of regulation with its ten revisions as the socio-economic situation was changing in the 2000s (MOLEG 2014). The Korean government also passed a new act just for the traditional market in 2004. This act clarified the promotion of the modernization of the traditional market and the balanced development of the distribution industry as the purpose of the legislation (MOLEG 2005)[4]. It was revised eleven times after its establishment and its name was also changed to 'Special act on the promotion of traditional marketplaces and shopping districts' (*Jeon-tong-si-jang mit sang-jeom-ga yuk-seong-eul rwi-han teuk-byeol-beop*) in 2009 (MOLEG 2014). The purpose of these three acts can be summed up as follows: support for the traditional markets and shopping districts, the enhancement of the competitiveness of the small and medium-sized retailers, networking and cooperation of the small and

4 The original name of the act was 'Special act on the promotion of traditional market' (*Jae-rae-si-jang yuk-seong-eul rwi-han teuk-byeol-beop*) when it was established in 2004.

medium-sized retailers, partnership between the big retail companies and the small and medium-sized retailers (Gim Sukgyeong et al. 2011: 115).

Apart from the change of the policy direction in the main law for the retail industry, the fact that the government established two more special acts for the support of the small and medium-sized retailers shows how much it was worried about their collapse. In particular, the government policy on the retail industry became more protective towards the small and medium-sized retailers together with the traditional markets around the year 2010 when the problem of the SSMs became a severely controversial social issue. It added the provision in its revision of the law for the development of the distribution industry in November 2010 that a local government can build a protective area for traditional markets where both the establishment and the operation of discount stores and SSMs can be restricted (MOLEG 2010). The size of the protection area for the traditional markets was expanded to one kilometre from the boundaries of the traditional commercial districts in the revision of the law in the year 2011 from 500 meters in the year 2010 (MOLEG 2011). This was not enough to protect the traditional markets. In addition, the Korean government established the provision that a local government can restrict both the operation times and the operation days of the discount stores and the SSMs in a further revision in 2012 (MOLEG 2012). Nevertheless, small and medium-sized retailers continue to fail, making it one of the most serious social problems at the present time.

It is natural that such social environment changes are being reflected in academic research. First of all, there are a number of researches being conducted concerning the reinvigorating of the traditional markets. Many of them have focused on practically reinvigorating the methods of the traditional markets through empirical study (I Jongin et al. 2009; Gim Seonghun et al. 2011; I Deokhun et al. 2013, etc.). In particular, they have explored the practical methods used in certain traditional markets because each traditional market could be operating in different conditions (I Jongin et al. 2009; I Deokhun et al. 2013). Some researchers have approached the same problem from the point of view of the small and medium-sized retailers in general rather than just certain cases. Some of them have argued that the building of public wholesale distribution centers was necessary in order to enhance the competitiveness of the small and medium-sized retailers (I Yeongchan et al. 2003). It has also been pointed out that an increase in consumer satisfaction by management innovation was a critical strategy for the survival of the small and medium-sized retailers (Yun Jeonggeun et al. 2009; Bak Juyeong et al. 2010). Others have stressed the importance of cooperative brand marketing as a strategy for enhancing their competitiveness because it is difficult for each of them to make an individual brand (Gim Gipyeong et al. 2011).

A number of pieces of research which have focused on the conflict between the modern retail format (the discount store and the SSM) and the traditional retailing sector have been produced since the 2000s. Many studies in this field have argued for enhancing the competitiveness of the traditional retailing sector as a basic method for resolving the problem, through comparative studies between both sides, even though there are somewhat different viewpoints among them (Gwak Wonil et al. 2009; Ma Sangyeol et al. 2012; Gim Junhwan et al. 2013). In particular, it is notable that a number of articles have appeared in the field of the law, not in the fields of economics and business studies (Jang Gyosik 2012; Baek Okseon 2013; Choe Bongseok et al. 2013). This situation arose after an association for the modern retail format filed a petition with the Constitutional Court in February 2012, arguing that the restrictions imposed by the government affect their rights. They argued that restrictions on the private sector have to secure their legal justification by appealing to a social consensus based upon considering all the stakeholders equally. This phenomenon means that conflicts between them have become a social problem that now has to be addressed in various fields.

Bibliography

Primary Sources

Bank of Korea (BOK) (1960), *Han-gug-eun-haeng 10nyeon-sa* (The History of the BOK over 10 years), Seoul: BOK

———, Consumer Price Indexes, annual

———, Financial Statement Analysis, annual (1990–2005)

———, Foreign Exchange Rate, annual

———, National Accounts, annual (1953–2006)

———, (2002), Press Release for the 39th Day of Savings

National Assembly Finance Committee (1976), Je 96hoe gug-hoe jae-mu-wi-won-hoe-hoe-ui-log je 13ho (Minutes No. 13 of the 96th National Assembly Finance Committee), Seoul: Dae-han-min-gug gug-hoe-sa-mu-cheo

National Assembly Committee of Trade and Industry (1986), Je 129hoe gug-hoe sang-gong-wi-won-hoe-hoe-ui-log je 4ho (Minutes No. 4 of the 129th National Assembly Committee of Trade and Industry), Seoul: Dae-han-min-gug gug-hoe-sa-mu-cheo

Credit Finance Association (CFA), Current Situation of Credit Card Lending, annual (1983–1996)

Daewoo Economic Institute (DEI) (1993–1995), Han-gug ga-gu-gyeongje hwal-dongjo-sa (Survey for Economic Activity of Korean Households)

Department of Trade and Industry (DTI) (1966), Yu-tonggu-jo gae-seon-e gwan-han jangdan-gi jonghab-dae-chaeg (Comprehensive Measures in the Long and Short Term for the Improvement of the Distribution System)

———, (1969), Yu-tong geun-dae-hwa 5gae-nyeon gye-hoeg (Five Year Plan for the Modernization of the Distribution System)

———, (1970), Si-jang geun-dae-hwa sa-eob (Plan for Modernisation of Traditional Market)

———, (1972), Yu-tong geun-dae-hwa gye-hoeg (Plan for Modernisation of Distribution Industry)

———, (1973), Yu-tonggu-jo gae-seon 3dae gi-bon-si-chaeg (Three Plans for Improvement of Distribution Industry)

———, (1974a), Pyo-jun-yu-tongma-jin-je (System for the Standardisation of Retail Margins)

———, (1974b), Yu-tonggu-jo gae-seon-dae-chaeg (Policy for Reform of Retailing Structure)

———, (1987), *Sanggongbaeg-seo* (White Paper of Trade and Industry)

Economic Planning Board (1974), Jonghab-mul-ga-an-jeongdae-chaeg (Comprehensive Measure for the Stability of Price)

———, (1976), *Gyeongje-baeg-seo* (White Paper of Economy)

———, (1987, 1990), *Han-gug-ui sa-hoe-ji-pyo* (Social Index of Korea), Seoul: EPB

Federation of Korean Industries (FKI) (1967), *1967nyeon-pan han-gug-gyeongje-yeon-gam* (Year Book of the Korean Economy in 1967), Seoul: FKI

———, (2001), *Jeon-gyeonglyeon 40nyeon-sa (sanggwon)* (History of FKI over 40 years I), Seoul: FKI

Financial Supervisory Service (FSS), Monthly Financial Statistics, annual (1990–1996)

Institute of Korean Distribution Industry (IKDI) (2000), *Jae-lae-si-jang sil-tae-bun-seog-gwa hwal-seonghwa bang-an* (State of the Traditional Market and the Measure of its Revitalisation)

Jeollanamdo Office of Education (JOE) (1997), *Gongjeog-jo-seo* (Written Evidence of the Meritorious Deeds)

Korea Chamber of Commerce and Industry (KCCI) (1954), *Donglan hu seo-ul ji-gu sang-gongsil-tae* (State of Business in Seoul after the Korean War), Seoul: KCCI

———, (1987, 1988, 1990, 1992, 1994, 1995, 1996, 1997, 1999), *So-mae-eob gyeong-yeong-dongtae jo-sa-bo-go* (Analysis of Current Retail Management)

———, (2001, 2002, 2003), *So-mae-eob gyeong-yeongdongtae bun-seog* (Analysis of Current Retail Management)

Korea Consumer Agency (KCA) (1990), Baeg-hwa-jeom-eob-ui bul-gongjeong geo-lae-wa so-bi-ja bo-ho (Unfair Trade of the Department Store and Protection of Consumer)

———, (1998), Dae-hyeong ga-gyeog-hal-in-jeom i-yonghyeon-hwanggwa so-bi-ja ui-sig-e gwan-han yeon-gu (Research on Purchasing in Discount Stores and on Consumers' Consciousness)

Korea Fair Trade Commission (KFTC) (1981), Hal-in-pan-mae-un-yongjun-chig (Working Standard of Discount Sales)

———, (1983), Yu-tong-eob-gye hal-in-teug-byeol-pan-mae-haeng-wi-e dae-han bul-gongjeong geo-lae-haeng-wi ji-jeong go-si (Specification on Behaviour of Unfair Trade concerning Discount Special Sales by Retail Companies)

Korea Chainstores Association (KOCA), *Monthly Retail Magazine*, each edition (2006-2011)

Korea Super-Chain Association (KOSCA) (1995), *KOSCA hyeob-hoe 20nyeon-ui bal-ja-chwi* (A Footmark of the KOSCA for 20 Years) Seoul: KOSCA

———, *Yu-tong-eob-che yeon-gam* (Yearbook of Retail Companies), annual (1996–2002)

Ministry of Construction and Transportation (MOCT), Survey of Land Prices, annual (1975–2006)

———, Survey of House Prices, annual (1987–2006)

Ministry of Finance (MOF) (1982), *Gan-jeob-gug-se tonggye 1* (Statistics of Indirect Taxes I),

Ministry of Government Administration and Home Affairs (MOGAHA) (2006), Gae-in-byeol-to-ji-so-yu-bun-po-hyeon-hwang-myeon-jeog-gi-jun (State of Distribution of Individual Landownership – In Owned Size)

Ministry of Labour (MOL), Annual Number of Strikes, annual (1997–2004)

Ministry of Government Legislation (MOLEG) (1949), Sangpyo-beob (Trademark Law)

———, (1951), Jung-angdo-mae-si-jangbeob (Law of the Central Wholesale Market)

———, (1961), Si-jangbeob (Law of the Market)

———, (1965), Jo-se-gammyeon-gyu-je-beob (Regulation Law on Tax Reduction and Exemption)

———, (1972), Yu-sin-heon-beob (Yushin Constitution)

———, (1974), Gug-min-saenghwal-ui an-jeong-eul wi-han dae-tonglyeong gin-geub-jo-chi (President's Emergency Measures for Stability of People's Living)

———, (1980), Dog-jeomgyu-je mich gongjeonggeo-lae-e gwan-han beob-lyul (Monopoly Regulation and Fair Trade Act)

———, (1980), Yu-tongsan-eob geun-dae-hwa chog-jin-beob (Law for the Stimulation of the Modernisation of the Distribution Industry)

———, (1981), Si-jangbeob jeon-myeon-gae-jeong-an (Whole Amendment of the Law of the Market)

———, (1982), Si-jangbeob si-haenglyeong (Dae-tonglyeonglyeong 10887) (Enforcement Decree of the Market Law (Presidential Decree No. 10887))

———, (1986), Do-so-mae-eob-jin-heungbeob (Law for the Promotion of the Wholesale and Retail Industry)

———, (1987), Si-jangbeob si-haenglyeong (Dae-tonglyeonglyeong 12211) (Enforcement Decree of the Market Law (Presidential Decree No. 12211))

———, (1991), Do-so-mae-eob-jin-heungbeob si-haenglyeong (Dae-tonglyeonglyeong 13411) (Enforcement of Decree of the Law for Promotion of Whole and Retail Industry (Presidential Decree No. 13411))

———, (1995), Do-so-mae-eob jin-heungbeob jeon-myeon gae-jeong-an (Whole Amendment of the Law for the Promotion of the Whole and of the Retail Industry)

———, (1995), Do-so-mae-eob-jin-heungbeob si-haenglyeong (Dae-tonglyeonglyeong 14718) (Enforcement of Decree of the Law for Promotion of Whole and Retail Industry (Presidential Decree No. 14718))

———, (1997), Yu-tongsan-eob bal-jeon-beob (Law for the Development of the Distribution Industry)

———, (2005), Jaeraesijang yugseongeul wihan teugbyeolbeob (Special Act on the Promotion of Traditional Market)

———, (2008), Sanghun-beob (Law of Citation of Merit)

———, (2010), Yu-tongsan-eob bal-jeon-beob (Law for the Development of the Distribution Industry)

———, (2011), Yu-tongsan-eob bal-jeon-beob (Law for the Development of the Distribution Industry)

———, (2012), Yu-tongsan-eob bal-jeon-beob (Law for the Development of the Distribution Industry)

———, (2014), Yu-tongsan-eob bal-jeon-beob (Law for the Development of the Distribution Industry)

———, (2014), Sogieob mich sosanggongin jiwoneul wihan teugbyeoljochibeob (Act on special measures for the development of small and micro enterprises)

———, (2014), Jeontongsijang mich sangjeomga yugseongeul wihan teugbyeolbeob (Special act on the promotion of traditional Marketplaces and shopping districts)

No, Taeu dae-tonglyeong (1988a), 13dae dae-tonglyeong chwi-imsa (Inaugural Address of the 13th President)

Penn World Tables Version 6.2 (PWT 6.2) (1950–2004)

Securities Supervisory Board (1997), *Jeunggwon-gamdog-won 20nyeon*-sa (History of Secutiries Supervisory Board for 20 years), Seoul: Securities Supervisory Board

Shinsegae Department Store (1987), *Sin-se-gye 25nyeon-ui bal-ja-chwi* (Histroy of Shinsegae over 25 Years), Seoul: Shinsegae Department Store.

Si-min-ui sin-mun (2003), *Han-gug-min-gan dan-che chonglam* (Directory of Korean NGOs), Seoul: Si-min-ui sin-mun

Statistics Korea (SK), Monthly Income and Expenditure per Urban Household, annual (1970–2006)

———, Population and Housing Census, annual (1970–2005)

———, (1968), Commerce Census

———, (1971, 1976, 1979, 1982), Wholesale and Retail Trade Census

———, (1986, 1991), Wholesale and Retail Trade Census with the Overall Establishment Statistics

———, (1988, 1989, 1990, 1992, 1993, 1995, 1997, 1998, 1999, 2000, 2002, 2003, 2004), Wholesale and Retail Trade Survey

———, (1996, 2001), Wholesale, Retail Trade and Service Industry Census

———, (1995), *Han-gug-ui sa-hoe-ji-pyo* (Social Index in Korea), Seoul: SK

———, Economically Active Population Survey, annual (1970–2006)

———, Index of Income Distribution, annual

Newspaper and Magazine Articles

Fashion Insight (2002), 'Bag-seongcheol-ssi seomsan-yeon hoe-jang jae-chu-dae' (Chairman Bag Reappointed as the Head of the KOFOTI), 25 Ferburary

Gyo-tong-il-bo (2008), 'Ja-gonghyeob sanggeun-bu-hoe-jang-e Heo Mun jeon san-ja-bu-sil-jang' (The Vice Chairman of the KAMA, Heo Mun Former Director of DTI), 8 May

Han-gug-gyeongje-sin-mun (Korea Economic Daily) (2002), 'Hal-in-jeom-ui geo-chim-eobsneun jil-ju' (Running of the Discount Store), 14 October

Han-gyeo-le 21 (Weekly) (2002), 'Jeon-cheol-hwan chongjae' (The President of the BOK, Jeon Cheolhwan), 14 March, Vol. 399

I-de-il-li (E-Daily) (2007), 'Ma-teu-ga go-geub-ui-lyu-kka-ji, baeg-hwa-jeom seong-yeog-bunggoe bi-sang' (Discount Store Dealing with Luxurious Apparel, Department Store in Crisis), 9 October (http://www.edaily.co.kr/news/NewsRead.edy?DCD=A601&newsid=01502246583291280) (Early-March 2008)

Jo-seon-il-bo (1970), 'Bag-dae-tonglyeong, so-bi-bo-da jeo-chug-meon-jeo' (President Park said, Savings before Consumption]), 26 September

———, (1972a), 'Gu-du-dakk-i jeo-chug-wang gimgwangcheon-ssi-e bag-dae-tonglyeong-i geum-il-bong bo-nae-wa' (President Park gives a gift of money to a shoeblack Mr Kim, King of Savings of the Year), 23 January

———, (1972b), 'Oe-lae-pum do-kkae-bi-si-jang geub-seub da-seos teu-leog ab-su' (A Raid on the Market of Foreign Goods in which goods as much as Five trucks was confiscated), 30 July

———, (1973a), 'Se-mu-sa-chal chi-myeongjeog gi-eob-su-sa, jingse-oe-jeog mog-jeog hwal-yongdo' (Tax Investigation Executed Regardless of Tax Collection), 24 May

———, (1973b), 'Geom-yag-eu-lo nae-ja-dong-won geug-dae-hwa' (Maximisation of Investment through people's frugality), 26 October

———, (1974a), 'Ga-jog-i oe-lae-pum sseu-myeon hae-dang gongmu-won-do mun-chaeg' (Civil Servants will be punished due to the use of foreign goods by their family), 6 June

———, (1974b), 'Bo-sa-bu, oe-lae-pum bul-mae-un-dong' (Ministry of Health and Social Affairs, Starting the Campaign of Boycott of Foreign Goods), 12 June

———, (1975a), 'Oe-lae-pum il-je-dan-sog, 6wol han-dal dong-an' (Strong Investigation on Foreign Goods in June]), 30 May

———, (1975b), 'Gug-se-cheong, ju-sig-i-dong-jae-beol 2se yu-heungbi jo-sa' (Tax Authority, Investigation on the Relationship between the Stock Trade of and Entertainment Costs of *Chaebol* Family), 6 July

———, (1977a), 'Pyeonghwa-si-jang cheol-si-neun jeungse-e tta-leun jeo-hang' (Closing up Shops of Pyounghwa Traditional Market in Resistance to a Tax Increase), 14 October

———, (1977b), 'Bu-ga-se-je-do sil-pae, sin-min pyeonghwa-si-jang sa-geon-jo-sa bal-pyo' (Failure of the VAT, the Opposition Party Announced after Investigation on the Pyounghwa Traditional Market in Resistance) 16 October

———, (1979a), 'Gug-se-cheong, ho-hwa-saenghwal eumseongso-deug se-geumbu-gwa' (Tax Authority, Taxation on Extravagance and Illegal Income), 3 June

———, (1979b), 'Ho-tel losde nae-gug-in baeg-hwa-jeom gae-seol-umjig-im-e geo-sen-ban-gi' (Strong Opposition to Establishment of the Department Store by Hotel Lotte', 6 July

———, (1979c), 'Losde-syo-pingsen-teo gae-gwan, baeg-hwa-jeom-e sae-pan-do' (Establishment of Lotte Shopping Center, New Wave in the Department Store), 18 December

———, (1992), 'Han-eun dog-lib-seong-wi-sangganghwa gwan-sim jo-sun jeon bu-chongli han-eun-chongjae chwi-im' (Attention to the Independence of the BOK, the Former Vice Prime Minster Jo Sun Taking over the President of the BOK), 26 March

———, (1997a), articles, 4 and 5 December

———, (1997b), articles, 5 and 11 December

———, (2000), 'Jae-beol-che-je mu-neo-ji-na (2)' (Does *Chaebol* System break down? (2)), 2 June

———, (2001), 'So-deug-tta-la so-bi yanggeug-hwa simhwa, go-geub seung-yongcha jal pal-li-go 300won-jja-li ppang-eun an-pal-lyeo' (Serious Polarisation of Consumption in Income Levels, High Turnover of Luxurious car but Low Turnover of Small Bread), 17 August

———, (2005a), 'Go jeongju-yeonghoe-jang gu-du gub gal-myeo 30nyeon sin-eo' (The Late Chairman Jeong Juyeong had repaired his own heels for 30 years), 14 April

———, (2005b), '131gae dan-che yanggeug-hwa hae-so gug-min-yeon-dae chul-beomsig' (Launch of National Confederation of 131 institutes for Decrease in Economic Inequality), 23 September

———, (2005c), '3bun-gi GDP 4.4% seongjang, gyeonggi jin-jja sal-a-na-na' (GDP 4.4 % Increase in the Third Quarter, Is Economic Situation Improved), 26 October

———, (2005d), 'Yo-jeum baeg-hwa-jeom, son-nim jul-eo-do mae-chul-eun neul-eo, so-bi yanggeug-hwa ttu-lyeos' (Decrease in Customs but Increase in Sales in the Department Store, Clear Polarisation of Consumption), 13 December

———, (2006), 'Mossa-neun jib a-i, gongbu mosha-neun a-i, jeong-ui-jang yanggeug-hwa haengbogye-sog' (Poverty linked to Low Academic Performance of Children, the Opposition Party Leader said), 25 February

———, (2007), 'Keon-syu-meo li-po-teu, 'go-geub-hal-in-jeom' geu mo-sun-ui ma-ke-ting' (Consumer Report, Luxurious Discount Store, Its Contradictory Marketing), 27 September

Mae-il-gyeongje-sin-mun (Maeil Business Newspaper) (2007), 'Hompeul-leo-seu, sang-pum-a-nin ga-chi-leul pan-da' (Homeplus, Sell the Value, instead of Goods), 18 September

Shinsegae Department Store (1996a), *Wol-gan sin-se-gye* (Monthly Shinsegae), June.

———, (1996b), *Wol-gan sin-se-gye ga-jog* (Monthly Shinsegae Family), Mar.

Seo-ul-gyeongje-sin-mun (Seoul Economic Daily) (1961), 'Bi-eo-ga-neun baeg-hwa-jeom' (Department Store Becoming Vacant Due to Closing up Stores), 11 September

The Economist (1997), 'Bargain hunters', Vol. 343, No. 8014, April.

Yonhap News Agency (2005a), 'MBC, jeon-du-hwan jeonggwon-ui 3s jeongchaeg-eul mal-han-da' (Chun's Regime, 3s Policies), 18 May

———, (2005b), 'Cham-yeo-jeongbu-ui bu-dongsan si-jang an-jeongdae-chaeg' (Measurements for stabilisation of Real Estate Market by the Governemnt), 31 August

Internet sites (Date of access in brackets)

Anyang Central Market <http://www.anyang.go.kr> (Mid-May 2008)

Carrefour <http://www.carrefour.com/cdc/group/history> (Early-March 2008)

CAEO <http://cceo.or.kr> (Mid-May 2005)

Daiei <http://www.daiei.co.jp/corporate/company/step/1960.html> (Mid-March 2008)

E-Mart <http://about.shinsegae.com/company/COHistoryV.asp> (Early-April 2006)

Homeplus <http://corporate.homeplus.co.kr> (Late-September 2006)

Hyundai Department Store <http://www.ehyundai.com/home/ir/ir_history.jsp> (Mid-January 2006)

KAMA <http://www.kama.or.kr> (Early-March 2008)

KOFOTI <http://www.kofoti.or.kr> (Early-March 2008)

Korea Federation of Small and Medium Business, (2013), 'Sangpum gonggeubjeom jubyeon sangga gyeongyeongsiltae josa' (Management Report of Supermarkets near the SSM), <http://stat2.smba.go.kr/index.jsp> (Early-February 2014)

KOSA <http://www.kosa.or.kr> (Mid-October 2007)

Lotte Department Store <http://dpt.lotteshopping.com/shopping/company/history.jsp> (Mid-January 2006)

Lotte-Mart <http://company.lottemart.com/company/history_2007.jsp> (Early-April 2006)

Si-dae-baeg-hwa-jeom, Ga-go-pa-baeg-hwa-jeom <http://stock.koscom.co.kr/giup/giup_info.jsp?code=A004010&market=A&upcode=16> (Early-October 2008)

Saemaul Movement, Naver Encyclopaedia <http://naver.com> (Early-February 2005)

Shinsegae Department Store <http://about.shinsegae.com/company/COHistoryV.asp> (Mid-January 2006)

Sukyo Supermarket <http://firstplus.co.kr> (Early-January 2005)

Tesco <http://www.tescocorporate.com> (Ealy-March 2008) <http://www.mt.co.kr/view/mtview.php?type=1&no=2013100915075696837&outlink=1> (Early-February 2014)

Secondary Sources in Korean, English and Japanese

Abramovitz, M. (1986), 'Catching Up, Forging Ahead, and Falling Behind', *Journal of Economic History*, Vol. 46, No. 2

———, (1991), 'The Elements of Social Capability', Presented at the Korea Development Institute (KDI), The Twentieth Anniversary Symposium on *Economic Growth and Social Capability*, July 1–3, Seoul, Korea

Aghion, P., E. Caroli, and C. Garcia-Penalosa (1999), 'Inequality and Economic Growth: The Perspective of the New Growth Theories', *Journal of Economic Literature*, Vol. 37, December, pp. 1615–1660

Alesina, A. and A. Drazen (1991), 'Why are Stabilizations Delayed?', *American Economic Review*, Vol. 81, No. 5

Alesina, A. and D. Rodrik (1994), 'Distribution Politics and Economic Growth', *Quarterly Journal of Economics*, May

Alesina, A. and R. Perotti (1996), 'Income Distribution, Political Instability, and Investment', *European Economic Review*, 40, pp. 1203–1228

Alexander, N. and G. Akehurst (1999), 'Introduction: The Emergence of Modern Retailing, 1750–1950', in Alexander, N. and G. Akehurst (eds), *The Emergence of Modern Retailing 1750–1950*, London: Frank Cass

Amsden, A. (1989), *Asia's Next Giant: South Korea and Late Industrialisation*, New York: Oxford University Press

An, Gwangho and Jo Jaeun (2003), *Yu-tonggwan-li won-lon* (Introduction to Marketing Channel Management), Seoul: Hag-hyeon-sa

Baek, Insu (2003), 'The Evolutionary Process of the Retail System in Korea', Doctoral Thesis of Department of Commerce, Waseda University (Japanese)

———, (2004), 'Han-gug baeg-hwa-jeom-ui seongjanggwa so-mae-gyeong-yeong hyeog-sin' (Development of department store and its retailing management innovations in Korea since the 1980s), *Han-il gyeongsangnon-jib*, Vol. 29, pp. 165–202 (Japanese)

Baek, Insu, Seo Yonggu, Gim Hyeoncheol and Gim Inho (2006), *Yu-tongsi-jang gae-bang 10nyeon, yu-tongsan-eob gu-jo-byeon-hwa-wa eob-tae-byeol haeg-sim i-syu* (10 Years since Opening of Domestic Market, the Structural Change of the Retail Industry and Key Issues in Each Retail Format), Seoul: KIET

Baek, Insu (2006), 'Conclusion and Policy Implication' in Baek Insu, Seo Yonggu, Gim Hyeoncheol and Gim Inho (eds), *Yu-tongsi-jang gae-bang 10nyeon, yu-tongsan-eob gu-jo-byeon-hwa-wa eob-tae-byeol haeg-sim i-syu* (10 Years since Opening of Domestic Market, the Structural Change of the Retail Industry and Key Issues in Each Retail Format), Seoul: KIET

Baek, Okseon (2013), 'Daehyeongmateu mich gieobhyeongsyupeomakes yeongeobilsi gyujee gwanhan beobjeog gochal' (Legal Analysis of Major Supermarkets and Super

Supermarket Business Hour Regulations), *Haengjeongbeob yeongu*, Vol. 36, pp. 319–349

Baek, Ukin (1994), 'Ggye-geub-byeol saenghwal-sangtae yeon-gu: bu-ui bul-pyeong-deunggwa so-bi-gu-jo byeon-hwa-leul jungsim-eu-lo' (A Study on Income Inequality and Life Condition: with Reference to Changes of Consumption Structure in 1980s), Doctoral Thesis of Department of Sociology, Graduate School, Seoul National University

Bak, Heonju, Jeong Huinam, Bak Cheol and Mun Gyeonghui (2000), *To-ji-si-jang-ui gu-jo-byeon-hwa mich jeon-mang yeon-gu* (Structural Changes in Korean Land Market with Short Term Prospective), Seoul: Korea Research Institute for Human Settlements (KRIHS)

Bak, Jingeun (2000), *Se-gye-gyeongje sog-ui han-gug-gyeongje 40nyeon: geu heu-leumgwa gwa-je* (The Korean Economy for 40 Years in World Economy), Seoul: Bag-yeongsa

Bak, Jinyong (1998), 'So-mae-eob-che-wa gonggeub-eob-che-ui sin-loe mich gyeol-sog-e gwan-han yeon-gu' (A Study on Trust and Commitment of Retailer-Supplier Relationship), Doctoral Thesis of Business Administration, Yonsei University

Bak, Juyeong and Sin Gidong (2010), 'SSMe daeeunghan jungsosyupeomakesui gyeong-jaengryeog ganghwabangan' (How to increase Small Retailers' Competitiveness against Super-Supermarket), *Yutongyeongu*, Vol. 15, No. 5, pp. 1–18

Bak, Taegyun (2007a), 'Han-gug-jeon-jaeng i-hu i-seungman jeongbu-ui gyeongje-bu-heung jeon-lyag' (The Economic Development Plans of the Rhee Government after the Korean War), *Se-gye-jeongchi 8*, Vol. 28, No. 2. pp. 203–249

———, (2007b), *Won-hyeonggwa byeon-yong: han-gug gyeongje-gae-bal gye-hoeg-ui gi-won* (Archetype and Metamorphosis: The Origin of Korea's Economic Development Plans), Seoul: Seoul National University Press

Bardhan, P. (1993), 'Symposium on Democracy and Development', *Journal of Economic Perspectives*, Vol. 7, No. 3

Barro, R.J. (1991), 'Economic Growth in a Cross-Section of Countries', *The Quarterly Journal of Economics*, May

———, (2000), 'Inequality and Growth in a Panel of Countries', *Journal of Economic Growth*, 5, pp. 5–32

Barro, R.J. and J-W. Lee (2001), 'International Data on Educational Attainment: Updates and Implications', *Oxford Economic Papers* 3, pp. 541–563

Benson, J.K. (1975), 'The Interorganizational Network as a Political Economy', *Administrative Science Quarterly*, Vol. 20, June

Bertola, G. (1993), 'Factor Shares and Savings in Endogenous Growth', *American Economic Review*, Vol. 83, No. 5

Brown, S. (1987), 'Institutional Change in Retailing: A Review and Synthesis', *European Journal of Marketing*, Vol. 21, No. 6

———, (1990), 'Innovation and Evolution in UK Retailing: The Retail Warehouse', *European Journal of Marketing*, Vol. 24, No. 9

Bucklin, L.P. (1972), *Competition and Evolution in the Distribution Trades,* Englewood Cliffs: Prentice Hall

Campbell, N.C.G. (1985), 'Buyer/Seller Relationship in Japan and Germany: An Interaction Approach', *European Journal of Marketing,* Vol. 19, Issue, 3

Castello, A and R. Domenech (2002), 'Human Capital Inequality and Economic Growth: Some New Evidence', *Economic Journal*, Vol. 112, No. 478

Cha, Sinheung (1995), 'Yu-tongsi-jang gae-bang-e tta-leun yu-tongsan-eob-ui jeongchaeg-dae-eung: do-so-mae-eob-eul jungsim-eu-lo' (Policy Response of Distribution Industry to the Distribution Market Opening: with Emphasis on Wholesale and Retail Trade), Dissertation of Master of Graduate School of Public Administration, Sungkyunkwan University

Chandler, A. (1999), *The Visible Hand*, Cambridge, Massachusetts and London: The Belknap Press of Harvard University Press

Chang, H-J. (1996), *The Political Economy of Industrial Policy,* London: Macmillan Press

Chang, H-J., H-J. Park, and C.G. Yoo (1998), 'Interpreting the Korean Crisis: Financial Liberalization, Industrial Policy and Corporate Governance', *Cambridge Journal of Economics,* Vol. 22, No. 6

Choe, Bongseok and Gu Jiseon, (2013), 'Daehyeongmateuwa SSMui jayulgyujee gwanhan beobjeog geomto' (A Legal Study on the Self-regulations of Large-scale Discount Stores and SSM), *Haengjeongbeob yeongu*, Vol. 36, pp. 293–318

Choe, Gwang and Hyeon Jingwon (1996), 'Bun-bae bul-gyun-deung chu-i-wa jo-se-ui so-deug-jae-bun-bae hyo-gwa: mun-heon-go-chal-eul jungsim-eu-lo' (The Trends of Distribution Inequality and the Effects of Tax on Income Redistribution), in Hyeon Jingwon (ed.), *Jo-se-jeongchaeg-gwa so-deug-jae-bun-bae* (Taxation Policy and Redistribution of Income), 96–01, Seoul: Korea Institute of Public Finance (KIPF)

Choe, Ilhyeong (1997), 'Han-gug-gi-eob-ui junggug yu-tongsan-eob jin-chul jeon-lyag: (ju)sin-se-gye-baeg-hwa-jeom sa-lye-leul jungsim-eu-lo' (The Strategy of the entry into the Chinese Retail Industry by the Korean Company – with the Case of Shinsegae Department Store), Dissertation of Master of Business Administration, Korea University

Choe, Jangho, Baek Insu and Gim Sui (1994), *Yu-tongsi-jang gae-bang-i ga-jeon-yu-tong-e mi-chi-neun yeonghyanggwa dae-eungbang-an* (Influence and Prospective Plan of Opening of the Distribution Industry on Distribution of Consumer Electronics), Seoul: KIET

Choe, Jeongpyo (1993), *Jae-beol-hae-che* (Dismantlement of Chaebol), Seoul: bi-bongchul-pan-sa

Choe, Jinseok and Gim Yeongdeok (2007), 'Oe-hwan-wi-gi jeon-hu-ui no-dongso-deug wi-heomgwa ye-bi-jeog jeo-chug sil-jeungbun-seog' (An Empirical Analysis of

Precautionary Savings: Before and After the Period of Korean Financial Crisis), *Gyeongje-yeon-gu,* Vol. 25, No. 2, pp. 131–151

Choi, S.C. (2003), 'Moves into the Korean market by global retailers and the response of local retailers', in Dawson, J.A., M. Mukoyama, S.C. Choi, and R. Larke (eds), *The Internationalization of Retailing in Asia*, London: RoutledgeCurzon

Cole, D.C. and Bak Yeongcheol (1984), *Han-gug-ui geum-yungbal-jeon: 1945–80* (Korea's Financial Development: 1945–80), Seoul: KDI

Coughlan, A.T., E. Anderson, L.W. Stern and A.I. El-Ansary (2001), *Marketing Channels*, Upper Saddle River, New Jersey: Prentice-Hall

Croix, D. and M. Doepke (2003), 'Inequality and Growth: Why Differential Fertility Matters', *American Economic Review*, Vol. 93, No. 4

Cundiff, E.W. (1965), 'Concepts in Comparative Retailing', *Journal of Marketing,* Vol. 29, Issue, 1

Davidson, W.R. (1970), 'Changes in Distribution Institutions', *Journal of Marketing*, Vol. 34, Issue, 1

Davidson, W.R., A.D. Bates and S.J. Bass (1976), 'The Retail Life Cycle', *Harvard Business Review,* Vol. 54, Nov.-Dec.

Davis, D.E. (2004), *Discipline and Development: Middle Classes and Prosperity in East Asia and Latin America*, Cambridge University Press

Dawson, J.A. (2002), 'Structural-spatial Relationships in the Spread of Hypermarket Retailing', in Findlay, A.M. and L. Sparks (eds), *Retailing: Critical Concepts*, London and New York: Routledge

Dent, C.M. (2003), 'Taiwan's Foreign Economic Policy: The 'Liberalization Plus' Approach of an Evolving Developmental State', *Modern Asian Studies*, 37, 2, pp. 461–483

Dreesman, A.C.R. (1968), 'Patterns of Evolution in Retailing', *Journal of Retailing,* Vol. 44, Issue, 1

Easterly, W. (2001), 'The Middle Class Consensus and Economic Development', *Journal of Economic Growth*, 6, pp. 317–335

Evans, P. (1994), 'Class, State, and Dependence in East Asia: Lessons for Latin Americanists', in Deyo, F.C. (ed.), *The Political Economy of the New Asian Industrialism*, Ithaca and London: Cornell Univ. Press

Ferreira, F.H.G. and M. Walton (2006), 'Inequality of Opportunity and Economic Development', World Bank Policy Research Working Paper 3816, January

Forbes, K. (2000), 'A Reassessment of the Relationship Between Inequality and Growth', *American Economic Review*, Vol. 90, No. 4

Fraser, W.H. (1981), *The Coming of the Mass Market, 1850–1914*, London: Macmillan

Gang, Aeri (1996), 'Ga-gyeog-pa-goe-hyeong yu-tong-eob-tae-ui ma-ke-ting jeon-lyag yeon-gu' (A Study on Marketing Strategy of Mass-discount Stores), Dissertation of Master of Business Administration, Sookmyung Women's University

Gang, Gwangha (2000), *Gyeongje-gae-bal 5gae-nyeon gye-hoeg: mog-pyo mich jib-haeng-ui pyeongga* (The Five-year Plan for Economic Development), Seoul: Seoul National University Press

Gilboy, E.W. (1967), 'Demand as a Factor in the Industrial Revolution', in Hartwell, R.M. (ed.), *The Causes of the Industrial Revolution in England*, London: Methuen Young Books

Gim, Beomsu (1997), 'Je-jo-eob-che-dae-li-jeomgan gwan-gye-gwan-li bang-an-e gwan-han yeon-gu' (A Study on the Management Plan in Manufacturer-Distributor Relationship), Dissertation of Master of Business Administration, Seoul National University

Gim, Chang (1994), 'Teug-byeol-so-bi-se-je-e gwan-han yeon-gu: je-pumga-gyeog-e mi-chi-neun yeonghyang-eul jungsim-eu-lo' (A Study on the Special Excise Tax System: Effectiveness on the Product Price), Dissertation of Master of Business Administration, Hanyang University

Gim, Cheolho (1992), 'Nongsan-mul ga-gyeog mich yu-tongjeongchaeg-ui hoe-go-wa jeon-mang' (The Past and the Future of Farm Prices and Agricultural Distribution Policy), *Nong-eob-jeongchaeg yeon-gu*, Vol. 19, No. 1, pp. 161–172

Gim, Deokjung (1984), 'Gug-je-su-ji bang-eo-myeon-e-seo bon su-ib-ja-yu-hwa-ui chu-jin-banghyang' (The Policy of Import Liberalisation in Respect of the Balance of Payment), Dissertation of Master of Graduate School of Public Administration, Seoul National University

Gim, Gipyeong and Yun Gichang, (2011), 'Jungsoyutongeobui gongdongbeuraendeu ma-ketingmigseu jeonryagi gogaegmanjog mich chungseongdoe michineun yeonghyang' (The Effects of Cooperative Brand Marketing Mix Strategies on the Customer Satisfactions and Loyalties), *Yutonggyeongyeonghaghoeji*, Vol. 14, No. 2, pp. 29–53

Gim, Ilyeong (1995), 'Bag-jeonghui che-je 18nyeon: bal-jeon-gwa-jeong-e dae-han bun-seog-gwa pyeongga' (Park's 18 years' Regime: Analysis and Appraisal on the Development in the Period), *Han-gug-jeongchi-hag-hoe-bo*, Vol. 29, No. 2, pp. 181–215

Gim, Inho (2006), 'Innovation of the Department Stores', in Baek Insu, Seo Yonggu, Gim Hyeoncheol and Gim Inho (eds), *Yu-tongsi-jang gae-bang 10nyeon, yu-tongsan-eob gu-jo-byeon-hwa-wa eob-tae-byeol haeg-sim i-syu* (10 Years since Opening of Domestic Market, the Structural Change of the Retail Industry and Key Issues in Each Retail Format), Seoul: KIET

Gim, Jeongeun (1998), 'Baeg-hwa-jeom ui-lyu-sangpum-ui Private Brandui hyeon-hwang mich jeon-mang' (The Present Situations and Prospects of Korean Department Store's Private Brand of Clothing), Dissertation of Master of Clothing and Textiles, Kon-kuk University

Gim, Jeongman (1990), 'Hae-oe-yeo-haeng-e dae-han han-gug-in ui-sig-e gwan-han yeon-gu' (Research on Korean Attitude to Foreign Travel), *Gwan-gwanghag yeon-gu* [*Study on Tourism*], Vol. 15

Gim, Juheon (2005), 'Te-seu-ko-ui han-gug-si-jang jin-chul-jeon-lyag sa-lye' (Entry Strategies of TESCO into the Korean Market), *Gyeong-yeonggyo-yug yeon-gu* [*Management Education Review*], Vol. 8, No. 2

Gim, Jundong, Gim Jongil and Gang Jungu (2003), *Gug-nae yu-tongseo-bi-seu si-jang gae-bang-ui gyeongje-jeog hyo-gwa-wa jeog-eung ji-won-jeongchaeg* (Economic Effects of the Liberalisation of Distribution Services in Korea and Adjustment Policies), Seoul: Korea Institute for International Economic Policy (KIEP)

Gim, Junhwan and Gim Hyeonsun (2013), 'Daehyeongmateuwa jeontongsijang iyong-haengtae chaie gwanhan siljeungyeongu-sudogwon jumineul daesangeuro-' (A Study on Difference of Shopping Behaviour between Super Store and Traditional Market Customer – The Case of Residents in Metropolitan Area-, *Hangug jugeohwangyeong haghoeji*, Vol. 11, No. 1, pp. 63–75

Gim, Juyeong and Bak Jeongeun (2011), 'Jaeraesijangui sijang jihyangjeog bunryue tta-reun baljeonbanghyang' (Market Oriented Typology and Development Directions of Conventional Market), *Yutongyeongu*, Vol. 16, No. 5, pp. 63–83

Gim, Myeongseop (2003), 'Han-gug-jeon-jaeng-i naengjeongche-je-ui gu-seong-e mi-chin yeonghyang' (The Impact of the Korean War on the Construction of the Cold War System), *Gug-je-jeongchi-non-chong*, Vol. 43, No. 1, pp. 115–133

Gim, Sangjo (1998), 'Je 3jang, geum-yung ja-bon-si-jang' (The Third Chapter, The Financial and Money Market), in Han-gug-sa-hoe-gwa-hag-yeon-gu-so [Korea Institute of Social Science (KISS)] (eds), *Gae-jeongpan, da-i-eo-geu-laem han-gug-gyeongje,* Seoul: ui-amchul-pan-mun-hwa-sa

Gim, Seongcheon (2000), 'Sangpumgwon geo-lae gyu-je-ha-neun ib-beob pil-yo' (The Need for Regulation on the Gift-voucher), *So-bi-ja si-dae,* September

Gim, Seonghun and Han Jaehwan (2011), 'Sobija insig bunseogeul tonghan jaeraesijangui hwalseonghwa bangan dochul' (Reinvigorating Method of the traditional market through analysis of Consumer's Recognition), *Nongchongyeongje*, Vol. 34, No. 3, pp. 59–77

Gim, Seongsu (1998), 'Han-gug-jae-beol-ui gyeong-yeongsa-jeog yeon-gu' (Historical Study for Korean Chaebol Companies), *Gyeong-yeongsa-hag,* Vol. 18

Gim, Sukgyeong, Gim Cheongon and Gim Gihwan (2011), Yutongsaneobui gujobyeon-hwa mich gyeongjaengryeog ganghwabangan-somaeyutongeul jungsimeuro-(Structural Change Analysis and Policy Suggestions for Strengthening Competitiveness of Korean Retail Industry-), Seoul: KIET

Gim, Uyeong, Bak Sunchan and I Changsu (2005), *Mu-yeog-ja-yu-hwa-ga go-yong mich imgeum yanggeug-hwa-e mi-chin yeonghyang: han-gug je-jo-eob-eul jungsim-eu-lo*

(The Effects of Trade Liberalization on Employment and Wage Inequality: the Korean Manufacturing Sector), Seoul: KIEP

Gim, Yeongmyeong (1992), *Han-gug hyeon-dae jeongchi-sa: jeongchi-byeon-dong-ui yeog-hag* (The Contemporary Political History of Korea), Seoul: Eul-yu-mun-hwa-sa

Gist, R.R. (1968), *Retailing: Concepts and Decisions,* New York: Wiley and Sons

Goldman, A. (1974), 'Outreach of Consumers and the Modernization of Urban Food Retailing in Developing Countries', *Journal of Marketing,* Vol. 38, Issue, 4

———, (1991), 'Japan's Distribution System: Institutional Structure, Internal Political Economy, and Modernization', *Journal of Retailing,* Vol. 67, Issue, 2

———, (1992), 'Evaluating the Performance of the Japanese Distribution System', *Journal of Retailing,* Vol. 68, Issue, 1

———, (2001), 'The Transfer of Retail Formats into Developing Economies: The Example of China', *Journal of Retailing,* Vol. 77, Issue, 2

Greenley, G.E. and D. Shipley (1992), 'A comparative Study of Operational Marketing Practices among British Department Stores and Supermarkets', *European Journal of Marketing,* Vol. 26, No. 5

Gross, W. (1964), 'Strategies Used by Major Department Stores to Compete with Low-Margin Retailers', *Journal of Retailing,* Summer

Grossman, G.M. and E. Helpman (1994), 'Endogenous Innovation in the Theory of Growth', *Journal of Economic Perspectives,* Vol. 8, No. 1

Gu, Hyeongsuk (1995), 'Jeompo i-mi-ji bun-seog-eul tonghan jeon-lyag su-lib-e gwan-han yeon-gu: myeongdong sin-se-gye baeg-hwa-jeom-ui sa-lye-leul jungsim-eu-lo' (A Study of Formulating Strategies by Analysis of Store Images), Dissertation of Master of Business Administration, Hanyang University

Gwak, Wonil, Nam Inu and No Jeonggu (2009), 'Jaeraesijanggwa daehyeongmateuui bangmunuidoe daehan hwangyeong mich gamjeongjeog yeonghyange gwanhan yeongu' (A Study on the Environmental and Affective Influences Visiting Attention in Small Traditional Markets and Large Discount Stores), *Yutongyeongu,* Vol. 14, No. 3, pp. 77–104

Gwon, Sunwon, Go Ildong, Gim Gwanyeong and Gim Seonung (1992), *Bun-bae bul-gyun-deung-ui sil-tae-wa ju-yo jeongchaeg-gwa-je* (The Situation of Unequal Distribution and Policy Task), Seoul: KDI

Haggard, S. (1994), *Pathways from the Periphery: The Politics of Growth in the Newly Industrializing Countries,* Ithaca and London: Cornell University Press

Hall, R.E. and C.I. Jones (1999), 'Why Do some Countries Produce so much more Output per Worker than Others?', *The Quarterly Journal of Economics,* February

Han-gug-sa-hoe-gwa-hag-yeon-gu-so [Korea Institute of Social Science (KISS)] (1998), *Gae-jeongpan, da-i-eo-geu-laem han-gug-gyeongje* (The Korean Economy in Diagram), Seoul: ui-amchul-pan-mun-hwa-sa

Hill, S.R. (1974), 'Distribution in Britain – The Next Ten Years', *Journal of Retailing*, Vol. 50, No. 2

Hirano, T. (1999), 'Retailing in Urban Japan, 1868–1945', *Urban History*, Vol. 26, No. 3. pp. 373–392

Hitoshi, T. (2003), 'The Development of Foreign Retailing in Taiwan: the Impact of Carrefour', in Dawson, J.A., M. Mukoyama, S.C. Choi, and R. Larke (eds), *The Internationalisation of Retailing in Asia*, RoutledgeCurzon: London

Hollander, S.C. (1966), 'Notes on the Retail Accordion', *Journal of Retailing*, Vol. 42, Issue, 2

Huber, E., D. Rueschemeyer, and J. Stephens (1993), 'The Impact of Economic Development on Democracy', *Journal of Economic Perspectives*, Vol. 7, No. 3

Hwang, Myeongsu, et al. (1992), *Han-gug-ui si-jang sang-eob-sa* (The Business History of the Korean Market), Seoul: Shinsegae Department Store Press

Hyeon, Jingwon (1996), 'To-ji-so-yu-ui pyeon-jungsil-tae-wa jonghab-to-ji-se-ui se-bu-dam bun-seog' (Unequal Distribution of Land Ownership and Analysis on Tax Burden of Aggregate Land Tax), in Hyeon Jingwon (ed.), *Jo-se-jeongchaeg-gwa so-deug-jae-bun-bae* (Taxation Policy and Redistribution of Income), 96–01, Seoul: KIPF

I, Byeongcheon (1998), 'Bal-jeon-gug-ga ja-bon-ju-ui-wa bal-jeon dil-le-ma' (Capitalism of the Developmental State and Dilemma of Development), in I, Byeongcheon and Gim Gyun (eds), *Wi-gi geu-li-go dae-jeon-hwan* (The Crisis and Big Change), Seoul: Do-seo-chul-pan dangdae

I, Byeonggi (1998), *Han-gug-ui gyeongje-seongjang yo-in-gwa san-eob-jeongchaeg-ui yeog-hal* (Factors for Growth of Korean economy and the Role of Industrial Policy), Seoul: Korean Economic Research Institute (KERI)

I, Daegeun (2002), *Hae-banghu 1950nyeon-dae-ui gyeongje* (The Economy of After-independence and the 1950s), Seoul: Samseonggyeongje-yeon-gu-so chul-pan-bu

I, Deokhun and I Yeongseok (2013), 'Jeongbuui jeontongsijang jiwonjeongchaegi sijan-ghwalseonghwae michineun yeonghyange gwanhan yeongu: daegu, daejeonui dosi-jiyeog jeontongsijangeul jungsimeuro' (A Study on the Effect of Government Policy for the traditional market: Focused on the traditional market in Daegu and Daejeon), *Saneobgyeongjeyeongu*, Vol. 26, No. 5, pp. 2337–2360

I, Inpyo (1999), 'Oe-gug dae-hyeong so-mae-jeom-ui gug-nae jin-ib-e tta-leun han-gug dae-hyeong so-mae-jeom-ui dae-eungjeon-lyag-e gwan-han yeon-gu' (A Study on the Corresponding Strategy of Korean Large Retailers according to the Domestic Entry of Foreign Large Retailers), Doctoral Thesis of Business Administration, Hannam University

I, Janggyu, et al. (1995), *Sil-log 6gonggyeongje-heug-ja-gyeongje-ui chimmol* (A True Record, Economy of the Sixth Republic), Seoul: JoongAng Daily

I, Jeongu and Hwang Seonghyeon (1998), *Han-gug-ui bun-bae-mun-je: hyeon-hwang, mun-je-jeomgwa jeongchaeg-banghyang* (The Problem of Korean Distribution: Reality, Problem and Policy Direction), Seoul: KDI

I, Jeongu and I Seongrim (2001), 'Gyeongje-wi-gi-wa bin-bu-gyeog-cha: 1997nyeon wi-gi i-hu-ui so-deug-bun-bae-wa bin-gon' (Economic Crisis and Income Disparity: Income Distribution and Poverty before and after the 1997 Crisis), *Gug-je-gyeongje-yeon-gu*, Vol. 7, No. 2, pp. 79–109

I, Jinsun (1993), 'Han-gug-ui ji-ga: to-ji-tu-gi-wa si-jangsil-pae' (Land Prices in Korea: Speculation on Lands and Market Failure), in Son Jaeyeong (ed.), *To-ji-si-jang-ui bun-seog-gwa jeongchaeg-gwa-je* (Analysis on Land Market and Task of Policy), 93–02, Seoul: KDI

I, Jongin, No Seonghun, Sin Haesik and Jeong Yunpil, (2009), 'Chuncheon jaeraesijangui hwalseonghwa bangan yeongu-jaeraesijanggwa daehyeongmateu iyonggogaegui siltaejosareul jungsimeuro-' (A Study on Vitality for Traditional Markets in Chunchon-In Case of Research on the Actual Condition for Customers of Traditional Market and Discount Stores-), *Sigpumyutongyeongu*, Vol. 26, No. 3, pp. 51–74

I, Jongseon (2001), 'IMFgyeongje-wi-gi-wa han-gug-ui no-sa-gwan-gye byeon-hwa' (IMF Economic Crisis and the Change of the Labour-management Relationship in Korea), *Han-gug-sa-hoe,* Vol. 4, Seoul: Institute of Social Research

I, Samseong (1993), *Mi-gug-ui dae-han jeongchaeg-gwa han-gug min-jog-ju-ui* (The Foreign Policy of America to Korea and Korean Nationalism), Seoul: Han-gil-sa

I, Sanghyeon (1996), 'U-li-na-la ga-jeon yu-tong dae-li-jeom-ui se-mu, hoe-gye-cheo-li gae-seon-e gwan-han yeon-gu: Ssa-ui sa-lye jungsim-eu-lo' (A Critical Research on the Improvement of the Process of Taxation and Accounting in General Electronic Goods Distributors in Korea), Dissertation of Taxation in Hongik University

I, Seoktae (1998), 'Yu-tonghwan-gyeong byeon-hwa-e tta-leun dae-eungjeon-lyag gae-bal-e gwan-han yeon-gu: han-gug ga-jeon-eob-gye gye-yeol dae-li-jeom-eul jungsim-eu-lo' (A Study of the Development of the Strategy to Adapt Changing in Distributing Industry – Centring on Korean Distributing Agents of Electronic Home Appliance Makers), Dissertation of Master of Administration, Kyunghee University

Ikeo, K. (1997), '3. 小売業態の発展' (The Development of the Retail Format, Chapter 3), in Tajima, Y. and H. Harada (eds), ゼミナール流通入門 (Seminar, Introduction of Retailing), Tokyo: Nihonkeizai shinbun (Japanese)

Im, Hyeokbaek (1994), *Si-jang gug-ga min-ju-ju-ui: han-gug-min-ju-hwa-wa jeongchi-gyeongje-i-lon* (The Market, the State, and the Democracy: Korean Democratic Transition and Theories of Political Economy), Seoul: Na-nam

Im, Hwicheol (1998), 'Chapter I, Industrial Economy', in KISS (eds), *Gae-jeongpan, da-i-eo-geu-laem han-gug-gyeongje* (The Korean Economy in Diagram), Seoul: Ui-amchul-pan-mun-hwa-sa

Im, Jongwon (1989), *Hyeon-dae ma-ke-ting won-lon* (The Principle of the Modern Marketing), Seoul: Beob-mun-sa

Im, Yeonggyun, An Gwanghoa and Gim Sangyong (2002), *Yu-tonggyeonglo gwan-li* (Marketing Channel Management), Seoul: Gyeongmun-sa

Ishihara, T. (1997), '2. 消費と小売構造の変化' (Consumption and the Change of Retail Structure, Chapter 2), in Tajima, Y. and H. Harada (eds), ゼミナール流通入門 (Seminar, Introduction of Retailing), Tokyo: Nihonkeizai shinbun (Japanese)

I, Yeongchan and Choe Jinsu (2003), 'Jungsoyutongeobui mulryugongdonghwae gwan-han yeongu' (A Study on the Physical Distribution Cooperation in the Small and Medium Distribution Industry), *Mulryuhaghoeji*, Vol. 13, No. 1. pp. 123–144

Izraeli, D. (1970), 'The Cyclical Evolution of Marketing Channels', *British Journal of Marketing*, Vol. 5, No. 3

Jang, Gyosik (2012), 'Daehyeongmateu yeongeobgyujejoryee gwanhan gochal' (A Study of Regulations on Major Discount Stores' Conduct of Business), *Beobhagyeongu*, Vol. 48, pp. 49–73

Jang, Sehun (2006), 'Jungsan-cheung-ui ju-geo-hyeon-sil-e bi-chwo-bon jungsan-cheung yug-seongjeongchaeg-ui banghyang' (The Way of Bringing up the Middle Class in the View of the Residential State) in the paper presented in *Han-gug-sa-hoe-hag-hoe jungsan-cheung po-leom 3cha bal-pyo-ja-lyo-jib*, pp. 121–149

Jefferys, J.B. (1954), *Retailing Trading in Britain, 1850–1950: A Study of Trends in Retailing with Special Reference to the Development of Cooperative, Multiple Shop, and Department Store Methods of Trading*, Cambridge, England: Cambridge University Press

Jeon, Byeongyu (2007), 'Han-gug no-dongsi-jang-ui yanggeug-hwa-e gwan-han yeon-gu: junggan il-ja-li mich junggan imgeumgye-cheung-eul jungsim-eu-lo' (Labour Market Polarization in Korea: Vanishing Middle Class?), *Han-gug-gyeongje-ui bun-seog*, Vol. 13, No. 2, pp. 171–230

Jeon, Changhwan (1998), 'Geum-yungse-gye-hwa-wa oe-hwan geum-yung wi-gi' (Financial Globalization, Currency and Financial Crisis), in I, Byeongcheon and Gim Gyun (eds.), *Wi-gi geu-li-go dae-jeon-hwan* (The Crisis and Big Change), Seoul: Do-seo-chul-pan dangdae

Jeon, Huijae (1980), 'Yu-tong-ui gyeongje-gu-jo-sang bi-junggwa mun-je-jeom mich geu gae-seon-bang-an yeon-gu: gongsan-pum yu-tonggu-jo gae-seon-eul wi-han haengjeongje-do-leul jungsim-eu-lo' (A Study on the Weight of Distribution in the Korea Economy, Problem and Proposal for its Improvement: On the Administrative Institutions for the Improvement of the Distribution Channel of Industrial Products), Dissertation of Master of Graduate School of Public Administration, Seoul National Universtiy

Jeon, Sangu (1995) 'Han-gug yu-tongsan-eob jeongchaeg 50nyeon-ui hyeon-hwanggwa gwa-je' (The present and Task of the Korean Policies for distribution industry for 50 years), *Bi-gyo-sa-beob,* Vol. 2, No. 2. pp. 21–27

Jeong, Byeonggwon (1996), 'Yu-tongsi-jang gae-bang-e dae-eunghan ga-jeon-san-eob yu-tongdae-li-jeom-ui gyeongjaenglyeog ganghwa-bang-an yeon-gu' (A Study of the Scheme for the Competitiveness Strengthening of Circulation Agency for the Household Electric Appliance Industry to Cope with the Opening of the Circulation Market), Dissertation of Master of Trade, Sungkyunkwan University

Jeong, Geonhwa (1987), 'Han-gug-ui do-si-bin-min-ui hyeongseong mich jon-jae-hyeongtae-e gwan-han il-yeon-gu: do-si bi-gongsig bu-mun-lon bi-pan-eul jungsim-eu-lo' (A Study on the Formation and Forms of the Urban Poor in Korea – A Critique of the Urban Informal Sector Theory), Dissertation of Master of the Department of Economics, Seoul National University

———, (1998), 'Chapter 7, People's Living', in KISS (eds), *Gae-jeongpan, da-i-eo-geu-laem han-gug-gyeongje* (The Korean Economy in Diagram), Seoul: Ui-amchul-pan-mun-hwa-sa

Jeong, Ho (1996), 'Yu-tongsi-jang gae-bang-e tta-leun jungso-ga-jeon-eob-gye-ui dae-eungbanghyang-e gwan-han yeon-gu' (A Study on Countermeasures of Small-Medium Home Appliance Industries as Open Circulation Market), Dissertation of Master of Administration, Sungkyunkwan University.

Jeong, Unchan (1985), *Geo-si-gyeongje-lon* (Macroeconomics), Seoul: Da-san-chul-pan-sa

———, (1998), *Han-gug-gyeongje jug-eo-ya san-da* (The Study for Survival of the Korean Economy), Seoul: Do-seo-chul-pan na-mu-wa sup

———, (1999), *Han-gug-gyeongje a-jig-do meol-eossda* (The Problems in Korean Economy), Seoul: Do-seo-chul-pan na-mu-wa sup

Jeong, Yunjae (1995), 'Je 3, 4 gonghwa-gug-ui seonggyeog-gwa li-deo-swib: bag-jeonghui dae-tonglyeong-ui geun-dae-hwa li-deo-sib-e gwan-han yeon-gu' (The Character and the Leadership of the Third and the Fourth Republics: A Study on President Park's Leadership for Modernization)', *Dongbug-a-yeon-gu,* Vol. 1, pp. 239–272

Jo, Byeongchan (1993), *Han-gug-si-janggyeongje-sa* (The Economic History of The Korean Market), Seoul: Dongkuk University Press

Jo, Changuk (1991), 'U-li-na-la ju-yo so-bi-jae-ui mul-jeog yu-tongjeongbo-hwa-e gwan-han sil-jeungjeog yeon-gu: teug-hi saenghwal-yongpum-ui POS si-seu-tem do-ib un-yeong-eul jungsim-eu-lo' (An Empirical Study of Physical Distribution Information System on Major Consumer Goods in Korea, with Emphasis on the Condition for Introduction and Operating of Point-Of-Sale (POS) System of Convenience Goods), Doctoral Thesis of Business Administration, Korea University

Jo, Donggi (2006), 'Jungsan-cheung-ui sa-hoe in-gu-hag-jeog teug-seonggwa ju-gwan-jeog gye-cheung-ui-sig' (The Social-Demographic Characteristic of the Middle Class and the Subjective Class Indentification), *Han-gug in-gu-hag,* Vol. 29, No. 3, pp. 89–109

Jo, Dongseong (1990), *Han-gug-jae-beol-yeon-gu* (The Study of Korean Chaebol), Seoul: Mae-il-gyeongje-sin-mun-sa

Jo, Gwansu (1981), 'Gongsan-pum-yu-tonggu-jo-gae-seon' (the Improvement of the Distribution Structure in the Manufactured Goods), in *Yu-tongsan-eob-geun-dae-hwa-gi-bon-gye-hoeg-hae-seol,* Seoul: EPB

Jo, Jinsang (1985), 'Dae-hyeong baeg-hwa-jeom-ui bu-sim-ib-ji-e tta-leun so-bi-ja gong-gan-i-dong-e gwan-han yeon-gu' (A Study on Moving Area of Consumers after Location of the Big Department Store at Sub-center), Dissertation of Master of Graduate School of Environmental Studies, Seoul National University

Jones, L. and Il. Sakong (1980), *Government, Business, and Entrepreneurship in Economic Development: The Korean Case,* Cambridge, Mass.: Harvard University Press

Ju, Hakjung (1979), 'Gye-cheungbyeol so-deug-bun-po-ui chu-gye-wa byeon-dong-yo-in' (Income Distribution of Income Levels and its Main Factors), *Han-gug-gae-bal-yeon-gu,* Vol. 1, No. 1, pp. 22–43

———, (1979), *Han-gug-ui so-deug-bun-bae-wa gyeol-jeong-yo-in (sang)* (Income Distribution and its Decisive Factor in Korea (Vol 1)), Seoul: KDI

———, (1982), *Han-gug-ui so-deug-bun-bae-wa gyeol-jeong-yo-in (ha)* (Income Distribution and its Decisive Factor in Korea (Vol. 2)), Seoul: KDI

Kaldor, N. (1955–1956), 'Alternative Theories of Distribution', *Review of Economic Studies,* Vol. 23, No. 2

———, (1957), 'A Model of Economic Growth', *Economic Journal,* Vol. 67, No. 268

KCCI (1985), *Han-gug-ui yu-tongsan-eob* (The Korean Distribution Industry), Seoul: KCCI

KCCI and Center for Korean Economic Research (CKER) (1977), *U-li-na-la su-peo-che-in-e gwan-han yeon-gu* (Research on Korean Superchain), Seoul: KCCI

KCCI (1999), *21se-gi-leul hyanghan yu-tongsan-eob bal-jeon-jeon-lyag-gwa jeongchaeg-gwa-je* (The Strategy for Development and Policy of Distribution Industry forward to 21st century), Seoul: KCCI

Kibarian, B. (1960–1961), 'Why Department Stores Can Meet Discount House Competition', *Journal of Retailing,* 36 (4), Winter

Kim, J.I. and L.J. Lau (1994), 'The sources of growth of the East Asian newly industrialized countries', *Journal of the Japanese and International Economies* 8 (3), pp. 235–271

Koo, H. and E.M. Kim (1992), 'The Development State and Capital Accumulation in South Korea', in Appelbaum, R.P. and J. Henderson (eds), *State and Development in the Asia Pacific Rim,* Newbury Park, England: Sage Publication

Koo, H. (1994), 'The Interplay of State, Social Class, and World System in East Asian Development: the Cases of South Korea and Taiwan', in Deyo, F.C. (ed.), *The Political Economy of the New Asian Industrialism,* Ithaca and London: Cornell Univ. Press

Krugman, P. (1994), 'The Myth of Asia's Miracle', *Foreign Affairs,* Nov./Dec. Vol. 73, Issue, 6, pp. 62–78

Kuznets, S. (1955), 'Economic Growth and Income Inequality', *American Economic Review*, Vol. 45, No. 1

Larke, R. (1994), *Japanese Retailing*, London: Routledge

Leightner, J.E. (1992), 'The Compatibility of Growth and Increased Equality: Korea', *Journal of Development Studies,* Vol. 29, No. 1

———, (2003), 'Equality and Growth in Asia', *Journal of Economic Issues*, Vol. XXXVII, No. 2

Lewis, W.A. (1954), 'Economic Development with Unlimited Supplies of Labour', *The Manchester School*, 22, pp. 139–191

Li, H. and H. Zou (1998), 'Income Inequality is not Harmful for Growth: Theory and Evidence', *Review of Development Economics*, 2 (3), pp. 318–334

Luedde-Neurath, R. (1988), 'State Intervention and Export-Oriented Development in South Korea', in White, G. (ed.), *Development States in East Asia*, London: Macmillan Press

Lyon, P., A. Colquhoun and D. Kinney (2004), 'UK food shopping in the 1950s: the social context of customer loyalty', *International Journal of Consumer Studies*, Vol. 28, No. 1, pp. 28–39

Ma, Sangyeol and An Jeompan (2012), *Daehyeongmateu yeongeobgyujeui uimiwa jung-soyutongeobgwaui sangsaengbaljeon bangan*, Changwon-si: Gyeongnam Development Institute

Matsuyama, K. (2002), 'The Rise of Mass Consumption Societies', *Journal of Political Economy*, Vol. 110, No. 5, pp. 1035–1070

McNair, M.P. (1931), 'Trends in Large Scale Retailing', *Harvard Business Review*, Vol. 10, October

———, (1958), 'Significant Trends and Developments in the Post War Period', in Smith, A.B. (ed.), *Competitive Distribution in a Free High Level Economy and its Implications for the University,* Pittsburg: University of Pittsburg Press

McNair, M.P. and E.C. May (1976), *The Evolution of Retail Institutions in the United States*, Cambridge, Marketing Science Institute

———, (1978), 'The Next Revolution of the Retailing Wheel', *Harvard Business Review,* Vol. 56, Sept.-Oct.

Meltzer, A.H. and S.F. Richard (1981), 'A Rational Theory of the Size of Government', *Journal of Political Economy*, 89, pp. 914–927

Min, Gyeonghwi, Jeong Jongseok, Seo Yonggu and An Yeonghyo (2000), *Yu-tong sin-jo-lyo-wa mul-lyu-hyeog-sin* (New Trend and Innovation of the Distribution Industry), Seoul: Eul-yu-mun-hwa-sa

Mokyr, J. (1977), 'Demand vs. Supply in the Industrial Revolution', *Journal of Economic History*, Vol. 37, No. 4, pp. 981–1008

Moore, M. (1984–1985), 'Mobilization and Disillusion in Rural Korea: The Saemaul Movement in Retrospect', *Pacific Affairs*, Vol. 57, No. 4, pp. 577–598

Murphy, K.M., A. Shleifer and R. Vishny (1989a), 'Income Distribution, Market Size and Industrialization', *Quarterly Journal of Economics*, Vol. 104, No. 3, pp. 537–564

———, (1989b), 'Industrialization and the Big Push', *Journal of Political Economy*, Vol. 97, No. 5. pp. 1003–1026

Nam, Ilchong (1992), *Han-gug-ui yu-tongsan-eob* (Korean Distribution Industry), Seoul: KDI

O, Sejo and Bak Jinyong (2004), *Gae-jeongpan, si-jang ji-hyangjeog yu-tonggwan-li* (Marketing Channel), Seoul: Bag-yeongsa

O, Sejo and Sekine Takasi (2002), *Han nun-e bo-neun han-il so-mae-yu-tong jeon-jaeng* (The War of the Retail Industry in Korea and Japan), Seoul: Jung-anggyeongje-pyeonglon-sa

O, Seyeong and Gim Ilsan (2003), 'A Comparative Analysis on the Marketing Mix Strategies of Foreign and Domestic Super Discount Stores', *Mu-yeog-hag-hoe-ji*, Vol. 28, No. 2, pp. 185–220

Okubo, T. (1992), 韓国の流通産業 (The Korean Distribution Industry), Tokyo: Sanno University Press (Japanese)

Pack, H. (1994), 'Endogenous Growth Theory: Intellectual Appeal and Empirical Shortcomings', *Journal of Economic Perspectives*, Vol. 8, No. 1

Park, Y.C. (1992), 'Export-led Growth and Economic Liberation in South Korea', Korea Institute of Finance Working Paper No. 92–01

———, (1998), *Financial Liberalization and Opening in East Asia: Issues and Policy Challenges*, Seoul: Korea Institute of Finance.

Partner, S. (1999), *Assembled in Japan*, Berkeley, Los Angeles and London: University of California Press

Pasdermadjian, H. (1954), *The Department Store: Its Origins, Evolution and Economics*, London: Newman Books

Pasinetti, L. (1962), 'Rate of Profit and Income Distribution in Relation to the Rate of Economic Growth', *Review of Economic Studies*, 29, pp. 267–279

Perkins, J. and C. Freedman (1999), 'Organizational Form and Retailing Development: The Department and the Chain Store, 1860–1940', *Service Industries Journal*, Vol. 19, No. 4, pp. 123–146

Perotti, R. (1993), 'Political Equilibrium, Income Distribution, and Growth', *Review of Economic Studies*, 60, pp. 755–776

———, (1996), 'Growth, Income Distribution, and Democracy: What the Data Say', *Journal of Economic Growth*, 1, pp. 149–187

Persson, T. and G. Tabellini (1994), 'Is Inequality Harmful for Growth? Theory and Evidence', *American Economic Review*, Vol. 84, No. 3

Pioch, E.A. and R.A. Schmidt (2000), 'Consumption and the Retail Change Process: a Comparative Analysis of Toy Retailing in Italy and France', *International Review of Retail, Distribution and Consumer Research,* Vol. 10, No. 2, pp. 183–203

Przeworski, A. and F. Limongi (1993), 'Political Regimes and Economic Growth', *Journal of Economic Perspectives,* Vol. 7, No. 3

Przeworski, A., M.E. Alvarez, J.A. Cheibub and F. Limongi (2006), *Democracy and Development: Political Institutions and Well-Being in the World, 1950–1990,* Cambridge, New York: Cambridge University Press

Purvis, M. (1999), 'Stocking the Store: Co-operative Retailers in North-East England and Systems of Wholesale Supply, circa 1860–77' in Alexander, N. and G. Akehurst (eds), *The Emergence of Modern Retailing 1750–1950,* London: Frank Cass

Robert, R.H. (1963), 'The Carriage Trade Myth?', *Journal of Retailing,* Vol. 39. (Fall)

Rodrik, D. (1995), 'Getting Interventions Right: How South Korea and Taiwan Grew Rich', *Economic Policy,* Vol. 10, No. 20, pp. 55–107

———, (1997), 'Has Globalization Gone Too Far?', *California Management Review,* Vol. 39, No. 3

———, (1999a), 'Democracy Pay Higher Wages', *Quarterly Journal of Economics,* August

———, (1999b), 'The Asian Financial Crisis and the Virtues of Democracy', *Challenge,* Vol. 42, No. 4, July/August

———, (2000a), 'Institutions for High-Quality Growth: What They Are and How to Acquire Them', *Studies in Comparative International Development,* Vol. 35, No. 3

———, (2000b), 'Participatory Politics, Social Cooperation, and Economic Stability', *American Economic Review,* Vol. 9, No. 2

———, (2000c), 'How Far Will International Economic Integration Go?', *Journal of Economic Perspectives,* Vol. 14, No. 1

Romer, P.M. (1994), 'The Origins of Endogenous Growth', *Journal of Economic Perspectives,* Vol. 8, No. 1

Romer, T. (1975), 'Individual Welfare, Majority Voting, and the Properties of a Linear Income Tax', *Journal of Public Economics,* 14, pp. 163–185

Rosenbloom, B. and M. Dupuis (1994), 'Low price, low cost, high service: a new paradigm for global retailing?', *International Review of Retail, Distribution and Consumer Research,* Vol. 4, No. 2, pp. 149–158

Sarel, M. (1997), 'Growth and Productivity in ASEAN Countries', IMF Working Paper

Seo, Geunu (1997), *Sin-yongka-deu-eob-ui hyo-yul-seong je-go bang-an* (The Way for Increase in Efficiency of the Credit Card Industry), Seoul: Korea Institute of Finance (KIF)

Seo, Yonggu (2006), 'The Distribution Industry and Economic Growth' in Baek, Insu, Seo Yonggu, Gim Hyeoncheol and Gim Inho, *Yu-tongsi-jang gae-bang 10nyeon, yu-tongsan-eob gu-jo-byeon-hwa-wa eob-tae-byeol haeg-sim i-syu* (10 Years after Openness of the Domestic Market, The Structural Change of the Retail Industry and Essential Issues in Each Format), Seoul: KIET

Seo, Yonggu and An Yeonghyo (1999), *Yu-tong sin-san-eob gyeongjaenglyeog yeon-gu* (Research on Competitiveness of New Retail Formats), Seoul: KIET

Shimaguchi, M. and L.J. Rosenberg (1979), 'Demystifying Japanese Distribution', *Columbia Journal of World Business*, Spring

Shaw, G. (1992a), 'The Study of Retail Development', in Benson, J. and G. Shaw (eds), *The Evolution of Retail Systems*, c1800~1914, Leicester, London and New York: Leicester University Press

———, (1992b), 'The European Scene: Britain and Germany', in Benson, J. and G. Shaw (eds), *The Evolution of Retail Systems*, c1800~1914, Leicester, London and New York: Leicester University Press

Sim, Otaek (1986), 'Su-ib-ja-yu-hwa jeongchaeg-ui hyo-gwa-seong pyeongga' (Appraisal of Effectiveness on the Policy of Import Liberalisation), Dissertation of Master of Graduate School of Public Administration, Seoul National University

Sin, Gidong (2009), *Gieobhyeong syupeomakes(SSM) hwagsanui jiyeogsanggwon yeonghyanggwa daeeungbangan yeongu* (Impact of Super Supermarket Opening on Existing Grocery Stores and Policy Implications), Gyeonggi-do Suwon-si: Geonggi Research Institute

Sin, Sangjin (2002), 'Dae-man-ui min-ju-hwa: gwa-jeonggwa si-sa-jeom' (Taiwan's Democratization: the Procedure and the Implication), *Han-gug dongbug-a non-chong*, Vol. 23, pp. 155–171

Solow, R.M. (1994), 'Perspectives on Growth Theory', *Journal of Economic Perspectives*, Vol. 8, No. 1

Son, Jaeyeong (1991), 'Ji-ga-wa geo-si-gyeongje-byeon-su-gan-ui in-gwa-gwan-gye-e gwan-han sil-jeungbun-seog' (A Empirical Study on Causality between Land Price Increase and Macroeconomic Variables), *Han-gug-gae-bal-yeon-gu*, Vol. 13, No. 3, pp. 55–74

Song, Daehui (1994), *Gonggi-eob-ui gyeongjaenglyeog je-go-wa min-yeonghwa jeongchaeg banghyang* (The Improvement of Management and the Direction of Privatization Policy in the State Owned Companies in Korea), Seoul: KDI

Song, Mingyeong (1998), 'Gug-ga-ju-do-jeog seongjangche-je-wa jae-beol, gyeongje-wi-gi' (*Chaebol* and Structure of Growth Ruled by Government, Economic Crisis), in I, Byeongcheon and Gim Gyun (eds.), *Wi-gi geu-li-go dae-jeon-hwan* (The Crisis and Big Change), Seoul: Do-seo-chul-pan dangdae

Stern, L.W. and T. Reve (1980), 'Distribution Channels as Political Economies: A Framework for Comparative Analysis', *Journal of Marketing*, Vol. 44, Issue, 3

Seong, Myeongjae (2001), 'Se-beob gae-jeonghyo-gwa mich so-deug so-bi pae-teon byeon-hwa-e tta-leun se-bu-dam hyo-gwa-ui bun-li chu-jeong-e gwan-han yeon-gu' (A Study on Estimating the Effects of Changes in Tax Structures and Distributions of Income and Consumption on the Tax Burden), *Jae-jeong yeon-gu*, Vol. 7, No. 2. pp. 1–49, Seoul: KIPF

Synodinos, N.E. (2001), 'Understanding Japanese Consumers: Some Important Underlying Factors', *Japanese Psychological Research*, Vol. 43, No. 4, pp. 235–248

Tatsuki, M. (1995), 'The Rise of the Mass Market and Modern Retailers in Japan', *Business History*, Vol. 37, No. 2, pp. 70–88

Temple, J. and P.A. Johnson (1998), 'Social Capability and Economic Growth', *Quarterly Journal of Economics*, August

The World Bank (1993), *The East Asian Miracle-Economic Growth and Public Policy*, Oxford University Press

Trappey, C.V. and M.K. Lai (1996), 'Retailing in Taiwan: Modernization and the Emergency of New Formats', *International Journal of Retail and Distribution Management*, Vol. 24, No. 8

U, Eunyeong (1996), 'Yu-tonghwan-gyeong byeon-hwa-e dae-han gug-nae baeg-hwa-jeom-ui dae-eungjeon-lyag' (The Strategy of the Domestic Department Store against the Environmental Change in Distribution System)', Dissertation of Master of Business Administration, Sookmyung Women's University

Wade, R. (1990), *Governing The Market-Economic Theory and The Role of Government in East Asian Industrialization,* Princeton: Princeton University Press

Wadinambiaratchi, G.H. (1972), 'Theories of Retail Development', *Social and Economic Studies,* Vol. 21

Wamsley, G.L. and M.N. Zald (1976), *The Political Economy of Public Organizations,* Bloomington: Indiana University Press

White, G. and R. Wade (1988), 'Developmental States and Markets in East Asia: An Introduction', in White, G. (ed.), *Development States in East Asia*, London: Macmillan Press

Yokomori, T. (2003), *Retailing and Wholesaling in Europe and Japan: Structural Change, Issues and Problems*, Tokyo: Hakutoshobo (Japanese)

Yoshikawa, H. (2003), 'The Role of Demand in Macroeconomics', *Japanese Economic Review*, Vol. 54, No. 1, March, pp. 1–27

Young, A. (1994), 'Lessons from the East Asian NICs: A contrarian view', *European Economic Review,* 38, pp. 964–973

———, (1995), 'The tyranny of numbers: Confronting the statistical realities of the East Asian Growth', *Quarterly Journal of Economics* **110** (3), pp. 641–680

Young, L. (1999), 'Marketing the Modern: Department Stores, Consumer Culture, and the New Middle Class in Interwar Japan', *International Labour and Working-Class History*, No. 55, Spring, pp. 52–70

Yu, Cheolgyu (1992), '80nyeon-dae hu-ban i-hu nae-su-hwag-jang-ui seonggyeog' (The Character of Expansion of Domestic Demand since the late 1980s in the Korean Economy), *Donghyanggwa jeon-mang*, Vol. 18, pp. 189–218

Yu, Gijun (2004), *Yu-tonggyeongje gil-jab-i* (The Guide of the Distribution Economy), Seoul: Hyeongseol-chul-pan-sa

Yu, Haeung and Gim Wonhui (1997), *To-ji-si-jang an-jeongsi-chaeg-ui pyeongga-wa gae-seon-bang-an yeon-gu* (Land Speculation and Land Market Stabilization Policies in Korea: Evaluation and Policy Alternatives), Seoul: Korea Research Institute for Human Settlements

Yu, Jongil (1998), 'No-sa-gwan-gye byeon-hwa-ui jeongchi-gyeongje-hag' (Political Economy of the Change in Industrial Relations) in I, Byeongcheon and Gim Gyun (eds), *Wi-gi geu-li-go dae-jeon-hwan* (The Crisis and Big Change), Seoul: Do-seo-chul-pan dangdae

Yun, Jeonggeun and I Yeongchan (2009), 'Gieobhyeong yutongjeomgwa jungsoyuton-geobcheganui hyeobryeogjeog baljeonbangane gwanhan yeongu' (A Study on Cooperative Developing Methods between Corporate Distributors and Small and Medium Distributors), *Yutonggyeongyeonghaghoeji*, Vol. 12, No. 3, pp. 57–82

Zald, M.N. (1970), 'Political Economy: A Framework for Comparative Analysis', in Zald, M.N. (ed.), *Power in Organisations,* Nashville: Vanderbilt University Press

Index

Author(s)

Subject(s)

Source(s)

www.ingramcontent.com/pod-product-compliance
Lightning Source LLC
LaVergne TN
LVHW010625300926
849162LV00001B/65